Best Copy Available

The following titles are bound-with items. Exact duplicates could not be found. Irregularities do exist.

THE

NEW TESTAMENT.

TRANSLATED FROM THE

ORIGINAL GREEK,

BY

H. T. ANDERSON.

LOUISVILLE, KY.:
STEREOTYPED AND PRINTED FOR THE AUTHOR BY
JOHN P. MORTON & CO.
1866.

DEDICATION AND PREFACE.

To ALL Lovers of Truth, the Author dedicates his Translation of the New Testament.

The Author saw, very early in life, that a translation of the New Testament was necessary. He began his investigations at the age of twenty-one, and has faithfully studied the Original since that time. He has made his translation without reference to any version; that is, he adopted no version as a basis. His work is not a Revision of a version, but a Translation; for he was not disposed to be trammeled by any version, but desired to find the truth of God, as it is contained in the Original. The truth thus found, he has endeavored to express in the English language as now spoken. He has been careful to express the exact sense of the Original, without permitting himself to be confined to an imitation of the letter of the Greek. In revising his work, he re-examined the common version, and wherever that version has expressed the sense of the Original in good English, he has adopted it. In this way he has, as he hopes, embodied all the excellences of that version, and avoided its errors.

The author takes pleasure in acknowledging himself largely indebted, for the English dress of the Translation, to his friend, and brother in Christ, JOHN AUGUSTUS WILLIAMS, of Harrodsburg, Kentucky.

The work has been carried on under many adverse circumstances; but, by the good providence of God, it has been completed. May it go forth, under the Divine blessing, to establish and comfort the hearts of those who love the Truth.

H. T. ANDERSON.

HARRODSBURG, KY., *March*, 1864.

NEW TESTAMENT.

TESTIMONY OF MATTHEW.

I. 1 THE book of the genealogy of Jesus Christ, the son of
David, the son of Abraham.
2 Abraham begot Isaac: Isaac begot Jacob: Jacob begot Judah
and his brothers: 3 Judah begot Phares and Zarah of Thamar:
Phares begot Hezron: Hezron begot Aram: 4 Aram begot Aminidab: Aminidab begot Nahshon: Nahshon begot Salmon: 5 Salmon begot Boaz of Rachab: Boaz begot Obed of Ruth: Obed
begot Jesse: 6 Jesse begot David the king: David the king begot
Solomon of her who had been the wife of Uriah: 7 Solomon begot Rehoboam: Rehoboam begot Abia: Abia begot Asa: 8 Asa
begot Jehosaphat: Jehosaphat begot Jehoram: Jehoram begot
Uzziah: 9 Uzziah begot Jotham: Jotham begot Ahaz: Ahaz
begot Hezekiah: 10 Hezekiah begot Manasseh: Manasseh begot
Amon: Amon begot Josiah: 11 Josiah begot Jeconiah and his
brothers, about the time of the removal to Babylon.
12 And after the removal to Babylon, Jeconiah begot Shealtiel: Shealtiel begot Zerubbabel: 13 Zerubbabel begot Abiud:
Abiud begot Eliakim: Eliakim begot Azor: 14 Azor begot Sadok: Sadok begot Achim: Achim begot Eliud: 15 Eliud begot
Eleazer: Eleazer begot Matthan: Matthan begot Jacob: 16 Jacob
begot Joseph the husband of Mary, of whom was born Jesus,
who is called Christ.
17 So all the generations from Abraham till David are fourteen
generations: and from David till the removal to Babylon are
fourteen generations: and from the removal to Babylon till the
Christ are fourteen generations.
18 But Jesus Christ was begotten thus: After his mother Mary
had been betrothed to Joseph, before they had come together,
she was found to be with child of the Holy Spirit. 19 Then Joseph her husband, being a just man, and not choosing to make

an example of her, intended to put her away privately. 20 But
while he was thinking of these things, behold, an angel of the
Lord appeared to him in a dream, saying: Joseph, son of David,
fear not to take home Mary your wife; for that which is begotten in her is of the Holy Spirit. 21 And she will bear a son, and
you shall call his name Jesus; for he will save his people from
their sins. 22 Now all this was done, that the word might be
fulfilled, which was spoken by the Lord through the prophet,
saying: 23 Behold, a virgin shall be with child, and shall bear a
son, and his name shall be called Immanuel, which, when translated, is, God with us. 24 And Joseph awoke from his sleep, and
did as the angel of the Lord had commanded him; and he took
home his wife, 25 and knew her not till she had brought forth
her first-born son. And he called his name Jesus.

II. 1 Now after Jesus was born in Bethlehem of Judea, in the
days of Herod the king, behold, Magi from the east came to
Jerusalem, 2 saying: Where is he that is born king of the Jews?
For we have seen his star in the east, and have come to do him
homage. 3 When Herod the king heard *these things*, he was
troubled, and all Jerusalem with him. 4 And when he had
assembled all the chief priests and scribes of the people, he
inquired of them where the Christ should be born. 5 And they
said to him: In Bethlehem of Judea; for thus it is written by
the prophet: 6 And thou, Bethlehem, city of Judah, art by no
means the least among the chiefs of Judah; for out of thee shall
come a leader, that shall be a shepherd to my people Israel.

7 Then Herod, when he had secretly called the Magi, inquired
of them strictly how long since the star appeared: 8 and sending them to Bethlehem, he said: Go, make strict inquiry for
the young child: and when you have found him, bring me
word, that I also may go and do him homage. 9 When they
had heard the king, they departed; and lo, the star, which
they had seen in the east, went before them, till it came and
stood over the place where the young child was. 10 And when
they saw the star, they rejoiced with very great joy. 11 And
having come into the house, they saw the young child with
Mary his mother; and falling down, they did him homage.
And when they had opened their treasures, they offered to him
gifts, gold, frankincense, and myrrh. 12 And having been
warned in a dream not to return to Herod, they departed
into their own country by another way.

13 When they had departed, behold, an angel of the Lord
appeared to Joseph in a dream, saying: Arise, and take the
young child and his mother, and flee into Egypt, and be there
till I bring you word; for Herod is about to seek for the young
child, to destroy him. 14 And he arose and took the young child
and his mother by night, and departed into Egypt, 15 and was
there till the death of Herod; that the word might be fulfilled
which was spoken by the Lord through his prophet, saying:
Out of Egypt have I called my Son.

16 Then Herod, when he saw that he was deceived by the
Magi, was greatly enraged, and sent out and slew all the male
children that were in Bethlehem and in all its borders, from
the age of two years and under, according to the time which
he had strictly inquired of the Magi. 17 Then was fulfilled that
which was spoken by Jeremiah the prophet, saying: 18 A voice
was heard in Ramah, wailing and weeping, and great mourning;
Rachel weeping for her children, and refusing to be comforted
because they are no more.

19 But when Herod was dead, behold, an angel of the Lord
appeared in a dream to Joseph in Egypt, 20 saying: Arise and
take the young child and his mother, and go into the land of
Israel; for they are dead who sought the young child's life.
21 And he arose and took the young child and his mother, and
came into the land of Israel. 22 But when he heard that Arche-
laus was reigning in Judea in place of Herod his father, he was
afraid to go thither. But being warned in a dream, he withdrew into the regions of Galilee, 23 and came and dwelt in a city
called Nazareth, that the word might be fulfilled which was
spoken by the prophets: He shall be called a Nazarene.

III. 1 In those days came John the Immerser, preaching in
the wilderness of Judea, 2 and saying: Repent, for the kingdom
of heaven is at hand. 3 For this is he that was spoken of by
Isaiah the prophet, saying: The voice of one crying in the
wilderness, Prepare the way of the Lord, make his paths
straight. 4 But the same John had his clothing of camel's hair,
and a girdle of leather around his loins, and his food was locusts
and wild honey.

5 Then went out to him Jerusalem, and all Judea, and all the
region round about the Jordan, 6 and were immersed by him in
the Jordan, confessing their sins. 7 But when he saw many of
the Pharisees and Sadducees coming to his immersion, he said

to them: Generation of vipers, who has warned you to flee from
the coming wrath? 8 Bring forth, therefore, fruit worthy of
repentance: 9 and think not to say within yourselves, We have
Abraham for our father; for I say to you that God is able from
these stones to raise up children to Abraham. 10 Even now the
ax is lying at the root of the trees: therefore, every tree that
does not bring forth good fruit is cut down and thrown into the
fire. 11 I immerse you in water, in order to repentance; but he
that comes after me is mightier than I, whose sandals I am not
worthy to carry. He will immerse you in the Holy Spirit and
in fire: 12 Whose winnowing-shovel is in his hand, and he will
thoroughly cleanse his thrashing-floor, and gather his grain into
his granary; but the chaff he will burn with unquenchable fire.
13 Then came Jesus from Galilee to the Jordan to John, to be
immersed by him. 14 But John forbade him, saying: I have
need to be immersed by thee, and comest thou to me? 15 But
Jesus answering said to him: Permit it now; for thus it becomes us to perform fully every righteous act. Then he permitted him. 16 And after Jesus was immersed, he came up immediately from the water; and lo, the heavens were opened to
him, and he saw the Spirit of God descending like a dove, and
coming upon him. 17 And lo, a voice from heaven, saying: This
is my beloved Son, in whom I delight.

IV. 1 Then was Jesus led up by the Spirit into the wilderness,
to be tempted by the devil. 2 And when he had fasted forty
days and forty nights, he was afterward hungry. 3 And the
tempter came to him and said: If you are the Son of God, command that these stones become bread. 4 But he answered and
said: It is written, Man shall not live by bread alone, but by
every word that comes forth from the mouth of God. 5 Then
the devil took him into the holy city, and placed him on the
pinnacle of the temple, 6 and said to him: If you are the Son
of God, throw yourself down, for it is written: He will give
his angels charge concerning you; and in their hands shall they
take you up, lest you strike your foot against a stone. 7 Jesus
said to him: It is again written, You shall not put the Lord
your God to the proof.
8 Again, the devil took him to a very high mountain, and
showed him all the kingdoms of the world and the glory of
them, 9 and said to him: All these things will I give you, if you
will fall down and worship me. 10 Then Jesus said to him: Get

behind me, Satan, for it is written: You shall worship the Lord
your God, and him only shall you serve. 11 Then the devil left
him, and behold, angels came and ministered to him.

12 Now when Jesus heard that John was delivered up, he withdrew into Galilee; 13 and, leaving Nazareth, he went and dwelt
in Capernaum, which is upon the sea, in the borders of Zebulon
and Naphtali, 14 that the word might be fulfilled which was
spoken by Isaiah the prophet, saying: 15 The land of Zebulon,
and the land of Naphtali, toward the sea beyond the Jordan,
Galilee of the Gentiles; 16 the people that sat in darkness saw
great light; and upon those who sat in the region and shadow
of death light has risen. 17 From that time Jesus began to preach
and to say: Repent, for the kingdom of heaven is at hand.

18 And as he was walking by the sea of Galilee, he saw two
brothers, Simon who is called Peter, and Andrew his brother,
throwing a net into the sea, for they were fishers. 19 And he
said to them: Come after me, and I will make you fishers of
men. 20 And they immediately left their nets and followed him.
21 And going on thence, he saw other two brothers, James the son
of Zebedee, and John his brother, in the ship with Zebedee their
father, mending their nets; and he called them. 22 And they
immediately left the ship and their father, and followed him.

23 And Jesus went about all Galilee, teaching in their synagogues, and preaching the gospel of the kingdom, and curing
every disease, and every kind of sickness among the people.
24 And his fame went abroad into all Syria. And they brought
to him all that were sick, those who were afflicted with various
diseases and pains, and those who were possessed with demons,
and lunatics, and paralytics; and he cured them. 25 And many
multitudes followed him from Galilee, and Decapolis, and Jerusalem, and Judea, and from beyond the Jordan.

V. 1 And seeing the multitudes, he went up into the mountain; and when he had sat down, his disciples came to him;
2 and he opened his mouth and taught them, saying: 3 Blessed
are the poor in spirit; for theirs is the kingdom of heaven.
4 Blessed are they that mourn; for they shall be comforted.
5 Blessed are the meek; for they shall inherit the earth. 6 Blessed
are they that hunger and thirst for righteousness; for they
shall be filled. 7 Blessed are the merciful; for they shall receive
mercy. 8 Blessed are the pure in heart; for they shall see God.
9 Blessed are the peacemakers; for they shall be called sons of

God. 10 Blessed are they that are persecuted on account of
righteousness; for theirs is the kingdom of heaven. 11 Blessed
are you, when they shall reproach you, and persecute you, and
say every evil thing against you, falsely, on my account. 12 Rejoice, and leap for joy; for great is your reward in heaven: for
so did they persecute the prophets who were before you.

13 You are the salt of the earth: but if the salt has become
tasteless, by what means shall it become salt again? It is then
good for nothing but to be thrown out and trod upon by men.
14 You are the light of the world: a city that lies upon a mountain can not be hid: 15 neither do men light a lamp and place it
under the measure, but on the lamp-stand, and it gives light to
all that are in the house. 16 In this way let your light shine
before men, that they may see your good works, and glorify
your Father who is in heaven.

17 Think not that I have come to make the law or the prophets
of no effect. I have not come to make them of no effect, but to
give them their full efficiency. 18 For verily I say to you, Till
heaven and earth pass away, one yod or one point shall in no
way pass from the law till all be fulfilled. 19 Whoever, therefore, shall make void one of the least of these commandments,
and shall teach men so, shall be called least in the kingdom of
heaven. But whoever shall do and teach, he shall be called
great in the kingdom of heaven. 20 For I say to you, That, unless your righteousness excel that of the scribes and Pharisees,
you can by no means enter into the kingdom of heaven.

21 You have heard that it was said to the ancients: You shall
not kill; and whoever shall kill, shall be liable to the sentence
of the judges. 22 But I say to you, Whoever is angry with his
brother without a cause, shall be liable to the sentence of the
judges. And whoever shall say to his brother, Worthless fellow,
shall be liable to the sentence of the Sanhedrim. But whoever
shall say, Impious wretch, shall be in danger of hell-fire. 23 If,
therefore, you bring your gift to the altar, and there remember
that your brother has any thing against you, 24 leave your gift
there before the altar, and go, first be reconciled to your brother,
and then come and offer your gift. 25 Come to an agreement
with your opponent at law quickly, while you are on the road
with him, lest your opponent at law deliver you to the judge,
and the judge deliver you to the officer, and you be thrown into
prison. 26 Verily, I say to you, You shall by no means come out
thence, till you have paid the last farthing.

27 You have heard that it was said: You shall not commit
adultery. 28 But I say to you, Whoever looks upon a woman to
cherish desire for her, has already committed adultery with her
in his heart. 29 If, then, your right eye ensnare you, tear it out
and throw it from you; for it is profitable for you that one of
your members should perish, and not that your whole body
should be thrown into hell. 30 And if your right hand ensnare
you, cut it off, and throw it from you; for it is profitable for you
that one of your members should perish, and not that your
whole body should be thrown into hell.

31 It has been said: Whoever will put away his wife, let him
give her a bill of divorce. 32 But I say to you, Whoever shall
put away his wife, unless on account of lewdness, causes her to
commit adultery: and whoever marries her that is divorced,
commits adultery. 33 Again, you have heard that it was said to
the ancients: You shall not swear falsely, but shall pay to the
Lord your vows. 34 But I say to you, Swear not at all: neither
by heaven, for it is the throne of God; 35 nor by the earth, for
it is his footstool; nor by Jerusalem, for it is the city of the
great King: 36 neither shall you swear by your head, for you
can not make one hair white or black. 37 But let your word be,
Yes, yes; no, no; for whatever is more than these is of the
Evil One.

38 You have heard that it was said: An eye for an eye, and a
tooth for a tooth. 39 But I say to you, Resist not the injurious.
But whoever will smite you on your right cheek, turn to him
the other also. 40 And to him that will go to law with you, and
take away your coat, give your mantle also. 41 And whoever
will compel you to go one mile, go with him two. 42 Give to
him that asks of you; and from him that would borrow of you,
turn not away.

43 You have heard that it was said: You shall love your neighbor, and hate your enemy. 44 But I say to you, Love your enemies: bless those who curse you, do good to those who hate you,
and pray for those who insult you and persecute you: 45 that
you may be the sons of your Father who is in heaven; for he
makes his sun to rise upon the evil and the good, and causes it
to rain on the just and on the unjust. 46 For if you love those
who love you, what reward have you? Do not even the publicans the same? 47 And if you salute your brethren only, in what
do you excel? Do not even the publicans so? 48 Be you therefore perfect, as your Father who is in heaven is perfect.

VI. 1 Beware of doing your righteous deeds before men, to be
seen by them; otherwise you have no reward with your Father
who is in heaven. 2 When, therefore, you do a charitable deed,
do not cause a trumpet to be sounded before you, as the hypocrites do, in the synagogues and in the streets, that they may be
glorified by men. Verily, I say to you, They have their reward.
3 But when you do a charitable deed, let not your left hand know
what your right hand does; 4 that your charitable deeds may be
in secret; and your Father, who sees in secret, himself will reward you openly.

5 And when you pray, you shall not be like the hypocrites; for
they love to pray standing in the synagogues, and in the corners
of the streets, that they may be seen by men. Verily, I say to
you, They have their reward. 6 But do you, when you pray, go
into your closet, and when you have closed the door, pray to
your Father who is in secret: and your Father who sees in secret will reward you openly. 7 But when you pray, do not use
vain repetitions, as the heathen do: for they think that they
will be heard for their many words. 8 Be not, therefore, like
them; for your Father knows what things you need before you
ask him.

9 In this manner, therefore, pray you: Our Father who art in
heaven, hallowed be thy name. 10 Thy kingdom come. Thy
will be done on earth, as it is done in heaven. 11 Give us this
day the bread for our support. 12 And forgive us our debts, as
we also forgive our debtors. 13 And lead us not into temptation,
but deliver us from the Evil One. 14 For if you forgive men
their offenses, your heavenly Father will also forgive you.
15 But if you forgive not men their offenses, neither will your
Father forgive your offenses.

16 And when you fast, do not put on a sad countenance, as
the hypocrites do; for they disfigure their faces, that they may
appear to men to be fasting. Verily, I say to you, They have
their reward. 17 But do you, when you fast, anoint your head
and wash your face; 18 that you may not appear to men to be
fasting, but to your Father who is in secret. And your Father
who sees in secret will reward you.

19 Lay not up for yourselves treasures on earth, where moths
and rust consume, and where thieves break through and steal.
20 But lay up for yourselves treasures in heaven, where neither
moth nor rust consumes, and where thieves do not break
through, nor steal. 21 For where your treasure is, there will

your heart be also. 22 The lamp of the body is the eye: if,
therefore, your eye be sound, your whole body will be light:
23 But if your eye be diseased, your whole body will be dark. If,
therefore, the light that is in you is darkness, how great is that
darkness!

24 No one can serve two masters: for he will either hate the
one and love the other; or he will hold to the one, and neglect
the other. You can not serve God and riches. 25 For this reason I say to you, Be not anxious for your life, what you shall
eat, and what you shall drink; nor for your body, what you
shall put on. Is not your life a greater gift than food, and your
body than clothing? 26 Observe the birds of the air, that they
neither sow, nor reap, nor gather into granaries. Yet your
heavenly Father feeds them. Are you not much better than
they? 27 Which of you, by his anxiety, can add one span to his
life? 28 And why are you anxious about clothing? Consider
the lilies of the field how they grow: they toil not, nor do they
spin. 29 But I say to you, That Solomon, in all his glory, was
not clothed like one of these. 30 If then, God so clothes the
herb of the field, which to-day is, and to-morrow is thrown into
the oven, will he not much more clothe you, O you of little
faith? 31 Therefore, be not anxious, saying: What shall we eat?
or, what shall we drink? or, with what shall we be clothed?
32 For after all these things do the Gentiles seek: for your heavenly Father knows that you need all these things. 33 But seek
first the kingdom of God, and his righteousness, and all these
things shall be given to you in addition. 34 Therefore, be not
anxious about the morrow, for the morrow will have anxieties
of its own. Sufficient for the day is its own evil.

VII. 1 Judge not, that you may not be judged: 2 for with
what judgment you judge, you shall be judged: and with what
measure you measure, it shall be measured to you. 3 And why
do you look at the splinter that is in your brother's eye, but perceive not the beam that is in your own eye? 4 Or, how will
you say to your brother, Let me pull out the splinter from your
eye: and lo, a beam is in your own eye? 5 Hypocrite! first
pull the beam out of your own eye, and then you will see
clearly to pull the splinter out of your brother's eye.

6 Give not that which is holy to dogs, nor throw your pearls
before swine, lest they trample them under their feet, and turn
again and tear you.

7 Ask, and it shall be given you; seek, and you shall find;
knock, and it shall be opened to you. 8 For every one that asks,
receives; and he that seeks, finds; and to him that knocks, it
shall be opened. 9 What man is there of you, of whom if his
son ask bread, will he give him a stone? 10 And if he ask a
fish, will he give him a serpent? 11 If then you, being evil,
know how to give good gifts to your children, how much more
will your Father who is in heaven give good things to those
who ask him? 12 All things, therefore, whatever you would that
men should do to you, even so do you to them; for this is the
law and the prophets.

13 Enter in through the strait gate: for wide is the gate, and
broad is the way, that leads to destruction; and many there
are that go in through it. 14 How strait is the gate, and how
narrow the way, that leads to life! and few there are that
find it.

15 But beware of false prophets, who come to you in sheep's
clothing, but within are ravenous wolves. 16 By their fruits you
will know them. Are grapes gathered from thorns, or figs from
thistles? 17 So every good tree produces goodly fruit: but an
unsound tree produces diseased fruit. 18 A good tree can not
produce diseased fruit; nor can an unsound tree produce goodly
fruit. 19 Every tree that does not produce goodly fruit, is cut
down and thrown into the fire. 20 Therefore, by their fruits you
shall know them.

21 Not every one that says to me, Lord, Lord, shall enter into
the kingdom of heaven; but he that does the will of my Father
who is in heaven. 22 Many will say to me in that day, Lord,
Lord, have we not prophesied in thy name, and in thy name
cast out demons, and in thy name done many mighty works?
23 And then will I profess to them, I never knew you; depart
from me, you that work iniquity.

24 Therefore, whoever hears these words of mine and does
them, I will liken him to a wise man, who built his house on
the rock: 25 and the rain descended, and the torrents came, and
the winds blew, and they beat against that house, and it fell
not: for it was founded on the rock. 26 And every one that
hears these words of mine, and does them not, shall be likened
to a foolish man, who built his house upon the sand. 27 And
the rain descended, and the torrents came, and the winds blew,
and beat upon that house, and it fell: and great was its fall.

28 And it came to pass when Jesus had ended these words, that

the multitudes were astonished at his teaching: 29 for he taught
them as one that had authority, and not as the scribes.

VIII. 1 And when he had come down from the mountain,
many multitudes followed him.
2 And behold, a leper came and did him homage, saying:
Lord, if thou wilt, thou canst make me clean. 3 And Jesus
stretched out his hand and touched him, saying: I will; be
clean. And immediately his leprosy was cleansed. 4 And Jesus
said to him: See that you tell no one. But go, show yourself
to the priest, and offer the gift that Moses commanded, for a
testimony to them.
5 And when he entered Capernaum, there came to him a centurion,
beseeching him, 6 and saying: Lord, my servant lies in
my house, palsied, fearfully afflicted. 7 And Jesus said to him:
I will go and cure him. 8 And the centurion answering, said:
Lord, I am not worthy that thou shouldst come under my roof;
but say in a word only, and my servant shall be restored to
health. 9 For I am a man under authority, having soldiers
under me; and I say to this one, Go, and he goes; and to another,
Come, and he comes; and to my servant, Do this, and he
does it. 10 And when Jesus heard it, he was filled with admiration,
and said to those who followed him: Verily I say to you,
not even in Israel have I found so great faith. 11 I also say to
you, That many shall come from the east and the west, and shall
recline with Abraham, and Isaac, and Jacob in the kingdom of
heaven; 12 but the sons of the kingdom shall be cast into the
darkness that is without. There shall be weeping and gnashing
of teeth. 13 And Jesus said to the centurion: Go, and as you
have believed, so be it to you. And his servant was restored to
health in that hour.
14 And when Jesus had come into Peter's house, he saw his
mother-in-law lying, and ill of a fever. 15 And he touched her
hand, and the fever left her: and she arose and ministered to
him.
16 When the evening had come, they brought to him many
that were possessed with demons: and he cast out the spirits
with his word, and cured all that were sick; 17 that the word
might be fulfilled which was spoken by Isaiah the prophet, saying:
He himself took our infirmities, and bore our diseases.
18 But when Jesus saw many multitudes about him, he gave
orders to depart to the other side. 19 And a certain scribe came

and said to him: Teacher, I will follow thee wherever thou
goest. [20] And Jesus said to him: The foxes have dens, and the
birds of the air have roosts; but the Son of man has not where
to lay his head. [21] And another of his disciples said to him:
Lord, permit me first to go and bury my father. [22] But Jesus
said to him: Follow me, and let the dead bury their own dead.

[23] And when he had entered the ship, his disciples followed
him. [24] And behold, there was a great tempest in the sea, so
that the ship was covered by the waves: but he was asleep.
[25] And his disciples came to him, and awoke him, saying: Lord,
save us; we perish. [26] And he said to them: Why are you
fearful, O you of little faith? Then he arose, and rebuked the
winds and the sea: and there was a great calm. [27] But the men
were astonished, and said: What man is this, that even the
winds and the sea obey him!

[28] And when he had come to the opposite side, into the country
of the Gadarenes, there met him two men, coming out of the
tombs, possessed with demons, very fierce, so that no one could
pass that way. [29] And behold, they cried out, saying: What
have we to do with thee, Jesus, Son of God? Hast thou come
hither to torment us before the time? [30] Now there was, at a
distance from them, a herd of many swine, feeding. [31] And the
demons besought him, saying: If thou cast us out, permit us
to go away into the herd of swine. [32] And he said to them: Go.
And when they had come out, they went away into the herd of
swine. And behold, the whole herd of swine rushed down a
steep place into the sea, and perished in the waters. [33] And
those who fed them fled, and went into the city, and told every
thing, and what had happened to those who had been possessed
with the demons. [34] And, behold, all the city came out to meet
Jesus. And when they saw him, they besought him to depart
out of their borders.

IX. [1] And he entered the ship, and passed over, and came
into his own city. [2] And behold, they brought to him a man
sick of the palsy, lying on a bed. And Jesus, seeing their faith,
said to the palsied man: Son, be of good courage; your sins
are forgiven you. [3] And behold, some of the scribes said within
themselves: This man talks impiously. [4] And Jesus, perceiving their thoughts, said: Why do evil thoughts arise in your
hearts? [5] For, which is easier, to say, Your sins are forgiven;
or to say, Arise, and walk? [6] But that you may know that

the Son of man on earth has authority to forgive sins (then he
said to the palsied man): Arise, take up your bed, and go to
your house. 7 And he arose, and departed to his house. 8 And
when the multitude saw it, they were astonished, and glorified
God, who had given such authority to men.

9 And as Jesus passed by from that place, he saw a man named
Matthew, sitting at the custom-house; and he said to him:
Follow me. And he arose and followed him. 10 And it came to
pass that, while Jesus was reclining at table in his house, behold, many publicans and sinners came and reclined at table
with him and his disciples. 11 And when the Pharisees saw it,
they said to his disciples: Why does your teacher eat with
publicans and sinners? 12 When Jesus heard it, he said to them:
Those who are in health have no need of a physician, but those
who are sick. 13 But go and learn what this means: I desire
mercy, and not sacrifice. For I came not to call righteous men,
but sinners to repentance.

14 Then came to him the disciples of John, saying: Why do
we and the Pharisees fast often, but your disciples fast not?
15 And Jesus said to them: Can the sons of the bride-chamber
mourn while the bridegroom is with them? But the days will
come, when the bridegroom shall be taken from them, and then
will they fast. 16 No one puts a patch of new cloth on an old
garment; for that which is put in to fill it up, takes from the
garment, and a worse rent is made. 17 Nor do men put new
wine into old bottles; if so, the bottles burst, and the wine runs
out, and the bottles are lost. But they put new wine into new
bottles, and both are preserved. 18 While he was speaking these
things to them, behold, a certain ruler came and did him homage, saying: My daughter is already dead; but come, lay thy
hand upon her, and she shall live. 19 And Jesus and his disciples arose and followed him.

20 And behold, a woman that had been diseased with an issue
of blood for twelve years, came behind him, and touched the
fringe of his mantle. 21 For she said within herself: If I may
only touch his mantle, I shall be saved. 22 But Jesus turned,
and saw her, and said: Daughter, be of good courage; your
faith has saved you. And the woman was saved from that hour.

23 And when Jesus came into the house of the ruler, and saw
the minstrels and the multitude making lamentation, 24 he said
to them: Depart; for the maid is not dead, but sleeps. And
they derided him. 25 But when the multitude had been sent out,

he went in, and took the maiden by the hand, and she arose.
26 And the fame of this went abroad in all that land.

27 And as Jesus was departing thence, two blind men followed
him, crying out and saying: Son of David, have mercy on us.
28 And when he had entered the house, the blind men came to
him. And Jesus said to them: Do you believe that I am able
to do this? They said to him, Yes, Lord. 29 Then he touched
their eyes, and said: According to your faith, be it to you.
30 And their eyes were opened; and Jesus strictly charged them,
saying: See that no one know it. 31 But they went out and
spread his fame abroad in all that land.

32 And as they were going out, behold, they brought to him a
dumb man possessed with a demon. 33 And after the demon had
been cast out, the dumb man spoke. And the multitudes were
astonished, and said: Never was it seen thus in Israel. 34 But
the Pharisees said: He casts out the demons by the prince of
the demons.

35 And Jesus went through all the cities and villages, teaching
in their synagogues, and preaching the gospel of the kingdom,
and curing every disease and every infirmity. 36 And when he
saw the multitudes, he was moved with compassion for them,
because they were troubled and scattered as sheep that had
no shepherd. 37 Then he said to his disciples: The harvest is
abundant, but the laborers are few. 38 Therefore pray the Lord
of the harvest to send out laborers into his harvest.

X. 1 And he called to him his twelve disciples, and gave them
authority over unclean spirits, so that they might cast them
out, and cure every disease and every infirmity.

2 Now these are the names of the twelve apostles: the first,
Simon, who is called Peter, and Andrew his brother; James the
son of Zebedee, and John his brother; 3 Philip and Bartholomew, Thomas, and Matthew the publican; James the son of Alphæus, and Lebbæus, who was surnamed Thaddæus; 4 Simon
the Canaanite, and Judas Iscariot, who also delivered him up.

5 These twelve Jesus sent forth after he had charged them,
saying: Go not into the road that leads to the Gentiles, and
enter not a city of the Samaritans. 6 But go rather to the lost
sheep of the house of Israel. 7 And as you go, preach, saying:
The kingdom of heaven is at hand. 8 Cure the sick, cleanse the
lepers, cast out demons. Freely you have received, freely give.
9 Provide for yourselves neither gold, nor silver, nor brass to

put into your purses, 10 nor bag for your journey, nor two coats,
nor sandals, nor staffs: for the laborer is worthy of his support.
11 Whatever city or village you enter, inquire who in it is
worthy, and there make your home till you go away. 12 When
you go into a house, salute it: 13 and if the house be worthy,
your peace shall come upon it; but if it be not worthy, your
peace shall return to you. 14 And whoever will not receive you,
nor hear your words, when you go out of that house or that
city, shake off the dust from your feet. 15 Verily I say to you,
It shall be more tolerable for the land of Sodom and Gomorrah,
in the day of judgment, than for that city.

16 Behold, I send you forth as sheep in the midst of wolves:
be, therefore, wise as serpents, and guileless as doves. 17 But
beware of men: for they will deliver you to the councils, and
scourge you in their synagogues; 18 and you will be brought
before governors and kings for my sake, for a testimony against
them and the Gentiles. 19 But when they deliver you up, be not
anxious how or what you shall speak; for that which you shall
speak shall be given you in that hour: 20 for it is not you that
speak, but it is the Spirit of your Father that speaks in you.
21 Brother will deliver up brother to death, and the father the
child; and children will rise up against their parents, and cause
them to be put to death. 22 And you will be hated by all men
on my account: but he that endures to the end shall be saved.

23 But when they persecute you in this city, flee into another:
for verily I say to you, You will not have made the circuit of
the cities of Israel before the Son of man shall come. 24 The
disciple is not above his teacher, nor the servant above his master. 25 It is enough for the disciple, that he be as his teacher;
and for the servant, that he be as his master. If they call
the master of the house Beelzebul, how much more those of his
household? 26 Fear them not, therefore; for there is nothing
covered that shall not be revealed, nor hidden that shall not be
made known. 27 What I tell you in darkness, speak in the light:
and what you hear in the ear, preach on the house-tops.

28 And fear not them that kill the body, but are not able to
kill the soul. But rather fear him who is able to destroy both
soul and body in hell. 29 Are not two sparrows sold for a farthing? and yet not one of them shall fall upon the ground without your father. 30 But even the hairs of your head are all
numbered. 31 Fear not, therefore: you are of more value than
many sparrows. 32 Whoever, therefore, will confess me before

men, him will I also confess before my Father who is in heaven.
[33] But whoever will deny me before men, him will I also deny
before my father who is in heaven.

[34] Think not that I have come to send peace on the earth. I
have not come to send peace, but a sword. [35] For I have come
to set a man at variance with his father, and the daughter with
her mother, and the daughter-in-law with her mother-in-law:
[36] and a man's enemies shall be those of his own household.
[37] He that loves father or mother more than me, is not worthy
of me: and he that loves son or daughter more than me, is not
worthy of me: [38] and whoever does not take his cross and follow after me, is not worthy of me. [39] He that finds his life shall
lose it; and he that loses his life for my sake, shall find it.
[40] He that receives you, receives me: and he that receives me,
receives him that sent me. [41] He that receives a prophet because he is a prophet, shall receive a prophet's reward: and he
that receives a righteous man because he is a righteous man,
shall receive a righteous man's reward. [42] And whoever will
give one of these little ones only a cup of cold water to drink,
because he is a disciple, verily I say to you, he shall not lose
his reward.

XI. [1] And it came to pass, when Jesus had made an end of
commanding his twelve disciples, he departed thence to teach
and to preach in their cities.

[2] Now when John had heard in the prison of the works of the
Christ, he sent two of his disciples, [3] and said to him: Art thou
he that was to come, or must we look for another? [4] And Jesus
answered and said to them: Go and tell John what you hear
and see. [5] The blind receive their sight, and the lame walk;
the lepers are cleansed, and the deaf hear; the dead are raised,
and the poor have the gospel preached to them; [6] and blessed is
he that shall find in me no cause of offense.

[7] As these were going away, Jesus began to say to the multitudes concerning John: What did you go out into the wilderness to see? A reed shaken by the wind? [8] But what did you
go out to see? A man clothed in soft raiment? Behold, those
who wear soft clothing are in kings' houses. [9] But what did
you go out to see? A prophet? Yes, I say to you, and more
than a prophet. [10] For this is he of whom it is written: Behold,
I send my messenger before thy face, who shall prepare thy way
before thee. [11] Verily, I say to you, Among those born of women,

there has not risen a greater than John the Immerser. But the
least in the kingdom of heaven is greater than he.

12 From the days of John the Immerser till now, the kingdom of heaven is taken by violence, and men of violence seize
upon it eagerly. 13 For all the prophets and the law prophesied
till John; 14 and if you are willing to receive it, he is Elijah
that was to come. 15 He that has ears to hear, let him hear.
16 But to what shall I liken this generation? It is like children
sitting in the markets, and calling to their companions, 17 and
saying: We have played on the pipe for you, and you have not
danced; we have wailed for you, and you have not lamented.
18 For John came, neither eating nor drinking, and they say:
He has a demon. 19 The Son of man has come eating and drinking, and they say: Behold, a glutton, and a drinker of wine,
a friend of publicans and sinners. Yet wisdom is vindicated by
her children.

20 Then he began to reprove the cities in which most of his
mighty works had been done, because they did not repent.
21 Alas for thee, Chorazin! alas for thee, Bethsaida! for if the
mighty works which have been done in you had been done in
Tyre and Sidon, they would have repented long ago in sackcloth and ashes. 22 But I say to you, It will be more tolerable
for Tyre and Sidon, in the day of judgment, than for you.
23 And thou, Capernaum, that hast been exalted to heaven,
shalt be brought down to hades. For if the mighty works
which have been done in thee had been done in Sodom, it would
have remained till this day. 24 But I say to you, It shall be
more tolerable for the land of Sodom, in the day of judgment,
than for thee.

25 At that time Jesus answered and said: I thank thee, Father,
Lord of heaven and of earth, because thou hast hid these things
from the wise and prudent, and hast revealed them to babes.
26 Even so, Father, for so it seemed good in thy sight. 27 All
things have been delivered to me by my Father; and no one
knows the Son, but the Father; nor does any one know the
Father, but the Son, and he to whom the Son will reveal him.
28 Come to me, all you that are weary, and heavily burdened,
and I will give you rest. 29 Take my yoke upon you, and learn
from me; for I am meek and lowly in heart; and you shall
find rest for your souls. 30 For my yoke is easy, and my burden is light.

XII. [1] At that time Jesus was going, on the Sabbath, through
the fields of grain; and his disciples were hungry, and began to
pull the ears of grain, and to eat. [2] But when the Pharisees saw
it, they said to him: Behold, your disciples are doing what it is
not lawful to do on the Sabbath. [3] But he said to them: Have
you not read what David did, when he and those who were with
him were hungry? [4] how he entered the house of God, and ate
the loaves of the presence, which it was not lawful for him to
eat, nor for those who were with him, but for the priests only?
[5] Or, have you not read in the law that on the Sabbath-days the
priests in the temple profane the Sabbath, and are blameless?
[6] But I say to you, that something greater than the temple is
here. [7] But if you had known what this means—I desire mercy,
and not sacrifice—you would not have condemned the blameless.
[8] For the Son of man is Lord of the Sabbath.

[9] And he departed thence, and went into their synagogue.
[10] And behold, a man was there that had a withered hand. And
they asked him, saying: Is it lawful to cure on the Sabbath-
days? that they might accuse him. [11] And he said to them:
What man shall there be among you, that shall have one sheep,
and if this fall into a pit on the Sabbath-day, will he not lay
hold on it and lift it out? [12] How much better, then, is a man
than a sheep! So it is lawful to do well on the Sabbath-days.
[13] Then he said to the man: Stretch forth your hand. And he
stretched it forth; and it was restored to soundness, like the
other. [14] But the Pharisees went out and took counsel against
him, that they might destroy him. [15] But Jesus perceived it,
and withdrew from that place. And many multitudes followed
him, and he cured them all. [16] And he charged them not to
make him known; [17] that the word might be fulfilled which
was spoken by Isaiah the prophet, saying: [18] Behold, my servant whom I have chosen; my beloved, in whom my soul delights. I will put my Spirit upon him, and he shall declare law
to the Gentiles. [19] He shall not contend, nor cry out; nor shall
any one hear his voice in the streets. [20] A bruised reed he shall
not break, and a smoking wick he shall not extinguish, till he
shall send forth his law for conquest. [21] And in his name shall
the Gentiles trust.

[22] Then was brought to him a demoniac, blind and dumb: and
he cured him, so that the blind and dumb man both spoke and
saw. [23] And all the people were amazed, and said: Is not this
the son of David? [24] But the Pharisees, when they heard it,

said: This man does not cast out the demons, unless by Beelzebul, the prince of the demons. [25] But Jesus, knowing their
thoughts, said to them: Every kingdom divided against itself
is brought to desolation. And no city or house divided against
itself shall stand. [26] And if Satan cast out Satan, he is divided
against himself; how then shall his kingdom stand? [27] And if
I cast out demons by Beelzebul, by whom do your sons cast
them out? For this reason, they shall be your judges. [28] But
if I cast out demons by the Spirit of God, then the kingdom of
God has already come upon you. [29] Or, how can any one enter
the house of the strong man and spoil his goods, unless he first
bind the strong man? and then he will plunder his house. [30] He
that is not with me, is against me; and he that gathers not
with me, scatters.

[31] Therefore I say to you, That every sin and impious speech
shall be forgiven men: but the impious speech against the Spirit
shall not be forgiven men. [32] And whoever shall speak a word
against the Son of man, it shall be forgiven him: but whoever
shall speak against the Holy Spirit, it shall not be forgiven him,
either in the present age, or in that which is to come. [33] Either
make the tree good, and its fruit good; or make the tree unsound, and its fruit unsound. For by the fruit the tree is
known. [34] Generation of vipers, how can you, being evil, speak
good things? For out of the abundance of the heart, the mouth
speaks. [35] The good man, out of his good treasury, brings forth
good things; and the evil man, out of his evil treasury, brings
forth evil things. [36] But I say to you, That for every idle word
which men speak, they shall give account in the day of judgment. [37] For by your words you shall be justified, and by your
words you shall be condemned.

[38] Then some of the scribes and Pharisees answered and said:
Teacher, we wish to see a sign from you. [39] But he answered
and said to them: A wicked and adulterous generation seeks for
a sign; and no sign shall be given to it, but the sign of Jonah
the prophet. [40] For as Jonah was three days and three nights
in the belly of the great fish, so shall the Son of man be three
days and three nights in the heart of the earth. [41] The men of
Nineveh shall rise in the judgment with this generation, and
condemn it; for they repented in accordance with the preaching
of Jonah; and behold, something greater than Jonah is here.
[42] The queen of the south shall rise in the judgment with this
generation, and shall condemn it; for she came from the most

distant parts of the earth to hear the wisdom of Solomon; and
behold, something greater than Solomon is here.
43 When the unclean spirit has gone out of a man, he goes
through dry places seeking rest, and finds none. 44 Then he
says: I will return to my house, out of which I came. And he
comes and finds it empty, swept, and set in order. 45 Then he
goes and takes with himself seven other spirits more wicked
than himself; and they enter in and dwell there. And the last
state of that man is worse than the first. So shall it be with
this wicked generation.
46 While he was yet speaking to the multitudes, behold, his
mother and his brothers stood without, desiring to speak to him.
47 And some one said to him: Behold, your mother and your
brothers stand without, desiring to speak to you. 48 But he answered and said to him that told him: Who is my mother? and
who are my brothers? 49 And he stretched out his hand toward
his disciples, and said: Behold my mother and my brothers.
50 For whoever will do the will of my Father who is in heaven,
the same is my brother, and sister, and mother.

XIII. 1 On that day Jesus went out of the house, and sat by
the sea. 2 And many multitudes came together to him, so that
he went into a ship and sat; and the whole multitude stood on
the shore.
3 And he spoke many things to them in parables, saying:
Behold, the sower went out to sow. 4 And as he sowed, some
seeds fell by the way: and the birds came and ate them up.
5 Others fell on stony places, where they had not much earth;
and they immediately sprung up, because they had no depth of
earth. 6 But when the sun was up, they were scorched; and
because they had no root, they withered away. 7 Others fell
among thorns, and the thorns sprung up and choked them.
8 Others fell upon good ground, and brought forth fruit, some a
hundred, some sixty, some thirty. 9 He that has ears to hear,
let him hear.
10 And the disciples came and said to him: Why dost thou
speak to them in parables? 11 He answered, and said to them:
Because it is given to you to know the mysteries of the kingdom of heaven; but to them it is not given. 12 For whoever
has, to him shall be given, and he shall have abundance; but
whoever has not, even that which he has shall be taken from
him. 13 For this reason I speak to them in parables; because

when they see, they see not; and when they hear, they hear
not, nor do they understand. 14 And in them is fulfilled the
prophecy of Isaiah, which says: You shall surely hear, and you
will not understand; and you shall surely see, and you will not
perceive. 15 For the heart of this people has become fat; and
with their ears they hear heavily; and their eyes they have
closed; lest they should see with their eyes, and hear with
their ears, and understand with their heart, and should turn
to me, and I should give them health. 16 But blessed are your
eyes, for they see; and your ears, for they hear. 17 For verily
I say to you, Many prophets and righteous men desired to see
what you see, and did not see; and to hear what you hear, and
did not hear.

18 Hear you, therefore, the parable of the sower. 19 When any
one hears the word of the kingdom, and understands it not, the
wicked one comes and catches away that which was sown in his
heart. This is he that received seed by the wayside. 20 He that
received seed on the stony places is he that hears the word, and
immediately receives it with joy. 21 Yet he has no root in himself, but endures for a while; and when affliction or persecution
arises on account of the word, he immediately takes offense.
22 He that received seed among the thorns, is he that hears the
word; and the cares of this age, and the deceitfulness of riches
choke the word, and it becomes unfruitful. 23 But he that received seed on the good ground, is he that hears the word and
understands it; who also produces fruit, and yields, one a hundred; another, sixty; another, thirty.

24 Another parable he laid before them, saying: The kingdom
of heaven is likened to a man that sowed good seed in his field.
25 But while men slept, his enemy came and sowed tares among
the wheat, and went away. 26 But when the blade sprung up,
and produced fruit, then appeared the tares also. 27 And the
servants of the master of the house came, and said to him, Sir,
did you not sow good seed in your field? Whence, then, has it
tares? 28 He said to them, An enemy has done this. The servants said to him, Is it your will, then, that we go and gather
them up? 29 But he said, No; lest while you are gathering the
tares, you root up the wheat with them. 30 Let both grow together till the harvest, and in time of harvest I will say to the
reapers, Collect first the tares, and bind them into bundles to
burn them; but gather the wheat into my granary.

31 Another parable he laid before them, saying: The kingdom

of heaven is like a grain of mustard, that a man took and
sowed in his field. 32 It is, indeed, the least of all seeds; but
when it is grown it is the largest of garden-plants, and becomes a tree, so that the birds of the air come and roost in its
branches.

33 He spoke another parable to them: The kingdom of heaven
is like leaven which a woman took and hid in three measures
of flour, till the whole was leavened.

34 All these things Jesus spoke to the multitudes in parables,
and without a parable he did not speak to them; 35 that the
word might be fulfilled which was spoken by the prophet, saying: I will open my mouth in parables; I will utter things
that have been kept secret from the foundation of the world.

36 Then Jesus left the multitudes, and went into the house.
And his disciples came to him and said: Explain to us the
parable of the tares of the field. 37 He answered and said to
them: He that sows the good seed is the Son of man; 38 the
field is the world; the good seed are the sons of the kingdom;
the tares are the sons of the Wicked One; 39 the enemy that
sowed them is the devil; the harvest is the end of the age;
and the reapers are angels. 40 As, therefore, the tares are collected and burned in fire, so shall it be in the end of this age.
41 The Son of man will send forth his angels, and collect out
of his kingdom all things that offend, and those who work iniquity, 42 and cast them into the furnace of fire; there shall be
weeping and gnashing of teeth. 43 Then shall the righteous
shine forth as the sun, in the kingdom of their Father. He
that has ears to hear, let him hear.

44 Again, the kingdom of heaven is like a treasure hid in a
field, which, when a man finds it, he hides; and for the joy it
gives, he goes and sells all that he has, and buys that field.

45 Again, the kingdom of heaven is like a merchant seeking
goodly pearls. 46 When he finds one pearl of great value, he
goes and sells all that he has, and buys it.

47 Again, the kingdom of heaven is like a net that is cast into
the sea, and that gathers of every kind: 48 when it is full, they
draw it to the shore; and sitting down, they collect the good
into vessels, but throw the bad away. 49 So shall it be in the
end of the age: the angels shall come forth and separate the
wicked from among the just, 50 and cast them into the furnace
of fire: there shall be weeping and gnashing of teeth.

51 Jesus said to them: Have you understood all these things?

They said to him: Yes, Lord. 52 He said to them: Therefore,
every scribe that is trained for the kingdom of heaven, is like
the master of a house, who brings out of his treasury things
new and old.

53 And it came to pass, when Jesus had finished these parables,
he departed from that place. 54 And he came into his own
country, and taught them in their synagogue, so that they were
astonished, and said: Whence has this man this wisdom, and
these mighty works? 55 Is not this the son of the carpenter?
Is not his mother called Mary? and his brothers, James and
Joses and Simon and Judas? 56 And his sisters, are they not
all with us? Whence, then, has this man all these things?
57 And they found in him occasion for offense. But Jesus said
to them: A prophet is not without honor, unless it be in his
own country and in his own house. 58 And he did not many
mighty works there, on account of their unbelief.

XIV. 1 At that time Herod the tetrarch heard of the fame of
Jesus; 2 and he said to his servants: This is John the Immerser;
ıe has risen from the dead; and for this reason the powers *of
he spiritual world* are active within him.

3 For Herod had laid hold of John, and bound him, and put
ıim in prison on account of Herodias, the wife of his brother
Philip. 4 For John said to him: It is not lawful for you to
ıave her. 5 And he intended to put him to death, but feared
he multitude, because they regarded him as a prophet. 6 But
when Herod's birthday was kept, the daughter of Herodias
anced in the midst, and pleased Herod. 7 Wherefore he promised, with an oath, to give her whatever she would ask. 8 And
eing previously instigated by her mother, she said: Give me
ere in a dish the head of John the Immerser? 9 And the king
as grieved: but on account of his oath, and those who reclined
t table with him, he commanded it to be given. 10 And he sent
ıd beheaded John in the prison. 11 And his head was brought
ı a dish, and given to the maiden: and she carried it to her
other. 12 And his disciples came and took away the body, and
ıried it; and went and told Jesus.

13 And when Jesus heard of it, he withdrew from that place,
ship, into a desert place apart: and the multitudes, when
ey heard of *his departure*, followed him, on foot, from the cities.
14 And when Jesus came out, he saw a great multitude, and
ıs moved with compassion for them, and cured their sick.

15 And when it was evening, his disciples came to him, and
said: this is a desert place, and the hour is now past; send the
multitudes away, that they may go into the villages, and buy
themselves food. 16 But Jesus said to them: They need not go
away; do you give them food. 17 They said to him: We have
here but five loaves and two fishes. 18 He said: Bring them
hither to me. 19 And he commanded the multitudes to recline
upon the grass: and he took the five loaves and the two fishes,
and looked up to heaven, and blessed, and broke, and gave the
bread to the disciples, and the disciples *gave it* to the multitudes.
20 And they all ate and were satisfied. And they took up what
remained of the broken pieces, twelve baskets full. 21 And
they that had eaten were about five thousand men, besides
women and children.

22 And he immediately constrained his disciples to get into the
ship, and go before him to the opposite side, while he sent the
multitudes away. 23 And when he had sent the multitudes away,
he went up into the mountain apart to pray. And when evening came, he was there alone. 24 But the ship was now in the
midst of the sea, tossed by the waves, for the wind was against
them.

25 And in the fourth watch of the night he came to them,
walking on the sea. 26 And when the disciples saw him walking
on the sea, they were alarmed, and said: It is a specter! and
they cried out for fear. 27 But Jesus immediately spoke to them,
and said: Take courage; it is I; be not afraid. 28 And Peter
answered him, and said: Lord, if it be thou, bid me come to
thee on the water. 29 And he said: Come. And Peter went
down from the ship, and walked upon the water to go to Jesus
30 But when he saw the wind strong, he was afraid; and begin
ning to sink, he cried out, saying: Lord, save me. 31 And
Jesus immediately stretched out his hand, and took hold of
him, and said to him: O you of little faith, why did you doubt
32 And when they had entered the ship, the wind ceased. 33 And
they that were in the ship came and worshiped him, saying
Truly, thou art the Son of God.

34 And when they had passed over, they came into the land of
Gennesaret. 35 And when the men of that place had knowledg
of him, they sent out into all the neighboring country, and
brought to him all that were sick; 36 and besought him tha
they might only touch the fringe of his mantle; and as many
as touched were perfectly saved.

XV. 1 Then came to Jesus scribes and Pharisees that were of
Jerusalem, saying: 2 Why do your disciples transgress the tradition of the elders? for they do not wash their hands when
they eat bread. 3 But he answered and said to them: And why
do you transgress the commandment of God for the sake of your
tradition? 4 For God commanded, saying, Honor your father
and your mother; and, He that curses father or mother shall
surely be put to death. 5 But you say, Whoever shall say to
his father or his mother, Whatever of mine might profit you, is
a gift, he must in no way honor his father or his mother; 6 and
you make the commandment of God of no effect for the sake
of your tradition. 7 Hypocrites! well did Isaiah prophesy of
you, saying, 8 This people draws near to me with their mouth,
and honors me with their lips; but their heart is far from me.
9 But in vain do they worship me, teaching precepts, the
commandments of men.

10 And he called the multitude to him, and said to them: Hear
and understand; 11 That which enters the mouth does not defile
the man; but that which comes out of the mouth, this defiles
the man.

12 Then came his disciples and said to him: Dost thou know
that the Pharisees, when they heard that saying, were offended?
13 But he answered and said: Every plant that my heavenly
Father has not planted, shall be rooted up. 14 Let them alone;
they are blind leaders of the blind; and if the blind lead the
blind, both will fall into the pit. 15 But Peter answered and
said to him: Explain to us this dark saying. 16 Jesus replied:
Are you also yet without understanding? 17 Do you not yet
understand that whatever enters the mouth passes into the
belly, and is cast out into the sink. 18 But those things which
go out from the mouth, come from the heart; and these defile
the man. 19 For from the heart come evil reasonings, murders,
adulteries, lewd conduct, thefts, false testimonies, impious
words. 20 These are the things that defile the man. But to eat
with unwashed hands does not defile the man.

21 And Jesus went out thence, and withdrew into the regions
of Tyre and Sidon. 22 And behold a woman of Chanaan came
out from those borders, and cried to him, saying: Have mercy
on me, Lord, son of David; my daughter is grievously vexed
with a demon. 23 But he answered her not a word. And his
disciples came and besought him, saying: Send her away, for
she cries after us. 24 But he answered and said: I am not sent

but to the lost sheep of the house of Israel. 25 But she came
and did him homage, saying: Lord, help me. 26 He answered
and said: It is not good to take the children's bread, and throw
it to the little dogs. 27 She replied: Yes, Lord; and yet *thou
canst help me;* for the little dogs eat of the crumbs which fall
from the table of their masters. 28 Then Jesus answered and
said to her: O woman, great is your faith; be it to you as you
desire. And her daughter was restored to health from that hour.

29 And Jesus departed thence, and came near the sea of Galilee, and went up into the mountain, and sat there. 30 And many
multitudes came to him, having with them the lame, the blind,
the deaf, the maimed, and many others; and laid them at the
feet of Jesus, and he cured them; 31 so that the multitudes were
astonished, when they saw the dumb speaking, the maimed
whole, the lame walking, and the blind seeing; and they glorified the God of Israel.

32 Then Jesus called his disciples to him, and said: I have
compassion on the multitude, because they have been with me
now three days, and have nothing to eat. And I am not willing
to send them away fasting, lest they faint on the road. 33 And
his disciples said to him: Whence should we have in the desert
as many loaves as would satisfy so great a multitude? 34 And
Jesus said to them: How many loaves have you? They said:
Seven, and a few little fishes. 35 And he commanded the multitude to recline on the ground. 36 And he took the seven loaves
and the fishes, and gave thanks, and broke, and gave them to
the disciples, and the disciples gave them to the multitude
37 And they all ate and were satisfied; and they took up wha
remained of the broken pieces, seven baskets full. 38 And those
who ate were four thousand men, besides women and children
39 And he sent the multitudes away, and entered the ship, and
went into the borders of Magdala.

XVI. 1 And the Pharisees and Sadducees came to tempt him
and asked him to show them a sign from heaven. 2 But he
answered and said to them: When it is evening, you say, Fai
weather; for the sky is red. 3 And in the morning, A storm
to-day; for the sky is red and lowering. Hypocrites! you
know how to judge of the face of the sky; but you can no
judge of the signs of the times. 4 A wicked and adulterou
generation seeks for a sign; and no sign shall be given it bu
the sign of Jonah the prophet. And he left them and departed

5 And his disciples came to the other side, and had forgotten
to take bread. 6 And Jesus said to them: Take heed and beware of the leaven of the Pharisees and Sadducees. 7 And they
reasoned among themselves, saying: It is because we took no
bread. 8 And Jesus perceiving it, said to them: O you of little
faith! why are you reasoning among yourselves because you
took no bread? 9 Do you not yet understand, nor remember the
five loaves of the five thousand, and how many baskets you took
up? 10 Nor the seven loaves of the four thousand, and how
many baskets you took up? 11 How is it that you do not understand, that I did not speak of bread when I commanded you to
beware of the leaven of the Pharisees and of the Sadducees?
12 Then they understood that he did not bid them beware of the
leaven of bread, but of the teaching of the Pharisees and of the
Sadducees.

13 When Jesus came into the regions of Cæsarea Philippi, he
asked his disciples, saying: Who do men say that I, the Son of
man, am? 14 They replied: Some say that thou art John the
Immerser; others, Elijah; others, Jeremiah, or one of the
prophets. 15 He said to them: But who say you that I am?
16 Simon Peter answered and said: Thou art the Christ, the Son
of the living God. 17 And Jesus answered and said to him:
Blessed are you, Simon, son of Jonah; for flesh and blood did
not reveal this to you, but my Father who is in heaven. 18 And
I say to you, That you are Peter, and on this rock I will build
my church: and the gates of hades shall not prevail against it.
19 And I will give to you the keys of the kingdom of heaven;
and whatever you shall bind on earth, shall be bound in heaven;
and whatever you shall loose on earth, shall be loosed in heaven.
20 Then he charged his disciples to tell no one that he was the
Christ.

21 From that time Jesus began to tell his disciples plainly,
that he must go to Jerusalem, and suffer many things from the
elders, and the chief priests, and the scribes, and be put to
death, and be raised again the third day. 22 And Peter took
him and began to rebuke him, saying: Be it far from thee,
Lord: this shall not be to thee. 23 But he turned and said to
Peter: Get behind me, adversary; you are a snare to me: for
you are not thinking of the things of God, but of the things
of men.

24 Then Jesus said to his disciples: If any one determines to
come after me, let him deny himself, and take up his cross, and

follow me. 25 For whoever will save his life, shall lose it. But
whoever will lose his life for my sake, shall find it. 26 For what
is a man profited, if he gain the whole world, but lose his own
life? Or, what will a man give as the ransom of his life? 27 For
the Son of man will come in the glory of his Father, with his
angels; and then he will reward every one according to his
deeds. 28 Verily I say to you, There are some standing here
that shall not taste of death, till they see the Son of man coming in his kingdom.

XVII. 1 And after six days, Jesus took with him Peter and
James and John his brother, and led them up into a high
mountain apart: 2 and he was transfigured before them: and
his face did shine as the sun, and his clothing was white as the
light. 3 And behold, there appeared to them Moses and Elijah,
talking with him. 4 And Peter answered and said to Jesus:
Lord, it is good for us to be here; if thou wilt, let us make here
three tents, one for thee, and one for Moses, and one for Elijah.
5 While he was yet speaking, behold, a bright cloud overshadowed
them; and lo, a voice from the cloud, saying: This is my beloved Son, in whom I delight; hear him. 6 And when the disciples heard it, they fell on their faces, and were greatly afraid.
7 And Jesus came and touched them, and said: Arise and be not
afraid. 8 And when they lifted up their eyes, they saw no one
but Jesus.

9 And as they came down from the mountain, Jesus charged
them, saying: Tell the vision to no one, till the Son of man has
risen from the dead. 10 And his disciples asked him, saying:
Why then do the scribes say that Elijah must come first?
11 Jesus answered and said to them: Elijah, indeed, comes first,
and he will restore all things. 12 But I say to you, That Elijah
has already come, and they did not recognize him, but did to
him what they wished; so also shall the Son of man suffer at
their hands. 13 Then the disciples understood that he spoke to
them of John the Immerser.

14 And when they had come to the multitude, there came to
him a man who knelt to him, 15 and said: Lord, have mercy on
my son; for he is a lunatic, and suffers grievously; for he often
falls into the fire, and often into the water. 16 And I brought
him to thy disciples, and they were not able to cure him.
17 Jesus answered and said: O faithless and perverse generation,
how long shall I be with you? How long shall I bear with you?

Bring him hither to me. [18] And Jesus rebuked the demon, and
he came out of him: and the child was cured from that hour.
[19] Then the disciples came to Jesus privately, and said: Why
were we not able to cast him out? [20] And Jesus said to them:
Because of your unbelief. For verily I say to you, If you have
faith like a grain of mustard-seed, you shall say to this mountain, Be removed from this place to that, and it shall be removed:
and nothing shall be impossible for you. [21] But this kind does
not go out but by prayer and fasting.
[22] And as they were making their journey in Galilee, Jesus
said to them: The Son of man is about to be delivered into the
hands of men; [23] and they will kill him, and on the third day
he will be raised again. And they were very sad.
[24] And when they had come into Capernaum, those who collected the didrachma came to Peter, and said: Does not your
teacher pay the didrachma? [25] He said: Yes. And when he
had come into the house, before he had spoken, Jesus said to
him: What think you, Simon? From whom do the kings of
the earth collect tax or tribute? From their own sons, or from
the sons of others? [26] Peter said to him: From the sons of
others. Jesus said to him: Then are their own sons free. [27] But
that we may give them no offense, go to the sea, and throw in a
hook, and take the fish that comes up first; and when you have
opened his mouth, you will find a stater; take that, and give to
them for me and you.

XVIII. [1] At that hour the disciples came to Jesus, and said:
Who then is greatest in the kingdom of heaven? [2] And Jesus
called a little child to him, and placed him in the midst of
them, [3] and said: Verily I say to you, Unless you turn and become as little children, you can not enter the kingdom of heaven.
[4] Whoever, therefore, humbles himself as this little child, is
greatest in the kingdom of heaven. [5] And whoever receives one
such little child on my account, receives me; [6] but whoever
ensnares one of these little ones that believe in me, it were better
for him that a millstone were hung about his neck, and that he
were drowned in the depth of the sea.
[7] Alas for the world because of snares! for it is necessary that
snares come: but alas for that man by whom the snare comes!
[8] If, then, your hand or your foot ensnares you, cut it off, and
throw it from you. It is better for you to enter into life lame
or maimed, than, having two hands or two feet, to be thrown

into the eternal fire. 9 And if your eye ensnares you, pull it out, and throw it from you. It is better to enter into life with one eye, than, having two eyes, to be thrown into hell-fire.

10 Take heed that you despise not one of these little ones: for I say to you, that their angels in heaven do always behold the face of my Father who is in heaven. 11 For the Son of man has come to save that which is lost. 12 What think you? If a man have a hundred sheep, and one of them go astray, does he not leave the ninety-nine, and go into the mountains, and seek for that which has gone astray? 13 And if it so be that he find it, verily I say to you, he rejoices over it more than over the ninety-nine that did not go astray. 14 Even so, it is not the will of your Father who is in heaven, that one of these little ones should be lost.

15 And if your brother sin against you, go and tell him of his fault between you and him alone; if he hear you, you have gained your brother. 16 But if he will not hear you, take with you one or two more, that, by the mouth of two or three witnesses, every word may be established. 17 But if he refuse to hear them, tell it to the church; and if he also refuse to hear the church, let him be to you as a heathen man and a publican.

18 Verily, I say to you, *my disciples*, Whatever you bind on earth, shall be bound in heaven; and whatever you loose on earth, shall be loosed in heaven. 19 Again, I say to you, that if two of you agree on earth about any thing for which they will ask, it shall be done for them by my Father who is in heaven. 20 For where there are two or three that have come together for my sake, there I am in the midst of them.

21 Then Peter came to him, and said: Lord, how often shall my brother sin against me, and I forgive him? Till seven times? 22 Jesus said to him: I say to you, Not till seven times, but till seventy times seven. 23 For this reason, the kingdom of heaven is likened to a king that wished to settle accounts with his servants. 24 And when he began to make a settlement, there was brought to him one that owed him ten thousand talents. 25 But as he was not able to pay, his lord commanded him, and his wife, and children, and all that he had, to be sold, and payment to be made. 26 Therefore, the servant fell down and besought him, saying, Have patience with me, lord, and I will pay you all. 27 And the lord of that servant was moved with compassion, and let him go, and forgave him the debt.

28 But that servant went out, and found one of his fellow-

servants, who owed him a hundred denarii; and he laid hold of
him, and took him by the throat, saying: Pay me what you
owe. 29 Then his fellow-servant fell down at his feet, and besought him, saying: Have patience with me, and I will pay you
all. 30 And he would not; but went and threw him into prison,
till he should pay the debt. 31 When his fellow-servants saw
what was done, they were very sad, and went and made known
to their lord all that was done. 32 Then his lord called him and
said to him: Wicked servant! I forgave you all that debt, because you besought me. 33 Ought you not to have had mercy
on your fellow-servant, even as I had mercy on you. 34 And his
lord was angry, and delivered him to the jailers, till he should
pay all that was due him. 35 So also will my heavenly Father
do to you, if, from your hearts, you forgive not every one his
brother's offenses.

XIX. 1 And it came to pass when Jesus had finished these
discourses, that he departed from Galilee, and came into the
borders of Judea, beyond the Jordan. 2 And many multitudes
followed him; and he cured them there.

3 And the Pharisees came to him to tempt him, and said to
him: Is it lawful for a man to put away his wife for every
cause? 4 He answered and said to them: Have you not read
that the Creator, at the beginning, created them male and female, 5 and said, For this cause shall a man leave his father
and his mother, and shall cleave to his wife, and the two shall
be one flesh? 6 So then, they are no longer two, but one flesh.
Therefore, what God has joined together, let not man put
asunder.

7 They said to him: Why, then, did Moses command us to give
a bill of divorce and put her away? 8 He said to them: Moses,
on account of the hardness of your hearts, permitted you to
put away your wives; but from the beginning it was not so.
9 But I say to you, That whoever puts away his wife, unless for
lewdness, and marries another, commits adultery; and he that
marries her that is put away, commits adultery.

10 His disciples said to him: If the relation of man and wife
be such, it is not good to marry. 11 But he said to them: All
can not accept this saying; only those to whom it is given.
12 For there are eunuchs that were born such from their mother's
womb; and there are eunuchs that have been made eunuchs by
men; and there are eunuchs that have made themselves eunuchs

for the sake of the kingdom of heaven. Let him accept it that
is able to accept it.

13 Then little children were brought to him, that he might lay
his hands on them and pray. And the disciples rebuked them.
14 But Jesus said: Let the little children come to me, and forbid
them not: for of such is the kingdom of heaven. 15 And he laid
his hands on them, and departed from that place.

16 And behold, one came and said to him: Good teacher, what
good thing must I do that I may have eternal life? He said to
him: 17 Why do you call me good? There is none good but one,
that is God. But if you desire to enter into life, keep the commandments. 18 He said to him: Which? Jesus replied: You
shall not kill; You shall not commit adultery; You shall not
steal; You shall not give false testimony; 19 Honor your father
and your mother; and, You shall love your neighbor as yourself. 20 The young man said to him: All these have I kept from
my youth, what do I lack? 21 Jesus said to him: If you would
be perfect, go, sell your possessions, and give to the poor, and
you shall have treasure in heaven; and come, follow me.
22 When the young man heard that saying, he went away
grieved; for he had great possessions.

23 Jesus said to his disciples: Verily I say to you, A rich man
will with difficulty enter into the kingdom of heaven. 24 And
again I say to you: It is easier for a camel to go through the
eye of a needle, than for a rich man to enter into the kingdom of God. 25 When the disciples heard it, they were greatly
amazed, and said: Who, then, can be saved? 26 But Jesus looked
on them, and said to them: With men, this is impossible; but
with God, all things are possible.

27 Then Peter answered and said to him: Behold, we have left
all and followed thee; what, then, shall we have? 28 Jesus said
to them: Verily I say to you, That, in the restoration, when
the Son of man shall sit on his glorious throne, you also who
have followed me shall sit on twelve thrones, judging the twelve
tribes of Israel. 29 And every one that has left houses, or
brothers, or sisters, or father, or mother, or wife, or children,
or lands, for my name's sake, shall receive a hundred-fold, and
shall inherit eternal life. But many that are first shall be last;
and the last first.

XX. 1 For the kingdom of heaven is like the master of a
house, who went out early in the morning to hire laborers for

his vineyard. 2 And when he had agreed with the laborers for a
denarius a day, he sent them into his vineyard. 3 And he went
out about the third hour, and saw others standing in the market, idle; 4 and he said to them: Go you also into my vineyard,
and whatever is right I will give you. 5 And they went. Again
he went out about the sixth, and about the ninth hour, and did
in like manner. 6 And about the eleventh hour he went out,
and found others standing idle, and said to them, Why do you
stand here all the day idle? 7 They said to him: No man has
hired us. He said to them: Go you also into the vineyard, and
whatever is right you shall receive.

8 When the evening came, the owner of the vineyard said to
his steward: Call the laborers, and, beginning with the last, pay
them their hire even to the first. 9 And when those came who
had been hired about the eleventh hour, they received each one
a denarius. 10 But when those came who had been hired first,
they thought that they would receive more; and they received
each one a denarius. 11 And when they received it, they murmured against the master of the house, 12 saying: these last have
worked one hour, and you have made them equal to us, who have
borne the burden of the day, and the heat. 13 But he answered
and said to one of them: Friend, I do you no injustice; did you
not agree with me for a denarius? 14 Take what is yours, and
go; I will give to this last even as to you. 15 Is it not allowed
me to do what I will with my own? Or, is your eye envious,
because I am good? 16 So the last shall be first, and the first last.
For many are called, but few are chosen.

17 And as Jesus was going up to Jerusalem, he took the twelve
disciples aside on his journey, and said to them: 18 Behold, we
are going up to Jerusalem, and the Son of man shall be delivered to the chief priests and the scribes, and they will condemn him to death, 19 and will deliver him to the Gentiles to
deride, and to scourge, and to crucify: and on the third day he
shall rise again.

20 Then came to him the mother of the sons of Zebedee, with
her sons, bowing down, and asking something of him. 21 He
said to her: What do you wish? She said to him: Command
that these two sons of mine may sit, the one on thy right hand,
and the other son on thy left, in thy kingdom. 22 But Jesus
answered and said: You know not what you ask. Are you able
to drink the cup that I am about to drink, and to be immersed
with the immersion with which I am immersed? They said to

him: We are able. 23 And he said to them: You shall drink
my cup, and be immersed with the immersion with which I am
immersed: but to sit on my right hand, and on my left, is not
mine to give; but it shall be given to them for whom it has
been prepared by my Father.

24 And when the ten heard it, their anger was aroused against
the two brothers. 25 But Jesus called them to him, and said:
You know that the rulers of the Gentiles act as lords over them,
and their great men have authority over them. 26 It shall not be
so among you. But whoever will be great among you, let him be
your minister. 27 And whoever will be first among you, let him be
your servant; 28 even as the Son of man came, not to be ministered to, but to minister, and to give his life a ransom for many.

29 And as they went out from Jericho, a great multitude followed him. 30 And behold, two blind men, sitting by the road,
when they heard that Jesus was passing by, cried out, saying:
Have mercy on us, Lord, son of David. 31 And the multitude
charged them to be silent. But they cried the more, saying:
Have mercy on us, Lord, son of David. 32 And Jesus stood still,
and called them, and said: What do you wish me to do for
you? 33 They said to him: Lord, that our eyes may be opened.
34 Jesus had compassion on them, and touched their eyes; and
their eyes immediately received sight, and they followed him.

XXI. 1 And when they drew near to Jerusalem, and had come
to Bethpage, to the mount of Olives, then Jesus sent two disciples, 2 saying to them: Go into the village opposite to you, and
immediately you will find an ass tied, and a colt with her: loose
them, and bring them to me. 3 And if any one say any thing
to you, you shall reply: The Lord has need of them: and he will
immediately send them. 4 All this was done, that the word
might be fulfilled which was spoken by the prophet, saying:
5 Say you to the daughter of Zion, Behold your king comes to
you, meek, and sitting upon an ass, and a colt the foal of an ass.

6 And the disciples went and did as Jesus commanded them;
7 and brought the ass and the colt, and put their mantles on
them, and caused him to sit upon them. 8 And a very great
multitude spread their mantles in the road: and others cut
branches from the trees, and spread them in the road. 9 And
the multitudes that went before, and that followed after, cried,
saying: Hosanna to the son of David. Blessed is he that comes
in the name of the Lord. Hosanna in the highest.

10 And when he entered Jerusalem, all the city was moved,
and said: Who is this? 11 And the multitude said: This is
Jesus the prophet, that is from Nazareth of Galilee.

12 And Jesus went into the temple of God, and drove out all
that sold and bought in the temple, and overthrew the tables of
the money-changers, and the seats of those who sold doves,
13 and said to them: It is written, My house shall be called a
house of prayer; but you have made it a den of robbers. 14 And
the blind and the lame came to him in the temple, and he cured
them. 15 But when the chief priests and the scribes saw the
wonderful things that he did, and the children crying in the
temple, and saying, Hosanna to the son of David, their anger
was aroused, 16 and they said to him: Do you not hear what
these say? And Jesus said to them: Yes; have you never read,
Out of the mouth of babes and sucklings thou hast perfected
praise? 17 And he left them, and went out of the city to Bethany, and there spent the night.

18 Now in the morning, as he was returning to the city, he
was hungry: 19 and seeing a fig-tree on the road, he went to it,
and found nothing on it but leaves; and he said to it: Let no
fruit grow on you henceforth forever. And the fig-tree immediately withered. 20 And when the disciples saw it, they were
astonished, and said: How soon has the fig-tree withered!
21 Jesus answered and said to them: Verily I say to you, If you
have faith, and doubt not, you shall do, not only what is done
to the fig-tree, but even if you shall say to this mountain, Be
taken up, and be thrown into the sea, it shall be done.
22 And all things that you ask for in prayer, believing, you
shall receive.

23 And after he had come into the temple, the chief priests
and elders of the people came to him as he was teaching, and
said: By what authority do you these things? And who gave
you this authority? 24 Jesus answered and said to them: I also
will ask you one thing, which if you will tell me, I also will tell
you by what authority I do these things. 25 The immersion of
John, whence was it? from heaven, or from men? But they
reasoned among themselves, and said, If we reply, From heaven,
he will say to us, Why then did you not believe him? 26 But if
we reply, From men, we fear the multitude; for all regard John
as a prophet. 27 And they answered and said to Jesus: We
know not. And he said to them: Neither do I tell you by what
authority I do these things.

28 But what think you? A man had two sons; and he went
to the first, and said, Son, go work to-day in my vineyard.
29 He answered and said, I will not. But he afterward regretted
it, and went. 30 And he came to the other, and spoke to him
in like manner. And he answered and said, I go, sir; and went
not. 31 Which of the two did the will of his father? They said
to him, The first. Jesus said to them: Verily I say to you, The
publicans and the harlots go into the kingdom of God before
you. 32 For John came to you in the way of righteousness, and
you believed him not. But the publicans and the harlots believed him. And you, when you had seen it, afterward felt no
regret, that you might believe him.

33 Hear another parable: There was a master of a house who
planted a vineyard, and put a hedge around it, and digged in
it a wine-press, and built a tower, and let it out to vine-dressers, and went into another country. 34 And when the time of
the fruit drew near, he sent his servants to the vine-dressers to
receive the fruits of it. 35 And the vine-dressers took his servants, and scourged one, and killed another, and stoned another.
36 Again he sent other servants more than the first: and they
treated them in like manner. 37 But afterward he sent to them
his son, saying, They will reverence my son. 38 But the vine-
dressers, when they saw the son, said among themselves, This
is the heir; come, let us kill him, and seize upon the inheritance.
39 And they took him, and carried him out of the vineyard, and
killed him. 40 Therefore, when the owner of the vineyard comes,
what will he do to those vine-dressers? 41 They said to him:
He will miserably destroy those wicked men, and let out his
vineyard to other vine-dressers, who will give him the fruits in
their season.

42 Jesus said to them: Did you never read in the Scriptures,
The stone which the builders rejected has become the head of
the corner? 43 This was from the Lord, and it is wondrous in
our eyes. For this reason, I say to you, The kingdom of God
shall be taken from you, and given to a nation that will bring
forth the fruits of it. 44 And he that falls upon this stone shall
be dashed to pieces; but him on whom it shall fall, it will make
like chaff for the wind.

45 And when the chief priests and Pharisees heard his parables, they knew that he spoke of them. 46 And when they
sought to lay hold of him, they feared the multitude, because
they regarded him as a prophet.

XXII. 1 And Jesus answering, spoke to them again in parables, saying: 2 The kingdom of heaven is like a king that made
a marriage feast for his son; 3 and sent his servants to call those
who had been invited to the marriage feast; and they refused
to come. 4 Again, he sent other servants, saying, Tell those
who have been invited, Behold, I have prepared my dinner; my
oxen and my fatlings are killed, and all things are ready: come
to the marriage feast. 5 But they were careless, and went away,
one to his farm, another to his merchandise. 6 And the rest
laid hold of his servants, and abused them and killed them.
7 And when that king heard of it, he was angry, and sent his
armies, and destroyed those murderers, and burned up their
city. 8 Then he said to his servants: The marriage feast is
ready, but those who were invited were not worthy. 9 Go,
therefore, to the cross-ways, and invite to the marriage feast
as many as you find. 10 And those servants went out into the
roads, and brought together all, as many as they found, both
bad and good: and the banquet-room was filled with guests.
11 And when the king came in to see the guests, he saw there a
man that had not put on a wedding-robe. 12 And he said to
him, Friend, how came you in hither without a wedding-robe?
And he was silent. 13 Then the king said to his servants, Bind
him hand and foot, and take him away, and throw him into the
darkness without: there shall be weeping and gnashing of teeth.
14 For many are called, but few chosen.
15 Then the Pharisees went and held a consultation, that they
might entrap him in his words. 16 And they sent to him their
disciples with the Herodains, saying: Teacher, we know that
you are true, and that you teach the way of God in truth, and
care not for any one: for you do not look upon the person of
men. 17 Tell us, therefore, what do you think? Is it lawful to
give tribute to Cæsar, or not? 18 But Jesus, knowing their wickedness, said to them: Why do you tempt me, hypocrites? 19 Show
me the tribute-money. And they brought him a denarius.
20 And he said to them: Whose image and superscription is
this? 21 They said to him: Cæsar's. Then he said to them:
Give, therefore, to Cæsar the things that are Cæsar's, and to
God the things that are God's. 22 And when they heard it, they
were astonished, and left him, and went away.
23 On that day there came to him the Sadducees, who say that
there is no resurrection; and they put a question to him, 24 saying: Teacher, Moses commanded, If any one die without chil-

dren, his brother shall marry his wife, and raise up children
for his brother. 25 Now there were with us seven brothers; and
the first took a wife, and died; and, having no child, left his
wife to his brother. 26 In like manner also the second, and the
third, to the seventh. 27 Last of all, the woman also died.
28 Therefore, in the resurrection, of which of the seven will she
be the wife? for they all had her.

29 Jesus answered and said to them: You err, because you
know neither the Scriptures nor the power of God. 30 For in
the resurrection they neither marry nor are given in marriage,
but are as the angels of God in heaven. 31 But, concerning the
resurrection of the dead, have you not read that which was
spoken to you by God, saying: 32 I am the God of Abraham,
and the God of Isaac, and the God of Jacob? God is not the
God of the dead, but of the living. 33 And when the multitude
heard this, they were astonished at his teaching.

34 When the Pharisees heard that he had put the Sadducees to
silence, they came together. 35 And one of them who was a lawyer, asked him a question, that he might tempt him, saying:
36 Teacher, which is the great commandment in the law? 37 Jesus said to him: You shall love the Lord your God with your
whole heart, and with your whole soul, and with your whole
mind. 38 This is the first and great commandment. 39 And
the second is like it: You shall love your neighbor as yourself.
40 On these two commandments hang the whole law and the
prophets.

41 While the Pharisees were together, Jesus asked them a
question, 42 saying: What think you of the Christ? whose son
is he? They said to him: The son of David. 43 He said to
them: How then does David in spirit call him Lord, saying,
44 The Lord said to my Lord, Sit thou at my right hand till I
make thy enemies thy footstool. 45 If then David calls him
Lord, how is he his son? 46 And no one was able to answer him
a word; nor did any one, from that day, dare to ask him another
question.

XXIII. 1 Then Jesus spoke to the multitudes, and to his
disciples, 2 saying: The scribes and the Pharisees sit in Moses'
seat: 3 therefore, all things that they command you to observe,
observe and do. But do not according to their works: for they
command, and do not. 4 For they bind up burdens that are
heavy and hard to be borne, and lay them on the shoulders of

men; but they refuse to move them with one of their fingers.
5 And they do all their works for the purpose of being seen by
men. They make their amulets broad, and enlarge the fringes
of their mantles. 6 They also love the most honorable places at
suppers, and the first seats in the synagogues, 7 and salutations
in the markets, and to be called by men, Rabbi, Rabbi.

8 But you must not be called Rabbi; for one is your teacher,
and all of you are brethren. 9 And call no man on earth your
father; for one is your Father, who is in heaven. 10 And be not
called leaders; for one is your leader, the Christ. 11 And the
greatest among you shall be your minister. 12 Whoever exalts
himself shall be humbled; and whoever humbles himself shall
be exalted.

13 But alas for you, scribes and Pharisees, hypocrites! for
you eat up the houses of widows, and for a pretext make long
prayers. For this reason, you shall receive the greater condemnation. 14 Alas for you, scribes and Pharisees, hypocrites!
for you close the kingdom of heaven in the face of men; for you
neither go in yourselves, nor do you suffer those who are entering, to go in. 15 Alas for you, scribes and Pharisees, hypocrites!
for you traverse sea and land to make one proselyte; and when
he is made, you make him twofold more a child of hell than
yourselves.

16 Alas for you, blind guides! who say, Whoever shall swear
by the temple, it is nothing; but whoever shall swear by the
gold of the temple, becomes a debtor. 17 Fools and blind! for
which is greater, the gold, or the temple that sanctifies the gold?
18 And, Whoever shall swear by the altar, it is nothing; but
whoever shall swear by the gift that is on it, becomes a debtor.
19 Fools and blind! for which is greater, the gift, or the altar
that sanctifies the gift? 20 Therefore, whoever swears by the
altar, swears by it, and by all that is on it. 21 And whoever
swears by the temple, swears by it, and by him that dwells in it.
22 And he that swears by heaven, swears by the throne of God,
and by him that sits upon it.

23 Alas for you, scribes and Pharisees, hypocrites! for you pay
tithes of mint and dill and cummin, and have neglected the
weightier matters of the law, its justice, its mercy, and its
faithfulness. These you ought to have done, and those you
ought not to have neglected. 24 Blind guides! who strain out a
gnat, but swallow a camel. 25 Alas for you, scribes and Pharisees, hypocrites! for you make clean the outside of the cup and

the plate; but within they are full of rapine and excess. 26 Blind
Pharisee! first make clean the inside of the cup and the plate,
that the outside of them also may be clean.

27 Alas for you, scribes and Pharisees, hypocrites! for you are
like whitened sepulchers, which without appear beautiful, but
within are full of dead men's bones, and of all uncleanness.
28 So also you outwardly appear to men to be just, but within
you are full of hypocrisy and lawlessness. 29 Alas for you,
scribes and Pharisees, hypocrites! for you build the tombs of
the prophets, and adorn the sepulchers of the righteous, 30 and
say: If we had been in the days of our fathers, we would not
have been partakers with them in the blood of the prophets.
31 So then you testify against yourselves, that you are the sons
of those who killed the prophets. 32 Do you also fill up the
measure of your fathers. 33 Serpents, generation of vipers, how
can you escape the condemnation of hell?

34 For this reason, behold, I send you prophets and wise men
and scribes; and some of them you will kill and crucify; and
some of them you will scourge in your synagogues, and persecute from city to city; 35 that upon you may come all the
righteous blood which has been shed upon the earth, from the
blood of Abel the just to the blood of Zachariah, the son of
Barachiah, whom you slew between the temple and the altar.
36 Verily I say to you, All these things shall come upon this
generation.

37 Jerusalem, Jerusalem, thou that killest the prophets and
stonest those who are sent to thee, how often have I desired to
gather thy children together, as a bird gathers her young under
her wings, and you refused. 38 Behold, your house is left to you
deserted. 39 For I say to you, That you shall not see me henceforth, till you shall say, Blessed is he that comes in the name
of the Lord.

XXIV. 1 And Jesus went out, and was departing from the
temple, and his disciples came to him to point out to him the
buildings of the temple. 2 But Jesus said to them: Do you not
see all these things? Verily I say to you, There shall not be left
here a stone upon a stone that shall not be thrown down.

3 And as he was sitting upon the mount of Olives, the disciples came to him privately, and said: Tell us, when shall these
things be? and what shall be the sign of thy coming, and of
the end of the age? 4 And Jesus answered and said to them:

Take heed that no one deceive you. 5 For many will come in my
name, saying, I am the Christ; and will deceive many. 6 And
you will hear of wars and rumors of wars: see that you be not
troubled, for all things must be fulfilled; but the end is not yet.
7 For nation will rise against nation, and kingdom against kingdom; and there will be famines and pestilences and earthquakes
in various places. 8 But all these are the beginning of sorrows.
9 Then they will deliver you up to affliction, and kill you; and
you will be hated by all nations on my account. 10 And then
will many be ensnared, and they will deliver one another up,
and hate one another; 11 and many false prophets will arise,
and deceive many; 12 and because iniquity abounds, the love of
many will grow cold. 13 But he that endures to the end, shall
be saved. 14 And this gospel of the kingdom shall be preached
in the whole habitable earth, for a testimony to all nations, and
then shall the end come.

15 When, therefore, you see that detestable thing that makes
desolate, spoken of by Daniel the prophet, standing in the holy
place, (let him that reads understand;) 15 then let those who are
in Judea flee to the mountains; 16 let not him that is on the
house-top come down to take his goods out of his house; 18 and
let not him that is in the field turn back to take his clothing.
19 But alas for those who are with child, and those who give
suck in those days! 20 Pray that your flight may not be in the
winter, nor on the Sabbath: 21 for then shall be great affliction,
such as has not been from the beginning of the world till now,
nor shall ever be. 22 And unless those days should be made few,
no flesh could be saved. But on account of the elect those days
shall be made few.

23 Then if any one shall say to you: Lo! here is the Christ, or
there; believe it not. 24 For false Christs and false prophets
will arise, and will show great signs and wonders, so as to deceive, if possible, even the elect. 25 Behold, I have told you beforehand. 26 Therefore, if they say to you: Behold, he is in the
desert; go not out: Behold, he is in the secret chambers; believe it not. 27 For as the lightning comes out from the east,
and shines even to the west, so also shall the coming of the Son
of man be. 28 For wherever the carcass is, there will the vultures come together.

29 Immediately after the affliction of those days, the sun shall
be darkened, and the moon shall not give her light, and the
stars shall fall from heaven; and the hosts of the heavens shall

be shaken. 30 And then shall appear the sign of the Son of man
in heaven; and then shall all the tribes of the land mourn, and
they shall see the Son of man coming in the clouds of heaven
with power and great glory. 31 And he will send his angels with
a trumpet of great voice, and they shall gather his elect from
the four winds, from one end of heaven to the other.

32 Learn now a parable from the fig-tree: As soon as its
branch becomes tender, and puts forth leaves, you know that
summer is near. 33 So also, when you see all these things, know
that it is near at the doors. 34 Verily I say to you, this generation shall not pass away till all these things shall have taken
place. 35 Heaven and earth shall pass away, but my words
shall not pass away.

36 But of that day and hour no one knows, not the angels of
heaven, but my Father only. 37 But as the days of Noah were,
so shall be the coming of the Son of man. 38 For as in the days
before the flood, they were eating and drinking, marrying and
giving in marriage, till the day in which Noah entered the ark,
39 and knew not, till the flood came and took them all away: so
shall be the coming of the Son of man. 40 Then two men shall
be in the field; one shall be taken, and the other left. 41 Two
women shall be grinding at the mill; one shall be taken, and
the other left.

42 Watch, therefore, for you know not at what hour your Lord
is coming. 43 But know this, That if the master of the house
had known at what watch the thief comes, he would have
watched, and would not have permitted his house to be broken
open. 44 For this reason, be you also ready; for at an hour in
which you think not, the Son of man comes. 45 Who then is
that faithful and wise servant, whom his master has made ruler
over his household servants, to give them their food in due time?
46 Blessed is that servant, whom his master, when he comes,
shall find so doing. 47 Verily I say to you, That he will make
him ruler over all his goods.

48 But if that wicked servant shall say in his heart, My master
delays his coming; 49 and shall begin to strike his fellow-servants, and shall eat and drink with the drunken; 50 the master
of that servant will come in a day in which he looks not for
him, and at an hour which he knows not, 51 and will cut him in
two, and appoint him his part with the hypocrites. There shall
be weeping and gnashing of teeth.

XXV. 1 Then shall the kingdom of heaven be likened to ten
virgins, who took their lamps and went out to meet the bridegroom. 2 Five of them were wise, and five were foolish. 3 Those
who were foolish took their lamps, and took no oil with them:
4 But the wise took oil in their vessels, with their lamps. 5 While
the bridegroom delayed, they all slumbered and slept. 6 And at
midnight a cry was made: Behold, the bridegroom comes! Go
you out to meet him. 7 Then all those virgins arose, and
trimmed their lamps. 8 And the foolish said to the wise: Give
us of your oil, for our lamps are going out. 9 But the wise answered, saying: Lest there may not be enough for us and you,
go rather to those who sell, and buy for yourselves. 10 While
they were going to buy, the bridegroom came; and those who
were ready went in with him to the marriage-supper; and the
door was closed. 11 Afterward the other virgins also came, and
said: Lord! Lord! open for us. 12 But he answered and said:
Verily I say to you, I know you not. 13 Watch, therefore, for
you know neither the day nor the hour.

14 For as a man, on leaving his country, called his own servants, and delivered to them his goods: 15 To one he gave five
talents; to another, two; and to another, one; to each one,
according to his own ability, and immediately left his country.
16 Then he that had received the five talents, went and traded
with them, and made other five talents. 17 In like manner also,
he that had received the two, gained other two. 18 But he that
had received the one, went and digged in the earth, and hid his
lord's money.

19 After a long time, the lord of those servants came and
settled with them. 20 And he that had received the five talents
came and brought other five talents, and said: Lord, you delivered to me five talents: see, I have gained other five talents in
addition to them. 21 His lord said to him: Well done, good and
faithful servant; you have been faithful over a few things, I will
make you ruler over many. Enter into the joy of your lord.

22 And he also that had received the two talents came, and
said: Lord, you delivered to me two talents; see, I have gained
other two talents in addition to them. 23 His lord said to him:
Well done, good and faithful servant; you have been faithful
over a few things, I will make you ruler over many. Enter into
the joy of your lord.

24 But he that had received the one talent came, and said:
Lord, I knew you, that you are a hard man, reaping where you

did not sow, and gathering where you did not scatter. 25 And
I was afraid, and went and hid your talent in the earth; see,
you have yours. 26 His lord answered and said to him: Wicked
and slothful servant; did you know that I reap where I did not
sow, and gather where I did not scatter? 27 Therefore, you
ought to have put my money with the bankers; and, when I
came, I could have received my own with interest. 28 Therefore,
take from him the talent, and give it to him that has the ten
talents. 29 For to every one that has, it shall be given, and he
shall have abundance. But from him that has not, even that
which he has shall be taken away. 30 And cast the unprofitable
servant into the darkness without. There shall be weeping and
gnashing of teeth.

31 When the Son of man shall come in his own glory, and all
the holy angels with him, then will he sit on the throne of his
own glory; 32 and all nations shall be gathered before him; and
he will separate them one from another, as a shepherd separates
his sheep from the goats. 33 And he will place the sheep on his
right hand, but the goats on his left. 34 Then the King will say
to those on his right hand: Come, you blessed of my Father,
inherit the kingdom prepared for you from the foundation of
the world. 35 For I was hungry, and you gave me food; I was
thirsty, and you gave me drink; I was a stranger, and you took
me to your houses; 36 naked, and you clothed me; I was sick,
and you visited me; I was in prison, and you came to me.
37 Then will the righteous answer him, saying: Lord, when did
we see thee hungry, and feed thee? or thirsty, and give thee
drink? 38 When did we see thee a stranger, and take thee to our
home? or naked, and clothe thee? 39 When did we see thee sick,
or in prison, and come to thee? 40 And the King will answer
and say to them: Verily I say to you, Inasmuch as you did it
to one of the least of these my brethren, you did it to me.

41 Then will he say to those on his left hand: Depart from me
you cursed, into the eternal fire, prepared for the devil and hi
angels. 42 For I was hungry, and you gave me no food; I wa
thirsty, and you gave me no drink; 43 I was a stranger, and yo
took me not to your houses; naked, and you did not clothe me
I was sick, and in prison, and you did not visit me. 44 The
they will also answer, and say: Lord, when did we see the
hungry, or thirsty, or a stranger, or naked, or sick, or in prison
and did not minister to thee? 45 Then will he answer them, say
ing: Verily I say to you, Inasmuch as you did it not to one o

the least of these, you did it not to me. [46] And these shall go
away into eternal punishment, but the righteous into eternal
life.

XXVI. [1] And it came to pass, when Jesus had finished all
these words, that he said to his disciples : [2] You know that after
two days the passover is kept, and the Son of man is delivered
up to be crucified.

[3] Then the chief priests, and the scribes, and the elders of the
people met together at the palace of the chief priest, who was
called Caiaphas. [4] And they consulted together that they might
take Jesus by craft and kill him. [5] But they said: Not during
the feast, lest there be a tumult among the people.

[6] When Jesus was in Bethany, in the house of Simon the leper,
[7] there came to him a woman who had an alabaster box of very
costly ointment; and she poured it on his head as he reclined at
table. [8] But when his disciples saw it, they were displeased, and
said: For what purpose was this waste? [9] For this could have
been sold for much, and given to the poor. [10] Jesus perceived
it, and said to them: Why do you trouble the woman? For she
has performed a good work upon me. [11] For you have the poor
always with you, but me you have not always. [12] For in pouring this ointment on my body, she has done it to prepare me for
burial. [13] Verily I say to you, wherever this gospel shall be
preached in the whole world, this also which she has done shall
be told for a memorial of her.

[14] Then one of the twelve, called Judas Iscariot, went to the
chief priests, [15] and said: What are you willing to give me, and
I will deliver him to you? And they weighed to him thirty
pieces of silver. [16] And from that time he sought an opportunity to deliver him up.

[17] On the first day of unleavened bread, the disciples came to
Jesus, and said to him: Where dost thou wish that we prepare
for thee to eat the passover? [18] He replied: Go into the city,
to a certain man, and say to him, The Teacher says, My time is
near; I will keep the passover at your house, with my disciples.
[19] And the disciples did as Jesus commanded them, and prepared
the passover.

[20] When the evening had come, he reclined at table with the
twelve. [21] And as they were eating, he said: Verily I say to
you, One of you will deliver me up. [22] And they were very sad,
and began each one of them to say to him: Lord, is it I? [23] He

answered and said: He that dips his hand with me in the dish,
will deliver me up. 24 The Son of man goes, as it is written of
him; but alas for that man by whom the Son of man is delivered up! It would have been good for that man, if he had not
been born. 25 And Judas, who delivered him up, answered and
said: Rabbi, is it I? He replied: You have said.

26 And as they were eating, Jesus took bread, and when he had
given thanks, he broke it, and gave it to the disciples, and said:
Take, eat; this is my body. 27 And he took the cup, and gave
thanks, and gave it to them, saying: Do you all drink of it:
28 for this is my blood of the new covenant, which is poured
out for many in order to the remission of sins. 29 But I say
to you I will not drink henceforth of this fruit of the vine, till
that day when I drink it with you new in the kingdom of my
Father.

30 And when they had sung a hymn, they went out into the
mount of Olives. 31 Then Jesus said to them: All of you will
be offended at me this night; for it is written, I will smite the
shepherd, and the sheep of the flock shall be scattered. 32 But
after I have risen, I will go before you into Galilee. 33 Peter
answered and said to him: Though all shall be offended at thee,
yet will I never be offended. 34 Jesus said to him: Verily I say
to you, This night, before the cock crows, you will deny me
three times. 35 Peter said to him: Though it should be necessary for me to die with thee, I will not deny thee. In like
manner said all the disciples.

36 Then Jesus came with them to a place called Gethsemane,
and said to his disciples: Sit here, till I go and pray yonder.
37 And he took with him Peter and the two sons of Zebedee,
and began to be in deep distress and anguish of soul. 38 Then
Jesus said to them: My soul is encompassed with sorrow even
to death; remain here, and watch with me. 39 And he went
forward a little, and fell on his face in prayer, saying: My
Father, if it is possible, let this cup pass from me; yet not as I
will, but as thou willest. 40 And he came to his disciples, and
found them sleeping; and he said to Peter: Was it so, that you
had not strength to watch with me one hour? 41 Watch and
pray, lest you enter into temptation. The spirit is willing, but
the flesh is weak.

42 Again, a second time, he went away, and prayed, saying:
My Father, if this cup can not pass from me, unless I drink it,
thy will be done. 43 And he came and found them sleeping

again, for their eyes were heavy. 44 And he left them, and went
away again, and prayed the third time, saying the same thing.
45 Then he came to his disciples, and said to them: Sleep what
time is left, and take your rest; behold, the hour draws near,
and the Son of man is delivered into the hands of sinners.
46 Arise, let us go; behold, he that delivers me up is at hand.

47 And while he was yet speaking, behold, Judas, one of the
twelve, and with him a great multitude with swords and clubs,
came from the chief priests and elders of the people. 48 He that
delivered him up had given them a sign, saying: The one that I
shall kiss is he; hold him fast. 49 And immediately he came to
Jesus, and said: Hail, Rabbi! and kissed him. 50 Jesus said to
him: Friend, for what purpose have you come? Then they
came, and laid hands on Jesus, and held him fast.

51 And behold, one of those who were with Jesus stretched out
his hand, and drew his sword, and struck the servant of the
chief priest, and cut off his ear. 52 Then Jesus said to him: Put
back your sword into its place; for all that take the sword,
shall perish by the sword. 53 Do you think that I can not now
call upon my Father, and he would cause more than twelve legions
of angels to stand by me? 54 But how then shall the
Scriptures be fulfilled, that thus it must be?

55 At the same time Jesus said to the multitudes: Have you
come out as against a robber, with swords and clubs, to take
me? I sat daily with you in the temple and taught, and you
did not take me. 56 All this was done, that the Scriptures of
the prophets might be fulfilled. Then all the disciples left him
and fled.

57 And those who took Jesus led him away to Caiaphas the
chief priest, where the scribes and elders had come together.
58 But Peter followed him, at a distance, to the palace of the
chief priest, and went in and sat with the attendants, to see the
end. 59 And the chief priests and the elders, and the whole Sanhedrim,
sought false testimony against Jesus, that they might
put him to death, 60 and found none. Though many false witnesses
came, yet they found none. At last two false witnesses
came, 61 and said: This man said, I am able to destroy the temple
of God, and to build it in three days. 62 And the chief priest
arose, and said to him: Do you make no answer? What do
these testify against you? 63 But Jesus remained silent.

And the chief priest answered and said to him: I adjure you,
by the living God, that you tell us whether you are the Christ, the

Son of God? 64 Jesus said to him: You have said. Moreover,
I say to you, Hereafter you shall see the Son of man sitting on
the right hand of the Almighty, and coming upon the clouds of
heaven. 65 Then the chief priest rent his clothes, and said: He
has spoken impiously; what further need have we of witnesses?
See now, you have heard his impious words: 66 What think you?
They answered and said: He is a subject for death. 67 Then did
they spit in his face, and strike him with their fists; some
struck him with the open hand, 68 and said: Give an answer to
us, Christ: Who is he that struck you?

69 But Peter was sitting without in the court; and a maid-
servant came to him, and said: You also were with Jesus of
Galilee. 70 But he denied before them all, saying: I know not
what you say. 71 And when he went out into the entrance, another maid-servant saw him, and said to those who were there:
This man was also with Jesus the Nazarene. 72 And again he
denied, with an oath: I know not the man. 73 After a little
while, those who stood by came and said to Peter: Of a truth
you also are one of them, for your speech betrays you. 74 Then
he began to curse and to swear, I know not the man. And immediately the cock crew. 75 And Peter remembered the word
which Jesus had spoken to him: Before the cock crows, you
will deny me three times. And he went out and wept bitterly.

XXVII. 1 When the morning came, all the chief priests and
elders of the people held a consultation against Jesus, that they
might put him to death. 2 And they bound him and led him
away, and delivered him to Pontius Pilate the governor.

3 Then Judas, who had delivered him up, when he saw that he
was condemned, stung by remorse, brought back the thirty
pieces of silver to the chief priests and elders, 4 saying: I have
sinned in having delivered up innocent blood. They replied:
What is that to us? You will see to that. 5 And he threw down
the money in the temple, and departed, and went and hanged
himself. 6 And the chief priests took the money, and said: It
is not lawful to put it into the sacred treasury, because it is the
price of blood. 7 And they took counsel, and bought with it
the potter's field, as a burial-place for foreigners. 8 For this
reason, that field is called the field of blood, to this day. 9 Then
the word was fulfilled which was spoken by Jeremiah the prophet,
saying: And they took the thirty pieces of silver, the price of
him that had a price set upon him, on whom some of the chil-

dren of Israel did set a price, [10] and gave them for the potter's
field, as the Lord appointed me.

[11] And Jesus stood before the governor; and the governor
asked him, saying: Are you the king of the Jews? Jesus replied to him: You say it. [12] And when he was accused by the
chief priests and elders, he made no answer. [13] Then Pilate said
to him: Do you not hear how many things they testify against
you? [14] And he gave him answer to not one word, so that the
governor was greatly astonished.

[15] Now at the feast, the governor was in the habit of releasing
to the multitude one prisoner, whom they chose. [16] They then
had a notorious prisoner, called Barabbas. [17] Therefore, while
they were together, Pilate said to them: Which do you wish me
to release to you, Barabbas, or Jesus, who is called Christ?
[18] For he knew that through envy they had delivered him up.

[19] While he was sitting on the judgment-seat, his wife sent to
him, saying: Have nothing to do with that just man, for I have
suffered much to-day in a dream, because of him.

[20] But the chief priests and the elders persuaded the multitude
to ask Barabbas, and destroy Jesus. [21] The governor answered
and said to them: Which of the two do you wish me to release
to you? They replied: Barabbas. [22] Pilate said to them: What
then shall I do with Jesus, who is called Christ? They all said
to him: Let him be crucified. [23] But the governor said: Why,
what evil has he done? But they cried vehemently, saying:
Let him be crucified. [24] When Pilate saw that he gained nothing, but rather that a tumult was rising, he took water, and
washed his hands before the multitude, and said: I am innocent
of the blood of this just man; you will see to it. [25] And all the
people answered and said: His blood be upon us and upon our
children. [26] Then he released to them Barabbas; but after he
had scourged Jesus, he delivered him up to be crucified.

[27] Then the soldiers of the governor took Jesus into the palace,
and brought together to him the whole band. [28] And they
stripped him, and put on him a scarlet cloak; [29] and when they
had plaited a crown of thorn branches, they put it upon his
head, and a reed in his right hand; and kneeling before him,
they derided him, saying: Hail, King of the Jews! [30] And they
spit upon him, and took the reed, and struck him on the head.
[31] And when they had derided him, they took off the cloak from
him, and put his own clothes on him, and led him away to
crucify him.

32 And as they were going out, they found a man of Cyrene,
named Simon: this man they compelled to carry his cross.
33 And when they had come to a place called Golgotha, which,
when translated, is the place of a skull, 34 they gave him vinegar to drink, mingled with gall; and when he had tasted it, he
refused to drink. 35 And when they had crucified him, they
divided his clothing among themselves, by casting the lot.
36 And they sat down and watched him there. 37 And they placed
above his head the charge that was made against him, written:
THIS IS JESUS THE KING OF THE JEWS. 38 Then were
two robbers crucified with him; one on his right hand, and the
other on his left.

39 And they that passed by reviled him, shaking their heads,
40 and saying: You that destroy the temple, and build it in
three days, save yourself; if you are the Son of God, come down
from the cross. 41 In like manner also the chief priests, with
the scribes and elders, derided him, and said: 42 He saved others;
himself he can not save. If he is the King of Israel, let him
now come down from the cross, and we will believe on him.
43 He trusted in God; let him deliver him now, if he delights
in him; for he said: I am the Son of God. 44 The robbers also
that were crucified with him, uttered the same reproaches
against him.

45 From the sixth hour there was darkness over all the land
till the ninth hour. 46 But about the ninth hour, Jesus cried
out with a loud voice, saying: Eli, Eli, lamah sabachthani?
that is, My God, my God, why hast thou forsaken me? 47 Some
of those who were standing there, when they heard it, said:
This man calls for Elijah. 48 And immediately one of them
ran, and took a sponge, and having filled it with vinegar, put it
on a reed, and gave it to him to drink. 49 The rest said: Wait,
let us see if Elijah is coming to save him.

50 And Jesus again cried with a loud voice, and gave up his
spirit. 51 And behold, the vail of the temple was rent in two
from top to bottom. And the earth did shake, and the rocks
were rent: 52 and the sepulchers were opened, and many bodies
of the saints that slept, arose. 53 And they came out of their
sepulchers after his resurrection, and entered the holy city, and
appeared to many.

54 Now the centurion, and those who were with him watching
Jesus, when they saw the earthquake, and what was done, were
greatly afraid, and said: Of a truth, this was the Son of God.

55 Many women that had followed Jesus from Galilee, and
had ministered to him, were there, looking on from a distance.
56 Among these was Mary Magdalene, and Mary the mother of
James and Joses, and the mother of the sons of Zebedee.

57 When the evening had come, there came a rich man of
Arimathea, named Joseph; and he also was a disciple of Jesus.
58 This man went to Pilate, and asked for the body of Jesus.
Then Pilate commanded the body to be given. 59 And Joseph
took the body and wrapped it in clean linen, 60 and laid it in
his own new tomb, which he had hewn out in the rock. And
he rolled a great stone to the door of the tomb, and departed.
61 And Mary Magdalene was there, and the other Mary, sitting
opposite the tomb.

62 On the morrow, which was the day after the preparation,
the chief priests and the Pharisees came together to Pilate,
63 and said: Sir, we remember that that deceiver said, while he
was yet alive, After three days I will arise. 64 Therefore, command that the sepulcher be made safe till the third day, lest
his disciples come and steal him away, and say to the people,
He has risen from the dead; and the last error will be worse
than the first. 65 Pilate said to them: You have a guard; go,
make it as safe as you know how. 66 And they went and made
the sepulcher safe, by placing a seal upon the stone, and setting
the guard.

XXVIII. 1 And after the Sabbath, as it began to dawn
toward the first day of the week, Mary Magdalene and the other
Mary came to see the sepulcher. 2 And behold, there had been
a great earthquake; for an angel of the Lord having descended
from heaven, came and rolled away the stone from the door,
and sat upon it. 3 His appearance was like lightning, and his
raiment was white as snow. 4 From fear of him the keepers did
shake and become like dead men. 5 But the angel answered and
said to the women: Fear not; for I know that you seek Jesus,
who was crucified. 6 He is not here; for he has risen, as he said.
Come, see the place where the Lord lay. 7 And go quickly, and
tell his disciples, that he has risen from the dead: and behold,
he goes before you into Galilee. There you shall see him. Lo,
I have told you.

8 And they went out quickly from the sepulcher, with fear and
great joy, and ran to tell his disciples. 9 And as they were going to tell his disciples, behold, Jesus met them, saying: Hail!

And they came and laid hold of his feet, and worshiped him.
10 Then Jesus said to them: Fear not; go, tell my brethren to
go into Galilee, and there they shall see me.

11 While they were going, behold, some of the guard came
into the city, and told the chief priests all things that were
done. 12 And when they came together with the elders, they
held a consultation, and gave much money to the soldiers,
13 saying: Say that his disciples came by night and stole him
away, while we were asleep. 14 And if this shall be heard in the
presence of the governor, we will persuade him, and make you
secure. 15 And they took the money, and did as they were
taught. And their report of this matter is every-where published among the Jews to this day.

16 And the eleven disciples went away into Galilee, into the
mountain, where Jesus had appointed *to meet* them. 17 And
when they saw him, they worshiped him; but some doubted.
18 And Jesus came and spoke to them, saying: All authority in
heaven and on earth is given to me. 19 Go, therefore, make disciples of all nations, immersing them (the disciples) into the
name of the Father, and of the Son, and of the Holy Spirit;
20 teaching them to observe all things whatever I have commanded you: and lo, I am with you all the days, even to the
end of the age.

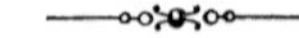

TESTIMONY OF MARK.

I. 1 THE beginning of the gospel of Jesus Christ, the Son of
God; 2 as it is written in Isaiah the prophet: Behold,
I send my messenger before my face, who shall prepare thy way.
3 The voice of one crying in the wilderness, Make ready the way
of the Lord, make his paths straight. 4 John was immersing
in the wilderness, and preaching the immersion of repentance
in order to the remission of sins. 5 And all the country of Judea and the inhabitants of Jerusalem went out to him, and
were all immersed by him in the river Jordan, confessing their
sins. 6 And John was clothed with camel's hair, and had a
girdle of leather around his loins, and he ate locusts and wild
honey: 7 and he preached, saying: There comes after me One
mightier than I, the strap of whose sandals I am not worthy to
stoop down and loose. 8 I immerse you in water; but he will
immerse you in the Holy Spirit.

9 And it came to pass in those days, that Jesus came from
Nazareth of Galilee, and was immersed by John in the Jordan.
10 And immediately on coming up from the water, he saw the
heavens opened, and the Spirit like a dove descending upon him.
11 And there was a voice from the heavens: Thou art my beloved
Son, in whom I delight.

12 And immediately the Spirit compelled him to go forth into
the wilderness. 13 And he was there in the wilderness forty
days, to be tempted by Satan; and he was with the wild beasts;
and the angels ministered to him.

14 But after John was delivered up, Jesus came into Galilee,
preaching the gospel of the kingdom of God, 15 and saying: The
time has fully come, and the kingdom of God is at hand; repent,
and believe the gospel. 16 And as he walked by the sea of Galilee, he saw Simon, and Andrew the brother of Simon, throwing
a net about in the sea; for they were fishers. 17 And Jesus said
to them: Come after me, and I will make you fishers of men.
18 And immediately they left their nets, and followed him.

19 And when he had gone a little further thence, he saw James
the son of Zebedee, and John his brother, who also were in the
ship, mending their nets. 20 And he immediately called them:
and they left their father Zebedee in the ship with the hired
servants, and went after him.

21 And they went into Capernaum; and immediately, on the
Sabbath, he entered the synagogue, and taught. 22 And they
were astonished at his teaching; for he taught them as one that
had authority, and not as the scribes. 23 And there was in their
synagogue a man who had an unclean spirit; and he cried out,
24 saying: Let us alone; what have we to do with thee, Jesus,
thou Nazarene? Hast thou come to destroy us? I know thee
who thou art, the Holy One of God. 25 And Jesus rebuked him,
saying: Be silent, and come out of him. 26 And the unclean
spirit threw him into convulsions, and cried with a loud voice,
and came out of him. 27 And all were amazed, so that they
questioned one another, saying: What means this? What new
teaching is this, that with authority he commands even the
unclean spirits, and they obey him? 28 And his fame immediately went abroad into all the surrounding country of Galilee.

29 And forthwith, having gone out of the synagogue, they
went into the house of Simon and Andrew, with James and
John. 30 Now the mother-in-law of Simon lay sick of a fever.
And at once they told him of her. 31 And he went to her, and

took her by the hand, and raised her up, and the fever left her
instantly; and she ministered to them.

32 And at evening, when the sun had gone down, they brought
to him all that were sick, and those who were possessed with
demons. 33 And the whole city came together to the door.
34 And he cured many that were sick of various diseases, and
cast out many demons, and did not suffer the demons to speak,
because they knew him.

35 And very early in the morning, while it was yet dark, he
arose and went out, and departed to a desert place, and there
prayed. 36 And Simon, and those who were with him, followed
after him. 37 And when they had found him, they said to him:
All are seeking for thee. 38 And he said to them: Let us go into
the neighboring towns, that I may preach there also; for I
have come forth for this purpose. 39 And throughout the whole
of Galilee he continued to preach in their synagogues, and to
cast out demons.

40 And there came to him a leper, beseeching him, and kneeling down to him, and saying to him: If thou wilt, thou canst
make me clean. 41 And Jesus, moved with compassion, stretched
forth his hand, and touched him, and said to him: I will; be
clean. 42 And when he had spoken, the leprosy immediately departed from him, and he was cleansed. 43 And he strictly
charged him, and forthwith sent him away, 44 and said to him:
See that you tell no one; but go, show yourself to the priest, and
offer for your cleansing the things which Moses commanded, for
a testimony to them. 45 But he went out, and began to proclaim
it much, and to publish the matter abroad, so that he was no
longer able to enter a city openly, but was without in desert
places: and they came to him from every quarter.

II. 1 And again he entered Capernaum, after some days; and
they heard that he was in the house. 2 And immediately many
came together, so that the house could contain them no longer,
nor could the space about the door. And he preached the word
to them.

3 And they came to him, bringing a paralytic, who was carried
by four men. 4 And not being able to come near him, on account of the multitude, they took off the roof where he was,
and having broken through, they let down the bed on which the
paralytic lay. 5 And Jesus, seeing their faith, said to the paralytic: Son, your sins are forgiven you. 6 But some of the scribes

were sitting there, and reasoning in their hearts: 7 Why does
this man thus speak impiously? Who can forgive sins but God
only? 8 And Jesus, immediately perceiving in his spirit that
they thus reasoned within themselves, said to them: Why are
you reasoning thus in your hearts? 9 Which is easier, to say to
the paralytic, Your sins are forgiven; or to say, Arise, take up
your bed and walk? 10 But that you may know that the Son of
man on earth has authority to forgive sins, (he said to the paralytic,) 11 I say to you, Arise, take up your bed and go to your
house. 12 And he arose forthwith, and took up his bed, and went
out before them all; so that they were all amazed, and glorified
God, saying: We have never seen it thus.

13 And he went out again by the sea: and all the multitude
came to him, and he taught them. 14 And as he passed by, he
saw Levi the son of Alphæus sitting at the custom-house; and
he said to him: Follow me. And he arose and followed him.
15 And it came to pass, as Jesus reclined at table in his house,
that many publicans and sinners reclined with him and his
disciples; for there were many, and they followed him. 16 And
when the scribes and Pharisees saw him eating with publicans
and sinners, they said to his disciples: Why is it that he eats
and drinks with publicans and sinners? 17 And when Jesus
heard it, he said to them: Those who are well have no need of
a physician, but those who are sick. I have not come to call
righteous men, but sinners.

18 And the disciples of John and of the Pharisees were in the
habit of fasting; and they came, and said to him: Why do the
disciples of John and of the Pharisees fast, but your disciples
fast not? 19 And Jesus said to them: Can the sons of the bride-
chamber fast, while the bridegroom is with them? As long as
they have the bridegroom with them, they can not fast. 20 But
the days will come when the bridegroom shall be taken from
them, and then they will fast in those days. 21 No one sews a
patch of new cloth on an old garment; if so, the new piece
which fills it up, takes from the old, and a worse rent is made.
22 And no one puts new wine into old bottles; if so, the new
wine bursts the bottles, and the wine is spilled, and the bottles
are destroyed. But new wine must be put into new bottles.

23 And it came to pass, that he was going on the Sabbath-day
through the fields of grain: and his disciples began, as they
went, to pull the ears of grain. 24 And the Pharisees said to
him: See, why are they doing on the Sabbath-day what is not

lawful? [25] And he said to them: Did you never read what David
did, when he had need and was hungry, he and those who were
with him? [26] How he entered the house of God in the days of
Abiathar the chief priest, and ate the loaves of the presence,
which it is not lawful, except for the priests, to eat, and gave to
those also who were with him? [27] And he said to them: The
Sabbath was made for man, not man for the Sabbath. [28] Therefore, the Son of man is Lord also of the Sabbath.

III. [1] And again he entered the synagogue, and a man was
there who had a withered hand. [2] And they watched him,
whether he would cure him on the Sabbath-day, that they might
accuse him. [3] And he said to the man who had the withered
hand: Arise, and come into the midst. [4] And he said to them:
Is it lawful to do good on the Sabbath-day, or to do evil? to save
life, or to kill? But they were silent. [5] And looking around on
them with anger, being grieved for the hardness of their heart,
he said to the man: Stretch forth your hand; and he stretched
it forth: and his hand was restored. [6] And the Pharisees immediately went out with the Herodians, and held a consultation
against him, that they might destroy him.

[7] And Jesus withdrew with his disciples to the sea; and there
followed him a great multitude from Galilee, and from Judea,
[8] and from Jerusalem, and from Idumea, and from beyond the
Jordan: and those about Tyre and Sidon, a great multitude,
when they heard what things he was doing, came to him.
[9] And he spoke to his disciples, that a small ship should continue
near him, because of the multitude, that they might not press
upon him. [10] For he cured many, so that as many as had diseases rushed upon him, that they might touch him. [11] And unclean spirits, when they saw him, fell down before him, and cried
out, saying: Thou art the Son of God. [12] And he strictly
charged them, that they should not make him known.

[13] And he went up into a mountain, and called to him such as
he wished, and they came to him. [14] And he appointed twelve,
that they should be with him, and that he might send them
forth to preach, [15] and to have authority to cure diseases, and
to cast out demons. [16] And Simon he surnamed Peter; [17] and
James the son of Zebedee, and John the brother of James: and
these he surnamed Boanerges, which means, sons of thunder:
[18] and Andrew, and Philip, and Bartholomew, and Matthew, and
Thomas, and James the son of Alphæus, and Thaddæus, and

Simon the Canaanite, 19 and Judas Iscariot, who also delivered
him up.

And they went into a house: 20 and the multitude came together again, so that they were not able even to eat bread.
21 And when his relatives heard of it, they came out to take
him; for they said: He is beside himself. 22 And the scribes
who had come down from Jerusalem said: He has Beelzebul;
and by the prince of the demons he casts out the demons.
23 And he called them to him, and spoke to them in parables:
How can Satan cast out Satan? 24 And if a kingdom be divided
against itself, that kingdom can not stand. 25 And if a house
be divided against itself, that house can not stand.

26 And if Satan rise up against himself, and be divided, he can
not stand, but has an end. 27 No one can enter the house of the
strong man, and spoil his goods, unless he first bind the strong
man; and then he will plunder his house. 28 Verily I say to
you, All sins shall be forgiven the sons of men, and whatever
impious speeches they may utter; 29 but whoever will speak impiously against the Holy Spirit shall never have forgiveness,
but is subject to eternal condemnation. 30 For they said: He
has an unclean spirit.

31 His mother and his brothers came, therefore, and standing
without, sent to him, and called him. 32 And the multitude was
sitting about him; and they said to him: Behold, your mother
and your brothers are without, seeking you. 33 And he answered them and said: Who is my mother, or my brothers?
34 And he looked round about on those who were sitting near
him, and said: Behold, my mother and my brothers; 35 for
whoever will do the will of God, is my brother, and my sister,
and mother.

IV. 1 And again he began to teach by the sea; and a great
multitude came together to him, so that he went into a ship,
and sat in the sea: and the whole multitude was on the land
near the sea. 2 And he taught them many things in parables,
and said to them in his teaching: 3 Hear; Behold, the sower
went forth to sow; 4 and it came to pass, as he sowed, that
some seed fell by the wayside, and the birds came and ate it up.
5 Other seed fell on stony ground, where it had not much earth:
and it immediately sprung up, because it had no depth of earth.
6 And when the sun was up, it was scorched; and because it had
no root, it withered away. 7 And other seed fell among thorns,

and the thorns grew up and choked it, and it produced no fruit.
8 And other seed fell in the good ground, and produced fruit that
grew up and increased, and produced, one thirty, one sixty, and
one a hundred. 9 And he said: He that has ears to hear, let
him hear.

10 And when he was alone, those who were about him, with
the twelve, asked him the meaning of the parable. 11 And he
said to them: To you it is given to know the mystery of the
kingdom of God; but to those who are without, all things are
done in parables; 12 that they may surely see, and not perceive;
and that they may surely hear, and not understand; lest they
should turn to me, and their sins should be forgiven them.
13 And he said to them: Do you not understand this parable?
And how then will you understand all parables? 14 The sower
sows the word. 15 These are they that received seed by the wayside, where the word is sown; and when they hear, Satan immediately comes and takes away the word that was sown in
their hearts. 16 And these are they that, in like manner, received seed in stony places: who, when they hear the word, immediately receive it with joy: 17 and they have no root in themselves, but endure for a time; afterward, when affliction or
persecution arises on account of the word, they immediately
take offense. 18 And these are they that received seed among
thorns; who hear the word, 19 and the anxieties of this age, and
the deceitfulness of riches, and desires for other things enter in
and choke the word, and it becomes unfruitful. 20 And these
are they that received seed on the good ground; who hear the
word, and receive it, and bring forth fruit, one thirty, and one
sixty, and one a hundred.

21 And he said to them: Is a lamp brought in that it may be
put under the measure, or under the divan? Is it not brought
that it may be put on the lamp-stand? 22 For there is nothing
hid that shall not be made known; nor has any thing been
concealed, but that it may come into open view. 23 If any one
has ears to hear, let him hear. 24 And he said to them: Take
heed how you hear; with what measure you measure, it shall
be measured to you; and to you that hear, more shall be given
25 for whoever has, to him shall be given; and whoever has not
even that which he has shall be taken from him.

26 And he said: So is the kingdom of God, as if a man should
sow seed in the ground, 27 and should sleep and rise, night
and day, and the seed should spring up and grow, he knows no

how. [28] For the earth, of its own accord, produces fruit, first
the blade, then the ear, then the full grain in the ear. [29] But
when the fruit is ripe, immediately he sends forth the sickle,
because the harvest is ready.

[30] And he said: To what shall we liken the kingdom of God?
Or, by what similitude shall we illustrate it? [31] It is like a
grain of mustard, which, when it is sown in the ground, is less
than all seeds that are in the ground; [32] yet, when it is sown, it
grows up, and becomes larger than all garden-plants, and sends
out great branches, so that the birds of the air can roost under
its shadow.

[33] And with many such parables he spoke the word to them,
as they were able to hear. [34] But without a parable he did not
speak to them; but when alone, he explained all things to his
disciples.

[35] And on the same day, when it was evening, he said to them:
Let us go over to the opposite side. [36] And when they had sent
the multitude away, they took him with them, as he was in the
ship; and there were other little ships with him. [37] And there
arose a great storm of wind, and the waves dashed into the
ship, so that it was now full. [38] And he was in the hinder part
of the ship, asleep on the pillow. And they awoke him, and
said to him: Teacher, carest thou not that we perish? [39] And
he arose, and rebuked the wind, and said to the sea: Peace,
be still. And the wind ceased, and there was a great calm.
[40] And he said to them: Why are you so fearful? How is it
that you have no faith? [41] And they were greatly afraid, and
said one to another: Who, then, is this, that even the wind and
the sea obey him?

V. [1] And they came to the opposite side of the sea, into the
country of the Gadarenes. [2] And when he had come out of the
ship, immediately there met him from the tombs a man with an
unclean spirit, [3] who had his dwelling among the tombs; and
no one could keep him bound even with chains; [4] because he
had often been bound with fetters and chains, and the chains
had been pulled to pieces by him, and the fetters had been
broken, and no one had strength to subdue him; [5] and always,
night and day, he was in the tombs, and in the mountains,
crying out, and cutting himself with stones.

[6] And when he saw Jesus at a distance, he ran and did him
homage; [7] and crying out with a loud voice, he said: What

have I to do with thee, Jesus, Son of God Most High? I adjure thee by God, that thou torment me not. 8 For he had said
to him: Unclean spirit, come out of the man. 9 And he asked
him: What is your name? And he said to him: My name is
Legion; for we are many. 10 And he earnestly besought him
that he would not send them out of the country.

11 Now a great herd of swine was feeding there near the
mountain. 12 And the demons besought him, saying: Send us
to the swine, that we may enter into them. 13 And Jesus immediately gave them leave. And the unclean spirits came out and
entered into the swine; and the herd (they were about two
thousand,) rushed down a steep place into the sea, and were
strangled in the sea. 14 And those who fed them fled, and told
it in the city, and in the country. And they came out to see
what had been done; 15 and they came to Jesus and saw the demoniac, who had had the legion, sitting, and clothed, and in
his right mind: and they were afraid.

16 And those who had seen it, told them how it had happened
to the demoniac, and also concerning the swine. 17 And they
began to beseech him to depart from their borders. 18 And
when he had entered the ship, he that had been possessed with
the demons besought him that he might be with him. 19 And
he did not permit him, but said to him: Go home to your relatives, and make known to them what things the Lord has done
for you, and that he has had compassion on you. 20 And he
went away and began to proclaim in Decapolis what things
Jesus had done for him. And all were astonished.

21 And when Jesus had again gone over in the ship to the opposite side, a great multitude came together to him; and he was
near the sea. 22 And behold, there came one of the rulers of the
synagogue, named Jairus; and when he saw him, he fell at his
feet, 23 and besought him earnestly, saying: My little daughter
is at the point of death; come, lay thy hands on her, that she
may be saved, and she will live. 24 And he went with him; and
a great multitude followed him, and pressed upon him.

25 And a certain woman who had had an issue of blood for
twelve years, 26 and had suffered much from many physicians,
and had spent all that she had, and was in no way benefited,
but rather grew worse, 27 when she heard of Jesus, came behind him in the multitude, and touched his mantle; 28 for she
said: If I may even touch his clothes, I shall be saved. 29 And
immediately the fountain of her blood dried up, and she knew

in her body that she was cured of that plague. 30 And Jesus,
immediately perceiving in himself that power had gone forth
from him, turned around in the multitude and said: Who
touched my clothes? 31 And his disciples said to him: Thou
seest the multitude pressing upon thee, and dost thou say, Who
touched me? 32 And he looked around to see her that had done
this. 33 But the woman, fearing and trembling, knowing what
had been done within her, came and fell down before him,
and told him all the truth. 34 And he said to her: Daughter,
your faith has saved you; go in peace, and be cured of your
plague.

35 While he was yet speaking, some came from the ruler of the
synagogue, who said: Your daughter is dead; why give the
Teacher further trouble? 36 But as soon as Jesus heard what
was spoken, he said to the ruler of the synagogue: Fear not,
only believe. 37 And he suffered no one to follow him, except
Peter and James and John the brother of James. 38 And he
came to the house of the ruler of the synagogue, and saw the
tumult, and those who were weeping and wailing greatly.
39 And he went in and said to them: Why do you make a tumult and weep? The child is not dead, but sleeps. 40 And
they derided him. But when he had put them all out, he took
the father and mother of the child, and those who were with
him, and went in where the child was lying. 41 And he took the
child by the hand, and said to her: Talitha kumi; which is,
when translated, Maiden, (I say to you,) arise. 42 And the
maiden immediately arose and walked, for she was twelve years
old. And they were greatly astonished. 43 And he charged
them strictly that no one should know this. And he commanded that something should be given her to eat.

VI. 1 And he departed thence, and came into his own country; and his disciples followed him. 2 And when the Sabbath
came, he began to teach in the synagogue. And many that
heard him were astonished, and said: Whence has this man
these things? and what wisdom is this which is given to him,
that even such mighty deeds are done by his hands? Is not
this the carpenter, the son of Mary, the brother of James and
Joses and Judah and Simon? And are not his sisters here with
us? And they found in him cause for offense. 4 But Jesus said to
them: A prophet is not without honor, unless in his own country, and among his own relatives, and in his own house. 5 And

he was unable to do any mighty deed there, except that he laid
his hands on a few sick persons and cured them; 6 and he wondered at their unbelief.

And he went to the villages round about, and taught. 7 And
he called to him the twelve, and began to send them out, two
and two, and gave them authority over unclean spirits. 8 And
he commanded them to take nothing for their journey, but a
staff only; no bag, no bread, no money in their purses; 9 but
to be shod with sandals, and not to put on two coats. 10 And
he said to them: Wherever you enter a house, there make your
home till you depart from that place. 11 And whoever will not
receive you, nor hear you, when you go out from that place,
shake off the dust under your feet, for a testimony against
them. Verily I say to you, It shall be more tolerable for Sodom or Gomorrah in the day of judgment, than for that city.
12 And they went out and preached that men should repent;
13 and they cast out many demons, and anointed with oil many
that were sick, and cured them.

14 And Herod the king heard of him, for his name had become
known; and he said: John the Immerser has risen from the
dead, and for this reason, the powers of the spiritual world are
active within him. 15 Others said: He is Elijah. Others said:
He is a prophet like one of the prophets. 16 But when Herod
heard of him, he said: John, whom I beheaded, has risen from
the dead.

17 For Herod himself had sent and taken John, and bound him
in prison on account of Herodias, the wife of his brother Philip;
for he had married her. 18 For John said to Herod: It is not
lawful for you to have your brother's wife. 19 And Herodias
was angry with him, and desired to have him killed, and was
not able; 20 for Herod feared John, because he knew him to be a
just and holy man; and he kept him in safety. And having
heard him, he did many things, and heard him with pleasure.

21 And a suitable day having come, when Herod, on his birthday, made a supper for his great men, and his chief officers, and
the first men of Galilee; 22 and the daughter of this Herodias
having come in, and danced, and pleased Herod and his guests,
the king said to the maiden: Ask me what you will, and I will
give it to you. 23 And he swore to her: Whatever you ask, I
will give you, to the half of my kingdom.

24 But she went out, and said to her mother: What shall I
ask? She replied: The head of John the Immerser. 25 And she

came in immediately, with haste, to the king, and made her request, saying: I desire that you give me, at once, in a dish, the
head of John the Immerser. [26] And the king was very sad; yet,
on account of his oath and his guests, he would not reject her.
[27] And the king immediately sent one of his guards, and commanded his head to be brought. [28] And he went and beheaded
him in the prison, and brought his head in a dish, and gave it
to the maiden; and the maiden gave it to her mother. [29] And
when his disciples heard of it, they came and took away his
body, and laid it in a tomb.

[30] And the apostles came together to Jesus, and told him all
things, both what they had done and what they had taught.
[31] And he said to them: Come yourselves privately into a desert
place, and rest awhile. For there were many coming and going,
and they had not leisure even to eat. [32] And they went away,
by ship, into a desert place, privately.

[33] And many saw them departing, and recognized him; and
they ran thither on foot from all the cities, and went before
them, and came together to him. [34] And when Jesus came out,
he saw a great multitude, and had compassion on them, because
they were as sheep that had no shepherd. And he began to
teach them many things.

[35] And when much of the day was now spent, his disciples
came to him, and said: This is a desert place, and much of the
day is now spent; [36] send them away, that they may go into the
country and the villages round about, and buy bread for themselves: for they have nothing to eat. [37] He answered and said
to them: Do you give them food. And they said to him:
Shall we go and buy two hundred denarii worth of bread, and
give them food? [38] He said to them: How many loaves have
you? Go and see. And when they had learned, they said:
Five, and two fishes. [39] And he commanded them to make all
recline in table parties upon the green grass. [40] And they reclined in oblong squares, by hundreds, and by fifties. [41] And
he took the five loaves and the two fishes, and looked up to
heaven, and blessed; and he broke the loaves, and gave them
to the disciples to place before them. And he divided the two
fishes among them all. [42] And they all ate, and were satisfied;
[43] and they took up twelve baskets full of the broken pieces,
and of the fishes. [44] And those who ate of the loaves were about
five thousand men.

[45] And he immediately compelled his disciples to get into the

ship, and to go before him to the opposite side, to Bethsaida,
while he sent the multitude away. 46 And when he had sent
them away, he went into the mountain to pray.
47 And when evening came, the ship was in the midst of the
sea, and he alone upon the land. 48 And he saw them toiling in
rowing; for the wind was against them. And about the fourth
watch of the night, he came to them, walking on the sea, and
intended to pass by them. 49 But when they saw him walking
on the sea, they thought it was a specter, and cried out; 50 for
they all saw him, and were troubled. And he immediately
spoke to them, and said: Take courage; it is I; be not afraid.
51 And he went up to them into the ship; and the wind ceased.
And they were greatly amazed in themselves beyond measure,
and wondered; 52 for they had learned nothing from the loaves:
for their heart was hardened.
53 And when they had passed over, they came to the land of
Genesaret, and drew the ship ashore. 54 And when they had come
out of the ship, the people immediately recognized him, 55 and
ran through the whole of that region round about, and began
to carry the sick on beds, wherever they heard that he was.
56 And whatever place he entered, whether villages or cities or
country, they laid the sick in the market-places, and besought
him that they might touch even the fringe of his mantle: and
as many as touched him were saved.

VII. 1 And there came together to him the Pharisees, and
some of the scribes, who had come from Jerusalem: 2 and when
they saw some of his disciples eating bread with common, that
is, with unwashed hands: 3 (for the Pharisees and all the Jews
eat not, unless they wash their hands carefully, because they
hold the tradition of the elders: 4 and when they come from
the market, they do not eat, unless they immerse themselves.
And there are many other things, which they have received to
hold, as the immersion of cups and pitchers and brazen vessels
and beds:) 5 then the Pharisees and the scribes asked him:
Why do your disciples not walk according to the tradition of
the elders, but eat bread with unwashed hands? 6 He answered
and said to them: Well did Isaiah prophesy of you hypocrites,
as it is written, This people honors me with their lips, but their
heart is far from me. 7 In vain do they worship me, teaching
precepts, the commandments of men. 8 For, neglecting the
commandment of God, you hold the tradition of men, the im-

mersion of pitchers and cups; and many other things like
these you do.
9 And he said to them: Well do you reject the commandment
of God, that you may keep your own tradition. 10 For Moses
said: Honor your father and your mother; and, He that curses
father or mother shall surely be put to death. 11 But you say:
If a man shall say to his father or mother, Whatever of mine
might benefit you, is Corban, (which means, a gift,) 12 you no
longer suffer him to do any thing for his father or mother,
13 making the word of God of no effect by your tradition, which
you have delivered; and many things like these you do.
14 And he called the whole multitude to him, and said to them:
Hear me, all of you, and understand. 15 There is nothing without that, by entering into a man, can defile him. But those
things which come out of the man, defile him. 16 If any one
has ears to hear, let him hear.
17 And when he had gone into the house, away from the multitude, his disciples asked him about the dark saying. 18 And
he said to them: Are you also so void of understanding? Do
you not perceive that nothing from without, by entering into a
man, can defile him? 19 Because it does not enter into his
heart, but into his belly, and goes out into the sink, cleansing
all food. 20 And he said: What comes out of the man, is that
which defiles the man. 21 For from within, out of the heart of
men, proceed the purposes which are evil: adulteries, lewd conduct,
murders, 22 thefts, schemes for extortion, wicked deeds, deceit,
wantonness, an evil eye, calumny, haughtiness, impiety. 23 All
these evil things come forth from within, and defile the man.
24 And he arose and departed thence to the borders of Tyre
and Sidon. And he entered a house, and desired that no one
should know it; but he could not escape notice. 25 For a woman,
whose little daughter had an unclean spirit, heard of him, and
came and fell at his feet; 26 (the woman was a Greek, a Syrophenician by nation,) and she besought him to cast the demon out
of her daughter. 27 But Jesus said to her: Let the children be
satisfied first; for it is not good to take the children's bread and
throw it to the little dogs. 28 She answered and said to him:
Yes, Lord; and *yet you can help me*, for the little dogs under the
table eat of the children's crumbs. 29 And he said to her: For this
saying, go your way: the demon has gone out of your daughter.
30 And she went to her house, and found the demon gone out,
and her daughter lying upon the bed.

31 And again he went out from the borders of Tyre and Sidon,
and came to the sea of Galilee, through the midst of the borders
of Decapolis. 32 And they brought to him a deaf man, who spoke
with difficulty; and they besought him to lay his hand upon
him. 33 And he took him aside from the multitude, and put his
fingers into his ears, and he spit, and touched his tongue; 34 and
looking up to heaven, he sighed, and said to him: Ephphatha,
which means, Be opened. 35 And immediately his ears were
opened, and the band of his tongue was loosed, and he spoke
plainly. 36 And he charged them to tell no one; but the more
he charged them, the more earnestly they published it. 37 And
they were amazed beyond measure, and said: He has done all
things well: he makes the deaf hear and the dumb speak.

VIII. 1 In those days, the multitude being very great, and
having nothing to eat, Jesus called his disciples to him and
said to them: 2 I have compassion on the multitude, because
they have continued with me now three days, and have nothing
to eat. 3 And if I send them home fasting, they will faint on
the way; for some of them have come from afar. 4 And his
disciples answered him: Whence will any one be able to satisfy
these men with bread, here in the wilderness? 5 And he asked
them: How many loaves have you? And they said: Seven.
6 And he commanded the multitude to recline on the ground.
And he took the seven loaves, and gave thanks, and broke them,
and gave them to the disciples to set before them: and they set
them before the multitude. 7 And they had a few small fishes;
and he blessed, and commanded that they also be set before
them. 8 And they ate, and were satisfied; and they took up
what remained of the broken pieces, seven baskets. 9 And those
who had eaten were about four thousand; and he sent them
away.

10 And he immediately entered the ship with his disciples, and
went into the regions of Dalmanutha. 11 And the Pharisees
came out, and began to put questions to him, asking of him a
sign from heaven, that they might tempt him. 12 And he sighed
deeply in his spirit, and said: Why does this generation seek
for a sign? Verily I say to you, no sign will be given to this
generation. 13 And he left them, and entered the ship again,
and departed to the opposite side.

14 And they had forgotten to take bread; and they had but one
loaf with them in the ship. 15 And he charged them, saying:

Take heed, and beware of the leaven of the Pharisees, and of
the leaven of Herod. 16 And they reasoned with one another,
saying: It is because we have no bread. 17 And Jesus perceived
it, and said to them: Why do you reason, because you have no
bread? Do you not yet perceive, nor understand? Is your
heart still hardened? 18 Having eyes, do you not see? and having ears, do you not hear? and do you not remember? 19 When
I broke the five loaves among the five thousand, how many
baskets full of broken pieces did you take up? They said to him:
Twelve. 20 When I broke the seven among the four thousand,
how many baskets full of broken pieces did you take up? They
replied: Seven. 21 And he said to them: How is it that you do
not understand?

22 And he came to Bethsaida; and they brought to him a blind
man, and besought him to touch him. 23 And he took the blind
man by the hand, and led him out of the village. And he spit
on his eyes, and laid his hands on him, and asked him if he saw
any thing. 24 And he looked up and said: I see men, like trees,
walking. 25 Then he again laid his hands on his eyes, and made
him look up. And he was restored, and saw all things clearly.
26 And he sent him away to his house, and said: Neither go into
the village, nor tell it to any one in the village.

27 And Jesus and his disciples went out into the villages of
Cæsarea Philippi. And on the road, he asked his disciples,
saying to them: Who do men say that I am? 28 They answered:
John the Immerser; and others, Elijah; and others, one of the
prophets. 29 And he said to them: But who say you that I am?
Peter answered and said to him: Thou art the Christ. 30 And
he charged them to tell no one concerning him.

31 And he began to teach them, that the Son of man must
suffer many things, and be rejected by the elders, and the chief
priests, and the scribes, and be put to death, and after three
days rise again. 32 And he spoke this saying plainly. And Peter took him aside and began to rebuke him. 33 But he turned
about, and, looking on his disciples, rebuked Peter, saying: Get
behind me, adversary: for you are not thinking of the things
of God, but of the things of men.

34 And he called to him the multitude with his disciples, and
said to them: Whoever determines to follow after me, let him
deny himself, and take up his cross, and follow me. 35 For
whoever will save his life, shall lose it; but whoever will lose
his life for my sake and the gospel's, shall save it. 36 For what

will it profit a man, if he gain the whole world, and lose his
own life? [37] Or, what will a man give as a ransom for his life?
[38] For whoever will be ashamed of me, and my words, in this
sinful and adulterous generation, of him the Son of man also
will be ashamed, when he comes in the glory of his Father, with
the holy angels.

IX. [1] And he said to them: Verily I say to you, There are
some of these standing here who shall not taste of death, till
they see the kingdom of God come in power.

[2] And after six days, Jesus took with him Peter and James
and John, and led them up alone into a high mountain apart;
and he was transfigured before them; [3] and his raiment became
shining, exceeding white like snow, as no fuller on earth could
whiten them. [4] And there appeared to them Elijah, with Moses;
and they were talking with Jesus. [5] And Peter answering, said
to Jesus: Rabbi, it is good for us to be here; and let us make
three tents, one for thee, and one for Moses, and one for Elijah.
[6] For he knew not what to say, for they were greatly afraid.
[7] And there was a cloud that overshadowed them; and a voice
came from the cloud, This is my beloved Son; hear him.
[8] And suddenly looking around, they no longer saw any one but
Jesus only with themselves.

[9] And as they were coming down from the mountain, he
charged them to tell no one what they had seen, till the Son of
man should rise from the dead. [10] And they kept the matter to
themselves, inquiring of one another what the rising from the
dead could mean. [11] And they asked him, saying: Why do the
scribes say that Elijah must come first? [12] And he answered
and said to them: Elijah comes first, and restores all things,
and, as it is written of the Son of man, that he must suffer
many things, and be despised, *so Elijah is to suffer.* [13] But I say
to you, that Elijah has already come, and they have done to
him what they wished: [as it is written of him.]

[14] And when he came to his disciples, he saw a great multitude
about them, and scribes disputing with them. [15] And at once,
all the multitude, on seeing him, were struck with awe, and
ran to him and saluted him. [16] And he asked the scribes: Why
are you disputing with them? [17] And one of the multitude answered and said: Teacher, I brought to you my son, who has a
dumb spirit. [18] And wherever it seizes him, it throws him into
convulsions; and he foams, and gnashes with his teeth, and pines

away: and I spoke to your disciples to cast him out, and they
were not able. 19 And he answered them, and said: O faithless
generation! how long shall I be with you? how long shall I
bear with you? Bring him to me. 20 And they brought him to
him. And when he saw him, the spirit immediately threw him
into convulsions; and he fell on the ground, and rolled himself,
foaming.

21 And he asked his father: How long is it since this came upon
him? He replied: From childhood. 22 And often it throws him
into the fire, and into the water, to destroy him. But if you
are able to do any thing, have compassion on us, and help us.
23 Jesus said to him: If you are able to believe, all things are
possible to him that believes. 24 And immediately the father of
the child cried out, and with tears said: Lord, I believe; help
my unbelief. 25 When Jesus saw that a multitude came running
together, he rebuked the unclean spirit, and said to it: Dumb
and deaf spirit, I command you, come out of him, and enter
into him no more. 26 And the spirit cried out, and threw him
into strong convulsions, and came out of him; and he was like
one dead, so that many said: He is dead. 27 But Jesus took him
by the hand, and lifted him up, and he arose.

28 And when he had come into the house, his disciples asked
him privately: Why were we not able to cast it out? 29 And he
said to them: This kind can go out by nothing, but by prayer
and fasting.

30 And they departed thence, and passed through Galilee; and
he wished no one to know it. 31 For he taught his disciples,
and said to them: The Son of man is to be delivered into the
hands of men, and they will put him to death; and after he is
put to death, he will rise on the third day. 32 But they did not
understand this saying, and they were afraid to question him.

33 And he came into Capernaum; and when he was in the
house, he asked them: What were you disputing about among
yourselves along the road? 34 But they were silent. For they
had been disputing with one another along the road which was
greatest. 35 And he sat down and called the twelve, and said to
them: If any one desires to be first, he shall be last of all, and
servant of all. 36 And he took a little child, and placed it in the
midst of them; and when he had taken it in his arms, he said
to them: 37 Whoever will receive one of such children on my account, receives me; and whoever will receive me, receives not
me, but him that sent me.

38 And John answered him and said: Teacher, we saw one
casting out demons in thy name, and he does not follow us: and
we forbade him, because he does not follow us. 39 But Jesus said:
Forbid him not; for there is no one that will do a mighty deed
in my name, and be able readily to speak evil of me. 40 For he
that is not against us, is for us. 41 For whoever will give you a
cup of water to drink on this account, because you are Christ's,
verily I say to you, he shall not lose his reward.

42 And whoever will ensnare one of these little ones that believe on me, it would be better for him if a millstone were hung
about his neck, and he were thrown into the sea. 43 And if your
hand ensnare you, cut it off: it is better for you to enter maimed
into life, than having two hands to go away into hell, into the
fire that is not quenched, 44 where their worm dies not, and the
fire is not quenched. 45 And if your foot ensnare you, cut it off:
it is better for you to enter into life lame, than having two feet
to be thrown into hell, into the fire that is not quenched, 46 where
their worm dies not, and the fire is not quenched. 47 And if your
eye ensnare you, pull it out: it is better for you to enter into the
kingdom of God with one eye, than having two eyes to be thrown
into hell-fire, 48 where their worm dies not, and the fire is not
quenched. 49 For every one shall be salted with fire, and every
sacrifice shall be seasoned with salt. 50 Salt is good; but if the
salt shall have become saltless, by what means will you season
it? Have salt in yourselves, and be at peace with one another.

X. 1 And he arose and went thence into the borders of Judea,
by the other side of the Jordan. And the multitudes again
came together to him; and, as his custom was, he taught them
again.

2 And the Pharisees came to him, and that they might tempt
him, asked him the question: Is it lawful for a man to put away
his wife? 3 He answered and said to them: What commandment
did Moses give you? 4 They replied: Moses permitted us to
write a bill of divorce, and put her away. 5 And Jesus answered
and said to them: On account of the hardness of your hearts,
he wrote this commandment for you. 6 But from the beginning
of the creation, God made them male and female. 7 For this
cause shall a man leave his father and mother, and shall be
joined to his wife; 8 and the two shall be one flesh. So, then,
they are no longer two, but one flesh. 9 Therefore, what God
has joined together, let not man put asunder.

[10] And in the house, his disciples again asked him about the
same matter. [11] And he said to them; Whoever puts away his
wife, and marries another, commits adultery against her; [12] and
if a woman puts away her husband, and is married to another,
she commits adultery.

[13] And they brought little children to him, that he might
touch them: but his disciples rebuked those who brought them.
[14] And when Jesus saw it, he was displeased, and said to them:
Let the little children come to me, and forbid them not; for of
such is the kingdom of God. [15] Verily I say to you, Whoever
will not receive the kingdom of God as a little child, shall not
enter into it. [16] And he took them in his arms, laid his hands
on them, and blessed them.

[17] And as he was going forth into the road, one ran and bowed
the knee to him, and asked him: Good Teacher, what shall I do
that I may inherit eternal life? [18] Jesus said to him: Why do
you call me good? None is good but one, that is God. [19] You
know the commandments, You shall not commit adultery; You
shall not kill; You shall not steal; You shall not give false
testimony; You shall not defraud; Honor your father and
mother. [20] He answered and said to him: Teacher, all these I
have kept from my youth. [21] And Jesus, looking on him, loved
him, and said to him: One thing you lack; go, sell whatever
you have, and give to the poor, and you shall have treasure in
heaven: and come, take up the cross, and follow me. [22] But
becoming sad at that saying, he went away sorrowful: for he
had great possessions.

[23] And Jesus looked around, and said to his disciples: With
what difficulty will those who have riches enter into the kingdom of God! [24] And his disciples were amazed at his words.
But Jesus, answering again, said to them: Children, how hard
it is for those who trust in riches to enter the kingdom of God!
[25] It is easier for a camel to go through the eye of a needle, than
for a rich man to enter into the kingdom of God. [26] And they
were astonished beyond measure, and said among themselves:
Who, then, can be saved? [27] Jesus looked on them and said:
With men this is impossible, but not with God: for with God
all things are possible.

[28] And Peter began to say to him: Behold, we have left all and
followed thee. [29] And Jesus answering, said: Verily I say to
you, There is no one that has left house, or brothers, or sisters,
or father, or mother, or wife, or children, or lands, for my sake,

and for the sake of the gospel, [30] who shall not receive a hundred-fold, now in this time, houses and brothers and sisters and
mothers and children and lands, with persecutions; and in the
age to come, eternal life. [31] But many that are first shall be
last: and the last first.

[32] And they were in the road going up to Jerusalem; and
Jesus went before them; and they were amazed, and as they
followed, they were afraid. And again taking the twelve aside,
he began to tell them what was about to befall him. [33] Behold,
we are going up to Jerusalem, and the Son of man will be delivered to the chief priests and the scribes, and they will condemn him to death, and deliver him to the Gentiles; [34] and they
will deride him, and scourge him, and spit upon him, and kill
him, and on the third day he will rise again.

[35] And James and John the sons of Zebedee came to him, and
said: Teacher, we desire you to do for us whatever we shall
ask. [36] He said to them: What do you wish me to do for you?
[37] They said to him: Grant to us that we may sit, one on thy
right hand, and one on thy left, in thy glory. [38] Jesus said to
them: You know not what you ask. Are you able to drink the
cup that I drink, and to be immersed with the immersion with
which I am immersed? [39] They said to him: We are able.
Jesus said to them: You shall drink the cup that I drink, and
you shall be immersed with the immersion with which I am
immersed. [40] But to sit on my right hand and on my left, is
not mine to give; but it shall be given to those for whom it is
prepared.

[41] And when the ten heard it, they began to be displeased with
James and John. [42] But Jesus called them to him, and said to
them: You know that those who think they rule the Gentiles,
act as lords over them; and their great men exercise authority
over them. [43] But it shall not be so among you. But whoever
desires to be great among you, shall be your minister; [44] and
whoever among you desires to be first, shall be servant of all.
[45] For the Son of man came not to be ministered to, but to
minister, and to give his life a ransom for many.

[46] And they came to Jericho: and as he was going out of
Jericho, with his disciples and a great multitude, blind Bar-
timæus, the son of Timæus, was sitting on the roadside, begging. [47] And when he heard that it was Jesus the Nazarene, he
began to cry out and say: Jesus, son of David, have mercy on
me! [48] And many rebuked him, that he should be silent. But

he cried out yet the more: Son of David, have mercy on me!
[49] And Jesus stood still, and commanded him to be called. And
they called the blind man, and said to him: Take courage;
arise, he calls you. [50] And throwing away his mantle, he arose,
and came to Jesus. [51] And Jesus answered and said to him:
What do you wish me to do for you? The blind man said to
him: Rabboni, that I may receive my sight. [52] And Jesus said
to him: Go, your faith has saved you. And he immediately
received his sight, and followed Jesus on the road.

XI. [1] And when they drew near to Jerusalem, as far as Bethphage and Bethany, at the mount of Olives, he sent two of his
disciples, [2] and said to them: Go into the village opposite you;
and as soon as you enter it, you will find a colt tied, on which
no man ever sat. Loose him and bring him. [3] And if any say
to you: Why are you doing this? say that the Lord has need
of him; and he will immediately send him hither. [4] And they
went and found the colt tied near the door without, in the
street. And they loosed him. [5] And some of those who were
standing there, said to them: Why are you loosing the colt?
[6] And they said to them as Jesus had commanded; and they
gave them permission. [7] And they brought the colt to Jesus,
and put their mantles upon him, and he sat on him.

[8] And many spread their mantles in the road, and others cut
branches from the trees, and spread them in the road. [9] And
those who went before, and those who followed after, cried, saying: Hosanna. Blessed is he that comes in the name of the
Lord. [10] Blessed is the coming kingdom of our Father David.
Hosanna in the highest.

[11] And Jesus entered Jerusalem, and went into the temple;
and when he had looked around on all things, the hour being
now late, he went out to Bethany with the twelve.

[12] And on the morrow, as they were coming from Bethany, he
was hungry; [13] and he saw at a distance a fig-tree that had
leaves; and he went, if perhaps he might find, any thing on it.
And when he came to it, he found nothing but leaves; for it
was not the time for figs. [14] And he answered and said to it:
No more may any one ever eat fruit from you. And his disciples heard it.

[15] And they came into Jerusalem; and Jesus entered the
temple, and began to drive out those who sold, and those who
bought in the temple; and he overturned the tables of the

money-changers, and the seats of those who sold doves. [16]And
he suffered no one to carry a vessel through the temple. [17]And
he taught, saying to them: Is it not written, My house shall be
called the house of prayer for all nations? But you have made
it a den of robbers. [18]And the scribes and the chief priests
heard him; and they sought how they might destroy him; for
they feared him, because all the multitude were astonished at
his teaching. [19]And when evening had come, he went out of
the city.

[20]And in the morning, as they were passing by, they saw
the fig-tree withered from the roots. [21]And Peter, calling his
words to mind, said to him: Rabbi, see! the fig-tree which
thou didst curse has withered. [22]And Jesus answered and said
to them: Have faith in God. [23]For, verily I say to you, that
whoever will say to this mountain, Be removed, and be cast
into the sea, and will not doubt in his heart, but believe that
what he says will come to pass, he shall have whatever he says.
[24]For this reason I say to you: All things that you ask for in
prayer, believe that you will receive them, and they shall be
yours. [25]And when you stand praying, forgive, if you have
any thing against any one, that your Father also who is in
heaven may forgive you your offenses. [26]But if you do not
forgive, your Father who is in heaven will not forgive your
offenses.

[27]And they came again into Jerusalem; and as he was walking in the temple, there came to him the chief priests and the
scribes and the elders, [28]and said to him: By what authority
do you these things? and who gave you this authority to do
these things? [29]And Jesus answered and said to them: I also
will ask you one thing, and if you answer me, I will also tell
you by what authority I do these things. [30]Was the immersion
of John from heaven, or from men? answer me. [31]And they
reasoned with themselves, saying: If we say, From heaven, he
will reply, Why, then, did you not believe him? [32]But if we
say, From men, they feared the people; for all regarded John
as a prophet indeed. [33]And they answered and said to Jesus:
We do not know. And Jesus answering, said to them: Neither
do I tell you by what authority I do these things.

XII. [1]And he began to speak to them in parables: A man
planted a vineyard, and set a hedge around it, and digged a
wine-press, and built a tower, and let it out to vine-dressers,

and went into another country. [2]And at the proper time, he
sent a servant to the vine-dressers, that he might receive from
the vine-dressers of the fruit of the vineyard. [3]And they took
him and scourged him, and sent him away without any thing.
[4]And again he sent to them another servant; and at him they
threw stones and wounded him in the head, and sent him away
shamefully treated. [5]And again he sent another; and him
they killed. And he sent many others, some of whom they
scourged, and some they killed. [6]Therefore, having yet one
son, his beloved, he sent him also to them last, saying, They
will reverence my son. [7]But those vine-dressers said one to
another, This is the heir; come, let us kill him, and the inheritance will be ours. [8]And they took him, and killed him, and
threw him out of the vineyard. [9]What, then, will the owner
of the vineyard do? He will come and destroy those vine-
dressers, and give his vineyard to others. [10]Have you not read
this Scripture: The stone which the builders rejected has become the head of the corner; [11]this was from the Lord, and it is
wondrous in our eyes?

[12]And they sought to take him, but feared the multitude; for
they knew that he had spoken the parable against them; and
they left him, and went away.

[13]And they sent to him some of the Pharisees and of the
Herodians, that they might entrap him in his words. [14]And
they came and said to him: Teacher, we know that you are
true, and that you care for no one; for you do not regard the
person of men, but teach the way of God in truth. Is it lawful to give tribute to Cæsar, or not? [15]Must we give, or must
we not give? But, knowing their hypocrisy, he said to them:
Why do you tempt me? Bring me a denarius, that I may see
it. [16]They brought it; and he said to them: Whose image
and superscription is this? They said to him: Cæsar's. [17]And
Jesus answered and said to them: Give to Cæsar the things
that are Cæsar's, and to God the things that are God's. And
they were astonished at him.

[18]And the Sadducees, who say that there is no resurrection,
came to him, and put a question to him, saying: [19]Teacher,
Moses wrote for us, If any man's brother die, and leave a wife,
and leave no children, his brother shall take his wife, and raise
up children for his brother. [20]Now there were seven brothers;
and the first took a wife, and dying, left no child; [21]and the
second took her, and he died, and left no child; and the third,

likewise; 22 and the seven took her, and left no child. Last of
all, the woman also died. 23 Therefore, in the resurrection,
when they rise, of which of them shall she be the wife? for the
seven had her as a wife. 24 And Jesus answered and said to
them: Do you not err for this reason, because you know not
the Scriptures, nor the power of God? 25 For when they rise
from the dead, they neither marry, nor are given in marriage,
but are as the angels in heaven. 26 But concerning the dead,
that they do rise, have you not read in the book of Moses, at
The Bush, how God spoke to him, saying, I am the God of
Abraham, and the God of Isaac, and the God of Jacob? 27 He is
not the God of the dead, but of the living. Therefore, you do
greatly err.

28 And one of the scribes came, and heard them reasoning
together; and perceiving that he had answered them well, he
asked him: Which is the first commandment of all? 29 And
Jesus answered him: The first commandment of all is, Hear,
O Israel, the Lord our God is one Lord. 30 And you shall love
the Lord your God with your whole heart, and with your whole
soul, and with your whole mind, and with your whole strength.
This is the first commandment. 31 And the second, which is
like it, is this: You shall love your neighbor as yourself.
There is no other commandment greater than these. 32 And the
scribe said to him: Teacher, in truth you have well said, that
there is one God, and there is no other beside him; 33 and to love
him with the whole heart, and with the whole understanding,
and with the whole soul, and with the whole strength, and to
love one's neighbor as himself, is more than all whole burnt-
offerings and sacrifices. 34 And Jesus perceiving that he answered with understanding, said to him: You are not far from
the kingdom of God. And no one, after that, ventured to ask
him a question.

35 And Jesus, as he was teaching in the temple, answered and
said: How say the scribes that the Christ is the son of David?
36 For David himself said by the Holy Spirit: The Lord said to
my Lord, Sit at my right hand, till I make thy enemies thy
footstool. 37 David himself, then, calls him Lord; and how is
he his son? And the great multitude heard him with pleasure.

38 And he said to them in his teaching: Beware of the scribes,
who love to walk in robes, and love salutations in the markets,
39 and the first seats in the synagogues, and the first places at
suppers; 40 who eat up the houses of widows, and, as a pretext,

make long prayers: these shall receive more abundant condemnation.
41 And Jesus, sitting opposite the treasury, observed how the
multitude threw money into the treasury. And many rich
persons threw in much. 42 And there came one poor widow,
and she threw in two mites, which make a farthing. 43 And he
called his disciples to him, and said to them: Verily I say to
you, this poor widow has thrown in more than all that have
thrown into the treasury. 44 For all have thrown in out of their
abundance; but she, out of her poverty, has thrown in all that
she had, her whole living.

XIII. 1 And as he was going out from the temple, one of his
disciples said to him: Teacher, see what stones and what buildings! 2 And Jesus answering, said to him: Do you see these
great buildings? There shall not be left one stone upon another,
that shall not be thrown down.
3 And as he sat on the mount of Olives, opposite the temple,
Peter and James and John and Andrew asked him privately:
4 Tell us, when shall these things be? And what shall be the
sign when all these things are about to be accomplished? 5 Jesus
answering them, began to say: Take heed, lest any one deceive
you. 6 For many will come in my name, saying, I am he, and
will deceive many. 7 But when you hear of wars and rumors of
wars, be not troubled; for these things must be: but not yet is
the end. 8 For nation will rise against nation, and kingdom
against kingdom: and there will be earthquakes in various
places, and there will be famines, and tumults. 9 These are the
beginning of sorrows. But take heed to yourselves; for they
will deliver you up to councils, and you will be scourged in the
synagogues; and you will stand before governors and kings for
my sake, for a testimony against them. 10 And the gospel must
first be preached among all the nations.
11 But when they lead you to deliver you up, be not anxious
beforehand, nor premeditate what you shall speak; but whatever shall be given you in that hour, that do you speak; for it
is not you that speak, but the Holy Spirit. 12 Brother will deliver up brother to death, and the father the child; and children
will rise up against their parents, and cause them to be put to
death; 13 and you will be hated by all on my account. But he
that endures to the end shall be saved.
14 But when you see that detestable thing that makes desolate,

which is spoken of by Daniel the prophet, standing where it
ought not, (let him that reads understand,) then let those who
are in Judea flee to the mountains; [15] let not him that is on the
house-top go down into his house, nor enter in to take any thing
from his house; [16] and let not him that is in the field turn back
to take his mantle. [17] But alas for those who are with child,
and for those who give suck in those days. [18] And pray that
your flight may not be in the winter. [19] For these will be the
days of affliction, such as has not been from the beginning of
the creation which God created, till this time, and will never be.
[20] And unless the Lord had made those days few, no flesh could
be saved: but for the sake of the elect whom he has chosen, he
has made those days few. [21] And then, if any one say to you:
Lo! here is the Christ, or, Lo! there; believe him not. [22] For
false Christs and false prophets will arise, and will show signs
and wonders, in order to lead astray, if possible, even the elect.
[23] But do you take heed: behold, I have told you all things beforehand.

[24] But in those days, after that affliction, the sun will be
darkened, and the moon will not give her light, [25] and the stars
of heaven will fall, and the hosts that are in the heavens will
be shaken. [26] And then shall they see the Son of man coming
in clouds with great power and glory. [27] And then will he send
his angels, and gather his elect from the four winds, from the
most distant part of earth to the most distant part of heaven.

[28] But learn a parable from the fig-tree: As soon as its branch
becomes tender, and puts forth leaves, you know that summer
is near. [29] So, also, when you see these things coming to pass,
know that it is near, at the doors. [30] Verily I say to you, this
generation shall not pass away, till all these things take place.
[31] Heaven and earth shall pass away, but my words shall not
pass away. [32] But of that day or that hour no one knows:
neither the angels who are in heaven, nor the Son, but the
Father.

[33] Take heed, watch and pray: for you know not when the
time is. [34] As a man, going into another country, leaves his
house, and gives authority to his servants, and to each one his
own work, and commands the door-keeper to watch; [35] watch
you therefore; for you know not when the master of the house
comes, whether at evening, or at midnight, or at the crowing
of the cock, or in the morning; [36] lest he come suddenly, and
find you sleeping. [37] What I say to you, I say to all, Watch.

XIV. [1] After two days was the passover and the feast of unleavened bread; and the chief priests and the scribes sought
how they might take him by craft, and kill him. [2] But they
said: Not during the feast, lest there be a tumult of the people.
[3] And while he was in Bethany, in the house of Simon the
leper, as he reclined at table, there came a woman that had an
alabaster box of ointment of pure nard, very costly; and she
broke the box, and poured it on his head. [4] And some of them
were displeased within themselves, and said: For what purpose
was this waste of the ointment? [5] For this ointment could
have been sold for more than three hundred denarii, and given
to the poor. And they murmured against her.
[6] But Jesus said: Let her alone; why do you trouble her?
She has performed a good work on me. [7] For you have the poor
with you always; and whenever you choose, you can do them
good; but me you have not always. [8] She has done what she
could; she has come beforehand to anoint my body for its burial.
[9] Verily I say to you, wherever this gospel shall be preached
throughout the whole world, this also which she has done shall
be told, for a memorial of her.
[10] And Judas Iscariot, one of the twelve, went away to the
chief priests, that he might deliver him up to them. [11] And
when they heard it, they were glad, and promised to give him
money. And he sought how he might conveniently deliver
him up.
[12] And on the first day of unleavened bread, when they killed
the passover, his disciples said to him? Where dost thou wish
that we go and prepare that thou mayest eat the passover?
[13] And he sent two of his disciples, and said to them: Go into
the city, and there will meet you a man carrying a pitcher of
water; [14] follow him, and wherever he enters, say to the master
of the house: The Teacher says, Where is the room in which I
may eat the passover with my disciples? [15] And he will show
you a large upper room, furnished and made ready; there make
ready for us. [16] And his disciples went out, and came into the
city, and found as he had said to them; and they prepared the
passover.
[17] And in the evening, he came with the twelve. [18] And while
they were reclining at table, and were eating, Jesus said *to them:*
Verily I say to you, One of you, he that eats with me, will deliver me up. [19] And they began to be sad, and to say to him,
one by one, Is it I? and another said, Is it I? [20] He answered

and said to them: It is one of the twelve, he that dips with me
into the dish. 21 The Son of man goes, as it is written of him;
but alas for that man by whom the Son of man is delivered up!
It would have been good for that man if he had never been born.

22 And while they were eating, Jesus took bread, and blessed,
and broke it, and gave it to them, and said: Take, eat; this is
my body. 23 And he took the cup, and when he had given
thanks, he gave it to them; and they all drank of it. 24 And
he said to them: This is my blood of the new covenant, which
is poured out for many. 25 Verily I say to you, I shall drink
no more of the fruit of the vine, till that day when I shall
drink it new in the kingdom of God.

26 And when they had sung a hymn, they went out into the
mount of Olives. 27 And Jesus said to them: All of you will find
in me an occasion for offense this night; for it is written: I will
smite the shepherd, and the sheep shall be scattered. 28 But
after I have risen, I will go before you into Galilee. 29 Peter
said to him: Though all should find occasion for offense, yet I
will not. 30 And Jesus said to him: Verily I say to you, this
day, during this very night, before the cock crows twice, you
will deny me three times. 31 But he said with the more vehe-
mence: Though it should be necessary for me to die with thee,
I would not deny thee. And so said they all. 32 And they came
to a place called Gethsemane; and he said to his disciples: Sit
here, while I pray. 33 And he took with him Peter and James
and John, and began to be in dismay and anguish of soul.
34 And he said to them: My soul is encompassed with sorrow,
even to death; remain here, and watch. 35 And he went forward a little, and fell upon the ground, and prayed, that, if it
were possible, the hour might pass from him; 36 and he said:
Abba, Father, all things are possible to thee; let this cup pass
from me: but not what I will, but what thou willest. 37 And
he came and found them sleeping; and he said to Peter: Simon,
do you sleep? Had you not strength to watch one hour?
38 Watch, and pray, *all of you*, lest you enter into temptation.
The spirit indeed is willing, but the flesh is weak.

39 And again he went away, and prayed, saying the same
thing. 40 And he returned, and found them sleeping again, for
their eyes were heavy; and they knew not what to answer him.
41 And he came the third time, and said to them: Sleep the remaining time, and take your rest. It is enough; the hour has
come; behold, the Son of man is delivered into the hands of

sinners. [42] Arise, let us go; behold, he that delivers me up draws near.

[43] And immediately, while he was yet speaking, came Judas, one of the twelve, and with him a great multitude, with swords and clubs, from the chief priests and the scribes and the elders.
[44] And he that delivered him up had given them a sign, saying: The one that I shall kiss, is he; take him, and lead him away securely.
[45] And when he came, he immediately went up to him and said: Rabbi, Rabbi, and kissed him.
[46] And they laid their hands on him and took him.

[47] And one of those who were standing by, drew a sword, and struck the servant of the chief priest, and cut off his ear.
[48] And Jesus answering, said to them: Have you come out as against a robber, with swords and clubs, to take me?
[49] I was daily with you in the temple, and taught, and you did not take me; but *this is so*, that the Scriptures may be fulfilled.
[50] And they all forsook him and fled.
[51] And there followed him a certain young man, who had a linen garment around his naked body. And the young men laid hold of him;
[52] and he left the linen garment, and fled from them naked.

[53] And they led Jesus away to the chief priest; and with him were assembled all the chief priests, and the elders, and the scribes.
[54] And Peter followed him, at a distance, even into the palace of the chief priest, and sat with the attendants, and warmed himself at the fire.
[55] And the chief priests and the whole Sanhedrim sought for testimony against Jesus, in order to put him to death, and found none.

[56] For many testified falsely against him, and their testimony did not agree.
[57] And some rose up, and testified falsely against him, saying:
[58] We heard him say, I will destroy this temple that is made with hands, and in three days I will build another made without hands.
[59] And not even in this did their testimony agree.
[60] And the chief priest stood up in the midst, and asked Jesus, saying: Do you make no answer? What do these testify against you?
[61] But he was silent, and made no answer.

Again, the chief priest asked him, and said to him: Are you the Christ, the Son of the Blessed?
[62] Jesus replied: I am. And you shall see the Son of man sitting at the right hand of the Almighty, and coming with the clouds of heaven.
[63] And the chief priest rent his clothes, and said: What further need have we of witnesses?
[64] You have heard his impious speech. What think you? They all condemned him to be a subject of death.

65 And some began to spit on him, and to cover his face, and to
strike him with their fists, and to say to him: Give an answer.
And the attendants struck him with their open hands.

66 And while Peter was in the court below, one of the maid-
servants of the chief priest came; 67 and when she saw Peter
warming himself, she looked at him, and said: You also were
with Jesus the Nazarene. 68 But he denied, saying: I neither
know, nor understand what you say. And he went out into the
entrance, and the cock crew. 69 And the maid-servant saw him
again, and began to say to those who stood by: This man is one
of them. 70 He again denied. And again, after a little while,
those who stood by said to Peter: Surely, you are one of them;
for you are a Galilean, and your speech is like theirs. 71 But he
began to curse and to swear, saying: I know not this man of
whom you speak. 72 And immediately the cock crew the second
time. And Peter remembered the word that Jesus had spoken
to him: Before the cock crows twice, you will deny me three
times. And when he thought upon it, he wept.

XV. 1 And forthwith in the morning, the chief priests, with
the elders and scribes, and the whole Sanhedrim, having held a
consultation, and having bound Jesus, led him away, and delivered him to Pilate. 2 And Pilate asked him: Are you the
King of the Jews? And he answering, said: You say it. 3 And
the chief priests accused him of many things. 4 Pilate again
asked him, saying: Do you make no answer? See, how many
things they testify against you. 5 But Jesus gave no further
answer; so that Pilate was astonished.

6 Now it was his custom to release to them, at the feast, one
prisoner, whomever they desired. 7 And there was one called
Barabbas, lying bound with his fellow-insurgents, who had
committed murder in the insurrection. 8 And the multitude
cried out, and began to ask him to do as he had always done for
them. 9 But Pilate answered them, saying: Do you wish me
to release to you the King of the Jews? 10 For he knew that,
through envy, the chief priests had delivered him up. 11 But
the chief priests instigated the multitude, that he should rather
release Barabbas to them. 12 And Pilate answered and said
again to them: What, then, do you wish me to do with him
whom you call the King of the Jews? 13 They again cried out:
Crucify him. 14 But Pilate said to them: Why, what evil has
he done? But they cried vehemently: Crucify him. 15 And Pi-

late, willing to gratify the multitude, released to them Barabbas:
and delivered Jesus, after he had scourged him, to be crucified.
16 And the soldiers led him away within the court, which is
the governor's house, and called together the whole band. 17 And
they clothed him in purple; and having plaited a crown of thorn
branches, they put it on him, 18 and began to salute him: Hail,
King of the Jews! 19 And they struck him on the head with a
reed, and spit upon him, and bowing their knees, did him homage. 20 And when they had derided him, they took off the purple from him, and put his own clothes on him, and led him out
to crucify him.
21 And they compelled one Simon, a Cyrenian, (the father of
Alexander and Rufus,) who was passing by, coming in from the
country, to bear his cross. 22 And they brought him to the place
Golgotha, which is, when translated, the place of a skull. 23 And
they gave him wine mingled with Myrrh, to drink: but he did
not receive it. 24 And when they had crucified him, they divided
his clothes among themselves, casting lots for them, what each
one should take.
25 And it was the third hour, and they crucified him. 26 And
the superscription containing his accusation was written above
him: THE KING OF THE JEWS. 27 And with him they
crucified two robbers, one on his right hand, and the other on
his left. 28 And the Scripture was fulfilled, which says: And he
was numbered with transgressors. 29 And those who passed by
reviled him, shaking their heads, and saying: Aha! you that
destroy the temple, and build it in three days, 30 save yourself,
and come down from the cross. 31 Likewise the chief priests,
with the scribes, speaking in derision one to another, said: He
saved others; himself he can not save. 32 Let the Christ, the
King of Israel, come down now from the cross, that we may
see and believe. Those also who were crucified with him, reproached him.
33 And when the sixth hour had come, there was darkness over
the whole land, till the ninth hour. 34 And at the ninth hour,
Jesus cried with a loud voice, saying: Eloi, Eloi, lamma sabachthani? which is, when translated, My God, my God, why hast
thou forsaken me? 35 And some of those who stood by, when
they heard it, said: Behold, he calls for Elijah. 36 And one ran,
and filled a sponge with vinegar, and put it on a reed, and gave
it to him to drink, saying: Wait; let us see if Elijah is coming
to take him down.

37 But Jesus, having cried with a loud voice, gave up his spirit.
38 And the vail of the temple was rent in two, from the top to the
bottom. 39 And when the centurion that was standing opposite
him, saw that he thus cried out, and gave up his spirit, he said:
Truly, this man was the Son of God.

40 And there were, at a distance, women also, looking on;
among whom were Mary Magdalene, and Mary the mother of
James the younger and of Joses, and Salome; 41 who also, when
he was in Galilee, followed him, and ministered to him; and
many other women, who had come up with him to Jerusalem.

42 And when the evening had come, because it was the preparation, which is the eve of the Sabbath, 43 Joseph of Arimathea,
an honorable counselor, who was himself looking for the kingdom of God, came, and went in boldly to Pilate, and asked for
the body of Jesus. 44 But Pilate was astonished that he was already dead; and having called the centurion to him, he inquired
of him whether he had been any while dead. 45 And having
learned the fact from the centurion, he gave the body to Joseph.
46 And he bought fine linen, and took him down, and wrapped
him in the linen, and laid him in a sepulcher that had been
hewed out of a rock: and he rolled a stone to the door of the
sepulcher. 47 And Mary Magdalene and Mary the mother of
Joses saw where he was laid.

XVI. 1 And when the Sabbath had passed, Mary Magdalene,
and Mary the mother of James, and Salome, bought spices, that
they might come and anoint him. 2 And very early, on the
first day of the week, when the sun had risen, they came to the
sepulcher. 3 And they said among themselves: Who will roll
away the stone for us from the door of the sepulcher? 4 for it was
very great. And looking up, they saw that the stone had been
rolled away. 5 And they entered the sepulcher, and saw a young
man sitting on the right side, clothed in a white robe: and they
were frightened. 6 But he said to them: Be not frightened; you
seek Jesus the Nazarene, who was crucified. He has risen; he
is not here: see the place where they laid him. 7 But go, tell his
disciples, and Peter, that he goes before you into Galilee; there
you shall see him, as he told you. 8 And they went out, and fled
from the sepulcher; for trembling and astonishment seized upon
them. And they said nothing to any one, for they were afraid.

9 Now when Jesus had risen early on the first day of the week,
he appeared first to Mary Magdalene, out of whom he had cast

seven demons. 10 And she went and told it to those who had been
with him, as they mourned and wept. 11 And though they heard
that he was alive, and had been seen by her, they did not believe.

12 After this he appeared in another form to two of them, as
they walked and went into the country. 13 And they went and
told it to the rest. But they did not believe them.

14 Afterward he appeared to the eleven as they reclined at
table; and he reproached them for their unbelief and hardness
of heart, because they did not believe those who had seen him
after he had risen.

15 And he said to them: Go into all the world, and preach the
gospel to every creature. 16 He that believes and is immersed,
shall be saved; he that believes not, shall be condemned.
17 And these signs shall attend those who believe. In my name
they shall cast out demons; they shall speak with new tongues;
18 they shall take up serpents; and, if they drink any deadly
thing, it shall not hurt them; they shall lay hands on the sick,
and they shall recover.

19 The Lord, therefore, after he had spoken to them, was
taken up into heaven: and he sat down at the right hand of
God. 20 And they went forth and preached every-where, the
Lord working with them, and confirming the word with signs
following.

TESTIMONY OF LUKE.

I. 1 SINCE many have undertaken to compose a history of
the things that are fully believed among us, 2 even as
they were delivered to us by those who were, from the beginning, eye-witnesses and ministers of the word; 3 it seemed good
to me also, having obtained exact information of all things
from the very first, to write them in order for you, most excellent Theophilus, 4 that you might know the certainty of the
things in which you have been instructed.

5 There was, in the days of Herod the king of Judea, a certain priest named Zachariah, of the class of Abijah; and his
wife was of the daughters of Aaron, and her name was Elizabeth. 6 They were both righteous before God, walking in all
the commandments and ordinances of the Lord, blameless.
7 And they had no child, because Elizabeth was barren, and
they were both advanced in years.

8 It came to pass, while he was officiating as priest before
God, in the order of his class, that, 9 according to the custom of
the priest's office, his lot was to burn incense, when he went
into the temple of the Lord. 10 And all the multitude of the
people were praying without, at the time of incense. 11 And
there appeared to him an angel of the Lord, standing at the
right side of the altar of incense.

12 And Zachariah was troubled at the sight, and fear fell upon
him. 13 But the angel said to him: Fear not, Zachariah; for
your prayer is heard, and your wife Elizabeth shall bear you a
son, and you shall call his name John. 14 And you shall have
joy and gladness, and many shall rejoice at his birth. 15 For he
shall be great before the Lord; and he shall drink neither wine
nor strong drink; and he shall be filled with the Holy Spirit
even from his mother's womb. 16 And many of the sons of
Israel shall he turn to the Lord their God. 17 And he shall go
before him in the spirit and power of Elijah to turn the hearts
of the fathers to the children, and the disobedient, by the wisdom
of the just, in order to make ready for the Lord a prepared people.

18 And Zachariah said to the angel: By what *sign* shall I
know this? for I am old, and my wife is advanced in years.
19 And the angel answered and said to him: I am Gabriel, who
stands in the presence of God; and I am sent to speak to you,
and to announce to you this good news. 20 And behold, you
shall be dumb and not able to speak, till the day in which
these things shall take place, because you did not believe my
words, which shall be fulfilled in their proper time. 21 And the
people were waiting for Zachariah, and they wondered that he
stayed so long in the temple. 22 But when he came out, he was
not able to speak to them; and they perceived that he had seen
a vision in the temple; and he made signs to them, and remained
speechless.

23 And it came to pass, when the days of his service were completed, that he departed to his own house. 24 And after those
days, his wife Elizabeth conceived, and kept herself retired for
five months, saying: 25 Thus has the Lord dealt with me in the
days in which he has looked with regard upon me, to take away
my reproach among men.

26 And in the sixth month, the angel Gabriel was sent from
God into a city of Galilee, named Nazareth, 27 to a virgin betrothed to a man whose name was Joseph, of the house of David;
and the name of the virgin was Mary.

28 And the angel came into her presence, and said: Hail, gra-
ciously accepted: the Lord is with you; blessed are you among
women. 29 And she was perplexed at his words, and reasoned,
what this salutation could mean. 30 And the angel said to her:
Fear not, Mary; for you have found favor with God. 31 And
behold, you shall conceive and bear a son, and you shall call
his name Jesus. 32 He shall be great, and shall be called the
Son of the Most High; and the Lord God will give to him the
throne of David his father; 33 and he shall reign over the house
of Jacob forever, and of his kingdom there shall be no end.

34 But Mary said to the angel: How shall this be, since I
know not a man? 35 And the angel answered and said to her:
The Holy Spirit will come upon you, and the power of the Most
High will overshadow you; for which reason, also, that which
is begotten, being holy, shall be called the Son of God. 36 And
behold, Elizabeth your kinswoman, even she has conceived a
son in her old age; and this is the sixth month with her who
is called barren; 37 for nothing shall be impossible with God.
38 And Mary said: Behold the handmaid of the Lord; let it be
to me according to your word. And the angel departed from
her.

39 And Mary arose in those days, and went with haste into the
mountainous country, into a city of Judah; 40 and she came
into the house of Zachariah, and saluted Elizabeth. 41 And it
came to pass, when Elizabeth heard the salutation of Mary,
that the babe in her womb leaped for joy. 42 And Elizabeth
was filled with the Holy Spirit, and spoke with a loud voice,
and said: Blessed are you among women, and blessed is the
fruit of your womb. 43 And whence is this to me, that the
mother of my Lord should come to me? 44 For, behold, when
the voice of your salutation sounded in my ears, the babe in
my womb leaped for joy. 45 And blessed is she who believed;
for there shall be a fulfillment of the things which were spoken
to her from the Lord.

46 And Mary said: My soul magnifies the Lord, 47 and my
spirit rejoices in God, my Savior; 48 for he has looked upon the
lowly condition of his handmaid. For, behold, from this time,
all generations shall call me blessed; 49 for He that is Mighty
has done great things for me, and holy is his name: 50 and his
mercy is from generation to generation upon those who fear
him. 51 He has done mighty deeds with his arm; he has scattered those who are proud in the understanding of their hearts.

52 He has cast down the mighty from their thrones, and exalted
the lowly. 53 He has filled the hungry with good things, but
the rich he has sent empty away. 54 He has helped Israel his
servant, (as he spoke to our fathers,) 55 by remembering his
mercy to Abraham and to his posterity forever.

56 And Mary remained with her about three months, and returned to her own house.

57 Now the time for Elizabeth to be delivered had fully come;
and she gave birth to a son. 58 And her neighbors and relatives
heard that the Lord had showed great mercy to her, and they
rejoiced with her.

59 And it came to pass, on the eighth day, that they came to
circumcise the child; and they called him by the name of his
father, Zachariah. 60 And his mother answered and said: Not
so: but he shall be called John. 61 And they said to her: There
is no one among your relatives that is called by this name.
62 And they made signs to his father, to know what he wished
him to be called. 63 And having asked for a writing tablet, he
wrote, saying: His name is John. And they were all astonished.

64 And immediately his mouth was opened, and his tongue was
loosed, and he spoke, and praised God. 65 And fear came on all
that dwelt round about them; and all these things were talked
of every-where throughout the mountainous country of Judea.
66 And all that heard them, laid them up in their hearts, and
said: What, then, will this child be? And the hand of the
Lord was with him.

67 And Zachariah his father was filled with the Holy Spirit,
and prophesied, saying: 68 Blessed be the Lord God of Israel;
for he has visited and redeemed his people; 69 and he has raised
up for us, in the house of David his servant, a horn of salvation, (70 as he spoke by the mouth of all his holy prophets of
ancient times,) 71 salvation from our enemies, and from the
hand of all that hate us, 72 in order to show the mercy promised to our fathers, and to remember his holy covenant, 73 the
oath which he swore to Abraham our father, 74 that he would
grant to us, that being delivered from the hands of our enemies,
we might serve him without fear, 75 in holiness and righteousness
before him, all our days.

76 And you, child, shall be called the prophet of the Most
High; for you shall go before the face of the Lord, to make
ready his ways, 77 by giving to his people the knowledge of salvation in the remission of their sins, 78 through the tender

mercies of our God; by which the dawn from on high has
visited us, 79 to give light to those who sit in darkness and in
the shadow of death, by guiding our feet in the way of peace.
80 And the child grew and became strong in spirit; and he was
in the deserts till the day of his manifestation to Israel.

II. 1 And it came to pass in those days, that there went forth
a decree from Cæsar Augustus, that all the inhabitants of the
land should be enrolled. 2 This enrollment first took place when
Cyrenius was governor of Syria. 3 And all went to be enrolled,
each one to his own city. 4 And Joseph also went up from Galilee, out of the city of Nazareth, into Judea, to the city of David, which is called Bethlehem, (for he was of the house and
family of David,) 5 to be enrolled with Mary his betrothed wife,
who was with child.
6 And it came to pass while they were there, that the days
for her to be delivered were completed; 7 and she brought forth
her first-born son, and wrapped him in swathing-clothes, and
laid him in the stable, because there was no place for them in
the inn.
8 And there were in the same country shepherds, living in the
open field, and guarding their flock by night. 9 And, behold, an
angel of the Lord stood by them, and the glory of the Lord shone
round about them; and they were greatly afraid. 10 And the
angel said to them: Be not afraid; for, behold, I bring you good
news of great joy, which shall be for all people. 11 For there is
born for you this day, in the city of David, a Savior, who is
Christ the Lord. 12 And this shall be to you the sign: you will
find the babe wrapped in swathing-clothes, and lying in a stable.
13 And suddenly there was with the angel a multitude of the
heavenly host, praising God, and saying: 14 Glory to God in the
highest, and on earth peace, good will among men.
15 And it came to pass, that, after the angels had gone away
into heaven, the shepherds said one to another: Let us now go
to Bethlehem, and see this thing that has come to pass, which
the Lord has made known to us. 16 And they came with haste,
and found both Mary and Joseph, and the babe lying in the
stable. 17 And after they had seen it, they made known every-
where the words that had been spoken to them of this child.
18 And all that heard, wondered at those things which were told
them by the shepherds. 19 But Mary kept all these things in her
mind, and pondered them in her heart. 20 And the shepherds

returned, glorifying and praising God for all things which they
had heard and seen, as it had been told to them.

21 And when eight days were completed for circumcising him,
his name was called Jesus, as it had been called by the angel,
before he was conceived in the womb.

22 And when the days for their purification were completed
according to the law of Moses, they brought him to Jerusalem,
to present him to the Lord, (23 as it is written in the law of the
Lord: Every male that opens the womb shall be called holy to
the Lord;) 24 and to offer a sacrifice, according to that which is
commanded in the law of the Lord: A pair of turtle-doves, or
two young pigeons.

25 And, behold, there was a man in Jerusalem, whose name
was Simeon. And this man was just and devout, looking for
the consolation of Israel. And the Holy Spirit was upon him:
26 and it had been revealed to him by the Holy Spirit, that he
should not see death before he had seen the Lord's Anointed.
27 And he came by the Spirit into the temple; and when the
parents brought in the child Jesus, to do for him according to
the custom of the law, 28 he took him in his arms, and blessed
God, and said: 29 Now, Lord, thou dost let thy servant depart
in peace, according to thy word, 30 for my eyes have seen thy
salvation, 31 which thou hast prepared before the face of all
people; 32 a light for a revelation to the Gentiles, and the glory
of thy people Israel.

33 And Joseph and his mother wondered at the things which
were spoken of him. 34 And Simeon blessed them, and said to
Mary his mother: Behold, this child is appointed for the fall
and rising again of many in Israel, and for a sign to be spoken
against, 35 (and a sword shall pierce through your own soul,)
that the thoughts of many hearts may be revealed.

36 And there was a prophetess, Anna, the daughter of Phanuel,
of the tribe of Asher; she was of great age, and had lived with
a husband seven years from her virginity: 37 and she was a widow
of about eighty-four years, and she departed not from the temple, but served, day and night, with fastings and prayers. 38 And
she came in at that hour, and gave thanks to the Lord, and
spoke of him to all that looked for redemption in Jerusalem.

39 And when they had performed all things according to the law
of the Lord, they returned to Galilee, to their own city Nazareth.
40 And the child grew, and became strong in spirit, being filled
with wisdom: and the grace of God was upon him.

[41] And his parents went up every year to Jerusalem, at the
feast of passover. [42] And when he was twelve years old, they
went up to Jerusalem, according to the custom of the feast.
[43] And when they had kept the full number of days, and had set
out to return, the child Jesus staid behind in Jerusalem; and
Joseph and his mother knew it not. [44] But supposing that he
was in the company, they went a day's journey; and they sought
for him among their relatives and acquaintance; [45] and not
finding him, they returned to Jerusalem in search of him.
[46] And it came to pass, after three days, that they found him
in the temple, sitting in the midst of the teachers, both hearing
them, and asking them questions. [47] And all that heard him
were astonished at his understanding, and his answers. [48] And
when they saw him they were amazed. And his mother said to
him: Child, why have you acted thus toward us? Behold, your
father and I have sought for you in sorrow. [49] And he said to
them: Why did you seek for me? Did you not know that I
must be in my Father's house? [50] And they did not understand
the words which he spoke to them. [51] And he went down with
them, and came to Nazareth, and was obedient to them. And
his mother kept all these sayings in her heart. [52] And Jesus
increased in wisdom and in stature, and in favor with God and
with man.

III. [1] In the fifteenth year of the reign of Tiberius Cæsar,
when Pontius Pilate was governor of Judea, and Herod was
tetrarch of Galilee, and his brother Philip was tetrarch of Itu-
rea and of the region of Trachonitis, and Lysanias was tetrarch
of Abilene, [2] Annas and Caiaphas being chief priests, the word
of God came to John the son of Zachariah, in the wilderness.
[3] And he came into all the country about the Jordan, preaching the immersion of repentance in order to the remission of
sins; [4] as it is written in the book of the words of Isaiah the
prophet, saying: The voice of one crying in the wilderness,
Make ready the way of the Lord, make his paths straight;
[5] every ravine shall be filled, and every mountain and hill shall
be made level; and the crooked ways shall be made straight;
and the rough ways shall be made smooth; [6] and all flesh shall
see the salvation of God.
[7] Therefore he said to the multitudes that came out to be immersed by him: Generation of vipers, who has warned you to
flee from the coming wrath? [8] Bring forth, therefore, fruits

worthy of repentance. And begin not to say within yourselves,
We have Abraham for our father; for I say to you, that God
is able from these stones to raise up children for Abraham.
9 And now also the ax is lying at the root of the trees; therefore, every tree that does not produce good fruit, is cut down
and cast into the fire.

10 And the multitudes asked him, saying: What, then, shall
we do? 11 He answered and said to them: He that has two
coats, let him give to him that has none; and he that has food,
let him do likewise. 12 And the publicans also came to be immersed, and they said to him: Teacher, what shall we do?
13 And he said to them: Exact no more than that which is appointed you. 14 And soldiers also asked him, saying: And what
shall we do? And he said to them: Take nothing from any
one by extortion, nor by false accusation, and be content with
your pay.

15 While the people were in suspense, and all were reasoning
in their hearts about John, whether he was the Christ or not,
16 John answered them all, saying: I indeed immerse you in
water; but there comes One mightier than I, the strap of whose
sandals I am not worthy to loose; he will immerse you in the
Holy Spirit and in fire. 17 His winnowing shovel is in his hand,
and he will thoroughly cleanse his thrashing-floor, and gather
the grain into his granary, but the chaff he will burn with unquenchable fire. 18 With many other exhortations he proclaimed
the good news to the people.

19 But Herod the tetrarch having been reproved by him on account of Herodias, the wife of his brother Philip, and for all the
wicked deeds which Herod did, 20 added this also to them all,
that he shut up John in prison.

21 And it came to pass, while all the people were being immersed, that Jesus also was immersed; and as he was praying,
the heaven was opened, 22 and the Holy Spirit descended upon
him, in a bodily form, like a dove; and there came a voice
from heaven, which said: Thou art my beloved Son; in thee
I delight.

23 And Jesus was about thirty years old when he began *his
ministry*, being, as was supposed, the son of Joseph, son of Heli,
24 son of Matthat, son of Levi, son of Malchi, son of Janna, son
of Joseph, 25 son of Mattathiah, son of Amos, son of Nahum,
son of Esli, son of Naggæ, 26 son of Maath, son of Mattathiah,
son of Shimei, son of Joseph, son of Judah, 27 son of Joannah,

son of Rhesa, son of Zerubbabel, son of Shealtiel, son of Neri,
28 son of Malchi, son of Addi, son of Kosam, son of Elmodam,
son of Er, 29 son of Jose, son of Eliezer, son of Jorim, son of
Matthat, son of Levi, 30 son of Simeon, son of Judah, son of
Joseph, son of Jonan, son of Eliakim, 31 son of Meleah, son of
Mainan, son of Mattatha, son of Nathan, son of David,
32 Son of Jesse, son of Obed, son of Boaz, son of Salmon, son
of Nahshon, 33 son of Aminidab, son of Aram, son of Esrom,
son of Phares, son of Judah, 34 son of Jacob, son of Isaac, son
of Abraham, son of Terah, son of Nahor, 35 son of Serug, son
of Reu, son of Peleg, son of Eber, son of Salah, 36 son of Kenan, son of Arphaxad, son of Shem, son of Noah, son of La-
mech, 37 son of Methusalah, son of Enoch, son of Jared, son of
Mahalaleel, son of Kenan, 38 son of Enos, son of Seth, son of
Adam, son of God.

IV. 1 And Jesus, full of the Holy Spirit, returned from the
Jordan, and was led by the Spirit into the wilderness, 2 and
was there forty days, to be tempted by the devil. And he ate
nothing during those days; and when they were ended, he was
afterward hungry. 3 And the devil said to him: If you are
the Son of God, command this stone to become bread. 4 And
Jesus answered him, and said: It is written, Man shall not live
by bread alone, but by every word of God.
5 And the devil took him up into a high mountain, and showed
him all the kingdoms of the world, in a moment of time. 6 And
the devil said to him: I will give you all the authority and
glory of these, for it is delivered to me; and to whomever I
will, I give it. 7 If, therefore, you will bow with reverence before me, all shall be yours. 8 And Jesus answered and said to
him: Get behind me, Satan; it is written, You shall worship
the Lord your God, and him only shall you serve.
9 And he brought him to Jerusalem, and placed him on the
pinnacle of the temple, and said to him: If you are the Son of
God, throw yourself down from this place; 10 for it is written,
He will give his angels charge concerning you, to guard you
carefully; 11 and in their hands they shall take you up, lest you
strike your foot against a stone. 12 And Jesus answered and
said to him: It is said, You shall not put the Lord your God to
the proof. 13 And when the devil had ended all the temptation,
he departed from him for a time.
14 And Jesus returned in the power of the Spirit into Galilee;

and his fame went throughout the whole of that region. 15 And
he taught in their synagogues, being glorified by all.

16 And he came to Nazareth, where he had been brought up;
and, as his custom was, he entered the synagogue on the Sabbath-day, and stood up to read. 17 And the volume of Isaiah
the prophet was given to him: and when he had unrolled the
volume, he found the place where it was written: 18 The Spirit
of the Lord is upon me; because he has anointed me to preach
the gospel to the poor; he has sent me to heal the broken-
hearted; to proclaim liberty to the captives, and recovery of
sight to the blind; to set free the oppressed; 19 to proclaim the
acceptable year of the Lord. 20 And he rolled up the volume,
and gave it back to the attendant, and sat down; and the eyes
of all that were in the synagogue were earnestly fixed upon him.
21 And he began to say to them: This Scripture which you
have heard, is this day fulfilled. 22 And all extolled him; and
they wondered at the words of grace which proceeded out of
his mouth, and said: Is not this the son of Joseph? 23 And he
said to them: You will assuredly apply to me this proverb,
Physician, heal yourself. Whatever things we have heard were
done in Capernaum, do also here in your country. 24 And he
said: Verily I say to you, No prophet is accepted in his own
country. 25 And I tell you, in truth, there were many widows
in Israel in the days of Elijah, when the heaven was shut up for
three years and six months, so that a great famine was on all
the land: 26 and to no one of them was Elijah sent, but to Sa-
repta, a city of Sidon, to a woman that was a widow. 27 And
many lepers were in Israel, in the time of Elisha the prophet;
and no one of them was cleansed but Naaman the Syrian.

28 And all that were in the synagogue, when they heard these
things, were filled with anger, 29 and arose, and drove him out
of the city, and brought him to the brow of the hill on which
their city was built, that they might throw him down headlong.
30 But he passed through the midst of them, and went away.

31 And he went down to Capernaum, a city of Galilee. And
he was teaching them on the Sabbath-days. 32 And they were
astonished at his teaching, for his word was with authority.
33 And there was in the synagogue a man who had the spirit of
an unclean demon; and he cried out with a loud voice, 34 saying: Let us alone; what have we to do with thee, Jesus, thou
Nazarene? Hast thou come to destroy us? I know thee who
thou art, the Holy One of God. 35 And Jesus rebuked him, say-

ing: Be silent, and come out of him. And the demon threw
him into the midst, and came out of him, and hurt him not.
[36] And amazement came upon all, and they spoke one to another, saying: What teaching is this? for with authority and
power he commands the unclean spirits, and they come out.
[37] And his fame went abroad into every place of the country
round about.

[38] And he arose and went out of the synagogue into the house
of Simon. And Simon's mother-in-law was confined with a
violent fever: and they besought him in her behalf. [39] And he
stood over her, and rebuked the fever, and it left her: and she
arose immediately, and ministered to them.

[40] And when the sun had gone down, all that had any sick
with various diseases, brought them to him; and he laid his
hands on every one of them, and cured them. [41] Demons also
came out of many, crying out and saying: Thou art the Christ,
the Son of God. And he rebuked them, and did not permit
them to speak, because they knew that he was the Christ.

[42] And when it was day, he went out and departed into a
desert place; and the multitudes sought for him, and came to
him and endeavored to detain him, that he should not go away
from them. [43] But he said to them: I must make known the
good news of the kingdom of God to other cities also; for to
this end I have been sent. [44] And he continued to preach in the
synagogues of Galilee.

V. [1] And it came to pass while the multitude was pressing on
him to hear the word of God, and he was standing by the lake
of Gennesaret, [2] that he saw two ships standing by the lake:
but the fishermen had gone out of them, and were washing
their nets. [3] And he entered one of the ships, which was
Simon's, and requested him to push out a little from the land.
And he sat down and taught the multitude from the ship.

[4] And when he had made an end of speaking, he said to Simon: Push out into the deep water, and let down your nets for
a draught. [5] And Simon answered and said to him: Master, we
have toiled all night and have caught nothing; but at thy
command, I will let down the net. [6] And when they had done
this, they inclosed a great number of fishes, and their net began
to break; [7] and they beckoned to their partners who were in the
other ship, to come and help them. And they came and filled
both the ships, so that they began to sink.

8 And when Simon Peter saw it, he fell down at the knees of
Jesus, and said: Depart from me, Lord, for I am a sinful man.
9 For amazement at the draught of fishes which they had
caught had seized upon him and all that were with him; 10 and
in like manner also upon James and John the sons of Zebedee,
who were partners with Simon. And Jesus said to Simon: Fear
not; from this time forth you shall catch men. 11 And when
they had brought their ships to the land, they left all and followed him.

12 And it came to pass, that he was in one of their cities; and
behold, a man full of leprosy; and when he saw Jesus, he fell
on his face and besought him, saying: Lord, if thou wilt, thou
canst make me clean. 13 And stretching out his hand, he touched
him, and said: I will; be clean. And immediately his leprosy
departed from him. 14 And he charged him to tell no one; but
go, show yourself to the priest, and make offering for your
cleansing, as Moses commanded, that it may be a testimony to
them. 15 But his fame went abroad the more: and many multitudes came together to hear, and to be cured by him of their
infirmities. 16 And he withdrew to the deserts and prayed.

17 And it came to pass, on a certain day, that he was teaching,
and there were Pharisees and teachers of the law sitting by,
who had come from every village of Galilee and Judea and Jerusalem; and the power of the Lord was exerted to heal them.
18 And behold, men brought, on a bed, a man who was a paralytic. And they sought how they might bring him in, and lay
him before him. 19 And finding no way by which they could
bring him in, because of the multitude, they went up on the
top of the house, and, through the tiling, let him down, with
his bed, into the midst before Jesus. 20 And when he saw their
faith, he said to him: Man, your sins are forgiven you. 21 And
the scribes and Pharisees began to reason, saying: Who is this
that utters impious words? Who can forgive sins but God
alone?

22 But Jesus perceived their reasonings, and answered and said
to them: Why are you reasoning in your hearts? 23 Which is
easier, to say, Your sins are forgiven you; or to say, Arise and
walk? 24 But that you may know that the Son of man on the
earth has power to forgive sins, (he said to the paralytic,) I say
to you, Arise, and take up your bed, and go to your house.
25 And he immediately arose before them, took up that on which
he had been lying, and went away to his own house, glorifying

God. 26 And astonishment seized upon all, and they glorified
God, and were filled with fear, saying: We have seen strange
things to-day.

27 And after these things, he went out and saw a publican
named Levi, sitting at the custom-house; and he said to him:
Follow me. 28 And leaving all, he arose and followed him.
29 And Levi made him a great feast at his own house; and there
was a great multitude of publicans and others, who reclined at
table with them. 30 And the Pharisees and their scribes murmured against his disciples, saying: Why do you eat and drink
with publicans and sinners? 31 And Jesus answered and said
to them: They that are well have no need of a physician, but
they that are sick. 32 I have not come to call righteous men,
but sinners, to repentance.

33 And they said to him: Why do the disciples of John fast
often, and make prayers, and likewise the disciples of the
Pharisees, but yours eat and drink? 34 And he said to them:
Can you make the sons of the bride-chamber fast, while the
bridegroom is with them? 35 But the days will come when the
bridegroom shall be taken from them; then shall they fast in
those days.

36 And he spoke also a parable to them: No one patches an old
garment with a piece taken from a new garment. If so, the new
tears it, and the patch from the new suits not the old. 37 And
no one puts new wine into old bottles; if so, the new wine will
burst the bottles, and it will be spilled, and the bottles will be
destroyed. 38 But new wine must be put into new bottles, and
both will be preserved. 39 And no one, after drinking old wine,
immediately desires new; for he says: The old is better.

VI. 1 And it came to pass, on the first Sabbath after the second day of the feast, that he was going through the fields of
grain; and his disciples pulled the ears and ate, rubbing them
in their hands. 2 And some of the Pharisees said to them:
Why are you doing what it is not lawful to do on the Sabbath-
days? 3 And Jesus answered and said to them: Have you not
read even that which David did, when he was hungry himself,
and those who were with him, 4 that he entered the house of
God, and took the loaves of the presence, and ate, and gave to
those also who were with him, which it is not lawful, except
for the priests alone, to eat? 5 And he said to them: The Son
of man is Lord also of the Sabbath.

[6] And it came to pass, on another Sabbath, that he entered
the synagogue and taught; and a man was there, whose right
hand was withered. [7] And the scribes and Pharisees watched
closely, whether he would heal on the Sabbath-day, that they
might find an accusation against him. [8] But he knew their
thoughts; and he said to the man that had the withered hand:
Rise, and stand forth in the midst. And he arose, and stood.
[9] Then Jesus said to them, I will ask you a question: Which is
lawful on the Sabbath, to do good, or to do evil? to save life,
or to kill? [10] And looking round upon them all, he said to him:
Stretch forth your hand. And he did so; and his hand was restored like the other. [11] But they were filled with madness, and
began to consult with one another what they should do to
Jesus.

[12] And it came to pass in those days, that he went out into
the mountain to pray; and he spent the night in prayer to God.
[13] And when it was day, he called to him his disciples; and from
them he chose twelve, whom he also named apostles: [14] Simon,
whom he also named Peter, and Andrew his brother, James and
John, Philip and Bartholomew, [15] Matthew and Thomas, James
the son of Alphæus, and Simon who is called Zelotes, [16] Judas
the brother of James, and Judas Iscariot, who was also the
traitor. [17] And he came down with them, and stood in a plain;
and with him stood a multitude of his disciples, and a great
number of people from all Judea and Jerusalem, and the sea-
coast of Tyre and Sidon, who had come to hear him, and to be
healed of their diseases, [18] and those who were oppressed by evil
spirits; and they were cured. [19] And the whole multitude
sought to touch him: for power went forth from him, and
healed them all.

[20] And he lifted up his eyes on his disciples, and said: Blessed
are you that are poor, for yours is the kingdom of God. [21] Blessed
are you that hunger now, for you shall be satisfied. Blessed
are you that weep now, for you shall laugh. [22] Blessed are you
when men shall hate you, and shall withdraw themselves from
you, and reproach you, and cast out your name as evil, on account of the Son of man. [23] Rejoice in that day, and leap for
joy; for behold, your reward is great in heaven: for so did their
fathers to the prophets.

[24] But alas for you that are rich! for you have received your
consolation. [25] Alas for you that are full! for you shall be
hungry. Alas for you that laugh now! for you shall mourn

and weep. 26 Alas for you, when men shall speak well of you!
for so did their fathers to the false prophets.
27 But I say to you that hear: Love your enemies; do good to
them that hate you; 28 bless them that curse you; pray for them
that abuse you. 29 To him that strikes you on one cheek, offer
also the other; and from him that takes away your mantle,
withhold not your coat. 30 Give to every one that asks of you;
and of him that takes away your goods, ask them not again.
31 And as you would that men should do to you, do you also in
like manner to them. 32 And if you love them that love you,
what thanks have you? for even sinners love those who love
them. 33 And if you do good to them that do good to you, what
thanks have you? for even sinners do the same. 34 And if
you lend to them from whom you hope to receive, what thanks
have you? for even sinners lend to sinners, that they may receive the same. 35 But love your enemies, and do good, and lend,
hoping for nothing in return; and your reward shall be great,
and you shall be sons of the Most High: for he is kind to the
unthankful and the evil. 36 Be you, therefore, merciful, as your
Father also is merciful.
37 Judge not, and you shall not be judged; condemn not, and
you shall not be condemned. Forgive, and you shall be forgiven. 38 Give, and it shall be given to you; good measure,
pressed down, shaken together, and running over, shall men
give into your lap. For with the same measure with which
you measure, it shall be measured to you in return.
39 And he spoke a parable to them: Can the blind lead the
blind? Will not both fall into the pit? 40 The disciple is not
above his teacher; but every accomplished disciple shall be as
his teacher.
41 And why do you look at the splinter that is in your brother's
eye, but perceive not the beam that is in your own eye? 42 Or,
how can you say to your brother: Brother, let me pull out the
splinter that is in your eye, when you yourself see not the beam
that is in your own eye? Hypocrite, first pull the beam out of
your own eye, and then you shall see clearly to pull out the
splinter that is in your brother's eye. 43 For a good tree does
not produce unsound fruit; nor does an unsound tree produce
good fruit. 44 For every tree is known by its own fruit. For
figs are not gathered from thorns, nor are grapes gathered from
brambles. 45 The good man, out of the good treasury of his
heart, brings forth that which is good; and the evil man, out

of the evil treasury of his heart, brings forth that which is evil.
For out of the abundance of his heart his mouth speaks.
46 But why call me Lord, Lord, and do not the things which
I command? 47 Every one that comes to me, and hears my
words, and does them, I will show you to whom he is like.
48 He is like a man that, when building a house, digged deep,
and laid the foundation on the rock. And when a flood arose,
the torrent dashed against that house, and it was not able to
shake it, for it was founded on the rock. 49 But he that hears,
and does not, is like a man that built a house upon the earth,
without a foundation, against which the torrent dashed with
violence, and immediately it fell, and the ruin of that house
was great.

VII. 1 And when he had ended all his sayings in the hearing
of the people, he went into Capernaum. 2 And a certain centurion's servant, who was dear to him, was sick, and about to die.
3 But when he heard of Jesus, he sent to him elders of the Jews,
and besought him to come and save his servant. 4 And they
came to Jesus, and besought him earnestly, saying: He is
worthy for whom thou shouldst do this; 5 for he loves our nation, and of his own accord has built us a synagogue. 6 And
Jesus went with them.

And when he was now not far from the house, the centurion
sent friends to him, and said to him: Lord, give thyself no
trouble; for I am not worthy that thou shouldst come under
my roof. 7 For which reason, neither did I count myself worthy
to go to thee; but command in a word, and my servant shall be
healed. 8 For I am a man placed under authority, and have
soldiers under me; and I say to this one, Go, and he goes; and
to another, Come, and he comes; and to my servant, Do this,
and he does it. 9 And when Jesus heard these things, he was
filled with admiration for him; and, turning to the multitude
that followed, he said: I say to you, Not even in Israel have I
found so great faith. 10 And they that had been sent, returned to
the house, and found the servant that had been sick restored to
health.

11 And it came to pass, the next day, that he was going to a
city called Nain; and many of his disciples and a great multitude followed him. 12 And when he came near the gate of the
city, behold, they were carrying out a dead man, the only son
of his mother, and she was a widow; and a great multitude

from the city was with her. [13] And when the Lord saw her,
he had compassion on her, and said to her: Weep not. [14] And
he went and touched the bier; and those who were carrying it,
stood still. And he said: Young man, I say to you, Arise.
[15] And he that had been dead, sat up and began to speak; and
he gave him to his mother. [16] And fear seized on all; and they
glorified God, saying: A great prophet has arisen among us;
and, God has visited his people. [17] And this report concerning
him went abroad into all Judea and all the neighboring region.

[18] And the disciples of John told him of all these things. [19] And
John called to him two of his disciples, and sent them to Jesus,
and said: Art thou he that was to come, or must we look for
another? [20] And the men came to him and said: John the Immerser has sent us to thee, and says, Art thou he that was to
come, or must we look for another? [21] And in that very hour
he cured many of diseases and plagues and evil spirits, and bestowed sight on many that were blind. [22] And Jesus answered
and said to them: Go and tell John what you have seen and
heard; that the blind receive their sight, the lame walk, the
lepers are cleansed, the deaf hear, the dead are raised, the poor
have the gospel preached to them; [23] and blessed is he who shall
find no cause of offense in me.

[24] And when the messengers of John had departed, he began
to say to the multitudes concerning John: What did you go out
into the wilderness to see? A reed shaken by the wind? [25] But
what did you go out to see? A man clothed in soft raiment?
Behold, they that wear splendid apparel, and live in luxury, are
in kings' houses. [26] But what did you go out to see? A prophet?
Yes, I say to you, and much more than a prophet. [27] This is
he, of whom it is written, Behold, I send my messenger before
thy face, who shall prepare thy way before thee. [28] For I say to
you, Among those born of women, there is no prophet greater
than John the Immerser. But the least in the kingdom of God
is greater than he. [29] And all the people, and the publicans that
heard him, vindicated God, by being immersed with the immersion of John; [30] but the Pharisees and the lawyers rejected the
counsel of God in regard to themselves, by not being immersed
by him. [31] To what, then, shall I compare the men of this
generation? and to what are they like? [32] They are like children sitting in the market-place, who call to one another, and
say, We have played on the pipe for you, and you have not
danced; we have sung mournful songs for you, and you have not

lamented. 33 For John the Immerser came, neither eating
bread nor drinking wine, and you say, He has a demon. 34 The
Son of man has come, eating and drinking, and you say, Behold,
a gluttonous man and a drinker of wine, a friend of publicans
and sinners. 35 Yet wisdom is vindicated by all her children.

36 And one of the Pharisees invited him to eat with him. And
he went into the house of the Pharisee, and reclined at table.
37 And, behold, a woman of the city, who was a sinner, when
she knew that he reclined at table in the house of the Pharisee,
brought an alabaster box of ointment, 38 and stood behind at
his feet, weeping; and she began to wash his feet with her
tears; and she wiped them with the hair of her head, and
kissed his feet and anointed them with the ointment. 39 But
when the Pharisee who had invited him, saw it, he said within
himself: This man, if he were a prophet, would have known
who, and what sort of woman this is that touches him; for
she is a sinner.

40 And Jesus answered and said to him: Simon, I have something to say to you. He replied: Teacher, say on. 41 A certain
creditor had two debtors; the one owed him five hundred denarii, the other, fifty. 42 But as they had nothing to pay, he
forgave them both. Which of them, then, will love him the
more? 43 Simon answered and said: I suppose he to whom he
forgave the more. He said to him: You have decided correctly.

44 And turning toward the woman, he said to Simon: Do you
see this woman? I entered your house, you gave me no water
for my feet; but she has washed my feet with her tears, and
wiped them with her hair. 45 You gave me no kiss; but she,
from the time I came in, has not ceased to kiss my feet. 46 You
did not anoint my head with oil; but she has anointed my feet
with ointment. 47 Wherefore, I say to you, her sins, which are
many, are forgiven; for she loved much. But he to whom little
is forgiven, loves little. 48 And he said to her: Your sins are
forgiven. 49 And those who reclined at table with him began
to say within themselves: Who is this that also forgives sins?
50 But he said to the woman: Your faith has saved you; go in
peace.

VIII. 1 And it came to pass afterward, that he went through
every city and village, preaching, and making known the good
news of the kingdom of God; and the twelve were with him;
2 and also certain women that had been cured of evil spirits and

diseases; Mary, called Magdalene, out of whom had gone seven
demons, 3 and Joanna, the wife of Chuza, Herod's steward, and
Susanna, and many others, who ministered to him from their
means.

4 And when a great multitude had assembled, and they were
coming to him from every city, he spoke by a parable: 5 The
sower went forth to sow his seed; and as he sowed, some fell by
the wayside, and it was trodden down, and the birds of the air
ate it up. 6 And some fell upon the rock; and when it had
sprung up, it withered, because it had no moisture. 7 And some
fell in the midst of thorns; and the thorns grew up with it and
choked it. 8 And other seed fell into good ground, and sprung
up, and produced fruit a hundred-fold. When he had said these
things, he cried: He that has ears to hear, let him hear.

9 And the disciples asked him, saying: What does this parable
mean? 10 He replied: To you it is given to know the mysteries
of the kingdom of God: but to others in parables; that when
they see, they may not see, and when they hear, they may not
understand. 11 But the meaning of the parable is this: The
seed is the word of God; 12 those by the wayside are they that
hear; then comes the devil and takes the word from their heart,
lest they should believe and be saved. 13 Those on the rock are
they that, when they hear, receive the word with joy; and
these have no root, who, for awhile, believe, and in time of
temptation apostatize. 14 That which fell among thorns are
those who hear, and so conduct themselves, that they are choked
by the cares and riches and pleasures of life, and bring no fruit
to perfection. 15 But that on the good ground are those who, in
a good and honest heart, hear the word, and keep it, and bring
forth fruit with patience.

16 No one, when he has lighted a lamp, covers it with a vessel,
or puts it under a divan, but sets it on a lamp-stand, that they
who come in may see the light. 17 For there is nothing concealed, that shall not be made manifest, nor hid, that shall not
be known and brought into view. 18 Take heed, therefore, how
you hear; for whoever has, to him shall be given; and whoever has not, even that which he seems to have shall be taken
from him.

19 And his mother and his brothers came to him, but were not
able to get near him on account of the multitude. 20 And it was
told him by some that said: Thy mother and thy brothers stand
without, desiring to see thee. 21 But he answered and said to

them: My mother and my brothers are they that hear the word
of God and do it.

22 And it came to pass, on a certain day, that he entered a
ship with his disciples; and he said to them: Let us go over
to the other side of the lake. And they set sail. 23 And while
they were sailing, he fell asleep. And a storm of wind came
down upon the lake, and they began to be filled, and were in
danger. 24 And they came to him, and awoke him, saying:
Master, master, we perish. But he arose and rebuked the wind
and the raging of the water, and they ceased, and there was a
calm. 25 And he said to them: Where is your faith? And being afraid, they wondered, and said one to another: Who, then,
is this, that he commands even the wind and the water, and
they obey him?

26 And they sailed to the country of the Gadarenes, which is
opposite to Galilee. 27 And when he came out upon the land,
there met him a certain man from the city, who had been possessed with demons for a long time, and who wore no clothes,
and dwelt in no house, but in the tombs. 28 When he saw Jesus,
he cried out, and fell down before him, and said with a loud
voice: What have I to do with thee, Jesus, Son of God Most
High? I beseech thee, torment me not. 29 For he had commanded the unclean spirit to come out of the man. For it had
often seized upon him, and he had been bound with chains and
fetters, and kept in confinement; and he broke the bonds, and
was driven by the demon into the deserts. 30 And Jesus asked
him, saying: What is your name? He answered, Legion; for
many demons had entered into him. 31 And they besought him,
that he would not command them to go away into the abyss.

32 And there was in that place a herd of many swine feeding
on the mountain. And they besought him to permit them to go
into them. And he permitted them. 33 And the demons came
out of the man, and went into the swine; and the herd rushed
down a steep place into the lake, and were drowned. 34 And
when those who fed them saw what was done, they fled, and told
it in the city and in the country. 35 And they came out to see
what had been done; and they came to Jesus, and saw the man
out of whom the demons had gone, clothed, and in his right
mind, sitting at the feet of Jesus; and they were afraid. 36 And
those who had seen it, told them by what means the man who
had been possessed with the demons, was saved.

37 And the whole multitude of the neighboring country of the

Gadarenes besought him to depart from them; for they were
seized with great fear. And he entered the ship and returned.
38 And the man out of whom the demons had gone, besought him
that he might be with him. But Jesus sent him away, saying:
39 Return to your house, and tell what things God has done for
you. And he went away, proclaiming through the whole city
what Jesus had done for him.

40 And it came to pass, when Jesus returned, that the multitude
received him gladly; for they were all waiting for him. 41 And,
behold, there came a man, whose name was Jairus; and he was
a ruler of the synagogue; and he fell down at the feet of Jesus,
and besought him to come into his house; 42 for he had a daughter, his only child, about twelve years of age, and she was dying. And as he went, the multitude pressed upon him.

43 And a woman that had been afflicted with an issue of blood
for twelve years, who had spent her whole living upon physicians, and could be cured by no one, 44 came behind, and touched
the fringe of his mantle; and her issue of blood immediately
ceased. 45 And Jesus said: Who touched me? When they all
denied, Peter and those with him said: Master, the multitudes
press upon thee, and throng thee, and dost thou say, Who
touched me? 46 But Jesus said: Some one touched me; for I
perceive that power has gone forth from me. 47 And the woman,
seeing that she had not escaped notice, came trembling, and fell
down before him, and told him, before all the people, for what
cause she had touched him, and that she was immediately restored to health. 48 And he said to her: Take courage, daughter; your faith has saved you; go in peace.

49 While he was yet speaking, there came some one from the
house of the ruler of the synagogue, and said to him: Your
daughter is dead; trouble not the Teacher. 50 But when Jesus
heard it, he answered him, saying: Fear not, only believe, and
she shall be saved. 51 And when he came to the house, he permitted no one to go in but Peter and James and John, and the
father and the mother of the child. 52 And all were weeping
and lamenting her. But he said? Weep not; she is not dead,
but sleeps. 53 And they derided him, knowing that she was
dead. 54 But he put them all out, and took her by the hand,
and called, and said: Child, arise. 55 And her spirit returned,
and she arose immediately. And he commanded that food
should be given her. 56 And her parents were amazed. But he
charged them to tell no one what had been done.

IX. 1 And he called his twelve disciples to him, and gave
them power and authority over all demons, and to cure diseases: 2 and he sent them to preach the kingdom of God, and to
heal the sick. 3 And he said to them: Take nothing for your
journey, neither staff, nor bag, nor bread, nor money; nor have
two coats each. 4 And whatever house you enter, there remain,
and thence depart. 5 And whoever will not receive you, when
you go out of that city, shake off even the dust from your feet,
for a testimony against them. 6 And they departed, and went
through every village, preaching the gospel, and performing
cures every-where.

7 And Herod the tetrarch heard of all things that were done
by him; and he was perplexed, because it was said by some,
that John had risen from the dead; 8 and by some, that Elijah
had appeared; and by others, that a prophet of ancient times
had risen again. 9 And Herod said: John I have beheaded:
but who is this, of whom I hear such things? And he desired
to see him.

10 And the apostles returned, and told him all that they had
done. And he took them, and withdrew privately to a desert
place, that belonged to a city called Bethsaida. 11 But the multitudes knew it, and followed him; and he received them, and
spoke to them of the kingdom of God, and healed those who
had need of healing.

12 And the day began to decline; and the twelve came and said
to him: Send the multitude away, that they may go into the
villages, and the country round about, and lodge, and find food;
for we are here in a desert place. 13 But he said to them: Do
you give them food. They replied: We have nothing but five
loaves and two fishes, unless we go and buy food for all these
people. 14 For there were about five thousand men. And he
said to his disciples: Make them recline in companies of fifty.
15 And they did so, and made them all recline. 16 And he took
the five loaves and the two fishes, and looking up to heaven, he
blessed them, and broke, and gave them to the disciples, to set
before the multitude. 17 And they all ate, and were satisfied;
and there was taken up what remained to them of the broken
pieces, twelve baskets.

18 And it came to pass, as he was praying in a retired place,
that his disciples were with him; and he asked them, saying:
Who do the multitudes say that I am? 19 They answered and
said: John the Immerser; but some, Elijah; and others, that

some prophet of ancient times has risen again. 20 He said to them: But who do you say that I am? Peter answered and said: The Christ of God. 21 And he strictly charged them and commanded them to tell this to no one, 22 saying: The Son of man must suffer many things, and be rejected by the elders and chief priests and scribes, and be put to death, and be raised the third day.

23 And he said to them all: If any one determines to come after me, let him deny himself, and take up his cross, and follow me. 24 For whoever will save his life, shall lose it; but whoever will lose his life for my sake, shall save it. 25 For what will it profit a man, if he gain the whole world, and destroy himself, or be lost? 26 For whoever will be ashamed of me and my words, of him will the Son of man be ashamed, when he comes in his own glory, and that of the Father, and of the holy angels. 27 But I say to you, of a truth, there are some of these who stand here that shall not taste of death till they see the kingdom of God.

28 And it came to pass, about eight days after these words, that he took Peter and John and James, and went up into a mountain to pray. 29 And as he prayed, the appearance of his face was changed, and his raiment became white and glittering. 30 And, behold, two men conversed with him, who were Moses and Elijah; 31 they appeared in glory, and spoke of his departure, which he was about to accomplish in Jerusalem.

32 And Peter and those who were with him were heavy with sleep; but having fully awakened, they saw his glory, and the two men that stood with him. 33 And it came to pass, that, as they were withdrawing from him, Peter said to Jesus: Master, it is good for us to be here; let us make three tents, one for thee, one for Moses, and one for Elijah, not knowing what he said. 34 While he was saying these things, there came a cloud, and it overshadowed them; and they were afraid as those men entered the cloud. 35 And there came a voice from the cloud, saying: This is my beloved Son; hear him. 36 And when the voice was past, Jesus was found alone. And they kept it secret, and told no one, in those days, any of the things which they had seen.

37 And it came to pass, that, on the next day, when they had come down from the mountain, a great multitude met him. 38 And, behold, a man from the multitude cried out, saying: Teacher, I beseech thee, look upon my son, for he is my only

child; [39]and, behold, a spirit seizes him, and he suddenly cries
out, and it throws him into convulsions, and causes him to
foam, and after depriving him of strength, hardly departs from
him. [40]And I entreated thy disciples to cast it out; but they
were not able. [41]And Jesus answering, said: O unbelieving
and perverse generation, how long shall I be with you and bear
with you! Bring your son hither. [42]And while he was coming,
the demon cast him to the ground, and threw him into convulsions; but Jesus rebuked the unclean spirit, and restored the
child to health, and gave him back to his father. [43]And they
were all amazed at the mighty power of God.

And while they were all wondering at every thing that Jesus
did, he said to his disciples: [44]Let these words sink into your
ears; for the Son of man is about to be delivered into the hands
of men. [45]But they did not understand this saying, and it was
concealed from them, that they might not understand it; and
they were afraid to ask him about this saying.

[46]And there arose a contention among them, which of them
should be greatest. [47]But Jesus perceived the thought of their
heart, and he took a little child, and made it stand by him,
[48]and said to them: Whoever will receive this little child on my
account, receives me; and whoever will receive me, receives him
that sent me. For he that is least among you all, the same
shall be great.

[49]And John answered and said: Master, we saw a certain one
casting out demons in thy name; and we forbade him, because
he does not follow with us. [50]And Jesus said to him: Forbid
him not; for whoever is not against us, is for us.

[51]And it came to pass, as the time for him to be taken up into
heaven had fully come, that he set his face steadfastly to go up
to Jerusalem. [52]And he sent messengers before his face; and
they went, and entered a village of the Samaritans, to prepare
for him. [53]And they did not receive him, because his face was
turned toward Jerusalem. [54]And when his disciples James and
John saw this, they said: Lord, is it thy will that we command
fire to come down from heaven and destroy them, even as Elijah
did? [55]But he turned and rebuked them, and said: You know
not of what spirit you are. [56]And they went to another village.

[57]And it came to pass, as they were going on their journey,
that a certain man said to him: Lord, I will follow thee wherever thou shalt go. [58]And Jesus said to him: The foxes have
dens, and the birds of the air have roosts, but the Son of man

has not where to lay his head. [59]And he said to another: Follow me. But he replied: Lord, permit me first to go and bury
my father. [60]Jesus said: Let the dead bury their own dead;
but do you go and publish abroad the kingdom of God. [61]And
another said: I will follow thee, Lord; but first permit me to
take leave of those at home. [62]Jesus said to him: No one that
puts his hand to the plow, and looks back, is fit for the kingdom
of God.

X. [1]And after these things, the Lord appointed seventy others, also, and sent them, two and two, before his face, into every
city and place to which he himself was about to go. [2]He said,
therefore, to them: The harvest truly is great, but the laborers
are few; pray, therefore, the Lord of the harvest that he send
out laborers into his harvest. [3]Go; behold, I send you as lambs
in the midst of wolves. [4]Carry no purse, nor bag, nor sandals;
and salute no one on the road. [5]Whatever house you enter,
first say, Peace be to this house. [6]And if a son of peace be
there, your peace shall rest on him; but, if not, it shall return
upon you. [7]And in that house remain, eating and drinking
what they have to give; for the laborer is worthy of his hire;
go not from house to house.

[8]And whatever city you enter, and they receive you, eat what
is set before you; [9]and heal those in it who are sick, and say to
them: The kingdom of God has come near to you. [10]But whatever city you enter, and they receive you not, go out into the
streets of it, and say: [11]Even the dust of your city, which
cleaves to us, we do wipe off against you; yet know this, that
the kingdom of God has come near to you. [12]I say to you, It
shall be more tolerable, in that day, for Sodom, than for that
city. [13]Alas for thee, Chorazin! alas for thee, Bethsaida! for, if
the mighty works which have been done in you, had been done
in Tyre and Sidon, they would have repented long ago, sitting in
sackcloth and ashes. [14]But for Tyre and Sidon it shall be more
tolerable in the judgment, than for you. [15]And thou, Capernaum, who hast been exalted to heaven, shalt be brought down
to hades. [16]He that hears you, hears me; and he that rejects
you, rejects me; and he that rejects me, rejects him that sent
me.

[17]And the seventy returned with joy, and said: Lord, even
the demons are subject to us through thy name. [18]And he said
to them: I saw Satan, like lightning from heaven, falling.

19 Behold, I give you authority to tread on serpents and scorpions, and authority over all the power of the enemy; and
nothing shall by any means hurt you. 20 However, rejoice not
in this, that the spirits are subject to you; but rejoice that
your names are written in heaven.

21 In that hour Jesus rejoiced in spirit, and said: I thank
thee, Father, Lord of heaven and earth, because thou hast hid
these things from the wise and prudent, and hast revealed them
to babes; even so, Father, for so it seemed good in thy sight.
22 All things are delivered to me by my Father; and no one
knows who the Son is but the Father, and who the Father is but
the Son, and he to whom the Son will reveal him.

23 And he turned to his disciples, and said privately: Blessed
are the eyes that see what you see. 24 For I say to you, that
many prophets and kings desired to see what you see, and did
not see; and to hear what you hear, and did not hear.

25 And, behold, a certain lawyer stood up to tempt him, and
said: Teacher, what shall I do to inherit eternal life? 26 He
said to him: What is written in the law? How do you read?
27 He answered and said: You shall love the Lord your God with
your whole heart, and with your whole soul, and with your
whole strength, and with your whole understanding, and your
neighbor as yourself. 28 He said to him: You have answered
correctly; do this, and you shall live.

29 But, wishing to justify himself, he said to Jesus: And who
is my neighbor? 30 And Jesus answered and said: A certain
man went down from Jerusalem to Jericho, and fell among robbers, who stripped him of his raiment, and wounded him, and
went away, leaving him half dead. 31 And by chance a certain
priest went down along that road, and when he saw him, he
passed by on the other side. 32 In like manner, also, a Levite,
when he came to the place, went and looked on him, and passed
by on the other side. 33 But a certain Samaritan, who was on
a journey, came near him; and when he saw him, he had compassion on him. 34 And he went to him, and bound up his
wounds, pouring in oil and wine; and he put him on his own
beast, and carried him to an inn, and took care of him. 35 And
on the morrow, when he departed, he took out two denarii, and
gave them to the innkeeper, and said to him: Take care of
him; and whatever you spend more, on my return, I will repay
you.

36 Which, then, of these three do you think was neighbor to

him that fell among the robbers? [37] He replied: He that showed
mercy to him. Jesus said to him: Go, and do you likewise.

[38] And it came to pass, as they continued their journey, that
he entered a certain village, and a certain woman named Martha
received him into her house. [39] And she had a sister called
Mary, who also sat at the feet of Jesus, and heard his word.
[40] But Martha made herself busy with much serving; and she
came to him, and said: Lord, dost thou not care that my sister
has left me to serve alone? Bid her, therefore, that she help
me. [41] But Jesus answered and said to her: Martha, Martha,
you are anxious and troubled about many things: [42] one thing is
needful; and Mary has chosen the good part, which shall not be
taken from her.

XI. [1] And it came to pass, as he was in a certain place praying, that, when he ceased, one of his disciples said to him:
Lord, teach us to pray, as John also taught his disciples. [2] And
he said to them: When you pray, say, Our Father who art in
heaven, hallowed be thy name; thy kingdom come; thy will be
done, as in heaven, so on earth. [3] Give us, day by day, the
bread sufficient for our support; [4] and forgive us our sins, for
we also forgive every one that is indebted to us; and lead us not
into temptation, but deliver us from the evil one.

[5] And he said to them: Which of you shall have a friend, and
shall go to him at midnight, and say to him, Friend, lend me
three loaves; [6] for a friend of mine, who is on a journey, has
come to me, and I have nothing to set before him? [7] And he
from within shall answer and say, Trouble me not; the door is
already closed, and my children and myself are in bed; I can
not rise and give you. [8] I say to you, Although he will not arise
and give him, because he is his friend, yet, on account of his
importunity, he will arise and give him as many as he needs.
[9] And I say to you, Ask, and it shall be given you; seek, and
you shall find; knock, and it shall be opened to you. [10] For
every one that asks, receives; and he that seeks, finds; and to
him that knocks, it shall be opened.

[11] If a son ask bread of any one of you that is a father, will
he give him a stone? Or if he ask a fish, will he, instead of a
fish, give him a serpent? [12] Or if he ask an egg, will he give
him a scorpion? [13] If, then, you, being evil, know how to give
good gifts to your children, how much more will your heavenly
Father give the holy Spirit to them that ask him?

14 And he was casting out a demon, and it was dumb; and it
came to pass, when the demon had gone out, that the dumb
man spoke: and the multitudes wondered. 15 But some of them
said: He casts out demons by Beelzebul, the prince of the
demons. 16 And others, that they might tempt him, asked of
him a sign from heaven. 17 But, knowing their purpose, he
said to them: Every kingdom divided against itself, is brought
to desolation; and a house that is divided against a house, falls.
18 If Satan be divided against himself, how shall his kingdom
stand? For you say, that I cast out demons by Beelzebul.
19 But if I cast out demons by Beelzebul, by whom do your sons
cast them out? Therefore, they shall be your judges. 20 But if
I cast out demons by the finger of God, then has the kingdom
of God already come upon you.

21 When the strong man armed keeps guard over his palace,
his goods are in peace; 22 but when one stronger than he comes
upon him and overcomes him, he takes away all his armor in
which he trusted, and divides his spoils. 23 He that is not with
me, is against me; and he that gathers not with me, scatters.

24 When the unclean spirit has gone out of a man, he goes
through dry places, seeking rest; and finding none, he says, I
will return to my house out of which I came. 25 And he comes
and finds it swept, and set in order. 26 Then he goes and takes
with him seven other spirits, more wicked than himself, and
they enter in, and dwell there: and the last state of that man
is worse than the first. 27 And it came to pass, that, when he
said these things, a certain woman from among the multitude
lifted up her voice, and said to him: Blessed is the womb that
bore thee, and the breasts that thou didst suck. 28 And he said:
Yes, rather blessed are they that hear the word of God, and keep it.

29 And when the multitudes were crowded together, he began
to say: This is an evil generation; it asks for a sign, and no
sign shall be given to it but the sign of Jonah the prophet.
30 For as Jonah was a sign to the Ninevites, so the Son of man
shall also be to this generation. 31 The queen of the south shall
rise in the judgment with the men of this generation, and shall
condemn them; for she came from the most distant parts of the
earth to hear the wisdom of Solomon; and lo, something greater
than Solomon is here. 32 The men of Nineveh shall rise in the
judgment with this generation, and condemn it; for they repented in accordance with the preaching of Jonah; and lo,
something greater than Jonah is here.

33 No one, when he has lighted a lamp, puts it in a secret
place, nor under the measure, but upon the lamp-stand, that
those who come in may see the light. 34 The lamp of the body
is the eye; when, therefore, your eye is sound, your whole body
also is light; but if it be diseased, your body also is dark.
35 Take heed, therefore, lest the light that is in you be darkness.
36 If, therefore, your whole body is light, having no part dark,
the whole shall be light; as when a lamp, by its brightness,
gives you light.

37 And as he spoke, a certain Pharisee asked him to dine with
him. And he went in and reclined at table. 38 And when the
Pharisee saw it, he wondered that he had not first immersed
himself before dinner. 39 And the Lord said to him: Now you
Pharisees cleanse the outside of the cup and the plate; but your
inward part is full of extortion and wickedness. 40 Senseless
men, did not he who made the outside, make the inside also?
41 But give as charity the contents of the cup, and behold, all
things are clean for you.

42 But alas for you, Pharisees! for you tithe mint and rue
and every herb, and pass by the justice and the love of God;
these you ought to have done, and those you ought not to have
left undone. 43 Alas for you, Pharisees! for you love the chief
seat in the synagogues, and greetings in the markets. 44 Alas
for you, scribes and Pharisees, hypocrites! for you are like
graves that are not seen; and men that walk over them know
it not.

45 And one of the lawyers answered and said to him: Teacher,
in saying these things, you reproach us also. 46 He replied:
Alas for you, lawyers, also! for you bind upon men burdens
hard to be borne, and you yourselves touch not the burdens
with one of your fingers. 47 Alas for you! for you build the
sepulchers of the prophets, and your fathers killed them.
48 Therefore you attest and approve the deeds of your fathers;
for they indeed killed them, and you build their sepulchers.
49 For this reason also the Wisdom of God said: I will send
them prophets and apostles, and some of them they will kill,
and persecute, 50 that the blood of all the prophets, which has
been shed from the foundation of the world, may be required
of this generation; 51 from the blood of Abel to the blood of
Zachariah, who perished between the altar and the temple; yes,
I say to you, It shall be required of this generation. 52 Alas for
you, lawyers! for you have taken away the key of knowledge;

you did not go in yourselves, and those who were entering in,
you prevented.
53 And when he said these things to them, the scribes and the
Pharisees began to be very angry, and to put questions to him
about many things, 54 trying to entrap him, and seeking to lay
hold on something from his mouth, that they might accuse him.

XII. 1 In the mean time, when myriads of the people had
come together, so that they trod one upon another, he began to
say to his disciples first of all: Beware of the leaven of the
Pharisees, which is hypocrisy. 2 For there is nothing covered,
which shall not be revealed, and hid, which shall not be made
known. 3 Wherefore, what you have spoken in the darkness,
shall be heard in the light; and what you have spoken in the
ear in closets, shall be proclaimed upon the house-tops.
4 But I say to you, my friends, Fear not them that kill the
body, and after that have no more that they can do. 5 But I
will show you whom you shall fear: Fear him who, after he
has killed, has authority to cast into hell; yes, I say to you,
Fear him. 6 Are not five sparrows sold for two farthings? yet
not one of them is forgotten before God. 7 But even the hairs
of your head are all numbered. Fear not, therefore; you are
of more value than many sparrows.
8 And I further say to you, Whoever confesses me before men,
him will the Son of man also confess before the angels of God.
9 But he that denies me before men, shall be denied before the
angels of God. 10 And whoever shall speak a word against the
Son of man, it shall be forgiven him; but he that speaks impiously against the Holy Spirit, shall not be forgiven. 11 When
they bring you to the synagogue, and to rulers and authorities,
be not anxious how or what you shall answer, or what you shall
say; 12 for the Holy Spirit shall teach you in that hour what
you ought to say.
13 And a certain one of the multitude said to him: Teacher,
speak to my brother, that he divide the inheritance with me.
14 But he said to him: Man, who made me a judge or a divider
over you? 15 And he said to them: Take heed and beware of
covetousness; for a man's life depends not on the abundance of
his possessions.
16 And he spoke a parable to them, saying: The farm of a
certain rich man brought forth plentifully. 17 And he reasoned
within himself, saying: What shall I do? for I have no place

in which I can store my fruits. [18] And he said: This will I do:
I will pull down my barns and I will build larger ones; and
there I will store all my produce, and my good things; [19] and I
will say to my soul: Soul, you have many good things laid up
for many years; take your ease, eat, drink, be merry. [20] But
God said to him: Senseless man, this night shall your soul be
required of you; and who shall have the things which you have
provided? [21] So is he that lays up treasure for himself, and is
not rich toward God.

[22] And he said to his disciples: For this reason I say to you,
Be not anxious for your life, what you shall eat; nor for your
body, what you shall put on. [23] Life is a greater gift than food,
and the body, than clothing. [24] Consider the ravens, that they
neither sow nor reap; which have neither storehouse nor granary; yet God feeds them: you are of far more value than the
birds. [25] Which of you, by his anxiety, can add one span to his
life? [26] If, therefore, you can not do that which is the least,
why are you anxious about the rest? [27] Consider the lilies, how
they grow. They toil not, they spin not; yet I say to you, that
Solomon in all his glory was not clothed like one of these. [28] If,
then, God so clothes the herb of the field, which to-day is, and
to-morrow is cast into the oven, will he not much more clothe
you, O you of little faith?

[29] And seek not what you shall eat, or what you shall drink,
and be not in anxious suspense. [30] For all these things the nations of the world seek after; but your Father knows that you
have need of these things. [31] But seek the kingdom of God, and
all these things shall be given you in addition. [32] Fear not, little flock, for it is your Father's good pleasure to give you the
kingdom. [33] Sell what you have, and be charitable. Make for
yourselves purses that do not become old, an unfailing treasure
in the heavens, where no thief comes near, and no moth cor-
rupts. [34] For where your treasure is, there will your heart be
also.

[35] Let your loins be girded, and your lamps burning; [36] and be
like men that are waiting for their lord, when he shall return
from the wedding; that, when he comes and knocks, they may
open for him immediately. [37] Blessed are those servants whom
their lord, when he comes, shall find watching. Verily I say
to you, That he will gird himself and make them recline at
table, and will come forth and serve them. [38] And if he shall
come in the second watch, and if he shall come in the third

watch, and find them thus, blessed are those servants. 39 But
know this, that if the master of the house had known at what
hour the thief comes, he would have watched, and would not
have suffered his house to be broken through. 40 Be you, therefore, ready also; for at an hour when you think not, the Son of
man comes.
41 Then Peter said to him: Lord, dost thou speak this parable
to us, or also to all? 42 And the Lord said: Who, then, is that
faithful and wise steward, whom his lord shall make ruler over
his servants, to give them their portion of food at the proper
time? 43 Blessed is that servant whom his lord, when he comes,
shall find so doing. 44 Of a truth, I say to you, that he will
make him ruler over all that he has. 45 But if that servant
shall say in his heart, My lord delays his coming, and shall begin to strike the men-servants and the maid-servants, and to
eat and to drink, and to be drunk; 46 the lord of that servant
will come in a day in which he looks not for him, and at an
hour which he knows not; and will cut him asunder, and appoint him his portion with the unfaithful.
47 And that servant who knew his lord's will, but made no
preparation, nor did according to his will, shall be beaten with
many stripes; 48 but he that knew not, and did things worthy
of stripes, shall be beaten with few. To whomever much has
been given, of him shall much be required; and to whom men
have intrusted much, of him will they ask the more.
49 I have come to send fire on the earth; and how greatly do
I wish that it were already kindled! 50 I have an immersion
with which to be immersed, and how distressed I am till it be
accomplished! 51 Do you think that I have come to give peace
in the earth? I tell you, No; but rather dissension. 52 For
from this time forth there shall be five in one house at variance,
three with two, and two with three. 53 The father shall be at
variance with the son, and the son with the father; the mother
with the daughter, and the daughter with the mother; the
mother-in-law with her daughter-in-law, and the daughter-in-
law with her mother-in-law.
54 And he said also to the multitudes: When you see the cloud
rising from the west, you immediately say, There comes a
shower: and so it is. 55 And when the south wind blows, you
say, There will be heat: and it comes to pass. 56 Hypocrites,
you know how to judge of the face of the earth, and of the
heavens; but how is it that you do not judge of this time?

57 And why even of yourselves do you not judge what is right?
58 For when you are going with your opponent at law to the
ruler, while you are on the way, endeavor to be delivered from
him, lest he drag you to the judge, and the judge deliver you
to the collector, and the collector throw you into prison. 59 I
say to you, You shall not come out thence, till you have paid
the very last mite.

XIII. 1 And there were present, at that time, some that told
him of the Galileans, whose blood Pilate had mingled with their
sacrifices. 2 And Jesus answered and said to them: Do you
think that those Galileans were greater sinners than all other
Galileans, because they suffered such things? 3 I tell you, No;
but unless you repent, you shall all likewise perish. 4 Or, those
eighteen, on whom the tower in Siloam fell, and killed them;
do you think that they were greater debtors than all other men
that were living in Jerusalem? 5 I tell you, No; but unless you
repent, you shall all likewise perish.

6 And he spoke this parable: A certain man had a fig-tree that
was planted in his vineyard; and he came and sought fruit on
it, and found none. 7 Then he said to his vine-dresser, Behold,
for three years I have come and sought fruit on this fig-tree,
and I have found none; cut it down; why does it occupy the
ground unprofitably? 8 But he answered and said to him, Sir,
let it alone this year also, till I shall dig about it, and throw
in manure; 9 and it may bear fruit; but if not, afterward you
shall cut it down.

10 And he was teaching in one of the synagogues on the Sabbath. 11 And, behold, there was a woman who had had a spirit
of infirmity for eighteen years; and she was bowed together,
and was not able to raise herself up at all. 12 And when Jesus
saw her, he called her to him, and said to her: Woman, you are
released from your infirmity. 13 And he laid his hands on her;
and she immediately stood erect, and glorified God.

14 But the ruler of the synagogue, indignant because Jesus
had performed a cure on the Sabbath-day, answered and said to
the multitude: There are six days in which work ought to be
done; on these, therefore, come and be cured, and not on the
Sabbath-day. Then the Lord answered him and said: 15 Hypocrites, does not each one of you, on the Sabbath, loose his ox or
his ass from the stable, and lead him away, and give him water?
16 And ought not this woman, who is a daughter of Abraham,

whom Satan has bound, lo, these eighteen years, to be loosed
from this bond on the Sabbath-day? 17 And when he had said
these things, all his adversaries were ashamed; and all the multitude rejoiced on account of all the glorious things that were
done by him.

18 Then he said: To what is the kingdom of God like; and to
what shall I liken it? 19 It is like a grain of mustard, which a
man took, and sowed in his garden; and it grew, and became a
great tree; and the birds of the air roosted in its branches.

20 And again he said: To what shall I liken the kingdom of
God? 21 It is like leaven, which a woman took and hid in three
measures of flour, till the whole was leavened.

22 And he went through every city and village, teaching, and
journeying to Jerusalem.

23 And a certain man said to him: Lord, are there few that are
saved? And he said to them: 24 Strive to enter in through the
strait gate; for many, I say to you, will seek to enter in, and
shall not be able. 25 When once the master of the house has
risen, and closed the door, and you begin to stand without, and
to knock at the door, saying, Lord, Lord, open for us, and he
shall answer and say to you, I know you not, whence you are;
26 then, you will begin to say, We have eaten and drunk in thy
presence, and thou hast taught in our streets. 27 And he shall
say, I tell you, I know you not, whence you are; depart from
me, all you workers of iniquity. 28 There shall be weeping and
gnashing of teeth, when you see Abraham and Isaac and Jacob
and all the prophets in the kingdom of God, but yourselves cast
out. 29 And they shall come from the east and the west, and
from the north and the south, and shall recline at table in the
kingdom of God. 30 And behold, there are last that shall be
first, and there are first that shall be last.

31 On the same day, certain Pharisees came and said to him:
Depart, and get away from this place; for Herod intends to kill
you. 32 And he said to them: Go and tell that fox, Behold, I
cast out demons, and perform cures to-day and to-morrow, and
the third day I finish the work. 33 But I must continue my
journey to-day and to-morrow and the day following; for it is
not possible that a prophet perish out of Jerusalem. 34 Jerusalem, Jerusalem, that killest the prophets and stonest them
that are sent to thee: how often have I desired to gather thy
children together, as a bird gathers her young under her wings,
and you refused. 35 Behold, your house is deserted; and I say

to you, You shall not see me till the time come when you shall
say, Blessed is he that comes in the name of the Lord.

XIV. 1 And it came to pass, that he went, on the Sabbath-
day, into the house of one of the chief men of the Pharisees, to
eat bread; and they watched him. 2 And behold, there was a
man before him, who had the dropsy. 3 And Jesus answered
and spoke to the lawyers and Pharisees, saying: Is it lawful to
cure on the Sabbath-day? 4 But they were silent. And he
took him, and healed him, and let him go. 5 And he answered
and said to them: Which of you, if his son or his ox should
fall into a pit, would not immediately pull him out on the Sabbath-day? 6 And they were not able to give him an answer to
these things.

7 And he spoke a parable to those who had been invited, when
he observed how they were choosing the first places at table;
and he said to them: 8 When you are invited by any one to a
wedding, do not recline in the first place, lest a more honorable
man than you may have been invited by him; 9 and he that
invited you and him, come and say to you, Give place to this
man; and then you shall begin with shame to take the last
place. 10 But when you are invited, go and recline in the last
place, that when he that invited you shall come, he may say to
you, Friend, go up higher. Then you shall have honor in the
presence of those who recline with you. 11 For every one that
exalts himself shall be humbled; and he that humbles himself
shall be exalted.

12 Then he said also to him that had invited him: When you
make a dinner or a supper, call not your friends, nor your
brothers, nor your relatives, nor your rich neighbors, lest they
also invite you in return, and a recompense be made you. 13 But
when you make a feast, invite the poor, the maimed, the lame,
the blind; 14 and you shall be blessed; for they have no power
to repay you; but you shall be repaid at the resurrection of
the just.

15 And a certain one of those who reclined at table with him,
after hearing these things, said to him: Blessed is he who shall
eat bread in the kingdom of God. 16 And he said to him: A
certain man made a great supper, and invited many. 17 And he
sent his servant at the hour of supper, to say to those who had
been invited, Come, for all things are now ready. 18 And they
all, with one consent, began to make excuse. The first said to

him, I have bought a farm, and I must go and see it; I pray
you, have me excused. 19 And another said, I have bought five
yoke of oxen, and I am going to try them; I pray you, have
me excused. 20 Another said, I have married a wife, and, for
this reason, I can not come. 21 And that servant came and told
his lord these things.

Then the master of the house was angry, and said to his servant, Go out quickly into the streets and lanes of the city, and
bring in hither the poor and the maimed, the lame and the
blind. 22 And the servant said, Lord, it is done as you commanded, and yet there is room. 23 And the lord said to his servant, Go out into the roads, and among the hedges, and compel
them to come in, that my house may be full. 24 For I say to
you, that not one of those men who have been invited shall
taste of my supper.

25 And many multitudes were journeying with him; and he
turned and said to them: 26 If any one comes to me, and hates
not his father and mother and wife and children and brothers
and sisters, and his own life also, he can not be my disciple.

27 And whoever does not bear his cross, and come after me,
can not be my disciple. 28 For which of you, intending to build
a tower, does not first sit down, and count the cost, whether
he has the means to finish it? 29 Lest, when he has laid the
foundation, and is not able to finish, all that see it begin to
deride him, 30 saying, This man began to build, and was not able
to finish.

31 Or, what king, going to make war against another king,
does not first sit down, and deliberate whether he is able, with
ten thousand, to meet him that is coming against him with
twenty thousand? 32 And if not, while he is yet at a distance,
he sends an embassy, and asks for conditions of peace. 33 So,
then, whoever of you does not forsake all that he has, can not
be my disciple. 34 Salt is good; but if the salt become tasteless,
by what means shall it become salt again? 35 It is fit neither
for earth, nor for manure; but they cast it out. He that has
ears to hear, let him hear.

XV. 1 And all the publicans and the sinners came near to
him to hear him. 2 And the Pharisees and the scribes murmured, saying: This man receives sinners, and eats with them.
3 And he spoke this parable to them, saying: 4 What man of
you that has a hundred sheep, and loses one of them, does not

leave the ninety-nine in the desert, and go after that which is
lost, till he find it? 5 And when he finds it, he puts it on his
shoulders, rejoicing. 6 And when he comes home, he calls together his friends and neighbors, and says to them, Rejoice
with me, for I have found my sheep that was lost. 7 I say to
you, That thus there shall be joy in heaven over one sinner
that repents, more than over ninety-nine just persons, who need
no repentance.

8 Or, what woman that has ten drachmas, if she lose one
drachma, does not light a lamp, and sweep the house, and
search carefully till she find it? 9 And when she finds it, she
calls together her friends and neighbors, saying, Rejoice with
me, for I have found the drachma that I lost. 10 So, I say to
you, There is joy in the presence of the angels of God over one
sinner that repents.

11 Then he said: A certain man had two sons. 12 And the
younger of them said to his father, Father, give me the portion
of the property that falls to me. And he divided his estate between them. 13 And not many days after, the younger son,
taking with him all that was his, left home for a distant
country, and there wasted his property in riotous living.
14 When he had spent all, there was a great famine throughout
that country, and he began to be in want. 15 And he went and
attached himself to one of the citizens of that country, who
sent him into his fields to feed swine. 16 And he would gladly
have filled his stomach with the pods which the swine did eat.
And no one gave to him.

17 But when he came to himself, he said, How many of my
father's hired servants have bread enough and to spare, and I
am perishing with hunger! 18 I will arise and go to my father,
and I will say to him, Father, I have sinned against heaven
and in your sight, 19 and am no longer worthy to be called your
son: make me as one of your hired servants. 20 And he arose,
and came to his father. And while he was yet a great way off,
his father saw him, and had compassion on him, and ran and
fell upon his neck, and kissed him. 21 But his son said to him,
Father, I have sinned against heaven and in your sight, and
am no longer worthy to be called your son. 22 But the father
said to his servants, Bring forth the best robe, and put it on
him, and put a ring on his hand, and sandals on his feet. 23 And
bring hither the fatted calf, and kill it, and let us eat and be

merry; 24 for this my son was dead, and is alive again: he was
lost, and is found. And they began to be merry.
25 But his elder son was in the field; and as he came and drew
near to the house, he heard music and dancing. 26 And he called
to him one of the servants, and asked what these things meant.
27 And he said to him, Your brother has come, and your father
has killed the fatted calf, because he has received him in health.
28 And he was angry, and would not go in. Then his father
went out and entreated him. 29 But he answered and said to
his father, Behold, for so many years do I serve you, and never
have I transgressed your commandment, and yet you never
gave me a kid, that I might make merry with my friends.
30 But as soon as this your son has come, who has eaten up your
estate with harlots, you have killed for him the fatted calf.
31 And he said to him, Son, you are ever with me, and all that
I have is yours. 32 But it became us to make merry and rejoice;
for this your brother was dead, and is alive again: was lost, and
is found.

XVI. 1 And he said also to his disciples: There was a certain
rich man, who had a steward; and he was accused to him of
wasting his goods. 2 And he called him, and said to him:
What is this that I hear of you? Give an account of your
stewardship, for you can no longer act as steward. 3 And the
steward said within himself, What shall I do? for my lord
takes from me the stewardship. I have not strength to dig; I
am ashamed to beg. 4 I am resolved on what I shall do, that,
when I am put out of the stewardship, I may be received into
their houses.
5 And he called to him every one of his lord's debtors, and
said to the first, How much do you owe my lord? 6 He replied,
A hundred baths of oil. And he said to him, Take back your
note, and sit down quickly, and write fifty. 7 Then he said to
another, How much do you owe? He replied, A hundred ho-
mers of wheat. And he said to him, Take back your note, and
write eighty. 8 And the lord commended the unjust steward,
because he acted prudently. For the children of this age are
more prudent toward their generation than the children of
light.
9 And I say to you, Make for yourselves friends with the unrighteous riches, that when you fail, you may be received into
the everlasting habitations. 10 He that is faithful in the least,

is faithful also in much. He that is unjust in the least, is unjust also in much. 11 If, therefore, you have not been faithful
in the unrighteous riches, who will intrust you with the true?
12 And if you have not been faithful in that which is another's,
who will give to you that which is your own? 13 No servant
can serve two masters; for he will either hate the one, and love
the other; or he will cleave to the one, and despise the other.
You can not serve God and riches.

14 And the Pharisees also, who were lovers of money, heard
all these things, and they scoffed at him. 15 And he said to
them: You set yourselves forth as righteous before men, but
God knows your hearts; for that which is highly esteemed
among men, is detestable in the sight of God. 16 The law and
the prophets were till John. Since that time, the kingdom of
God is preached, and every one enters it by force. 17 But it is
easier for heaven and earth to pass away, than for one point
of the law to fail. 18 Whoever divorces his wife and marries
another, commits adultery: and whoever marries her that is
divorced, commits adultery.

19 There was a certain rich man, who was clothed in purple
and fine linen, and feasted sumptuously every day. 20 And there
was a certain poor man named Lazarus, who was laid at his
gate, full of sores: 21 and he would gladly have been fed with
the crumbs that fell from the rich man's table. And even the
dogs came and licked his sores. 22 And it came to pass, that
the poor man died, and was carried by angels to Abraham's
bosom. The rich man also died, and was buried; 23 and in hades
he lifted up his eyes, being in torments, and saw Abraham afar
off, and Lazarus in his bosom.

24 And he called to him and said, Father Abraham, have
mercy on me, and send Lazarus, that he may dip the tip of his
finger in water, and cool my tongue; for I am tormented in
this flame. 25 But Abraham said, Son, remember that, in your
lifetime, you received your good things, and likewise Lazarus
his evil things. But now he is comforted, and you are tormented. 26 And beside all this, between us and you there is a
great chasm fixed, so that they that would pass hence to you,
can not; nor can they that would, pass thence to us.

27 Then he said, I beseech you, therefore, father, that you
would send him to my father's house; 28 for I have five brothers;
that he may earnestly admonish them, lest they also come to
this place of torment. 29 Abraham said to him, They have

Moses and the prophets; let them hear them. 30 But he said,
Not so, Father Abraham; but if one should go to them from
the dead, they would repent. 31 But he said to him, If they
hear not Moses and the prophets, they will not be persuaded,
though one should rise from the dead.

XVII. 1 Then he said to his disciples: It is impossible that
causes of offense should not come; but alas for him by whom
they come! 2 It would be better for him that a millstone were
hung about his neck, and he were thrown into the sea, than
that he should cause one of these little ones to sin. 3 Take heed
to yourselves; if your brother sin against you, rebuke him; and
if he repent, forgive him. 4 And if he sin against you seven
times in a day, and seven times in a day turn again to you and
say, I repent, you shall forgive him.

5 And the apostles said to the Lord: Increase our faith. 6 And
the Lord said: If you had faith like a grain of mustard, you
might say to this sycamine-tree, Be uprooted, and be planted in
the sea, and it should obey you.

7 Which of you that has a servant plowing, or feeding a flock,
will say to him immediately, when he comes in from the field,
Go and recline at table? 8 But will he not say to him, Make
ready my supper, and gird yourself, and serve me, till I have
eaten and drunk; and afterward, you shall eat and drink?
9 Does he thank that servant, because he did what was commanded? I think not. 10 So also you, when you shall have
done all things that you are commanded to do, say, We are unprofitable servants; for we have done what was our duty to do.

11 And it came to pass, as he was journeying to Jerusalem,
that he passed through the midst of Samaria and Galilee.
12 And as he entered a certain village, there met him ten men
that were lepers, who stood at a distance. 13 And they lifted up
their voice, saying: Jesus, Master, have mercy on us. 14 And
when he saw them, he said to them: Go, show yourselves to
the priests. And it came to pass, that, as they went, they were
made clean.

15 But, one of them, seeing that he was restored to health,
turned back, and, with a loud voice, glorified God. 16 And he
fell on his face at his feet, and gave him thanks; and he was a
Samaritan. 17 And Jesus answered and said: Were not the ten
cleansed? but where are the nine? 18 Were there none found
to return and give glory to God, but this one of another race?

19 And he said to him: Arise, and go; your faith has saved
you.
20 And being asked by the Pharisees, when the kingdom of
God should come, he answered them and said: The kingdom
of God comes not so as to attract attention; 21 nor shall it be
said, Lo here! or Lo there! for, behold, the kingdom of God is
among you.
22 And he said to his disciples: The days will come, when you
will desire to see one of the days of the Son of man, and shall
not see it. 23 And they shall say to you, Lo here! or Lo there!
go not after them, nor follow them. 24 For as the lightning
that flashes out of one part under heaven, shines to another
part under heaven, so shall the Son of man be in his day.
25 But first he must suffer many things, and be rejected by this
generation.
26 And as it was in the days of Noah, so shall it be also in the
days of the Son of man. 27 They ate, they drank, they married,
they were given in marriage, till the day in which Noah entered
the ark, and the flood came and destroyed them all. 28 In like
manner also, as it was in the days of Lot: they ate, they drank,
they bought, they sold, they planted, they builded; 29 but in the
day in which Lot went out of Sodom, it rained fire and brimstone from heaven, and destroyed them all. 30 Even thus shall
it be in the day in which the Son of man is revealed.
31 In that day, let not him that is on the house-top, and whose
goods are in the house, come down to take them away. Likewise, he that is in the field, let him not turn back. 32 Remember Lot's wife. 33 Whoever will seek to save his life, shall lose
it; and whoever will lose his life, shall save it. 34 I say to you,
on that night two men shall be in one bed; the one shall be
taken, and the other left. 35 Two women shall be grinding together; the one shall be taken, and the other left. 36 Two men
shall be in the field; the one shall be taken, and the other left.
37 And they answered and said to him: Where, Lord? And he
said to them: Where the body is, there will the vultures be
gathered.

XVIII. 1 And he spoke a parable to them, that they ought
always to pray, and not to become weary, 2 saying: There was
in a certain city a judge, who neither feared God nor regarded
man. 3 And there was a widow in that city, and she came to
him, and said: Avenge me on my opponent at law. 4 And for

a while he refused. But afterward he said within himself:
Though I fear not God, nor regard man, 5 yet, because this widow
troubles me, I will avenge her, lest by her continual coming she
weary me.
6 And the Lord said: Hear what the unjust judge says; 7 and
will not God avenge his elect, who cry to him day and night,
though he delay long in respect to them? 8 I say to you, that
he will avenge them speedily. Yet, when the Son of man comes,
will he find the faith on the earth?
9 And he spoke this parable to some, who trusted in themselves that they were righteous, and who despised others. 10 Two
men went up into the temple to pray, the one a Pharisee, and
the other a publican. 11 The Pharisee stood and prayed thus
with himself: God, I thank thee that I am not as other men,
extortioners, unjust, adulterers, or even as this publican. 12 I
fast twice in the week; I give tithes of all that I possess. 13 And
the publican, standing afar off, would not even lift up his eyes
to heaven, but smote upon his breast, saying: God, be merciful
to me a sinner. 14 I say to you, this man went down to his
house justified, rather than the other. For every one that exalts himself, shall be humbled; but he that humbles himself,
shall be exalted.
15 And they brought to him infants also, that he might touch
them. But when his disciples saw it, they rebuked them. 16 And
Jesus called them to him, and said: Let the little children come
to me, and hinder them not; for of such is the kingdom of God.
17 Verily I say to you, Whoever shall not receive the kingdom
of God, as a little child, shall in no way enter into it.
18 And a certain ruler asked him, saying: Good teacher, what
shall I do to inherit eternal life? 19 And Jesus said to him:
Why do you call me good? None is good but one, *that is* God.
20 You know the commandments, Do not commit adultery; Do
not kill; Do not steal; Do not bear false testimony; Honor
your father and your mother. 21 He replied: All these have I
kept from my youth. 22 When Jesus heard this, he said to him:
One thing you yet lack; sell all that you have, and give to the
poor, and you shall have treasure in heaven: and come, follow
me. 23 And when he heard this, he was very sad, for he was
very rich.
24 When Jesus saw that he was very sad, he said: How difficult it is for those who have riches to enter into the kingdom
of God! 25 For it is easier for a camel to go through the eye

of a needle, than for a rich man to enter into the kingdom of
God. [26] And those who heard it said: Who, then, can be saved?
[27] He replied: Things that are impossible with men, are possible
with God.

[28] Then Peter said: Behold, we have left all and followed thee.
[29] And he said to them: Verily I say to you, There is no one
that has left house, or parents, or brothers, or wife, or children, for the sake of the kingdom of God, [30] who shall not receive manifold more in this time, and in the age to come, eternal
life.

[31] And he took the twelve aside, and said to them: Behold,
we are going up to Jerusalem, and all things that are written
by the prophets concerning the Son of man shall be accomplished. [32] For he shall be delivered to the Gentiles, and shall
be derided and insulted and spit upon; [33] and they shall scourge
him, and put him to death, and on the third day he shall rise
again. [34] And they understood none of these things; and this
saying was concealed from them; and they understood not the
things that were spoken.

[35] And it came to pass, that, as he came near to Jericho, a
certain blind man sat by the road begging. [36] And when he
heard the multitude passing by, he asked what this meant.
[37] And they told him that Jesus the Nazarene was passing by.
[38] And he cried out and said: Jesus, son of David, have mercy
on me. [39] And those who went before rebuked him that he
should be silent. But he cried so much the more: Son of David,
have mercy on me.

[40] And Jesus stood still, and commanded him to be brought to
him. And when he came near, he asked him, [41] saying: What
do you wish me to do for you? He replied: Lord, that I may
receive my sight. [42] And Jesus said to him: Receive your sight;
your faith has saved you. [43] And he immediately received his
sight, and followed him, glorifying God. And all the people,
when they saw it, gave praise to God.

XIX. [1] And he entered, and passed through Jericho. [2] And,
behold, there was a man called Zacchæus, who was a chief publican; and he was rich. [3] And he sought to see Jesus, who he
was, and was not able on account of the multitude, because he
was of small stature. [4] And he ran before, and climbed up a
sycamore-tree, that he might see him, for he was about to pass
that way. [5] And when Jesus came to the place, he looked up

and saw him, and said to him: Zacchæus, make haste and come
down, for I must spend this day at your house. 6 And he made
haste and came down, and received him joyfully.
7 And when they saw it, they all murmured, saying: He has
gone to be guest with a man that is a sinner. 8 And Zacchæus
stood, and said to the Lord: Behold, Lord, the half of my goods
I give to the poor; and if I have taken from any one by false
accusation, I restore him fourfold. 9 And Jesus said to him:
To-day has salvation come to this house, since he also is a son
of Abraham. 10 For the Son of man has come to seek and to save
that which was lost.

11 And as they heard these things, he also spoke a parable, because he was near Jerusalem, and they thought that the kingdom of God would immediately appear. 12 He said, therefore:
A certain nobleman went into a distant country to receive for
himself a kingdom, and to return. 13 And he called his ten servants, and gave them ten pounds, and said to them, Engage in trade
till I come. 14 But his citizens hated him, and sent an embassy
after him, saying, We will not have this man to reign over us.
15 And it came to pass, that, when he had returned, having
received the kingdom, he commanded those servants to be
called, to whom he had given the money, that he might know
what each had gained by trading. 16 And the first came and
said: Lord, your pound has gained ten pounds. 17 And he said
to him: Well done, good servant; because you have been faithful
in a very little, have authority over ten cities. 18 And the second came and said: Lord, your pound has gained five pounds.
19 And he said to him also: And be you over five cities. 20 And
another came and said: Lord, behold your pound, which I have
kept laid away in a napkin. 21 For I was afraid of you, because
you are a hard man; you take up that which you did not lay
down, and reap that which you did not sow.
22 Then he said to him: Out of your own mouth will I judge
you, you wicked servant. You knew that I was a hard man,
taking up what I did not lay down, and reaping what I did
not sow. 23 And why then did you not put my money into the
bank, that, when I came, I could have collected it with interest? 24 And he said to those who stood by: Take from him the
pound, and give it to him that has ten pounds. 25 And they said
to him: Lord, he has ten pounds. 26 For I say to you, To every
one that has, it shall be given; but from him that has not,
even that which he has shall be taken away. 27 But those who

are my enemies, who are not willing that I should rule over
them, bring hither, and slay them before me. [28] And when he
had said these things, he went before, going up to Jerusalem.

[29] And it came to pass, that, when he came near to Bethphage
and Bethany, to the mount called the mount of Olives, he sent
two of his disciples, [30] saying: Go into the opposite village, in
which, when you enter, you will find a colt tied, on which no
man ever sat. Loose him, and bring him. [31] And if any one
ask you why you loose him, thus shall you say to him: The
Lord has need of him.

[32] And those who were sent, went, and found as he had said
to them. [33] And as they were loosing the colt, the owners of
him said to them: Why do you loose the colt? [34] They replied:
The Lord has need of him. [35] And they brought him to Jesus,
and threw their mantles upon the colt, and sat Jesus on him.
[36] And as he was going on, they spread their mantles in the
road. [37] And when he was now near the descent of the mount
of Olives, the whole multitude of the disciples began to rejoice
and to praise God, with a loud voice, for all the mighty deeds
which they had seen, [38] saying: Blessed is the king that comes
in the name of the Lord; peace in heaven, and glory in the
highest. [39] And some of the Pharisees from among the multitude, said to him: Teacher, rebuke your disciples. [40] And he
answered, and said to them: I say to you, that if these had
been silent, the stones would have cried out.

[41] And when he came near, he looked upon the city, and wept
over it, [42] saying: Hadst thou known, even thou, at least in
this thy day, the things which were for thy peace! But now,
they are hid from thy eyes. [43] For the days will come upon
thee, when thy enemies will throw up a mound about thee, and
inclose thee around, and keep thee in on every side, [44] and will
destroy thee and thy children within thee, and will not leave in
thee one stone upon another, because thou knewest not the time
of thy visitation.

[45] And he went into the temple, and began to drive out those
who were selling in it, and those who were buying, [46] and said
to them: It is written, My house is a house of prayer; but you
have made it a den of robbers.

[47] And he was teaching daily in the temple. But the chief
priests, and the scribes, and the chief of the people sought to
destroy him, [48] and found nothing that they could do, for all the
people hung on his words.

XX. 1 And it came to pass, that, on one of those days, while
he was teaching the people in the temple, and preaching the
gospel, the chief priests and the scribes, with the elders, came
to him, 2 and spoke to him, saying: Tell us by what authority
you do these things? or, who is he that gave you this authority? 3 And he answered and said to them: I also will ask you
one thing, and do you answer me. 4 Was the immersion of
John from heaven, or from men? 5 And they reasoned among
themselves, saying: If we say, From heaven, he will reply:
Why, then, did you not believe him? 6 But if we say, From
men, all the people will stone us; for they believe that John
was a prophet. 7 And they answered, that they knew not
whence it was. 8 And Jesus said to them: Nor do I tell you
by what authority I do these things.

9 And he began to speak this parable to the people: A man
planted a vineyard, and let it out to vine-dressers, and was
absent from home for a long time. 10 And at the proper season,
he sent a servant to those vine-dressers, that they should give
him of the fruit of the vineyard. But the vine-dressers
scourged him, and sent him away empty-handed. 11 And he
then sent another servant. But they scourged him also, and
treated him shamefully, and sent him away empty-handed.
12 And he also sent a third; but they wounded him, and drove
him out.

13 And the owner of the vineyard said: What shall I do? I
will send my beloved son; perhaps, when they see him, they
will reverence him. 14 But when the vine-dressers saw him,
they reasoned among themselves, saying: This is the heir;
come, let us kill him, that the inheritance may be ours. 15 And
they drove him out of the vineyard, and killed him. What,
then, will the owner of the vineyard do to them? 16 He will
come and destroy these vine-dressers, and will give his vineyard
to others.

And when they heard it, they said: Be it not so! 17 And he
looked on them and said: What, then, does this mean, which is
written, The stone which the builders rejected has become the
head of the corner? 18 Whoever shall fall on this stone, shall be
dashed to pieces; but on whomever it shall fall, it will make
him as chaff for the wind. 19 And the chief priests and the
scribes sought to lay hands on him, the same hour; (and yet
they feared the people;) for they knew that he spoke this
parable against them.

20 And they watched him, and sent spies, who feigned themselves to be just men, that they might take hold of his words,
in order to deliver him up to the power and authority of the
governor. 21 And they asked him, saying: Teacher, we know
that you speak and teach rightly, and do not regard the person
of any, but teach the way of God in truth. 22 Is it lawful for
us to give tribute to Cæsar, or not? 23 But he perceived their
cunning, and said to them: Why do you tempt me? 24 Show me
a denarius. Whose image and superscription has it? They
answered and said: Cæsar's. 25 He said to them: Give, therefore,
to Cæsar the things that are Cæsar's, and to God the things
that are God's. 26 And they were not able to take hold of his
words before the people. And they were astonished at his
answer, and were silent.

27 Then there came to him some of the Sadducees, (these deny
that there is any resurrection,) and asked him, 28 saying: Teacher, Moses wrote for us, If any man's brother die, having a wife,
and he die without children, that his brother should take his
wife, and raise up children for his brother. 29 There were,
therefore, seven brothers; and the first took a wife, and died
without children; 30 and the second took his wife, and he died
without children; 31 and the third took her; and in like manner
also the seven; and they left no children, and died. 32 Last of all,
the woman also died. 33 Therefore, in the resurrection, of which
of them shall she be the wife? for the seven had her as a wife.

34 And Jesus answered and said to them: The children of this
age marry, and are given in marriage. 35 But those who shall
be accounted worthy to attain that age, and the resurrection
from the dead, neither marry, nor are given in marriage. 36 For
they can die no more; for they are like the angels, and are the
sons of God, being the sons of the resurrection. 37 But that
the dead are raised, even Moses showed at The Bush, since he
calls the Lord the God of Abraham, and the God of Isaac, and
the God of Jacob. 38 He is not a God of the dead, but of the
living; for all live to him. 39 And certain of the scribes answered and said: Teacher, thou hast answered well. 40 And
after this they durst not ask him any question at all.

41 But he said to them: How say they that the Christ is the
son of David? 42 Even David himself says, in the book of
Psalms: The Lord said to my Lord, Sit at my right hand, 43 till
make thy enemies thy footstool. 44 David, therefore, calls him
Lord; and how is he his son?

[45]And while all the people were listening, he said to his disciples: [46]Beware of the scribes, who delight to walk in robes,
and love greetings in the markets, and the first seats in the
synagogues, and the first places at suppers; [47]who eat up the
houses of widows, and, for a pretext, make long prayers. These
shall receive the greater condemnation.

XXI. [1]And he looked up, and saw the rich throwing their
gifts into the treasury. [2]And he saw also a certain poor widow
throw in thither two mites. [3]And he said: Of a truth, I say
to you, that this poor widow has thrown in more than they all.
[4]For all these, from their abundance, have thrown in among
the gifts of God; but she, from her poverty, has thrown in all
the living that she had.

[5]And as some were saying of the temple, that it was adorned
with beautiful stones and offerings, he said: [6]As for these things
which you see, the days will come in which there shall not be
left one stone upon another, that shall not be thrown down.
[7]And they asked him, saying: Teacher, when shall these things
be? And what shall be the sign when these things come to
pass? [8]He replied: Take heed that you be not deceived; for
many will come in my name, saying: I am he; and, The time
is near. Go not, therefore, after them. [9]But when you hear
of wars, and tumults, be not terrified; for these things must first
take place; but the end comes not immediately. [10]Then he said
to them: Nation shall rise against nation, and kingdom against
kingdom; [11]and there shall be great earthquakes in various
places, and famines, and pestilences; and there shall be fearful
sights and great signs from heaven.

[12]But before all these things, they will lay their hands on you,
and persecute you, delivering you up to synagogues, and into
prisons, after being brought before kings and governors for my
name's sake. [13]But this shall become to you the means of bearing testimony. [14]Therefore, determine in your hearts not to
meditate beforehand what you shall answer; [15]for I will give
you a mouth, and wisdom, which all your opposers shall not be
able to gainsay or withstand. [16]But you will be delivered up by
parents and brothers and relatives and friends; and some of
you they will put to death; [17]and you will be hated by all for
my name's sake. [18]Yet a hair of your head shall not perish.
[19]By your patient endurance, preserve your lives.

[20]But when you shall see Jerusalem besieged by armies, then

know that its desolation is near. 21 Then let those who are in
Judea flee to the mountains; and let those who are in the midst
of it, withdraw from it. Let those who are in the country, not
come within it. 22 For these are the days of vengeance, that all
things that are written may be fulfilled. 23 But alas for them
that are with child, and for them that give suck in those days!
for there shall be great distress upon the land, and wrath upon
this people. 24 And they shall fall by the edge of the sword, and
be led away captive among all nations; and Jerusalem shall be
trodden down by the Gentiles, till the times of the Gentiles be
fulfilled.

25 And there shall be signs in the sun and in the moon and in
the stars; and on the earth, distress of nations in perplexity;
the sea and its waves roaring; 26 men's hearts failing on account of the fearful expectation of the things that are coming
on the land; for the hosts of the heavens shall be shaken.
27 And then shall they see the Son of man coming in a cloud,
with power and great glory. 28 When these things begin to
take place, look up, and lift up your heads; for your redemption draws near.

29 And he spoke a parable to them: See the fig-tree, and all
the trees; 30 when they now put forth leaves, you see, and know
of yourselves that summer is near. 31 So likewise, when you
see these things taking place, you know that the kingdom of
God is near. 32 Verily I say to you, This generation shall not
pass away till all be fulfilled. 33 Heaven and earth shall pass
away, but my words shall not pass away.

34 And take heed to yourselves, lest your hearts become heavy
with reveling and drunkenness and the cares of life, and that
day come upon you when you look not for it. 35 For as a snare,
it shall come on all that dwell on the face of all the land.
36 Watch, therefore, and pray at all times, that you may be accounted worthy to escape all these things that shall come to pass,
and to stand before the Son of man.

37 And in the day-time he was teaching in the temple. But
he went out and passed the nights in the mount called the mount
of Olives. 38 And all the people came early in the morning to
him in the temple, in order to hear him.

XXII. 1 Now the feast of unleavened bread, which is called
the passover, was at hand. 2 And the chief priests and the
scribes sought how they might kill him; for they feared the

people. [3] But Satan entered into Judas surnamed Iscariot, who
was of the number of the twelve. [4] And he went away, and
conferred with the chief priests and the captains how he might
deliver him up to them. [5] And they were glad, and agreed to
give him money. [6] And he consented, and sought an opportunity to deliver him up to them without tumult.

[7] Then came the day of unleavened bread, when the passover
must be killed. [8] And he sent Peter and John, saying: Go,
make ready the passover for us, that we may eat it. [9] They
said to him: Where dost thou wish that we make it ready?
[10] And he said to them: Behold, as you go into the city, there
shall meet you a man carrying a pitcher of water; follow him
into the house that he enters; [11] and say to the master of the
house: The Teacher says to you, Where is the room in which I
may eat the passover with my disciples? [12] And he will show
you a large upper room furnished; there make ready. [13] And
they went, and found as he had said to them; and they made
ready the passover.

[14] And when the hour had come, he reclined at table, and the
twelve apostles with him. [15] And he said to them: I have
greatly desired to eat this passover with you before I suffer.
[16] For I say to you, I will eat of it no more till it is fulfilled in
the kingdom of God. [17] And he took the cup, and gave thanks,
and said: Take this, and divide it among yourselves; [18] for I
say to you, I will not drink of the fruit of the vine till the
kingdom of God has come.

[19] And he took bread, and gave thanks; and he broke, and
gave it to them, saying: This is my body, which is given for
you: do this in remembrance of me. [20] In like manner also,
the cup, after he had supped, saying: This cup is the new covenant in my blood, which is shed for you.

[21] But, behold, the hand of him that delivers me up is with
me on the table. [22] And the Son of man goes, as it is determined;
but alas for that man by whom he is delivered up. [23] And they
began to inquire among themselves, which of them it could be
that was about to do this thing.

[24] And there had been also a contention among them, which
of them was thought to be the greatest. [25] And he said to
them: The kings of the nations have dominion over them, and
those who exercise authority over them are called benefactors.
[26] But you shall not be so; but let the greatest among you be as
the younger, and him that is chief, as he that serves. [27] For

which is greater, he that reclines at table, or he that serves?
Is not he that reclines at table? But I am among you as one
that serves. 28 You are they that have continued with me in
my trials; 29 and I appoint to you a kingdom, as my Father
has appointed to me, 30 that you may eat and drink at my table
in my kingdom, and sit on thrones, judging the twelve tribes
of Israel.

31 And the Lord said: Simon, Simon, behold, Satan has demanded you apostles for himself, that he may sift you as wheat.
32 But I have prayed for you, Simon, that your faith fail not.
And when you have turned to me again, strengthen your brethren. 33 And he said to him: Lord, I am ready to go with thee,
both to prison and to death. 34 He replied: I tell you, Peter,
the cock shall not crow this day before you have three times
denied that you know me.

35 And he said to them: When I sent you without purse and
bag and sandals, did you need any thing? They replied: Nothing. 36 Then he said to them: But now, he that has a purse,
let him take it, and likewise a bag; and he that has no sword,
let him sell his mantle and buy one. 37 For I say to you, That
even this which is written must be fulfilled in me: And he was
numbered with transgressors. For the things concerning me
have an end. 38 And they said: Lord, behold, here are two
swords. He said to them: It is enough.

39 And after he had gone out, he went, according to custom,
to the mount of Olives; and his disciples followed him. 40 And
when he came to the place, he said to them: Pray, that you
enter not into temptation. 41 And he withdrew from them
about a stone's throw, and kneeled down, and prayed, 42 saying:
Father, if thou art willing that this cup should pass from me—
yet, not my will, but thine be done.

43 And there appeared to him an angel from heaven, to
strengthen him. 44 And he was in agony, and prayed more
earnestly. And his sweat was like great drops of blood falling to the ground. 45 And he arose from prayer, and came to
his disciples, and found them asleep for sorrow. 46 And he said
to them: Why do you sleep? Arise and pray, lest you enter
into temptation.

47 And while he was yet speaking, behold a multitude; and he
that was called Judas, one of the twelve, went before them, and
came near to Jesus to kiss him. 48 But Jesus said to him: Judas,
do you deliver up the Son of man with a kiss? 49 When those

who were about him saw what would be done, they said to him:
Lord, shall we strike with the sword? 50 And a certain one of
them struck the servant of the chief priest, and cut off his right
ear. 51 And Jesus answered and said: Let this matter proceed
thus far. And he touched his ear and healed him.

52 And Jesus said to the chief priests, and the captains of the
temple, and the elders that had come against him: Have you
come out with swords and clubs, as against a robber? 53 While
I was daily with you in the temple, you did not lay hands on
me. But this is your hour, and the authority of darkness.
54 And they took him, and led him away, and brought him into
the house of the chief priest.

But Peter followed at a distance. 55 And when they had
kindled a fire in the middle of the court, and had sat down together, Peter sat down in the midst of them. 56 And a certain
maid-servant saw him sitting by the fire; and, looking intently
at him, she said: This man also was with him. 57 But he denied,
saying: Woman, I know him not. 58 And after a little, another
saw him, and said: You also are one of them. Peter replied:
Man, I am not. 59 And about one hour after, another confidently affirmed, saying: Of a truth, this man also was with
him; for he is a Galilean. 60 But Peter said: Man, I know not
what you say. And immediately, while he was speaking, the
cock crew. 61 And the Lord turned and looked at Peter. And
Peter remembered the word of the Lord, that he had said to him,
Before the cock crows, you will deny me three times. 62 And
Peter went out and wept bitterly.

63 And the men that had Jesus in custody mocked him, and
smote him. 64 And when they had blindfolded him, they struck
him on the face, and asked him, saying: Give an answer; who
is it that struck you? 65 And many other impious things they
said to him.

66 And when it was day, the elders of the people, the chief
priests also and scribes, met together, and led him up to the
Sanhedrim, and said: 67 If you are the Christ, tell us. But he
said to them: If I tell you, you will not believe; 68 and if I
also ask you a question, you will not answer me, nor let me go.
69 Henceforth the Son of man shall sit on the right hand of the
power of God. 70 And they all said: You are, then, the Son of
God? He said to them: You say that I am. 71 They replied:
What further need have we of testimony? For we ourselves
have heard from his own mouth.

XXIII. [1] And the whole number of them arose, and led him
away to Pilate. [2] And they began to accuse him, saying: We
found this man turning the people away, and forbidding to give
tribute to Cæsar, saying that he himself is Christ, a king.
[3] And Pilate asked him, saying: Are you the king of the Jews?
He answered and said to him: You say it. [4] Pilate said to the
chief priests and to the multitudes: I find no fault in this man.
[5] But they became the more urgent, and said: He excites the
people, teaching throughout the whole of Judea, beginning from
Galilee to this place. [6] When Pilate heard of Galilee, he asked
if the man was a Galilean.

[7] And when he learned that he belonged to the dominion of
Herod, he sent him to Herod, who was at that time in Jerusalem. [8] When Herod saw Jesus, he rejoiced greatly; for he
had, for a long time, desired to see him, because he had heard
many things of him; and he hoped to see some sign done by
him. [9] And he questioned him concerning many things; but he
made him no answer. [10] And the chief priests and the scribes
stood by, and vehemently accused him. [11] But Herod and his
guards treated him with contempt; and having mocked him,
and put on him a gaudy robe, he sent him back to Pilate.
[12] And on the same day, Pilate and Herod became friends to each
other; for, before this, they had been at enmity the one toward
the other.

[13] And Pilate called together the chief priests and the rulers
and the people, [14] and said to them: You have brought to me
this man as one that turns the people away; and behold, I have
examined him before you, and have found in this man no fault,
with respect to the things of which you accuse him; [15] nor indeed did Herod; for I sent you to him, and behold, nothing
worthy of death has been done by him. [16] I will, therefore,
chastise him, and release him.

[17] For it was necessary that he should release to them one at
the feast. [18] And the whole multitude cried out, saying: Away
with this man, and release to us Barabbas. [19] He, for a certain
seditious movement that had been made in the city, and for
murder, had been thrown into prison. [20] Therefore Pilate, desiring to release Jesus, again called to them. [21] But they answered, saying: Crucify, crucify him. [22] He said to them the
third time: Why, what evil has he done? I have found nothing in him worthy of death. I will, therefore, chastise him, and
release him. [23] But they were urgent with loud voices, demand-

ing that he should be crucified. And their voices, and those of
the chief priests, prevailed. 24 And Pilate gave sentence that it
should be as they demanded. 25 And he released him that for a
seditious movement, and for murder, had been thrown into
prison, whom they demanded; but Jesus, he delivered up to
their will.

26 And as they led him away, they laid hold of Simon, a certain Cyrenian, who was coming from the country, and on him
they laid the cross, that he might carry it after Jesus. 27 And
there followed him a great number of the people, and of women
that bewailed and lamented him. 28 But Jesus turned, and said
to them, Daughters of Jerusalem, weep not for me, but weep for
yourselves and for your children. 29 For, behold, the days are
coming in which they will say, Blessed are the barren, and the
wombs that never bore, and the breasts that never gave suck.
30 Then shall they begin to say to the mountains, Fall on us;
and to the hills, Cover us. 31 For, if they do these things in the
green tree, what shall be done in the dry?

32 And two others, who were evil-doers, were led out to be put
to death with him. 33 And when they came to the place called
Skull, they there crucified him and the evil-doers; one on the
right, and the other on the left. 34 And Jesus said: Father,
forgive them, for they know not what they do. And dividing
his clothing into parts, they cast lots. 35 And the people stood
and looked on. And the rulers with them scoffed at him, saying: He saved others, let him save himself if he is the Christ,
the chosen of God. 36 The soldiers also derided him, coming to
him and offering him vinegar, 37 and saying: If you are the
King of the Jews, save yourself. 38 And a superscription was
also written over him in Greek and in Roman and in Hebrew
letters, THIS IS THE KING OF THE JEWS.

39 And one of the evil-doers that were hanged reviled him,
saying: If you are the Christ, save yourself and us. 40 But the
other answering, rebuked him, saying: Do you not fear God,
since you are in the same condemnation? 41 And we justly;
for we are receiving the due reward of our deeds; but this man
has done nothing wrong. 42 And he said to Jesus: Remember
me, Lord, when thou comest in thy kingdom. 43 And Jesus said
to him: Verily I say to you, to-day you shall be with me in
paradise.

44 And it was about the sixth hour, and there was darkness
over the whole land till the ninth hour. 45 And the sun was

darkened, and the vail of the temple was rent in the midst.
46 And Jesus cried with a loud voice, and said: Father, into thy
hands I commend my spirit. And when he had said this, he
gave up his spirit.

47 When the centurion saw what was done, he glorified God,
saying: Truly, this was a righteous man. 48 And all the multitudes that had come together to that sight, when they saw what
was done, returned, smiting their breasts. 49 And all his acquaintance, and the women that had followed him from Galilee,
stood at a distance looking on these things.

50 And, behold, there was a man named Joseph, a counselor,
a good and a just man; 51 (he had not given his consent to their
counsel and deed;) he was of Arimathea, a city of the Jews, and
he himself also waited for the kingdom of God: 52 this man
came to Pilate, and asked for the body of Jesus. 53 And he took
it down, and wrapped it in linen, and laid it in a sepulcher
that had been hewed in rock, in which no one had yet been
laid. 54 And the day was the preparation, and the Sabbath was
beginning.

55 And the women that had come with him from Galilee followed after and saw the sepulcher, and how his body was laid.
56 And they returned, and prepared spices and ointment; and
they rested on the Sabbath, according to the commandment.

XXIV. 1 And on the first day of the week, at early dawn,
they came to the sepulcher, bringing the spices which they had
prepared; and with them came certain others. 2 And they
found the stone rolled away from the sepulcher; 3 and they entered in, but found not the body of the Lord Jesus. 4 And it
came to pass, while they were much perplexed at this, Behold,
two men stood by them in shining raiment. 5 And while they
feared and bowed their faces to the earth, they said to them:
Why seek you among the dead for him that lives? 6 He is not
here, but he has risen; remember that he spoke to you while
he was yet in Galilee, 7 saying, The Son of man must be delivered into the hands of sinful men, and be crucified, and the
third day rise again.

8 And they remembered his words, 9 and returned from the
sepulcher, and told all these things to the eleven and to the
rest. 10 It was Mary Magdalene and Joanna and Mary the
mother of James, and the others with them, that told these
things to the apostles. 11 And their words seemed to them as

idle tales, and they believed them not. 12 But Peter arose and
ran to the sepulcher, and stooping down, he saw the linen
clothes lying by themselves; and he departed, wondering in
himself at that which had come to pass.

13 And, behold, two of them were going, on the same day, to
a village called Emmaus, distant from Jerusalem sixty furlongs.
14 And they were talking to one another about all these things
which had taken place. 15 And it came to pass, that, while they
conversed and reasoned together, Jesus himself drew near, and
went on with them. 16 But their eyes were restrained, so that
they did not recognize him. 17 And he said to them: What
matters are these which you are discussing with one another as
you walk and are sad?

18 And one of them, whose name was Cleopas, answered and
said to him: Are you only a stranger in Jerusalem, and have
not known the things that have taken place there in these days?
19 And he said to them: What things? They said to him: The
things concerning Jesus the Nazarene, who was a prophet
mighty in deed and in word before God and all the people; 20 and
how the chief priests and our rulers delivered him up to be condemned to death, and crucified him. 21 But we trusted that it
was he that was about to redeem Israel. And besides all this,
to-day is the third day since these things were done. 22 And
further, certain women of our company, who were early at the
sepulcher, astonished us: 23 for they found not his body, and
came and told that they had seen a vision of angels, who said
that he was alive. 24 And some of those who were with us went
to the sepulcher, and found it even as the women had said, but
him they saw not.

25 And he said to them: O inconsiderate, and slow of heart to
believe all things that the prophets have spoken! 26 Ought not
the Christ to have suffered these things, and to enter into his
glory? 27 And beginning from Moses, and all the prophets, he
explained to them, in all the Scriptures, the things concerning
himself. 28 And they drew near the village to which they were
going; and he made as if he would go further. 29 And they
constrained him, saying: Remain with us, for it is near the
evening, and the day has declined. And he went in to remain
with them.

30 And it came to pass, while he reclined at table with them,
that he took bread and blessed; and he broke, and gave it to
them. 31 And their eyes were opened, and they recognized him,

and he disappeared from them. 32 And they said one to another,
Did not our heart burn within us while he talked with us by
the way, and while he opened to us the Scriptures?
33 And they arose the same hour, and returned to Jerusalem,
and found the eleven, and those who were with them, assembled, 34 and saying: The Lord has risen indeed, and has appeared to Simon. 35 And they told what had taken place on
the way, and how he was made known to them in the breaking
of bread.
36 And while they were speaking of these things, Jesus himself stood in the midst of them, and said to them: Peace be to
you. 37 But they were terrified and frightened, and thought
that they saw a spirit. 38 And he said to them: Why are you
troubled, and why do doubts arise in your hearts? 39 See my
hands and my feet, that it is I myself; handle me and see; for a
spirit has not flesh and bones, as you see me have. 40 And when
he had said this, he showed them his hands and his feet. 41 And
while they did not believe as yet for joy, and were astonished,
he said to them: Have you any thing here to eat? 42 And they
gave him a piece of broiled fish, and of a honey-comb. 43 And
he took it, and did eat before them.
44 And he said to them: These are the words that I spoke to
you, while I was yet with you, that all things must be fulfilled
that are written in the law of Moses, and in the prophets, and
in the psalms, concerning me. 45 Then he opened their mind,
that they might understand the Scriptures, 46 and he said to
them: Thus it is written, and thus was it necessary that the
Christ should suffer, and rise again from the dead the third
day, 47 and that repentance and remission of sins should be
preached in his name among all nations, beginning at Jerusalem. 48 You are witnesses of these things. 49 And behold, I
send the promise of my Father upon you. But do you remain
in the city of Jerusalem, till you be clothed with power from
on high.
50 And he led them out as far as Bethany; and he lifted up his
hands and blessed them. 51 And it came to pass, that as he
blessed them, he was separated from them, and carried up into
heaven. 52 And they worshiped him, and returned to Jerusalem
with great joy; 53 and were continually in the temple, praising
and blessing God.

TESTIMONY OF JOHN.

I. 1 IN the beginning was the WORD, and the WORD was
with God, and the WORD was God. 2 He was in the
beginning with God. 3 All things were made by him, and without him not one thing was made that now exists. 4 In him was
life, and the life was the light of men. 5 And the light shines
in the darkness, and the darkness comprehended it not.

6 There was a man sent from God, whose name was John.
7 This man came as a witness, to testify of the Light, that all
through him might believe. 8 He was not the Light; but he
came to testify of the Light.

9 He was the true Light, which, coming into the world, gives
light to every man. 10 He was in the world, and the world was
made by him, and the world knew him not. 11 He came to his
own country, and his own people received him not. 12 But as
many as received him, to them he gave the privilege of becoming the children of God, even to those who believe on his name:
13 who were begotten, not of blood, nor of the will of the flesh,
nor of the will of man, but of God. 14 And the WORD became
flesh, and tabernacled among us, (and we beheld his glory, the
glory as of the only begotten of the Father,) full of grace and
of truth.

15 John testified of him, and cried, saying: This is he of
whom I said: He that comes after me, is now before me, for
he existed before me. 16 And from his fullness have we all received, even grace for grace; 17 for the law was given through
Moses, but the grace and the truth came through Jesus Christ.
18 No one has seen God at any time; the only begotten Son, who
is in the bosom of the Father, he has revealed him.

19 And this is the testimony of John, when the Jews sent
priests and Levites from Jerusalem to ask him: Who are you?
20 And he confessed, and did not deny; and he confessed: I am
not the Christ. 21 And they asked him: What then? Are you
Elijah? And he said: I am not. Are you the prophet? And
he answered: No. 22 They then said to him: Who are you?
that we may give an answer to those who sent us; what say
you of yourself? 23 He said: I am the voice of one crying in
the wilderness, Make straight the way of the Lord; as said the
prophet Isaiah.

24 And those who were sent were of the Pharisees; 25 and they

asked him, and said to him: Why, then, do you immerse, if you
are not the Christ, nor Elijah, nor the prophet? 26 John answered them, saying: I immerse in water; but there stands one
among you whom you know not. 27 He it is, who, though he
comes after me, is now before me; the strap of whose sandal I
am not worthy to loose. 28 These things were done in Bethany,
beyond the Jordan, where John was immersing.

29 The next day John saw Jesus coming to him, and said:
Behold the Lamb of God, that takes away the sin of the world.
30 This is he of whom I said, After me comes a man who is now
before me, for he existed before me. 31 And I knew him not;
but that he might be made manifest to Israel, for this reason I
have come immersing in water. 32 And John testified, saying:
I saw the Spirit descending from heaven like a dove, and it remained on him. 33 And I knew him not; but he that sent me
to immerse in water, said to me, On whom you shall see the
Spirit descending and remaining, this is he that immerses in
the Holy Spirit. 34 And I saw, and do testify that this is the
Son of God.

35 Again the next day, John was standing with two of his disciples. 36 And looking on Jesus as he walked, he said: Behold
the Lamb of God. 37 And the two disciples heard him speak,
and they followed Jesus. 38 And Jesus turned, and saw them
following, and said to them: 39 What do you seek? They said
to him: Rabbi, (which, when translated, is called Teacher,)
where abidest thou? 40 He said to them: Come and see. They
went and saw where he abode; and they remained with him
that day; for it was about the tenth hour. 41 One of the two
that heard John speak, and followed him, was Andrew, the
brother of Simon Peter. 42 He first found his own brother
Simon, and said to him: We have found the Messiah; (which,
when translated, is the Christ;) 43 and he brought him to Jesus.
Jesus looking on him, said: You are Simon, the son of Jonah;
you shall be called Cephas (which, when translated, is Rock).

44 The day following, Jesus wished to go into Galilee; and he
found Philip, and said to him: Follow me. 45 Now, Philip was
of Bethsaida, the city of Andrew and Peter. 46 Philip found
Nathaniel, and said to him: We have found him of whom Moses
in the law and the prophets did write, Jesus of Nazareth, the
son of Joseph. 47 And Nathaniel said to him: Can any thing
good come out of Nazareth? Philip said to him: Come and see.

48 Jesus saw Nathaniel coming to him, and said of him: Be-

hold, an Israelite in truth, in whom there is no guile. 49 Nathaniel said to him: How knowest thou me? Jesus answered
and said to him: Before Philip called you, while you were under
the fig-tree, I saw you. 50 Nathaniel answered and said to him:
Rabbi, thou art the Son of God; thou art the King of Israel.
51 Jesus answered and said to him: Do you believe, because I
said to you, I saw you under the fig-tree? You shall see
greater things than these. 52 And he said to him: Verily, verily
I say to you, From this time you shall see heaven opened, and
the angels of God ascending and descending upon the Son of
man.

II. 1 And on the third day there was a marriage in Cana of
Galilee; and the mother of Jesus was there. 2 And both Jesus
and his disciples were invited to the marriage. 3 And the wine
having failed, the mother of Jesus said to him: They have no
wine. 4 Jesus said to her: Woman, what have I to do with you?
my hour has not yet come. 5 His mother said to the servants:
Whatever he says to you, do. 6 Now, according to the Jewish
custom of purifying, six water-pots of stone had been set there,
containing each two or three baths.

7 Jesus said to them: Fill the water-pots with water. And
they filled them to the brim. 8 And he said to them: Draw out
now, and carry it to the governor of the feast. And they carried it. 9 When the governor of the feast had tasted the water
that had been made wine, (and he knew not whence it was, but
the servants that had drawn the water knew,) the governor of
the feast called the bridegroom, and said to him: 10 Every man
sets out the good wine first, and when they have drunk freely,
then that which is inferior; but you have kept the good wine
till now. 11 This beginning of signs Jesus made in Cana of Galilee, and manifested his glory; and his disciples believed on him.

12 After this he went down to Capernaum, he and his mother
and his brothers and his disciples. And they continued there
not many days.

13 And the passover of the Jews was near, and Jesus went up
to Jerusalem. 14 And he found in the temple those who were
selling oxen and sheep and doves, and the money-changers sitting. 15 And when he had made a whip of cords, he drove them
all out of the temple, the sheep also, and the oxen, and he
poured out the money of the money-changers, and overthrew
their tables; 16 and said to those who sold doves: Take these

things hence; make not my Father's house a house of merchandise. [17] And his disciples remembered that it was written, Zeal
for thy house consumes me.

[18] Then answered the Jews and said to him: What sign do you
show us, seeing that you do these things? [19] Jesus answered
and said to them: Destroy this temple, and I will raise it up in
three days. [20] Then the Jews said to him: Forty and six years
was this temple in building, and will you rebuild it in three
days? [21] But he spoke of the temple of his body. [22] When,
therefore, he was raised from the dead, his disciples remembered
that he had said this. And they believed the Scripture, and the
word that Jesus had spoken.

[23] And while he was in Jerusalem, during the feast of passover, many believed on his name, because they saw the signs
that he did. [24] But Jesus did not trust himself to them, because
he knew all men, [25] and had no need that any one should testify
of man, for he himself knew what was in man.

III. [1] There was a man of the Pharisees, named Nicodemus,
a ruler of the Jews. [2] This man came to Jesus by night, and
said to him: Rabbi, we know that thou hast come as a teacher
from God; for no man can do these signs which thou doest,
unless God be with him.

[3] Jesus answered and said to him: Verily, verily I say to you,
unless a man be born again, he can not see the kingdom of
God.

[4] Nicodemus said to him: How can a man be born when he is
old? Can he enter his mother's womb the second time, and be
born?

[5] Jesus answered: Verily, verily I say to you, unless a man be
born of water and of the Spirit, he can not enter into the kingdom of God. [6] That which is begotten of the flesh, is flesh; and
that which is begotten of the Spirit, is spirit. [7] Wonder not
that I said to you, you must all be born again. [8] The Spirit
breathes where he pleases, and you hear his voice, but you
know not whence he comes, and whither he goes; so is every
one that is begotten of the Spirit.

[9] Nicodemus answered and said to him: How can these things
be? [10] Jesus answered and said to him: Are you the teacher of
Israel, and do not understand these things? [11] Verily, verily, I
say to you, we speak that which we know, and testify to that
which we have seen; and you receive not our testimony. [12] If

I have told you of earthly things, and you believe not, how will
you believe, if I tell you of heavenly things? [13] And no man
has ascended into heaven, but he who came down from heaven,
the Son of man, who is in heaven. [14] And as Moses lifted up
the serpent in the wilderness, so must the Son of man be lifted
up; [15] that whoever believes on him may not perish, but have
eternal life. [16] For God so loved the world, that he gave his
only begotten Son, that whoever believes on him should not
perish, but have eternal life. [17] For God sent not his Son into
the world to condemn the world, but that the world, through
him, might be saved.

[18] He that believes on him is not condemned; but he that believes not is condemned already, because he has not believed on
the name of the only begotten Son of God. [19] And this is the
condemnation, that light has come into the world, and men
have loved darkness rather than light, because their deeds were
evil. [20] For every one that does evil, hates the light, and comes
not to the light, lest his deeds should be exposed. [21] But he that
does the truth, comes to the light, that his deeds may be made
manifest that they are done in God.

[22] After these things, Jesus and his disciples came into the
land of Judea, and he remained there with them, and immersed.
[23] And John also was immersing in Ænon, near Salim, because
there was much water there. And they came and were immersed; [24] for John had not yet been thrown into prison.

[25] There arose, therefore, a dispute between some of John's
disciples and a Jew, about purification. [26] And they came to
John, and said to him: Rabbi, he who was with you beyond the
Jordan, to whom you bore testimony, behold, he immerses, and
all are going to him.

[27] John answered and said: A man can receive nothing unless
it be given to him from heaven. [28] You yourselves will testify
for me, that I said, I am not the Christ, but that I am sent before him. [29] He that has the bride, is the bridegroom; but the
friend of the bridegroom, who stands and hears him, rejoices
greatly on account of the voice of the bridegroom. This, my
joy, is therefore complete. [30] He must increase, but I must
decrease.

[31] He that comes from above, is over all. He that is from the
earth, is from the earth, and speaks from the earth. He that
comes from heaven, is over all; [32] and what he has seen and
heard, this he testifies; and no one receives his testimony. [33] He

that has received his testimony has solemnly declared that God
is true. [34] For he whom God has sent, speaks the words of
God; for God gives not the Spirit by measure to him. [35] The
Father loves the Son, and has given all things into his hand.
[36] He that believes on the Son has eternal life. But he that believes not the Son, shall not see life, but the wrath of God
remains on him.

IV. [1] When, therefore, the Lord knew that the Pharisees had
heard that Jesus was making and immersing more disciples
than John, ([2] though not Jesus himself, but his disciples immersed,) [3] he left Judea, and went again into Galilee. [4] And it
was necessary that he should go through Samaria. [5] He came,
therefore, to a city of Samaria, called Sychar, near the field that
Jacob gave to his son Joseph. [6] And Jacob's well was there.
Jesus, therefore, wearied with his journey, sat thus on the well.
It was about the sixth hour.

[7] There came a woman of Samaria to draw water. And Jesus
said to her: Give me to drink. [8] For his disciples had gone into
the city to buy food. [9] Then the woman of Samaria said to him:
How is it that you, who are a Jew, ask drink of me, who am a
woman of Samaria? (For the Jews have no social intercourse
with the Samaritans.) [10] Jesus answered and said to her: If
you had known the gift of God, and who it is that said to you,
Give me to drink, you would have asked of him, and he would
have given you living water. [11] The woman said to him: Sir,
you have no vessel with which you can draw, and the well is
deep; whence have you that living water? [12] Are you greater
than our father Jacob, who gave us the well, and drank from it
himself, and his sons, and his cattle?

[13] Jesus answered and said to her: Whoever drinks of this
water, will thirst again; [14] but whoever drinks of the water
that I will give him, shall never thirst. But the water that I
will give him, shall be in him a fountain of water springing up
in order to eternal life.

[15] The woman said to him: Sir, give me this water, that I may
not thirst, nor come hither to draw.

[16] Jesus said to her; Go, call your husband, and come hither.
[17] The woman answered and said: I have no husband.

Jesus said to her: You have well said, I have no husband;
[18] for you have had five husbands, and he whom you now have
is not your husband. In this you have spoken truly. [19] The

woman said to him: Sir, I perceive that thou art a prophet.
20 Our fathers worshiped in this mountain, and you Jews
say that in Jerusalem is the place where we ought to
worship.
21 Jesus said to her: Woman, believe me, the hour is coming,
when neither in this mountain, nor in Jerusalem, will you worship the Father. 22 You worship you know not what; we know
what we worship; for salvation is of the Jews. 23 But the hour
is coming, and now is, when the true worshipers will worship
the Father in spirit and in truth; for the Father seeks such to
worship him. 24 God is spirit; and they that worship him, must
worship him in spirit and in truth. 25 The woman said to him:
I know that Messiah (who is called Christ) is coming; when he
comes, he will tell us all things.
26 Jesus said to her: I who speak to you am he. 27 And upon
this his disciples came, and were astonished that he was talking
with the woman. Yet no one said: What seekest thou? or, why
talkest thou with her?
28 Then the woman left her water-pot, and went into the city,
and said to the men: 29 Come, see a man who has told me all
things that I ever did. Is not this the Christ? 30 Then they
went out of the city and came to him.
31 In the mean time, the disciples besought him, saying:
Rabbi, eat. 32 But he said to them: I have food to eat of which
you know not. 33 Then the disciples said one to another: Has
any one brought him food? 34 Jesus said to them: My food is
to do the will of him that sent me, and to finish his work. 35 Do
you not say, There are yet four months, and harvest comes?
Behold, I say to you, Lift up your eyes, and look on the fields,
for they are already white for the harvest. 36 And he that reaps
receives wages, and gathers fruit for life eternal; that he that
sows, and he that reaps, may rejoice together. 37 For in this
is the saying true, One sows and another reaps. 38 I have sent
you to reap that on which you bestowed no labor. Others have
labored, and you have entered into their labors.
39 And many of the Samaritans of that city believed on him,
because of the word of the woman who testified, He told me all
things that I ever did. 40 When, therefore, the Samaritans came
to him, they besought him to abide with them. And he abode
there two days. 41 And many more believed because of his own
word; 42 and they said to the woman: We no longer believe
because of what you said, for we ourselves have heard, and

we know that this is in truth the Savior of the world, the
Christ.

[43] And after two days he departed thence, and went into Galilee; [44] for Jesus himself testified that a prophet has no honor in
his own country. [45] Therefore, when he came into Galilee, the
Galileans received him, because they had seen all things that he
had done in Jerusalem during the feast; for they themselves
had gone to the feast.

[46] Then Jesus came again into Cana of Galilee, where he had
made the water wine. And there was a certain courtier, whose
son was sick in Capernaum. [47] When he heard that Jesus had
come from Judea into Galilee, he went to him, and besought
him that he would come down, and restore his son to health,
for he was about to die. [48] Then said Jesus to him: Unless you
see signs and wonders, you will not believe. [49] The courtier
said to him: Sir, come down before my child die. [50] Jesus said
to him: Go, your child lives. And the man believed the word
that Jesus spoke, and departed. [51] And as he was going down,
his servants met him, and said: Your son lives. [52] Then he inquired of them the hour in which he was restored to health.
And they said to him: Yesterday, at the seventh hour, the fever
left him. [53] Then his father knew that it was in the same hour
in which Jesus said to him, Your son lives. And he himself,
and all his house, believed. [54] This is the second sign which
Jesus did, when he came out of Judea into Galilee.

V. [1] After this was the feast of the Jews; and Jesus went up
to Jerusalem. [2] Now there is in Jerusalem, near the sheep-gate,
a pool, called, in the Hebrew tongue, Bethesda, with five
porches. [3] In these lay a great multitude of sick persons,
blind, lame, withered, who waited for the moving of the water.
[4] For an angel went down at a certain season into the pool, and
stirred the water. Then he who entered first after the motion
of the water, was cured of whatever disease he had.

[5] And a certain man was there, who had been sick thirty-
eight years. [6] When Jesus saw him lying, and knew that he
had been already a long time in that condition, he said to him:
Do you wish to be restored to health? [7] The sick man answered him: Sir, I have no man to put me into the pool when
the water is stirred; but while I am coming, another goes
down before me. [8] Jesus said to him: Arise, take up your
bed and walk. [9] And the man was immediately restored to

health; and he took up his bed and walked. And that day
was the Sabbath.

10 The Jews, therefore, said to him that was cured: It is the
Sabbath; it is not lawful for you to carry your bed. 11 He answered them: He that restored me to health said to me, Take
up your bed and walk. 12 Then they asked him: Who is he that
said to you, Take up your bed and walk? 13 But he that had
been restored to health knew not who he was; for Jesus had
withdrawn himself, because a multitude was in the place.
14 After this Jesus found him in the temple, and said to him:
Behold, you have been restored to health; sin no more, lest
some worse thing befall you. 15 The man departed, and told the
Jews that it was Jesus that had restored him to health. 16 And
for this reason did the Jews persecute Jesus, and seek to kill
him, because he had done these things on the Sabbath.

17 But Jesus answered them: My Father works till now, and
I also work. 18 For this reason, therefore, the Jews sought the
more to kill him, because he had not only broken the Sabbath,
but also said that God was his own father, making himself equal
with God.

19 Then Jesus answered and said to them: Verily, verily I say
to you, the Son can do nothing of himself, but what he sees the
Father do; for whatever things he does, these also the Son does
in like manner. 20 For the Father loves the Son, and shows him
all things that he himself does; and he will show him greater
works than these, that you may be astonished. 21 For as the
Father raises the dead, and makes them alive, so also the Son
makes alive whom he will. 22 For the Father judges no one, but
has given all judicial authority to the Son; 23 that all may honor
the Son, as they honor the Father. He that honors not the Son,
honors not the Father who sent him.

24 Verily, verily I say to you, He that hears my word, and believes on him that sent me, has eternal life, and comes not into
condemnation, but has passed from death into life. 25 Verily,
verily I say to you, The hour is coming, and now is, when the
dead shall hear the voice of the Son of God, and those who hear,
shall live. 26 For as the Father has life in himself, so has he
given to the Son also to have life in himself; 27 and he has given
him authority to execute judgment also, because he is the Son
of man. 28 Be not astonished at this; for the hour is coming in
which all that are in the graves shall hear his voice, 29 and shall
come forth; those who have done good, to the resurrection of

life, and those who have done evil, to the resurrection of condemnation. 30 I can of myself do nothing. As I hear, I judge;
and my judgment is just, because I seek not my own will, but
the will of him that sent me.

31 If I testify concerning myself, my testimony is not worthy
of credit. 32 There is another that testifies concerning me, and
I know that the testimony which he testifies concerning me is
worthy of credit. 33 You sent to John, and he bore testimony to
the truth. 34 But I receive not testimony from man; yet I say
these things that you may be saved. 35 He was the burning and
shining lamp; and you were willing, for a time, to rejoice in his
light. 36 But I have testimony greater than that of John; for
the works which the Father has given me to finish, these very
works which I do, testify concerning me, that the Father has
sent me. 37 And the Father, who sent me, has testified concerning me. You have neither heard his voice at any time, nor seen
his shape. 38 And his word you have not remaining in you; for
whom he has sent, him you believe not.

39 You search the Scriptures, because in them you think you
have eternal life; and these are they which testify concerning
me: 40 and yet you refuse to come to me, that you may have
life. 41 I receive not honor from men. 42 But I know you, that
you have not the love of God in you. 43 I have come in my
Father's name, and you receive me not; if another should come
in his own name, him would you receive. 44 How can you believe who receive honor one from another, and seek not the honor
that comes from God alone? 45 Think not that I will accuse you
to the Father: there is one that accuses you, Moses, in whom
you trust. 46 For if you had believed Moses, you would have
believed me; for he wrote of me. 47 But if you believe not his
writings, how shall you believe my words?

VI. 1 After these things Jesus went away to the other side of
the sea of Galilee, which is the sea of Tiberias. 2 And a great
multitude followed him, because they had seen the signs which
he did in the case of the sick. 3 And Jesus went up into the
mountain, and sat there with his disciples. 4 And the passover,
the feast of the Jews, was near. 5 Then Jesus, lifting up his
eyes, and seeing that a great multitude was coming to him, said
to Philip: Whence shall we buy bread that these may eat?
6 But this he said to try him; for he himself knew what he was
about to do.

7 Philip answered him: Two hundred denarii worth of bread
is not enough for them, that each may take a little. 8 One of
his disciples, Andrew, the brother of Simon Peter, said to him:
9 There is a lad here that has five barley loaves, and two little
fishes; but what are these among so many? 10 But Jesus said:
Make the men recline. Now, there was much grass in the place.
So the men reclined, in number about five thousand. 11 And
Jesus took the loaves, and after giving thanks, distributed them
to the disciples, and the disciples to those who had reclined;
and in like manner of the fishes, as much as they wished.
12 And when they were satisfied, he said to his disciples: Gather
up the broken pieces which remain, that nothing be lost.
13 Then they gathered them up, and filled twelve baskets with
the broken pieces of the five barley loaves, which remained after
they had eaten.

14 Then the men, after having seen the sign which Jesus did,
said: This is, in truth, the prophet that was to come into the
world. 15 Therefore, Jesus perceiving that they were about to
come and take him by force, to make him king, withdrew into
the mountain himself alone.

16 And when evening had come, his disciples went down to
the sea, 17 and, having entered the ship, went across the sea
toward Capernaum. And it was now dark, and Jesus had not
come to them. 18 And the sea arose by reason of a great wind
that was blowing. 19 Then, having rowed about twenty-five or
thirty furlongs, they saw Jesus walking on the sea, and coming
near the ship; and they were afraid. 20 But he said to them:
It is I; be not afraid. 21 Then they willingly received him into
the ship; and immediately the ship was at the land to which
they were going.

22 The next day, the multitude that stood on the other side of
the sea, seeing that no other boat had been there but the one
which his disciples had entered, and that Jesus had not entered
the boat with his disciples, but that his disciples had gone away
alone; (23 but there came other boats from Tiberias near the
place where they had eaten bread, after the Lord had given
thanks;) 24 when, therefore, the multitude saw that neither
Jesus nor his disciples were there, they also entered the ships,
and came to Capernaum, seeking Jesus.

25 And finding him on the opposite side of the sea, they said
to him: Rabbi, when didst thou come hither? 26 Jesus answered
them, and said: Verily, verily I say to you, You seek me, not

because you saw the signs, but because you ate of the loaves,
and were satisfied. 27 Labor not for the food that perishes, but
for the food that endures to life eternal, which the Son of man
will give you; for him has God the Father attested. 28 Then
they said to him: What shall we do, that we may work the
works of God? 29 Jesus answered and said to them: This is
the work of God, that you believe on him whom he has sent.
30 Therefore, they said to him: What sign do you show, then,
that we may see, and believe you? What work do you perform?
31 Our fathers ate the manna in the wilderness; as it is written,
He gave them bread from heaven to eat.

32 Then Jesus said to them: Verily, verily I say to you, Moses
did not give you the bread from heaven; but my Father gives
you the true bread from heaven. 33 For the bread of God is he
who comes down from heaven, and gives life to the world.
34 Then they said to him: Lord, evermore give us this bread.
35 Jesus said to them: I am the bread of life; he that comes to
me shall never hunger; he that believes on me shall never thirst.
36 But I said to you, that you have seen me, and yet you do not
believe. 37 All that the Father gives me, will come to me; and
him that comes to me, I will by no means cast out. 38 For I
came down from heaven, not to do my own will, but the will of
him that sent me. 39 And this is the will of him who sent me,
that of all that he gives me, I shall lose nothing, but shall raise
it up at the last day. 40 For this is the will of him that sent me,
that every one who sees the Son, and believes on him, may have
eternal life; and I will raise him up at the last day.

41 Then the Jews murmured at him, because he said, I am the
bread that came down from heaven. 42 And they said: Is not
this Jesus, the son of Joseph, whose father and mother we
know? How, then, does he say, I came down from heaven?
43 Jesus answered and said to them: Murmur not among yourselves; 44 no man can come to me, unless the Father, who sent
me, draw him; and I will raise him up at the last day. 45 It
is written in the prophets, and they shall all be taught of God.
Every one that hears from the Father, and learns, comes to me.
46 Not that any one has seen the Father, but he who is from
God; he has seen the Father.

47 Verily, verily I say to you, He that believes on me has
eternal life. 48 I am the bread of life. 49 Your fathers ate the
manna in the wilderness, and died. 50 This is the bread which
comes down from heaven, that any one may eat of it, and not

die. 51 I am the bread that lives, which came down from heaven. If any one eat of this bread, he shall live forever. And the bread that I will give is my flesh, which I will give for the life of the world.

52 The Jews, therefore, contended among themselves, saying: How can this man give us his flesh to eat? 53 Then Jesus said to them: Verily, verily I say to you, Unless you eat the flesh of the Son of man, and drink his blood, you have no life in you. 54 He that eats my flesh and drinks my blood, has eternal life, and I will raise him up at the last day; 55 for my flesh is food indeed, and my blood is drink indeed. 56 He that eats my flesh and drinks my blood, dwells in me, and I in him. 57 As the living Father has sent me, and I live by the Father, so he that eats me, even he shall live by me. 58 This is the bread that came down from heaven; not as your fathers ate the manna, and died; he that eats this bread shall live forever.

59 These things he spoke in the synagogue, as he taught in Capernaum. 60 Therefore, many of his disciples, when they heard him, said: This is a hard saying; who can hear it? 61 But Jesus, knowing in himself that his disciples murmured at it, said to them: Does this offend you? 62 Then, what if you should see the Son of man go up where he was before? 63 It is the spirit that makes alive; the flesh profits nothing; the words that I speak to you are spirit and life. 64 But there are some among you who believe not. For Jesus knew from the beginning who they were that believed not, and who he was that would betray him. 65 And he said: For this reason I said to you: No one can come to me unless it be given him from my Father.

66 After this, many of his disciples went back, and walked with him no more. 67 Then Jesus said to the twelve: Will you also go away? 68 Simon Peter answered him: Lord, to whom shall we go? Thou hast the words of eternal life; 69 and we believe, and know that thou art the Christ, the Son of God. 70 Jesus answered them: Have I not chosen you twelve, and one of you is a devil? 71 He spoke of Judas Iscariot, the son of Simon; for he was about to deliver him up, being one of the twelve.

VII. 1 And after this Jesus walked in Galilee: for he would not walk in Judea, because the Jews sought to kill him.

2 Now the feast of tabernacles, a feast of the Jews, was near. 3 Then his brothers said to him: Depart hence, and go into

Judea, that your disciples may see your works which you do;
4 for no one does any thing in secret, while he himself seeks to
be before the public. If you do these things, show yourself to
the world. 5 For neither did his brothers believe on him. 6 Then
Jesus said to them: My time has not yet come; but your time
is always ready. 7 The world can not hate you; but me it hates,
because I testify of it, that its works are evil. 8 Do you go up
to this feast. I go not up now to this feast, because my time
has not yet fully come. 9 These things said he to them, and remained in Galilee. 10 But when his brothers had gone up, then
he also went up to the feast, not openly, but, as it were, in
secret.

11 Then the Jews sought for him at the feast, and said: Where
is he? 12 And there was much murmuring among the multitudes concerning him. Some said: He is a good man. Others
said: No; but he deceives the multitude. 13 However, no one
spoke openly of him, for fear of the Jews.

14 Now in the middle of the feast, Jesus went up into the
temple, and taught. 15 And the Jews were astonished, and said:
How has this man a knowledge of letters, having never been
taught? 16 Then Jesus answered and said: My teaching is not
mine, but his who sent me. 17 If any one will do his will, he
shall know with respect to the teaching, whether it is of God,
or I speak of myself. 18 He who speaks of himself, seeks his
own glory; he who seeks the glory of him that sent him, he is
true, and there is no unrighteousness in him. 19 Did not Moses
give you the law? and not one of you keeps the law. Why do
you seek to kill me? 20 The multitude answered and said: You
have a demon: who seeks to kill you?

21 Jesus answered and said to them: I have done one work,
and you are all astonished on account of this. 22 Moses gave
you circumcision, (not that it is of Moses, but of the fathers,)
and you circumcise a man on the Sabbath-day. 23 If a man receives circumcision on the Sabbath-day, that the law of Moses
may not be broken, are you angry with me, because I have restored the entire man to health on the Sabbath-day? 24 Judge
not according to appearance, but judge righteous judgment.

25 Then said some of the men of Jerusalem: Is not this he
whom they seek to kill? 26 and, lo, he is speaking boldly, and
they say nothing to him. Have the rulers really learned that
this is the Christ? 27 But we know this man, whence he is.
But when the Christ comes, no one knows whence he is.

[28] Then Jesus cried out in the temple, as he was teaching, and
said: You both know me, and you know whence I am; and I
have not come of myself, but he who sent me is true, whom you
know not. [29] But I know him, because I am from him, and he
has sent me. [30] Then they sought to take him; yet no one laid
his hand on him, because his hour had not yet come. [31] And
many of the multitude believed on him, and said: When the
Christ comes, will he do more signs than these which this man
has done?

[32] The Pharisees heard the multitude murmuring such things
concerning him; and the Pharisees and chief priests sent attendants to take him. [33] Then Jesus said to them: Yet a little
while I am with you, and I go away to him that sent me.
[34] You will seek me, and shall not find me; and where I am, you
can not come. [35] Then the Jews said among themselves:
Whither is this man about to go, that we shall not find him?
Is he about to go to those who are dispersed among the Greeks,
and to teach the Greeks? [36] What means this saying which he
uttered, You will seek me, and will not find me; and, Where I
am you can not come?

[37] On the last day, the great day of the feast, Jesus stood and
cried, saying: If any one thirst, let him come to me and drink.
[38] He that believes on me, as the Scripture has said, from his
inner self shall flow rivers of living water. [39] But this he spoke
of the Spirit, which those who believe on him were about to receive; for the Holy Spirit had not yet been given, because Jesus
had not yet been glorified. [40] Therefore, many of the multitude,
when they had heard this word, said: This is, in truth, the
prophet. [41] Others said: This is the Christ. But others said:
Does the Christ come out of Galilee? [42] Has not the Scripture
said that the Christ comes from the posterity of David, and
from Bethlehem, the town where David was? [43] So there was a
division among the multitude because of him. [44] And some of
them desired to take him; but no one laid hands on him.

[45] Then came the attendants to the chief priests and the Pharisees; and they said to them: Why have you not brought him?
[46] The attendants answered: Never did man speak like this man.
[47] Then the Pharisees answered them: Are you also deceived?
[48] Has any one of the rulers, or of the Pharisees believed on
him? [49] But this multitude that know not the law are cursed.
[50] Nicodemus said to them (he that came to Jesus by night, being
one of them): [51] Does our law condemn a man unless it first hear

from him, and know what he does? 52 They answered and said
to him: Are you also from Galilee? Search, and see that out
of Galilee arises no prophet.
53 And every one departed to his own house.

VIII. 1 But Jesus went to the mount of Olives. 2 And in the
morning he again entered the temple, and all the people came
to him, and he sat down and taught them. And the scribes
and Pharisees brought to him a woman who had been detected
in adultery; and they made her stand in the midst, 4 and said
to him: Teacher, this woman was detected in adultery; in the
very act. 5 Now Moses, in his law, commanded us, that such
should be stoned; but what say you? 6 This they said to tempt
him, that they might bring an accusation against him. But
Jesus stooped down, and with his finger wrote on the ground.
7 But as they continued to ask him, he stood up, and said to
them: Let him among you who is without sin, first throw a
stone at her. 8 And again he stooped down and wrote on the
ground. 9 But having heard him, and being convicted by their
conscience, they went out, one by one, beginning from the oldest,
even to the last. And Jesus was left alone, and the woman
standing in the midst. 10 And when Jesus stood up, and saw
no one but the woman, he said to her: Woman, where are those
who accused you? Has no one condemned you? 11 She said:
No one, sir. Jesus said to her: Neither do I condemn you; go,
and sin no more.
12 Then Jesus spoke to them again, saying: I am the light of
the world; he that follows me shall not walk in darkness, but
shall have the light of life. 13 Then the Pharisees said to him:
You testify concerning yourself; your testimony is not worthy
of credit. 14 Jesus answered and said to them: Though I testify
concerning myself, my testimony is worthy of credit; for I
know whence I came, and whither I go. But you know not
whence I came, and whither I go. 15 You judge according to
the flesh; I judge no man. 16 And yet if I judge, my judgment
is true, because I am not alone, but I and the Father who sent
me. 17 It is also written in your law, the testimony of two is
worthy of credit. 18 I am one that testify concerning myself,
and the Father who sent me, testifies of me.
19 Then they said to him: Where is your Father? Jesus answered: You know neither me, nor my Father. If you had
known me, you would have known my Father also. 20 These

words Jesus spoke in the treasury, as he taught in the temple;
and no one laid hands on him, because his hour had not yet
come.
[21] Then spoke Jesus to them again: I go away, and you will
seek me, and in your sin you shall die; whither I go, you can
not come. [22] Then said the Jews: Will he kill himself, because
he says, Whither I go, you can not come? [23] And he said to
them: You are from beneath, I am from above; you are of this
world, I am not of this world. [24] Therefore said I to you, that
you shall die in your sins. For if you believe not that I am
He, you shall die in your sins. [25] Then they said to him: Who
are you? And Jesus said to them: The same that I said to you
at the beginning. [26] I have many things to say, and to judge
with respect to you; but he that sent me is true; and what
things I have heard from him, these I speak to the world.
[27] They knew not that he was speaking to them of the Father.
[28] Then said Jesus to them: When you have lifted up the Son
of man, then you will know that I am He, and that I do nothing of myself, but as the Father has taught me I speak these
things. [29] And he that sent me is with me. The Father has
not left me alone, because I always do what is pleasing to
him.
[30] While he was speaking these words, many believed on him.
[31] Then said Jesus to those Jews that believed on him: If you
continue in my word, you are my disciples indeed, [32] and you
shall know the truth, and the truth shall make you free.
[33] They answered him: We are the posterity of Abraham, and
have never been in bondage to any one. How say you, You
shall be made free?
[34] Jesus answered them: Verily, verily I say to you, whoever
works sin is the servant of sin. [35] The servant continues not
in the house forever; but the Son continues forever. [36] Therefore, if the Son make you free, you shall be free indeed. [37] I
know that you are the posterity of Abraham; yet you seek to
kill me, because my word has no place in you. [38] I speak what
I have seen with my Father, and you do what you have seen
with your father. [39] They answered and said to him: Abraham
is our father.
Jesus said to them: If you were the children of Abraham,
you would do the works of Abraham. [40] But now you seek to
kill me, a man that has spoken to you the truth, which I have
heard from God; this Abraham did not. [41] You do the works of

your father. They said to him: We were not born of lewdness;
we have one father, God.
42 Jesus said to them: If God were your father, you would
love me; for I came forth from God and have come hither; nor,
indeed, did I come of myself, but he sent me. 43 Why do you
not know what I say? Because you can not understand my
words. 44 You are of your father, the devil; and the desires of
your father you will do. He was a murderer from the beginning, and stood not in the truth, because there is no truth in
him. When he speaks that which is false, he speaks from what
is his own; for he is a liar, and the father of it. 45 But because
I speak the truth, you believe me not. 46 Which of you convicts
me of sin? If I speak the truth, why do you not believe me?
47 He that is of God, hears God's words. For this reason you do
not hear them, because you are not of God.
48 The Jews answered, and said to him: Do we not well say
that you are a Samaritan, and have a demon? 49 Jesus answered: I have not a demon; but I honor my Father, and you
dishonor me. 50 I seek not my own glory; there is one that
seeks and judges. 51 Verily, verily I say to you, if any one will
keep my word, he shall never see death.
52 Then said the Jews to him: Now we know that you have a
demon. Abraham is dead, and the prophets; and you say, If a
man keep my word, he shall never taste of death. 53 Are you
greater than our father Abraham, who is dead? And the
prophets are dead; whom do you make yourself?
54 Jesus answered: If I honor myself, my honor is nothing;
it is my Father that honors me, of whom you say, that he is
your God. 55 And yet you have not known him. But I know
him; and if I should say that I do not know him, I should be
like yourselves, a liar. But I know him, and I keep his word.
56 Abraham, your father, rejoiced that he could see my day;
and he saw it, and was glad. 57 Then the Jews said to him:
You are not yet fifty years old, and have you seen Abraham?
58 Jesus said to them: Verily, verily I say to you, before Abraham came into being, I was. 59 Then they took up stones to
throw at him. But Jesus concealed himself, and went out of
the temple, going through the midst of them; and so passed by.

IX. 1 And as he passed by, he saw a man that had been blind
from his birth. 2 And his disciples asked him, saying: Rabbi,
who sinned, this man, or his parents, that he was born blind?

3 Jesus answered: Neither this man sinned, nor his parents;
but that the works of God might be made manifest in him.
4 I must work the works of him that sent me, while it is day;
the night comes, when no man can work. 5 While I am in the
world, I am the light of the world. 6 Having said this, he spit
on the ground, and made clay of the spittle, and spread the
clay on the eyes of the blind man, 7 and said to him: Go, wash
in the pool of Siloam; which, translated, means Sent. He
went, therefore, and washed and came seeing.

8 Then his neighbors, and those who had before seen him, that
he was blind, said: Is not this he that sat and begged? 9 Some
said: It is he. Others: He is like him. But he said: I am he.
10 Then they said to him: How were your eyes opened? 11 He
answered and said: A man called Jesus made clay and spread it
on my eyes, and said to me: Go to the pool of Siloam and wash.
After I had gone and washed, I received my sight. 12 Then they
said to him: Where is he? He said: I know not.

13 They brought to the Pharisees him that had formerly been
blind. 14 And it was the Sabbath when Jesus made the clay
and opened his eyes. 15 Then again the Pharisees also inquired
of him how he had received his sight. He said to them: He
put clay on my eyes, and I washed, and I see. 16 Then some of
the Pharisees said: This man is not from God, for he keeps not
the Sabbath. Others said: How can a man that is a sinner do
such signs? And there was a division among them.

17 Again they said to the blind man: What say you of him,
seeing that he opened your eyes? He said: He is a prophet.
18 The Jews did not, therefore, believe concerning him, that he
had been blind, and had received his sight, till they called the
parents of him that had received his sight, 19 and asked them,
saying: Is this your son, who, you say, was born blind? How,
then, does he now see? 20 His parents answered them, and said:
We know that this is our son, and that he was born blind; 21 but
how he now sees we know not; or who opened his eyes we know
not. He is of age; ask him; he will speak for himself.

22 His parents said this, because they feared the Jews. For
the Jews had already agreed, that if any one should confess him
to be the Christ, he should be put out of the synagogue. 23 For
this reason his parents said: He is of age; ask him.

24 Then, the second time, they called the man who had been
blind, and said to him: Give glory to God; we know that this
man is a sinner. 25 He answered and said: If he is a sinner, I

know it not. One thing I do know, that having been blind, I
now see. 26 They said to him again: What did he for you?
How did he open your eyes? 27 He answered them: I have
already told you, and you did not understand; why would you
hear it again? Do you also wish to become his disciples?
28 They reviled him, and said: You are the disciple of that man;
but we are the disciples of Moses. 29 We know that God spoke
to Moses; but as for this man, we know not whence he is.

30 The man answered and said to them: Why, there is something wonderful in this, that you know not whence he is, and
yet he has opened my eyes. 31 We know that God hears not sinners; but if any one be a worshiper of God, and do his will, him
he hears. 32 Since the beginning it has not been heard that any
one opened the eyes of one who had been born blind. 33 If this
man were not of God, he could do nothing. 34 They answered
and said to him: You were wholly born in sins, and do you
teach us? And they cast him out.

35 Jesus heard that they had cast him out. And having found
him, he said to him: Do you believe on the Son of God? 36 He
answered and said: Who is he, sir, that I may believe on him?
37 Jesus said to him: You have seen him; and it is he that talks
with you. 38 He said: Lord, I believe; and he worshiped him.
39 And Jesus said: For judgment have I come into this world,
that those who see not, may see; and that those who see, may
become blind.

40 And some of the Pharisees who were with him, heard these
things, and said to him: Are we also blind? 41 Jesus said to
them: If you were blind, you would not have sin; but now you
say, We see; therefore your sin remains.

X. 1 Verily, verily I say to you, he that goes not through the
door into the sheepfold, but climbs up some other way, he is a
thief, and a robber. 2 But he that enters through the door, is
the shepherd of the sheep. 3 To him the door-keeper opens;
and the sheep hear his voice, and he calls his own sheep by
name, and leads them out. 4 And when he puts his own sheep
out, he goes before them; and the sheep follow him; for they
know his voice. 5 And a stranger they will not follow, but will
flee from him; for they know not the voice of strangers.

6 This parable spoke Jesus to them; but they knew not the
meaning of the things which he spoke to them. 7 Therefore
Jesus spoke again to them: Verily, verily I say to you, I am

the door of the sheep. [8] All that came before me were thieves
and robbers; but the sheep did not hear them. [9] I am the door:
if any one enters through me, he shall be saved; and he shall
go in and out, and find pasture. [10] The thief comes only to steal
and kill and destroy. I have come that they may have life, and
have it in abundance. [11] I am the good shepherd: the good
shepherd lays down his life for the sheep. [12] But he that is a
hireling, and not the shepherd, to whom the sheep do not belong, sees the wolf coming, and leaves the sheep, and flees; and
the wolf catches the sheep, and scatters them. [13] The hireling
flees because he is a hireling, and cares not for the sheep.

[14] I am the good shepherd, and I know my sheep, and am
known by mine. [15] As the Father knows me, I also know the
Father, and I lay down my life for the sheep. [16] And other
sheep I have, which are not of this fold; those, also, must I
bring, and they will hear my voice: and there shall be one
flock, one shepherd. [17] For this reason, my Father loves me,
because I lay down my life that I may take it again. [18] No one
takes it from me, but I lay it down of myself. I have authority
to lay it down, and I have authority to take it again. This
commandment I have received from my Father.

[19] Again, therefore, there was a division among the Jews, on
account of these words. [20] And many of them said: He has a
demon, and is mad; why do you hear him? [21] Others said:
These are not the words of one that has a demon. Can a demon
open the eyes of the blind?

[22] And the feast of the dedication was celebrated in Jerusalem,
and it was winter: [23] and Jesus was walking in the temple, in
Solomon's porch.

[24] Then the Jews came round him, and said to him: How long
do you keep us in suspense? If you are the Christ, tell us
plainly. [25] Jesus answered them: I have told you, and you do
not believe. The works which I do in my Father's name, these
testify of me. [26] But you believe not, because you are not of
my sheep. As I said to you, [27] my sheep hear my voice, and I
know them, and they follow me: [28] and I give them eternal life;
and they shall never perish, and no one shall take them out of
my hand. [29] My Father, who gave them to me, is greater than
all; and no one is able to take them out of my Father's hand.
[30] I and my Father are one.

[31] Then the Jews took up stones again, to stone him. [32] Jesus
answered them: Many good works have I showed you from my

Father: for which of these works do you stone me? [33] The
Jews answered and said to him: We do not stone you for a good
work, but for your impious words; and because you, being man,
make yourself God. [34] Jesus answered them: Is it not written
in your law, I said, you are gods? [35] If he called them gods,
to whom the word of God was committed, (and the Scripture
can not be made void,) [36] do you say of him, whom the Father
has sanctified, and sent into the world, You speak impiously,
because I said, I am the Son of God? [37] If I do not the works
of my Father, believe me not; [38] but if I do, though you believe
not me, believe the works, that you may know and believe that
the Father is in me, and I in him.

[39] Then they sought again to take him, but he escaped from
their hands. [40] And he went away again beyond the Jordan,
to the place where John first immersed, and there he abode.
[41] And many came to him, and said: John did no sign; but all
things that John said of this man were true. [42] And many who
were there believed on him.

XI. [1] Now a certain man was sick, Lazarus, of Bethany, the
village of Mary and Martha her sister. [2] It was the Mary that
anointed the Lord with ointment, and wiped his feet with her
hair, whose brother Lazarus was sick. [3] Therefore his sisters
sent to him, saying: Lord, behold, he whom thou lovest is sick.

[4] But when Jesus heard it, he said: This sickness is not to
death, but for the glory of God, that by it the Son of God may
be glorified. [5] Now, Jesus loved Martha, and her sister, and
Lazarus. [6] When, therefore, he heard that he was sick, he still
remained two days in the place where he was. [7] Then after this,
he said to his disciples: Let us go into Judea again. [8] His disciples said to him: Rabbi, the Jews just now sought to stone
thee, and art thou going thither again? [9] Jesus answered: Are
there not twelve hours in the day? If any one walks during
the day, he does not stumble, for he sees the light of this world.
[10] But if any one walks in the night, he stumbles, because there
is no light in him.

[11] Thus spoke he; and after this he said to them: Our friend
Lazarus sleeps; but I go that I may awake him out of sleep.
[12] Then his disciples said: Lord, if he sleeps, he will be saved.
[13] Jesus spoke of his death; but they thought that he spoke
of taking rest in sleep. [14] Therefore, Jesus then said to them
plainly: Lazarus is dead. [15] And I rejoice, on your account,

that I was not there, in order that you may believe. But let us
go to him. 16 Then Thomas, who is called Didymus, said to his
fellow-disciples: Let us also go, that we may die with him.

17 Then when Jesus came, he found that he had already been
four days in the tomb. 18 Now Bethany was near Jerusalem,
about fifteen furlongs off. 19 And many of the Jews had come
to Martha and Mary, to comfort them concerning their brother.
20 Then Martha, when she heard that Jesus was coming, went
out to meet him; but Mary sat still in the house. 21 Then
Martha said to Jesus: Lord, if thou hadst been here my brother
would not have died. 22 But even now, I know that whatever
thou wilt ask of God, God will give thee.

23 Jesus said to her: Your brother shall rise again. 24 Martha
said to him: I know that he will rise, in the resurrection at the
last day. 25 Jesus said to her: I am the resurrection and the
life; he that believes on me, though he were dead, yet shall he
live; 26 and he that lives and believes on me, shall never die.
Do you believe this? 27 She said to him: Yes, Lord; I believe
that thou art the Christ, the Son of God, who was to come into
the world.

28 And when she had said this, she went away, and called
Mary, her sister, secretly, saying: The Teacher has come, and
calls for you. 29 When she heard it, she rose quickly and came
to him. 30 Now Jesus had not yet come into the village, but
was in the place where Martha met him. 31 Then the Jews that
were with her in the house, and were comforting her, seeing
Mary rise and go out quickly, followed her, saying: She is
going to the tomb to weep there. 32 Then, when Mary came
where Jesus was, and saw him, she fell at his feet, saying to
him: Lord, if thou hadst been here, my brother would not
have died.

33 Then, when Jesus saw her weeping, and the Jews that came
with her weeping also, he was greatly moved in spirit, and
troubled; 34 and he said: Where have you laid him? They
said to him: Lord, come and see. 35 Jesus wept. 36 Then said
the Jews: See how he loved him! 37 And some of them said:
Could not he, who opened the eyes of the blind man, have
caused that even this man should not have died? 38 Then Jesus,
again greatly moved within himself, came to the tomb. It was
a cave, and a stone was laid against it. 39 Jesus said: Take
away the stone. Martha, the sister of him that was dead, said to
him: Lord, the body is offensive; for he has been dead four days.

40 Jesus said to her: Did I not tell you, that, if you would
believe, you should see the glory of God? 41 Then they took
away the stone. And Jesus lifted up his eyes and said: Father,
I thank thee, that thou hast heard me. 42 I know, indeed, that
thou dost always hear me. But for the sake of the multitnde
who stand around me, I have said it, that they may believe that
thou hast sent me. 43 And when he had said these things, he
cried with a loud voice, Lazarus, come forth. 44 And he that
had been dead came forth, bound hand and foot with grave-
clothes; and his face was bound around with a handkerchief.
Jesus said to them: Loose him, and let him go.

45 Then many of the Jews that had come to Mary, and who
saw what he had done, believed on him. 46 But some of them
went away to the Pharisees, and told them what Jesus had done.

47 Then the chief priests and the Pharisees called together the
Sanhedrim, and said: What are we doing? For this man does
many signs. 48 If we thus let him alone, all will believe on him,
and the Romans will come and take away our place and our
nation. 49 But one of them, Caiaphas, who was chief priest
that year, said to them: You know nothing, 50 nor do you consider that it is profitable for us, that one man should die for the
people, and not that the whole nation should perish. 51 But
this he did not speak of himself; but being chief priest that
year, he prophesied that Jesus was about to die for the nation;
52 and not for the nation only, but that he should gather into
one the children of God that were scattered abroad. 53 From
that day, therefore, they consulted together to put him to
death.

54 Therefore, Jesus no longer walked openly among the Jews,
but withdrew thence to the region near the wilderness, to a
city called Ephraim, and there he remained with his disciples.
55 And the passover of the Jews was near; and many went up
from the country to Jerusalem, before the passover, to purify
themselves. 56 Then they sought for Jesus, and said one to
another, as they stood in the temple: What think you, that
he will not come to the feast? 57 Now the chief priests and the
Pharisees had given orders, that, if any one knew where he was,
he should inform them, that they might take him.

XII. 1 Then, six days before the passover, Jesus came to
Bethany, where Lazarus was, who had been dead, whom he had
raised from the dead. 2 There they made him a supper, and

Martha served; but Lazarus was one of those who reclined at
table with him.

3 Then Mary took a pound of ointment of pure nard, very
costly, and anointed the feet of Jesus, and wiped his feet with
her hair. And the house was filled with the perfume of the
ointment. 4 Then said one of his disciples, Judas Iscariot, the
son of Simon, who was about to deliver him up: 5 Why was not
this ointment sold for three hundred denarii, and given to the
poor. 6 But he said this, not because he cared for the poor, but
because he was a thief, and had the purse, and took what was
put in it. 7 Then Jesus said: Let her alone; she has kept this
for the day of my burial. 8 For the poor you have always with
you; but me you have not always.

9 Therefore, a great multitude of the Jews learned that he was
there; and they came, not on account of Jesus only, but that
they might see Lazarus also, whom he had raised from the dead.
10 But the chief priests consulted that they might kill Lazarus
also, 11 because on account of him many of the Jews went away,
and believed on Jesus.

12 On the next day, a great multitude that had come to the
feast, having heard that Jesus was coming into Jerusalem,
13 took branches of palm-trees, and went out to meet him, and
cried: Hosanna, blessed is the king of Israel that comes in the
name of the Lord. 14 And Jesus, having found a young ass, sat
upon him, as it is written: 15 Fear not, daughter of Zion; behold, your king comes, sitting on the colt of an ass. 16 His disciples did not understand these things at first; but when Jesus
was glorified, then they remembered that these things were
written of him, and that they had done these things to him.

17 The multitude therefore that was with him, testified that
he had called Lazarus out of the tomb, and raised him from the
dead. 18 For this reason, also, the multitude met him, because
they had heard that he had done this sign. 19 Then the Pharisees said among themselves: You see that you gain nothing.
Behold, the world has gone after him.

20 Among those who came to worship at the feast were certain
Greeks. 21 These then came to Philip, who was of Bethsaida
of Galilee, and asked him, saying: Sir, we wish to see Jesus.
22 Philip came and told Andrew; and then Andrew and Philip
told Jesus. 23 But Jesus answered them, saying: The hour has
come that the Son of man must be glorified. 24 Verily, verily I
say to you, unless a grain of wheat fall into the ground and die,

it remains alone; but if it die, it produces much fruit. [25] He
that loves his life shall lose it; and he that hates his life in
this world shall keep it to eternal life. [26] If any one serve me,
let him follow me; and where I am, there shall my servant also
be. If any one serve me, him will my Father honor.

[27] Now is my soul troubled; and what shall I say? Father,
save me from this hour? But for this purpose came I to this
hour. [28] Father, glorify thy name. Then there came a voice
from heaven: I have glorified it, and will glorify it again.
[29] Then the multitude that stood by and heard it, said: It
thundered. Others said: An angel spoke to him. [30] Jesus answered and said: This voice came not for my sake, but for
yours. [31] Now is the judgment of this world: now is the
prince of this world cast out. [32] And I, if I be lifted up from
the earth, will draw all men to myself. [33] This he said, signifying what death he was about to die.

[34] The multitude answered him: We have heard out of the
law, that the Christ remains forever: and how say you that
the Son of man must be lifted up? Who is this Son of man?
[35] Then Jesus said to them: Yet a little while is the light with
you: walk while you have the light, lest the darkness overtake
you. For he that walks in the darkness knows not whither
he goes. [36] While you have the light, believe in the light, that
you may become the sons of light. These things spoke Jesus,
and he departed, and concealed himself from them.

[37] But though he had done so many signs in their presence,
yet they believed not on him, [38] that the word of Isaiah the
prophet might be fulfilled, which he spoke: Lord, who has believed our report? and to whom has the arm of the Lord been
revealed? [39] For this reason they could not believe, because
Isaiah said again: [40] He has blinded their eyes, and hardened
their heart, lest they should see with their eyes, and understand
with their heart, and should turn, and I should give them
health. [41] These things said Isaiah, when he saw his glory, and
spoke of him. [42] But yet, many even of the rulers believed on
him; but on account of the Pharisees, they would not confess
him, lest they should be put out of the synagogue; [43] for they
loved the glory of men more than the glory of God.

[44] Jesus cried, and said: He that believes on me, believes not
on me, but on him that sent me. [45] And he that sees me, sees
him that sent me. [46] I have come a light into the world, that
he who believes on me, may not remain in darkness. [47] And

if any one hear my words, and believe not, I judge him not;
for I came not to judge the world, but to save the world. 48 He
that rejects me, and receives not my words, has that which
judges him: the word which I have spoken, that shall judge
him in the last day. 49 For I have not spoken of myself: but
the Father who sent me, he gave me commandment what I
should say, and what I should speak. 50 And I know that his
commandment is life eternal. What things I speak therefore,
as the Father has said to me, so I speak.

XIII. 1 Now before the feast of the passover, Jesus knew
that his hour had come that he must go out of this world to
his Father; and having loved his own that were in the world,
he loved them to the end. 2 And supper being over, the devil
having already put it into the heart of Judas Iscariot, the son
of Simon, to deliver him up, 3 Jesus, knowing that the Father
had delivered all things into his hands, and that he had come
from God, and was going to God, 4 arose from supper, and laid
aside his garments, and taking a towel, he girded himself.
5 Then he poured water into a basin, and began to wash his
disciples' feet, and to wipe them with the towel with which he
was girded.

6 Then he came to Simon Peter; and Peter said to him: Lord,
dost thou wash my feet? 7 Jesus answered and said to him:
What I am doing you know not now, but you will know hereafter. 8 Peter said to him: Thou shalt never wash my feet.
Jesus answered him: Unless I wash you, you have no part
with me. 9 Simon Peter said to him: Lord, not my feet only,
but my hands and my head. 10 Jesus said to him: He that has
bathed needs nothing else save to wash his feet, but is wholly
clean. And you are clean, but not all. 11 For he knew who
would deliver him up; for this reason he said, You are not all
clean.

12 Therefore, when he had washed their feet, and had taken
his garments, he reclined at table again, and said to them: Do
you understand what I have done for you? 13 You call me
Teacher and Lord; and you say well, for so I am. 14 If, then,
I, your Lord and your Teacher, have washed your feet, you also
ought to wash one another's feet. 15 For I have given you an
example, that you also may do as I have done for you. 16 Verily,
verily I say to you, the servant is not greater than his master,
nor is he that is sent greater than he that sent him. 17 If you

know these things, blessed are you, if you do them. 18 I speak not of you all. I know whom I have chosen: but that the Scripture may be fulfilled, He that eats bread with me has lifted up his heel against me. 19 I tell you this now, before it comes to pass, that when it comes to pass, you may believe that I am he.

20 Verily, verily I say to you, he that receives him that I shall send, receives me; and he that receives me, receives him that sent me.

21 When Jesus had spoken these things, he was troubled in spirit, and testified and said: Verily, verily I say to you, that one of you will deliver me up. 22 Then the disciples looked at one another, doubting of whom he spoke. 23 There was reclining on the bosom of Jesus, one of his disciples, whom Jesus loved. 24 Then Simon Peter beckoned to this one, that he should inquire who it was of whom he spoke. 25 And he that was reclining on Jesus' breast, said to him: Lord, who is it?

26 Jesus answered: It is he to whom I shall give this morsel after I have dipped it. And when he had dipped the morsel, he gave it to Judas Iscariot, the son of Simon. 27 And after the morsel *was given*, then Satan entered into him. Then Jesus said to him: What you do, do quickly. 28 But none of those who reclined at table with him knew for what purpose he said this to him. 29 For some thought, because Judas had the purse, that Jesus had said to him: Buy what we need for the feast; or, that he should give something to the poor. 30 Then, on receiving the morsel, he immediately went out; and it was night.

31 When he had gone out, Jesus said: Now is the Son of man glorified, and God is glorified in him. 32 If God is glorified in him, God will also glorify him in himself, and will immediately glorify him. 33 Little children, yet a little while I am with you. You will seek me; and, as I said to the Jews, whither I go, you can not come, so now I say to you. 34 A new commandment I give to you, That you love one another; as I have loved you, that you also love one another. 35 By this shall all men know that you are my disciples, if you have love one for another.

36 Simon Peter said to him: Lord, whither goest thou? Jesus answered him: Whither I go, you can not follow me now; but you shall follow me hereafter. 37 Peter said to him: Lord, why can I not follow thee now? I will lay down my life for thee. 38 Jesus answered him: Will you lay down your life for

me? Verily, verily I say to you, the cock will not crow till you
have denied me three times.

XIV. 1 Let not your heart be troubled; believe in God; believe also in me. 2 In my Father's house are many mansions;
if it were not so, I would have told you. I go to prepare a
place for you. 3 And if I go and prepare a place for you, I will
come again and take you with myself, that where I am, you may
be also. 4 And whither I go you know, and the way you know.
5 Thomas said to him: Lord, we know not whither thou goest,
and how can we know the way? 6 Jesus said to him: I am the
way, and the truth, and the life; no one comes to the Father,
but through me. 7 If you had known me, you would have
known my Father also. And from this time you know him,
and have seen him.
8 Philip said to him: Lord, show us the Father, and we shall
be content. 9 Jesus said to him: Have I been so long with you,
and have you not known me, Philip? He that has seen me,
has seen the Father; and how say you, Show us the Father?
10 Do you not believe that I am in the Father, and that the
Father is in me? The words that I speak to you, I speak not
of myself. The Father who dwells in me, he does the works.
11 Believe me, that I am in the Father, and that the Father is in
me. If not, believe me on account of the works themselves.
12 Verily, verily I say to you, he that believes on me, the works
that I do he also shall do. Even greater works than these
shall he do, because I go to my Father; 13 and whatever you
ask in my name, I will do, that the Father may be glorified in
the Son. 14 If you ask any thing in my name, I will do it.
15 If you love me, keep my commandments; 16 and I will pray
the Father, and he will give you another Advocate, that he may
dwell with you forever; 17 the Spirit of the truth, whom the
world can not receive, because it neither sees him nor knows
him. But you know him, because he dwells with you, and
shall be in you. 18 I will not leave you orphans; I am coming
to you. 19 Yet a little while, and the world sees me no more;
but you shall see me. Because I live, you also shall live.
20 In that day you shall know that I am in my Father, and
you in me, and I in you. 21 He that has my commandments
and keeps them, he it is that loves me; and he that loves me
shall be loved by my Father; and I will love him, and will
manifest myself to him.

[22] Judas, not Iscariot, said to him: Lord, how is it that thou
wilt manifest thyself to us, and not to the world? [23] Jesus answered and said to him: If any one loves me, he will keep my
word, and my Father will love him, and we will come to him,
and make our abode with him. [24] He that loves me not, keeps
not my words; and the word which you hear is not mine, but
the Father's who sent me.
[25] These things have I spoken to you, while I am yet with you.
[26] But the Advocate, the Holy Spirit, whom the Father will
send in my name, he shall teach you all things, and bring to
your remembrance all things that I have spoken to you. [27] Peace
I leave to you; my peace I give to you; not as the world gives,
do I give to you. Let not your heart be troubled, and let it not
be afraid. [28] You have heard that I said to you, I am going
away, and am coming again to you. If you loved me, you
would rejoice, because I go to the Father; for my Father is
greater than I. [29] And now I have told you before it comes to
pass, that when it does come to pass, you may believe. [30] I will
not talk much more with you; for the prince of this world is
coming, and has nothing in me. [31] But *this takes place* that the
world may know that I love the Father, and even as he gave
me commandment, so I do. Arise, let us go hence.

XV. [1] I am the true vine, and my Father is the vine-dresser.
[2] Every branch in me that bears no fruit, he takes away; and
every branch that bears fruit, he prunes, that it may bear more
fruit. [3] Now are you pure, through the word which I have
spoken to you. [4] Abide in me, and I will abide in you. As
the branch can not bear fruit of itself, unless it abide in the
vine, so neither can you, unless you abide in me. [5] I am the
vine, you are the branches. He that abides in me and I in him,
he will bear much fruit; for apart from me you can do nothing.
[6] If any one abide not in me, he is thrown out as a branch,
and withers; and such are gathered, and thrown into the fire,
and burned. [7] If you abide in me, and my words abide in you,
you shall ask what you will, and it shall be done for you. [8] In
this is my Father glorified, that you bear much fruit; and in
this you will be my disciples. [9] As the Father has loved me, so
have I loved you; abide in my love. [10] If you keep my commandments, you shall abide in my love, even as I have kept my
Father's commandments, and abide in his love.
[11] These things have I spoken to you, that my joy may remain

in you, and that your joy may be full. [12] This is my commandment: That you love one another, as I have loved you. [13] Greater
love has no man than this, that one should lay down his life for
his friends. [14] You are my friends, if you do whatever I command you. [15] I no longer call you servants, because the servant
knows not what his master does. But I have called you friends;
for all things that I have heard from my Father, I have made
known to you. [16] You have not chosen me, but I have chosen
you, and appointed you, that you may go and bring forth fruit,
and that your fruit may remain; that whatever you ask of the
Father in my name, he may give you. [17] These things I command
you, that you may love one another.

[18] If the world hates you, you know that it hated me before it
hated you. [19] If you were of the world, the world would love
its own. But because you are not of the world, but I have
chosen you out of the world, therefore the world hates you.
[20] Remember the word which I spoke to you, The servant is not
greater than his master. If they have persecuted me, they will
also persecute you; if they have kept my word, they will keep
yours also. [21] But all these things they will do to you on my
account, because they know not him that sent me. [22] If I had
not come and spoken to them, they would not have had sin; but
now they have no excuse for their sin. [23] He that hates me,
hates my Father also. [24] If I had not done among them the
works that no other man has done, they would have had no sin;
but now they have both seen, and hated both me and my Father.
[25] But this is so, that the word may be fulfilled which is written
in their law, They hated me without a cause.

[26] But when the Advocate has come, whom I will send to you
from my Father, the Spirit of the truth, which proceeds from
the Father, he will testify of me; [27] and you also will testify,
because you have been with me from the beginning.

XVI. [1] These things have I spoken to you, that you may not
be ensnared. [2] They will put you out of the synagogues; indeed,
the time is coming, when he that kills you, will think that he
is offering service to God. [3] And these things they will do, because they know neither the Father nor me. [4] But these things
I have told you, that, when the time has come, you may remember that I told you of them. But these things I did not tell you
at the beginning, because I was with you. [5] And now I go to
him that sent me, and no one of you asks me, Whither goest

thou? [6] But because I have spoken these things to you, sorrow
has filled your heart.

[7] But yet I tell you the truth: it is profitable for you that
I go away. For if I go not away, the Advocate will not come
to you. But if I go away, I will send him to you. [8] And when
he has come, he will convince the world of sin, and of righteousness, and of judgment. [9] Of sin, because they believe not
on me; [10] of righteousness, because I go to my Father, and you
see me no more; [11] of judgment, because the prince of this world
is judged.

[12] I have yet many things to say to you; but you can not
bear them now. [13] But when he, the Spirit of the truth, has
come, he will guide you into all the truth; for he will not speak
of himself; but what he hears, that will he speak, and he will
show you things to come. [14] He will glorify me; for he will
take of mine, and show it to you. [15] All things that the Father
has are mine; for this reason I said, that he will take of mine,
and show it to you. [16] A little while, and you will not see me;
and again, a little while, and you will see me, because I go to
the Father.

[17] Then some of his disciples said one to another: What is
this that he says to us, A little while, and you will not see me;
and again, a little while, and you will see me? and, Because I
go to the Father? [18] Therefore they said: What is this that he
says, The little while? We know not what he says. [19] Then
Jesus knew that they wished to ask him; and he said to them:
Are you inquiring of one another about this, because I said, A
little while and you will not see me; and again, a little while,
and you will see me? [20] Verily, verily I say to you, you shall
weep and lament, but the world will rejoice. You shall be sorrowful, but your sorrow shall be turned into joy. [21] A woman,
when she is in labor, has sorrow, because her hour has come;
but when the child is born, she no longer remembers the pain,
for joy that a man is born into the world. [22] You, therefore,
have sorrow now; but I shall see you again, and your heart will
rejoice, and your joy no one takes from you. [23] And in that day
you shall ask nothing of me; verily, verily I say to you, whatever you ask of the Father in my name, he will give you. [24] Till
this time you have asked for nothing in my name; ask, and you
shall receive, that your joy may be full.

[25] These things I have spoken to you in parables; the time is
coming when I will no longer speak to you in parables, but will

teach you plainly concerning the Father. 26 In that day you
shall ask in my name; and I say not to you, that I will ask the
Father in your behalf; 27 for the Father himself loves you, because you have loved me, and have believed that I came forth
from God. 28 I came forth from the Father, and have come into
the world: again I leave the world, and go to the Father.

29 His disciples said to him: Lo, now thou speakest plainly,
and speakest no parable. 30 Now we know that thou knowest
all things, and hast no need that any one should ask thee. By
this we believe that thou hast come forth from God. 31 Jesus
answered them: Do you now believe? 32 Behold, the hour is
coming, and has now come, in which you shall be scattered,
each one to his own home, and shall leave me alone: and yet I
am not alone, for the Father is with me. 33 These things I have
spoken to you, that in me you may have peace. In the world
you shall have affliction, but be of good courage; I have overcome the world.

XVII. 1 Jesus spoke these words, and lifted up his eyes to
heaven, and said: Father, the hour has come: glorify thy Son,
that thy Son may also glorify thee; 2 as thou hast given him
authority over all flesh, that he may give eternal life to all
that thou hast given him. 3 And this is life eternal, to know
thee, the only true God, and Jesus Christ whom thou hast sent.
4 I have glorified thee on the earth; I have finished the work
which thou gavest me to do. 5 And now, Father, glorify me
with thyself, with the glory which I had with thee before the
world was.

6 I have made known thy name to the men that thou gavest
me out of the world. Thine they were, and thou gavest them
to me, and they have kept thy word. 7 Now they know that all
things that thou hast given me are from thee; 8 for the words
which thou gavest me I have given them; and they have received
them, and they know surely that I came forth from thee, and
they believe that thou didst send me. 9 I pray for them; I pray
not for the world, but for them whom thou hast given me; for
they are thine. 10 And all mine are thine, and thine are mine,
and I am glorified in them. 11 And I am no longer in the
world; but these are in the world, and I come to thee. Holy
Father, keep in thy name those whom thou hast given me, that
they may be one, as we are one. 12 While I was with them in
the world, I kept them in thy name. Those whom thou gavest

me, I have kept; and none of them is lost but the son of perdition, that the Scripture may be fulfilled. 13 And now I come
to thee; and these things I speak in the world, that they may
have my joy fulfilled in themselves.

14 I have given them thy word; and the world has hated them,
because they are not of the world, even as I am not of the world.
15 I do not pray thee to take them out of the world, but to keep
them from the Evil One. 16 They are not of the world, as I am
not of the world. 17 Sanctify them through thy truth; thy word
is truth. 18 As thou hast sent me into the world, so I send them
into the world; 19 and for them I sanctify myself, that they also
may be sanctified through the truth. 20 I pray, not for these
only, but for those also who shall believe on me through their
word; 21 that they all may be one, as thou, Father, art in me,
and I in thee, that they may be one in us: that the world may
believe that thou hast sent me. 22 And the glory which thou
gavest me, I have given them, that they may be one, as we are
one; 23 I in them, and thou in me, that they may be made perfect in one, that the world may know that thou hast sent me,
and hast loved them, as thou hast loved me.

24 Father, I wish that they also, whom thou hast given me,
may be with me where I am, that they may behold my glory,
which thou hast given me; for thou didst love me before the
foundation of the world. 25 Righteous Father, though the world
has not known thee, yet I have known thee, and these have
known that thou hast sent me. 26 And I have made known to
them thy name, and will continue to make it known, that the
love with which thou hast loved me may be in them, and I in
them.

XVIII. 1 When Jesus had spoken these things, he went out
with his disciples beyond the brook Kedron, where was a garden, which he and his disciples entered. 2 And Judas, who delivered him up, also knew the place, because Jesus often went
thither with his disciples. 3 Judas, then, having received the
band of soldiers and attendants from the chief priests and Pharisees, came thither with torches and lamps and weapons.

4 Then Jesus, knowing all things that were coming upon him,
went forth, and said to them: Whom do you seek? 5 They answered him: Jesus the Nazarene. Jesus said to them: I am he.
Judas, also, who delivered him up, was standing among them.
6 Then, when he said to them, I am he, they went backward, and

fell to the ground. 7 Then he asked them again: Whom do
you seek? They said: Jesus the Nazarene. 8 Jesus answered:
I have told you that I am he. If, then, you seek me, let these
go away. 9 *This he said*, that the word might be fulfilled which
he had spoken: Of those whom thou hast given me, I have lost
none.
10 Then Simon Peter, who had a sword, drew it, and struck
the servant of the chief priest, and cut off his right ear. The
name of the servant was Malchus. 11 Then Jesus said to Peter:
Put up your sword into its scabbard. Shall I not drink the
cup that my Father has given me?
12 Then the band of soldiers, and the officer, and the attendants of the Jews, took Jesus and bound him, 13 and led him first
to Annas; for he was the father-in-law of Caiaphas, who was
chief priest that year. 14 It was Caiaphas who had given counsel to the Jews, that it was profitable that one man should die
for the people.
15 And Simon Peter followed Jesus, and so did another disciple.
And that other disciple was acquainted with the chief priest,
and he went in with Jesus into the palace of the chief priest.
16 But Peter stood without near the door. Then the other disciple, who was acquainted with the chief priest, went out and
spoke to the door-keeper, and brought Peter in. 17 Then the
maid-servant who kept the door said to Peter: Are you not also
one of the disciples of this man? He said: I am not. 18 And
the servants and attendants, having made a fire of coals, for it
was cold, were standing and warming themselves. And Peter
stood with them, and warmed himself.
19 Then the chief priest questioned Jesus concerning his disciples and his teaching. 20 Jesus answered him: I have spoken
openly to the world; I always taught in the synagogue, and in
the temple, where the Jews come together, and in secret I have
spoken nothing. 21 Why do you ask me? Ask those who have
heard, what things I said to them. Behold, they know what I
have said. 22 When he had spoken thus, one of the attendants,
who was standing by, struck Jesus with his open hand, saying:
Do you answer the chief priest thus? 23 Jesus answered him:
If I have spoken evil, testify of the evil; but if well, why do
you strike me? 24 Then Annas sent him bound to Caiaphas the
chief priest.
25 And Simon Peter was standing and warming himself. Then
they said to him: Are not you also one of his disciples? He

denied, and said: I am not. [26]One of the servants of the chief
priest, who was a kinsman of him whose ear Peter had cut off,
said: Did I not see you in the garden with him? [27]Then Peter
denied again. And immediately the cock crew.

[28]Then they led Jesus from Caiaphas to the governor's palace.
It was the morning hour. And, in order that they might not
be defiled, but that they might eat the passover, they did not
go into the governor's palace. [29]Then Pilate came out to them,
and said: What accusation do you bring against this man?
[30]They answered and said to him: If this man were not an
evil-doer, we would not have delivered him to you. [31]Then
Pilate said to them: Take him yourselves, and judge him according to your law. Then the Jews said to him: It is not
lawful for us to put any one to death; [32]that the word of Jesus
might be fulfilled, which he spoke, signifying by what death he
was about to die.

[33]Then Pilate again entered the governor's palace, and called
Jesus, and said to him: Are you the king of the Jews? [34]Jesus
answered him: Do you say this of yourself, or did others speak
to you of me? [35]Pilate answered: Am I a Jew? Your own
nation, and the chief priests have delivered you to me; what
have you done? [36]Jesus answered: My kingdom is not of this
world; if my kingdom were of this world, then would my servants fight, that I might not be delivered up to the Jews. But
now my kingdom is not hence. [37]Then Pilate said to him: You
are a king, then? Jesus answered: You say that I am a king.
For this purpose was I born, and for this purpose I came into
the world, that I might testify to the truth. Every one that is
of the truth, hears my voice. [38]Pilate said to him: What is
truth?

And when he had said this, he again came out to the Jews,
and said to them: I find no fault in him. [39]But you have a
custom, that I release to you one during the passover. Are you
willing, then, that I should release to you the king of the Jews?
[40]They all, then, cried out, saying: Not this man, but Barabbas.
Now Barabbas was a robber.

XIX. [1]Then Pilate, therefore, took Jesus and scourged him.
[2]And the soldiers plaited a crown of thorn-branches, and put it
upon his head; and they put on him a purple robe, [3]and said:
Hail, King of the Jews. And they struck him with their open
hands.

4 Then Pilate came out again, and said to them: Behold, I
bring him out to you, that you may know that I find no fault
in him. 5 Then Jesus came out, wearing the crown of thorn-
branches, and the purple robe. And Pilate said to them: Behold the man! 6 When the chief priests and their attendants
saw him, they cried out, saying: Crucify him, crucify him.
Pilate said to them: Do you take him and crucify him; for I
find no fault in him. 7 The Jews answered: We have a law, and
according to our law he ought to die, because he made himself
the Son of God.

8 Then, when Pilate heard this word, he was the more afraid;
9 and he went into the governor's palace again, and said to Jesus:
Whence are you? But Jesus gave him no answer. 10 Then
Pilate said to him: Do you not speak to me? Do you not know
that I have authority to crucify you, and authority to release
you? 11 Jesus answered: You could have no authority over me,
had it not been given you from above. Therefore, he that delivered me to you, has the greater sin.

12 After this Pilate sought to release him. But the Jews cried
out, saying: If you release this man, you are not Cæsar's friend.
Every one that makes himself a king, speaks against Cæsar.
13 Then Pilate, when he heard that word, led Jesus out, and sat
on the judgment-seat, in a place called the Pavement, but in
Hebrew, Gabbatha; 14 it was the preparation for the passover,
and about the third hour; and he said to the Jews, Behold your
king! 15 But they cried out: Away with him, away with him;
crucify him! Pilate said to them: Shall I crucify your king?
The chief priests answered: We have no king but Cæsar.
16 Then he, therefore, delivered him to them to be crucified.
And they took Jesus, and led him away.

17 And, bearing his cross, he went forth into a place called the
Place of a Skull, which is called, in Hebrew, Golgotha, 18 where
they crucified him, and with him two others, one on each side,
and Jesus in the middle.

19 And Pilate wrote a superscription, and put it on the cross;
and the writing was, JESUS THE NAZARENE, THE KING
OF THE JEWS. 20 Therefore many of the Jews read this
superscription, because the place where Jesus was crucified was
near the city. And it was written in Hebrew and in Greek and
in Latin. 21 Then the chief priests of the Jews said to Pilate:
Write not, The king of the Jews: but, that he said, I am the
king of the Jews. 22 Pilate answered: What I have written, I

have written. 23 Then the soldiers, when they had crucified
Jesus, took his clothing, and made four parts, to each soldier a
part; and they took his coat also. Now his coat was without
seam, woven from the top throughout. 24 Then they said, one
to another, let us not rend it, but cast lots for it, whose it shall
be. *This was done* that the Scripture might be fulfilled, which
says: They divided my clothing among them, and for my
vesture they did cast lots. The soldiers, therefore, did these
things.

25 Now there stood by the cross of Jesus his mother, and his
mother's sister, Mary the wife of Cleopas, and Mary Magdalene. 26 Then Jesus, seeing his mother and the disciple whom
he loved standing by, said to his mother: Woman, behold your
son. 27 Then he said to the disciple: Behold your mother. And
from that hour that disciple took her to his own home.

28 After this, Jesus knowing that all things were now accomplished, that the Scripture might be fulfilled, said: I thirst.
29 Now a vessel full of vinegar had been set there; and they
filled a sponge with vinegar, and put it upon a hyssop-stalk,
and put it to his mouth. 30 Therefore, when Jesus had received
the vinegar, he said: It is finished. And he bowed his head,
and gave up his spirit.

31 Then the Jews, as it was the preparation, that the bodies
might not remain on the cross on the Sabbath, for that Sabbath-
day was a great day, besought Pilate that their legs might be
broken, and that they might be taken down. 32 Then came the
soldiers, and broke the legs of the first, and of the other that
was crucified with him. 33 But when they came to Jesus, and
saw that he was already dead, they did not break his legs:
34 but one of the soldiers pierced his side with a spear; and
immediately there came out blood and water.

35 And he that saw it has given testimony, and his testimony
is true, and he knows that he speaks the truth, that you may
believe; 36 for these things were done that the Scripture might
be fulfilled: A bone of him shall not be broken. 37 And again
another Scripture says: They shall look on him whom they
pierced.

38 And after this, Joseph of Arimathea, who was a disciple of
Jesus, but secretly, for fear of the Jews, besought Pilate that
he might take away the body of Jesus. And Pilate gave him
permission. He then came and took away the body of Jesus.
39 Then came Nicodemus also, (who, at the first, had come to

Jesus by night,) bringing a mixture of myrrh and aloes, about
a hundred pounds. 40 Then they took the body of Jesus, and
bound it in linen cloths, with the spices, according to the Jewish custom of burying. 41 Now, in the place where he was crucified, there was a garden, and in the garden a new tomb, in
which no one had ever been laid. 42 There, then, on account
of the preparation-day of the Jews, they laid Jesus, for the
tomb was near.

XX. 1 And early on the first day of the week, while it was
yet dark, Mary Magdalene came to the tomb, and saw that the
stone had been taken away from the tomb. 2 Then she ran and
came to Simon Peter, and to the other disciple whom Jesus
loved, and said to them: They have taken away the Lord out
of the tomb, and we know not where they have laid him.
3 Then Peter and the other disciple went out, and came to the
tomb.

4 And the two ran together; and the other disciple outran
Peter, and came first to the tomb; 5 and he stooped down and
saw the linen cloths lying, but he did not go in. 6 Then came
Simon Peter, following him; and he went into the tomb, and
saw the linen cloths lying, 7 and the handkerchief that had been
on his head, not lying with the linen cloths, but folded in a
place by itself. 8 Then, therefore, the other disciple, who came
first to the tomb, went in, and saw, and believed. 9 For, as yet,
they did not know the Scripture, that he must rise from the
dead. 10 Then the disciples went away again by themselves.

11 But Mary stood without near the tomb, weeping; and as
she wept, she stooped down and looked into the tomb, 12 and saw
two angels in white raiment, sitting, the one at the head, and
the other at the foot, where the body of Jesus had lain. 13 And
they said to her: Woman, why do you weep? She said to them:
They have taken away my Lord, and I know not where they
have laid him. 14 Having said this, she turned back, and saw
Jesus standing, and knew not that it was Jesus.

15 Jesus said to her: Woman, why do you weep? Whom do
you seek? Supposing that it was the gardener, she said to him:
Sir, if you have taken him hence, tell me where you have laid
him, and I will take him away. 16 Jesus said to her: Mary.
She turned, and said to him: Rabboni; which is, translated,
Teacher. 17 Jesus said to her: Touch me not, for I have not
yet ascended to my Father: but go to my brethren, and say to

them, I ascend to my Father and your Father, and to my God
and your God. 18 Mary Magdalene came and told the disciples
that she had seen the Lord, and that he had said these things
to her.

19 Then, on that day, the first day of the week, when it was
evening, and the doors of the house in which the disciples were
assembled had been closed for fear of the Jews, Jesus came and
stood in the midst, and said to them: Peace be to you. 20 And
having said this, he showed them his hands and his side. Then
the disciples rejoiced, when they saw the Lord. 21 Then Jesus
said to them again: Peace be to you. As my Father has sent
me, so I send you. 22 And when he had said this, he breathed
on them, and said to them: Receive the Holy Spirit. 23 Whosever sins you forgive, they are forgiven them: whosever sins
you retain, they are retained.

24 But Thomas, one of the twelve, who is called Didymus, was
not with them when Jesus came. 25 Then the other disciples
said to him: We have seen the Lord. But he said to them:
Unless I see in his hands the print of the nails, and put my
finger in the print of the nails, and put my hand into his side,
I will not believe.

26 And after eight days, again his disciples were within, and
Thomas was with them. Then Jesus came, though the doors
had been closed, and stood in the midst, and said: Peace be to
you. 27 Then he said to Thomas: Reach hither your finger, and
behold my hands; and reach hither your hand, and put it into
my side; and be not faithless, but believing. 28 And Thomas
answered and said to him: My Lord and my God. 29 Jesus
said to him: Because you have seen me you have believed:
blessed are they who, though they have not seen, yet have believed.

30 Many other signs truly did Jesus in the presence of his disciples, which are not written in this book; 31 but these are written, that you may believe that Jesus is the Christ, the Son of
God, and that by believing you may have life through his name.

XXI. 1 After this, Jesus showed himself again to his disciples,
at the sea of Tiberias. And he showed himself in this way.
2 There were together, Simon Peter, and Thomas called Didymus, and Nathaniel of Cana of Galilee, and the sons of Zebedee,
and two others of his disciples. 3 Simon Peter said to them: I
am going a fishing. They said to him: We also are going with

you. They went out and entered the ship; and that night they
caught nothing.
[4] But when the morning had now come, Jesus stood on the
shore; but the disciples knew not that it was Jesus. [5] Then
Jesus said to them: Children, have you any food? They answered him: No. [6] He said to them: Throw the net on the
right side of the ship, and you will find. They threw it, therefore, and were no longer able to draw it for the multitude of
fishes. [7] Then that disciple whom Jesus loved said to Peter:
It is the Lord. And when Simon Peter heard that it was the
Lord, he girded on his outer coat, for he had on his inner garment only, and threw himself into the sea. [8] And the other
disciples came in a little ship, dragging the net with fishes, for
they were not far from the land, only about two hundred cubits.
[9] As soon as they had come to the land, they saw there a fire
of coals, and fish lying upon it, and bread. [10] Jesus said to them:
Bring of the fish that you have just taken. [11] Simon Peter went
and drew the net to the land, full of large fishes, a hundred and
fifty-three. And though they were so many, the net did not
break. [12] Jesus said to them: Come and breakfast. But no one
of the disciples durst ask him, Who art thou? because they
knew it was the Lord. [13] Then Jesus came and took the bread,
and gave it to them, and the fish likewise. [14] This was now the
third occasion on which Jesus showed himself to his disciples,
after he had risen from the dead.
[15] When, therefore, they had taken breakfast, Jesus said to
Simon Peter: Simon, son of Jonah, Do you love me more than
these? He said to him: Yes, Lord, thou knowest that I love
thee. He said to him: Feed my lambs. [16] He said to him again
a second time: Simon, son of Jonah, do you love me? He said
to him: Yes, Lord, thou knowest that I love thee. He said to
him: Be a shepherd to my sheep. [17] He said to him a third
time: Simon, son of Jonah, do you love me? Peter was grieved
because he said to him the third time, Do you love me? And he
said to him: Lord, thou knowest all things, thou knowest that
I love thee. Jesus said to him: Feed my sheep. [18] Verily, verily
I say to you, when you were young, you girded yourself, and
walked whither you chose; but when you have become old, you
shall stretch forth your hands, and another shall gird you, and
lead you whither you would not. [19] But this he said, signifying
by what death he would glorify God. And when he had spoken
this, he said to him: Follow me.

20 Then Peter, turning about, saw the disciple that Jesus loved
following, who also reclined at supper upon his breast, and
said: Lord, who is he that delivers thee up? 21 Peter seeing
this one, said to Jesus: Lord, what shall this one do? 22 Jesus
said to him: If I will that he remain till I come, what is that
to you? Do you follow me. 23 Therefore, this saying went out
among the brethren, that that disciple should not die. Yet
Jesus did not say to him, he shall not die; but, If I will that
he remain till I come, what is that to you?

24 This is the disciple who testifies of these things, and who
has written these things; and we know that his testimony is
true. 25 And there are also many other things that Jesus did;
if they should be written, every one of them, I suppose that
not even the world itself could contain the books that would
be written.

ACTS OF APOSTLES.

I. 1 THE former record I made, O Theophilus, of all things
that Jesus began both to do and to teach, 2 till the
day on which he was taken up, after he had, through the Holy
Spirit, given commandments to the apostles whom he had chosen.
3 To whom, after he had suffered, he also showed himself alive,
by many indubitable proofs; appearing to them for forty days,
and speaking of the things that pertain to the kingdom of God.
4 And calling them together, he commanded them not to depart
from Jerusalem, but to wait for the promise of my Father,
which, *said he*, you have heard from me; 5 for John indeed immersed in water, but you shall be immersed in the Holy Spirit,
not many days hence.

6 Therefore, when they came together, they asked him, saying: Lord, wilt thou at this time restore the kingdom to Israel?
7 But he said to them: It is not for you to know times or seasons
that the Father has reserved under his own control. 8 But you
shall receive power, after the Holy Spirit has come upon you,
and you shall be witnesses for me both in Jerusalem, and in
all Judea, and in Samaria, and to the most distant part of the
earth.

9 And when he had spoken these things, while they were looking on him, he was taken up, and a cloud received him out of

their sight. 10 And while they were looking earnestly toward
heaven, as he went up, behold, two men stood by them in white
raiment, 11 who also said: Men of Galilee, why stand you gaz-
ing up into heaven? This Jesus, who has been taken up from
you into heaven, shall come in the same manner in which you
saw him go into heaven.

12 Then they returned to Jerusalem from the mount called
Olivet, which is near Jerusalem, a Sabbath-day's journey.
13 And when they had come in, they went up into an upper
room, in which dwelt Peter and James, and John and Andrew,
Philip and Thomas, Bartholomew and Matthew, James the son
of Alphæus, and Simon Zelotes, and Judas the brother of James.
14 All these, with one mind, continued in prayer and supplication, with the women, and Mary the mother of Jesus, and with
his brothers.

15 And in those days Peter arose in the midst of the disciples,
(the number of the names together was about a hundred and
twenty,) and said:

16 Brethren, it was necessary for this Scripture to be fulfilled,
which the Holy Spirit had before spoken by the mouth of David, concerning Judas, who was a guide to those who took Jesus:
17 for he was numbered with us, and had been appointed to this
ministry. 18 Therefore he purchased a field with the reward of
his iniquity; and falling headlong, he burst asunder in the
midst, and all his bowels gushed out. 19 And it was known to
all that dwelt in Jerusalem, so that the field is called, in their
own language, Akeldama, that is, The field of blood. 20 For it
is written in the book of Psalms, Let his habitation be desolate,
and let no one dwell in it, and, His office let another take.
21 Therefore, of these men who have associated with us during
the whole time in which the Lord Jesus went in and out among
us, 22 beginning from the immersion of John till the day on
which he was taken up from us, must one be appointed as a
witness with us of his resurrection.

23 And they set apart two, Joseph called Barsabas, who was
surnamed Justus, and Matthias; 24 and praying, they said:
Thou, Lord, who knowest the hearts of all, make known which
of these two thou hast chosen, 25 that he may be appointed to
this ministry and apostleship, from which Judas by transgression fell, that he might go to his own place. 26 And they gave
in their lots, and the lot fell on Matthias: and he was numbered with the eleven apostles.

II. 1 And when the day of Pentecost had fully come, they
were all with one consent in one place. 2 And suddenly there
came from heaven a sound as of a rushing, violent wind, and it
filled the whole house in which they were sitting. 3 And there
appeared to them tongues like fire, which distributed themselves, and sat one on each of them. 4 And they were all filled
with the Holy Spirit, and began to speak with other tongues,
as the Spirit gave them utterance.

5 Now there were dwelling in Jerusalem devout Jews, from
every nation under heaven. 6 When the report of this had gone
abroad, the multitude came together; and they were perplexed,
for each one heard them speak in his own language. 7 They
were amazed and astonished, and said one to another: Are
not all these that are speaking, Galileans? 8 And how is it
that we hear, every one in our own language in which we
were born—9 Parthians and Medes and Elamites, and we who
dwell in Mesopotamia, Judea, and Cappadocia, Pontus and
Asia, 10 Phrygia and Pamphyla, Egypt and the parts of Libya
about Cyrene, Roman residents, Jews and proselytes, 11 Cretes
and Arabians—we hear them speaking, in our own tongues,
the wonderful works of God? 12 And they were all in amazement and doubt, and said, one to another: What can this mean?
13 But others deriding, said: They are full of new wine.

14 But Peter standing up with the eleven, lifted up his voice
and said to them: Men of Judea, and all you that dwell in Jerusalem, be this known to you, and give ear to my words.
15 For these men are not drunk, as you suppose: for it is the
third hour of the day. 16 But this is that which was spoken of
by the prophet Joel:

17 And it shall come to pass in the last days, says God, that I
will pour out of my Spirit on all flesh; and your sons and your
daughters shall prophesy, and your young men shall see visions,
and your old men shall dream dreams. 18 And also on my servants and on my handmaids, I will pour out of my Spirit in those
days, and they shall prophesy. 19 And I will show wonders in
heaven above, and signs in the earth beneath, blood and fire
and columns of smoke. 20 The sun shall be turned into darkness, and the moon into blood, before that great and terrible
day of the Lord comes. 21 And it shall come to pass, that whoever shall call on the name of the Lord shall be saved.

22 Men of Israel, hear these words: Jesus the Nazarene, clearly
pointed out to you as a man from God, by mighty deeds and

wonders and signs, which God did by him in your midst, as you
yourselves also know, 23 him, delivered up by the fixed purpose
and foreknowledge of God, you took, and with wicked hands
did crucify and slay: 24 whom God raised up, having loosed the
pains of death, because it was not possible for him to be held in
subjection by it. 25 For David speaks with reference to him:
I saw the Lord always in my presence: for he is at my right
hand, that I should not be moved. 26 Therefore my heart rejoiced, and my tongue sang praise. Moreover, my flesh shall
rest in hope; 27 because thou wilt not leave my soul in hades,
nor suffer thy Holy One to see corruption. 28 Thou didst make
known to me the ways of life; thou wilt make me full of joy
with thy countenance.

29 Brethren, I may say to you plainly of the patriarch David,
that he died, and was buried, and his sepulcher is with us to
this day. 30 Therefore, being a prophet, and knowing that God
had sworn to him with an oath, that he would cause one from
the fruit of his loins to sit on his throne; 31 foreseeing this, he
spoke of the resurrection of the Christ, that his soul was not
left in hades, nor did his flesh see corruption. 32 This Jesus has
God raised up, of which we all are witnesses. 33 Therefore, having been exalted to the right hand of God, and having received
from his Father the promise of the Holy Spirit, he has poured
out this, which you now see and hear. 34 For David has not
ascended into the heavens; but he himself says, The Lord said
to my Lord, Sit at my right hand, 35 till I make thy enemies
thy footstool. 36 Therefore, let all the house of Israel know assuredly, that God has made this same Jesus whom you crucified, both Lord and Christ.

37 When they heard this, they were pierced to the heart,
and said to Peter and the other apostles: Brethren, what shall
we do?

38 And Peter said to them: Repent, and be immersed, every
one of you, in the name of Jesus Christ, in order to the remission of sins; and you shall receive the gift of the Holy Spirit.
39 For the promise is to you, and your children, and to all that
are afar off, as many as the Lord our God shall call. 40 And
with many other words did he testify and exhort, saying: Save
yourselves from this wicked generation.

41 Then they that gladly received his word were immersed,
and on that day there were added to them about three thousand
souls. 42 And they attended constantly to the teaching of the

apostles, and the fellowship, and the breaking of bread, and the
prayers. 43 And fear came on every soul; and many wonders
and signs were done by the apostles. 44 And all that believed
were together, and had all things in common; 45 and they sold
their possessions and goods, and distributed them to all, as each
had need. 46 And with one consent, they continued daily in the
temple; and, breaking bread from house to house, they partook
of their food with gladness and simplicity of heart, 47 praising
God, and being in favor with all the people. And the Lord
added the saved daily to the Church.

III. 1 Now Peter and John were going up together into the
temple at the hour of prayer, which was the ninth hour. 2 And
a certain man, lame from his mother's womb, was carried along,
whom they laid daily at that gate of the temple which is called
Beautiful, that he might ask charity of those who were going
into the temple. 3 This man, seeing Peter and John about to
go into the temple, asked charity. 4 But Peter, fixing his eyes
on him with John, said: Look on us. 5 And he gave heed to
them, expecting to receive something from them.
6 But Peter said: Silver and gold I have none: but what I
have, this I give you. In the name of Jesus Christ the Nazarene, arise and walk. 7 And he took him by his right hand
and raised him up: and immediately his feet and ankles received strength. 8 And leaping up, he stood and walked, and
went with them into the temple, walking and leaping and praising God. 9 And all the people saw him walking and praising
God; 10 and they recognized him, that it was he that had sat for
charity at the Beautiful gate of the temple. And they were
filled with wonder and amazement at what had happened to him.
11 And while he was holding to Peter and John, all the people
ran together to them in the porch called Solomon's, greatly astonished. 12 But when Peter saw it, he answered the people:
Men of Israel, why are you astonished at this? or, why do
you look so earnestly on us, as if by our own power or godliness we had caused this man to walk? 13 The God of Abraham,
and of Isaac, and of Jacob, the God of our fathers, has glorified
his Son Jesus, whom you delivered up, and whom you rejected
in the presence of Pilate, when he was determined to release
him. 14 But you rejected the Holy and Just One, and demanded
that a murderer should be given to you; 15 and you slew the
Author of life, whom God has raised from the dead, of which

we are witnesses. 16 And his name, by faith in his name, has
made this man strong whom you see and know; even the faith
which is by him, has given him this entire soundness in the
presence of you all.
17 And now, brethren, I know that through ignorance you did
this, as did also your rulers. 18 But the things which God foretold by the mouth of all his prophets, that his Christ should
suffer, he has thus fulfilled. 19 Repent, therefore, and turn, in
order that your sins may be blotted out, so that seasons of re-
freshing may come from the presence of the Lord, 20 and that
he may send Jesus Christ, who was destined for you; 21 whom
heaven must retain, till the time for restoring all things that
God has spoken by the mouth of his holy prophets of ancient
times.
22 For Moses said to the fathers, A prophet like me shall the
Lord your God raise up for you from among your brethren;
him shall you hear in all things that he shall say to you. 23 And
it shall come to pass, that every soul that will not hear that
prophet, shall be destroyed from among the people. 24 And all
the prophets, from Samuel and those that follow after, as many
as have spoken, have also foretold these days. 25 You are the
sons of the prophets, and of the covenant that God made with
our fathers, saying to Abraham, And in your offspring shall all
the families of the earth be blessed. 26 To you first, God, having
raised up his Son Jesus, has sent him to bless you, in turning
every one of you away from his iniquities.

IV. 1 While they were speaking to the people, the priests,
and the captain of the temple, and the Sadducees came upon
them, 2 being vexed because they taught the people, and
preached through Jesus the resurrection from the dead. 3 And
they laid hands on them, and put them in prison till the next
day, for it was already evening. 4 But many of those who heard
the word, believed; and the number of the men was about five
thousand.
5 And it came to pass, on the next day, that their rulers and
elders and scribes, 6 and Annas the chief priest, and Caiaphas
and John and Alexander, and as many as were of the family
of the chief priest, met together in Jerusalem. 7 And when
they had made them stand in the midst, they asked: By what
power, or by what name have you done this? 8 Then Peter,
filled with the Holy Spirit, said to them: Rulers of the people,

and elders of Israel, [9] if we are this day examined with respect
to the good deed done to the infirm man, by what means he has
been saved, [10] be it known to you all, and to all the people of
Israel, that by the name of Jesus Christ the Nazarene, whom
you crucified, whom God raised from the dead, by him does
this man stand before you in health. [11] This is the stone that
was rejected with contempt by you builders, which has become
the head of the corner. [12] And there is salvation in no other;
nor, indeed, is there another name under heaven, given among
men, by which we must be saved.

[13] Now, when they saw the boldness of Peter and John, and
perceived that they were unlearned and plain men, they were
astonished; and they also recognized them, that they had been
with Jesus; [14] and, seeing the man who had been cured standing
with them, they had nothing to say in reply. [15] But, having
commanded them to go aside out of the Sanhedrim, they consulted with one another, [16] saying: What shall we do with these
men? For that an evident sign has been done by them, is manifest to all that dwell in Jerusalem, and we can not deny it.
[17] But that it may spread no further among the people, let us
severely threaten them, so that they speak no more to any man
in this name. [18] And they called them in, and commanded them
to speak no more at all, nor to teach, in the name of Jesus.

[19] But Peter and John answering them, said: Whether it is
right in the sight of God to obey you rather than God, judge
you. [20] For we can not but speak the things that we have seen
and heard. [21] And when they had further threatened them,
they let them go, finding nothing for which they could punish
them, because of the people; for they all glorified God on account of that which had been done; [22] for the man on whom
this sign of healing had been performed was more than forty
years old.

[23] And having been released, they went to their own, and told
all that the chief priests and elders had said to them. [24] And
when they heard it, they lifted up their voice with one consent
to God, and said: Lord, thou art God, who didst make the
heaven and the earth and the sea, and all things that are in
them; who, by the mouth of David thy servant, didst say,
[25] Why did the heathen rage, and the people devise vain things?
[26] The kings of the land stood up, and the rulers met together
against the Lord and against his anointed. [27] For, in truth,
against thy holy child Jesus, whom thou didst anoint, both

Herod and Pontius Pilate, with the Gentiles and the people of
Israel, did meet togther, 28 to do whatever thy hand and thy
counsel determined to be done. 29 And now, Lord, look upon
their threatenings, and grant to thy servants that they may
speak thy word with all boldness, 30 by stretching out thy hand
to heal, that both signs and wonders may be done through the
name of thy holy child Jesus.

31 And when they had prayed, the place in which they were
assembled was shaken; and they were all filled with the Holy
Spirit, and spoke the word of God with boldness.

32 And the multitude of believers were of one heart and of
one soul; and no one said that any part of his possessions was
his own; but they had all things in common. 33 And with
great power did the apostles bear testimony to the resurrection
of the Lord Jesus, and great grace was on them all. 34 Nor,
indeed, was there any needy person among them; for as many
as were owners of lands or houses, sold them, and brought the
prices of what had been sold, 35 and laid them down at the feet
of the apostles; and distribution was made to every one as he
had need.

36 And Joses, who, by the apostles, was surnamed Barnabas,
(which name, when translated, is, Son of consolation,) a Levite,
by birth a Cyprian, 37 having land, sold it, and brought the
money and laid it at the feet of the apostles.

V. 1 But a certain man named Ananias, with Sapphira his
wife, sold a possession, 2 and kept back part of the price, and
his wife was conscious of it; and he brought a certain part of
it, and laid it at the feet of the apostles. 3 But Peter said:
Ananias, why has Satan filled your heart, that you should at-
tempt to deceive the Holy Spirit, and keep back part of the
price of the land? 4 While it remained *unsold*, was it not your
own? And after it was sold, was it not at your own disposal?
Why have you purposed this thing in your heart? You have
not lied to men, but to God. 5 And when Ananias heard these
words, he fell down, and expired. And great fear came on all
that heard these things. 6 And the young men arose and
wound him in his mantle, and carried him out, and buried him.

7 And after an interval of about three hours, his wife, not
knowing what had been done, came in. 8 And Peter answered
her: Tell me, did you sell the land for so much? She replied:
Yes; for so much. 9 But Peter said to her: Why is it that you

have agreed together to tempt the Spirit of the Lord? Behold,
the feet of those who have buried your husband are at the door,
and they shall carry you out. [10] And she immediately fell down
at his feet, and expired. And the young men came in and found
her dead; and they carried her out, and buried her by the side
of her husband. [11] And great fear came on all the church, and
on all that heard these things.

[12] And many signs and wonders were done among the people
by the hands of the apostles; (and they were all with one consent in Solomon's porch. [13] And no one of the rest durst join
himself to them; but the people magnified them. [14] And believers in the Lord were more and more added to them, multitudes both of men and women;) [15] so that they brought the sick
out along the streets, and laid them on beds and couches, that
even the shadow of Peter, as he passed along, might fall on some
of them. [16] And many people of the cities round about came to
Jerusalem, bringing the sick, and those who were troubled by
evil spirits, all of whom were cured.

[17] But the chief priest arose, and all that were with him,
(which is the sect of the Sadducees,) and were filled with indignation; [18] and they laid their hands on the apostles, and put
them in the public prison. [19] But an angel of the Lord opened
the doors of the prison by night, and brought them out, and
said: [20] Go, stand in the temple, and speak to the people all the
words of this life. [21] And having heard this, they entered the
temple, early in the morning, and taught. But the chief priest,
and those who were with him, came and called together the
Sanhedrim, and all the eldership of the sons of Israel, and sent
to the prison to have them brought.

[22] But when the attendants came, and found them not in the
prison, they returned and reported, [23] saying: We found the
prison closed with all safety, and the guards standing before
the doors; but when we had opened, we found no one within.
[24] When the priest and the captain of the temple and the chief
priests heard these words, they were in doubt about them, what
this could mean. [25] And some one came and reported to them:
Behold, the men whom you put in prison are standing in the
temple, and teaching the people.

[26] Then went the captain with the attendants, and brought
them without violence; for they feared the people, lest they
should be stoned. [27] And when they had brought them, they
made them stand before the Sanhedrim; and the chief priest

asked them, 28 saying: Did we not strictly charge you not to
teach in this name? And behold, you have filled Jerusalem
with your teaching, and you intend to bring this man's blood
upon us.

29 But Peter and the apostles answered and said: We must
obey God rather than men. 30 The God of our fathers has
raised up Jesus, whom you slew by hanging him on a tree.
31 Him has God exalted to his right hand to be a Prince and a
Savior, in order to give to Israel repentance and remission of
sins: 32 and we are witnesses of these things, and so is the Holy
Spirit also, whom God has given to them that obey him.

33 And when they heard this, they were enraged; and they
determined to put them to death. 34 Then arose a certain man
in the Sanhedrim, a Pharisee, named Gamaliel, a teacher of the
law, who was honored by all the people; and he commanded
them to put the apostles out for a little while, 35 and said to
them: Men of Israel, consider well with yourselves what you
are about to do to these men. 36 For before these days Theudas
arose, declaring himself to be some great one; to whom a number of men, about four hundred, joined themselves; and he was
slain; and all, as many as believed him, were scattered and
brought to naught. 37 After this man, Judas the Galilean arose,
in the days of the enrollment, and drew over many people after
him; and he was destroyed, and all, as many as believed him,
were scattered. 38 And now I say to you, keep away from these
men, and let them alone; for if this counsel or this work be of
men, it will come to an end; 39 but if it is of God, you can not
bring it to an end: and take heed, lest you be found fighting
also against God.

40 And they were persuaded by him; and when they had called
the apostles in and scourged them, they commanded them not
to speak in the name of Jesus, and let them go. 41 Then, they
went from the presence of the Sanhedrim, rejoicing that they
were thought worthy to suffer shame for his name's sake. 42 And
daily in the temple, and from house to house, they ceased not to
teach and to preach Jesus the Christ.

VI. 1 In those days, when the disciples were increasing in
number, there arose a murmuring of the Hellenists against the
Hebrews, because their widows were neglected in the daily min-
istration. 2 And the twelve called the multitude of the disciples
to them, and said: It is not right that we should leave the word

of God, and serve tables. 3 Therefore, brethren, select from among yourselves seven men, of good report, full of the Holy Spirit and of wisdom, whom we may appoint over this business: 4 but we will give ourselves continually to prayer and to the ministry of the word.

5 And the speech pleased the whole multitude; and they chose Stephen, a man full of faith and of the Holy Spirit, and Philip and Prochorus and Nicanor and Timon and Parmenas, and Nicolas, a proselyte of Antioch, 6 whom they set before the apostles. And when they had prayed, they laid their hands on them.

7 And the word of God increased, and the number of the disciples in Jerusalem was greatly multiplied; and a great multitude of the priests became obedient to the faith.

8 And Stephen, full of faith and power, did great wonders and signs among the people. 9 Then there arose some who belonged to the synagogue called the synagogue of the Freedmen, and some of the Cyrenians and Alexandrians, and of those who were from Cilicia and Asia, and they disputed with Stephen. 10 And they were not able to resist the wisdom and the spirit with which he spoke. 11 Then they instigated men to say: We have heard him speak impious words against Moses, and against God.

12 And they excited the people, and the elders, and the scribes, and came upon him, and took him by violence, and brought him into the Sanhedrim. 13 And they brought forward false witnesses, who said: This man ceases not to speak words against this holy place, and the law. 14 For we have heard him say, that this Jesus the Nazarene will destroy this place, and will change the customs which Moses delivered to us. 15 And all that sat in the Sanhedrim, looking earnestly upon him, saw his face that it was like the face of an angel.

VII. 1 And the chief priest said: Are these things so? 2 He replied: Brethren and fathers, hear: The God of glory appeared to our father Abraham, while he was in Mesopotamia, before he dwelt in Charran, 3 and said to him: Get out from your land, and from your kindred, and come into a land that I will show you. 4 Then he departed from the land of the Chaldeans, and dwelt in Charran; and thence, after his father died, he removed into this land, in which you now dwell. 5 And he gave him no inheritance in it, not a foot-breadth; and yet he promised to

give it for a possession to him, and to his posterity after him,
when as yet he had no child.

6 And God spoke thus: That his posterity should sojourn in
a strange land, and they should enslave them and afflict them,
for four hundred years. 7 And the nation to which they shall
be in bondage I will judge, said God; and after that, they shall
come forth and serve me in this place. 8 And he gave him the
covenant of circumcision, and thus he begot Isaac, and circumcised him the eighth day; and Isaac begot Jacob, and Jacob
begot the twelve patriarchs.

9 And the patriarchs, moved with envy, sold Joseph into
Egypt: but God was with him, 10 and delivered him from all
his afflictions, and gave him favor and wisdom in the sight of
Pharaoh, king of Egypt: and he made him governor over
Egypt, and his whole house. 11 And there came a famine, and
great affliction on the whole land of Egypt, and of Chanaan:
and our fathers found no sustenance. 12 But when Jacob heard
that there was grain in Egypt, he sent forth our fathers the
first time: 13 and, on their second visit, Joseph made himself
known to his brothers, and the kindred of Joseph were made
known to Pharaoh. 14 And Joseph sent and called to him his
father Jacob, and all his kindred, seventy-five souls. 15 And
Jacob went down into Egypt, and died, himself and our fathers;
16 and they were carried over into Sychem, and laid in the sepulcher which Abraham bought for its value in silver, from the sons
of Emmor, the father of Sychem.

17 And as the time of the promise which God had made with
an oath to Abraham drew near, the people increased and multiplied in Egypt, 18 till another king arose, who knew not Joseph.
19 He dealt insidiously with our race, and afflicted our fathers,
so that they exposed their infants, in order that they might
not live.

20 At which time Moses was born; and he was exceedingly
beautiful, and was nursed three months in his father's house.
21 But having been exposed, the daughter of Pharaoh took him
up, and educated him as her own son. 22 And Moses was instructed in all the wisdom of the Egyptians, and was mighty
in words and in deeds. 23 When he had completed his fortieth
year, it came into his heart to visit his brethren, the sons of
Israel. 24 And seeing one of them unjustly treated, he defended
and avenged him that was oppressed, and smote the Egyptian.
25 And he supposed that his brethren would understand that,

by his hand, God would give them salvation: but they understood not.

26 And on the next day he showed himself to them, as they
were fighting, and endeavored to persuade them to peace, saying, Men, you are brothers: why do you injure one another?
27 But he that was doing the injury to his neighbor, thrust him
away, saying, Who made you a ruler or a judge over us? 28 Do
you intend to kill me, as you killed the Egyptian yesterday?
29 And at that saying Moses fled, and became a resident in the
land of Midian, where he begot two sons. 30 And when forty
years were completed, there appeared to him, in the wilderness
of Mount Sinai, an angel of the Lord in a flame of fire in a bush.
31 When Moses saw it, he wondered at the sight, and as he was
drawing near to observe it, the voice of the Lord came to him:
32 I am the God of your fathers, the God of Abraham, and the
God of Isaac, and the God of Jacob. And Moses trembled, and
durst not observe it. 33 Then said the Lord to him: Loose your
shoes from your feet; for the place in which you stand is holy
ground. 34 I have surely seen the affliction of my people who
are in Egypt, and I have heard their groaning, and I have come
down to deliver them; and now come, and I will send you into
Egypt.

35 This Moses, whom they rejected, saying, Who made you a
ruler and a judge? him God sent as a ruler and as a redeemer,
by the hand of the angel that appeared to him in the bush.
36 He brought them out, after he had performed wonders and
signs in the land of Egypt, and at the Red Sea, and in the wilderness, forty years. 37 This is that Moses, who said to the sons
of Israel, A prophet like me will the Lord your God raise up for
you from among your brethren; him shall you hear.

38 This is he who was in the congregation in the wilderness
with the angel that spoke to him in the mount Sinai, and with
our fathers; he received the living oracles, that he might give
them to us. 39 To him our fathers were not willing to be obedient; but they rejected him, and turned back in their hearts
to Egypt, 40 saying to Aaron: Make us gods that shall go before
us; for, as for this Moses, who brought us out of the land of
Egypt, we know not what has become of him. 41 And they
made a calf in those days, and offered sacrifice to the idol, and
rejoiced in the works of their own hands. 42 But God turned
and delivered them up to serve the host of heaven, as it is written in the book of the prophets: Your victims and your sacri-

fices did you offer to me for forty years in the wilderness, O house
of Israel? [43] Yes, you took up the tabernacle of Moloch, and
the star of your God Remphan, images which you made to
worship; and I will carry you away beyond Babylon.

[44] The tabernacle of the testimony was with our fathers in the
wilderness, *built* as he who spoke to Moses commanded him to
build it, according to the pattern which he had seen: [45] which
our fathers, who were with Joshua, received by succession, and
brought into the land possessed by the Gentiles, whom God continued to drive out from the face of our fathers till the days of
David, [46] who found favor before God, and desired to find a
dwelling-place for the God of Jacob. [47] But Solomon built him
a house. [48] Yet the Most High dwells not in temples made with
hands, as says the prophet: [49] Heaven is my throne, and the
earth is my footstool. What house will you build me? says the
Lord; or what is the place of my rest? [50] Has not my hand made
all these things?

[51] You stiff-necked, and uncircumcised in heart and in ears, you
do always resist the Holy Spirit; as your fathers did, so also do
you. [52] Which of the prophets did not your fathers persecute?
They slew also those who foretold the coming of the Just One,
of whom you have now become the betrayers and murderers;
[53] who received the law by the appointment of angels, and have
not kept it.

[54] When they heard these things, they were enraged in their
hearts, and gnashed upon him with their teeth. [55] But being
full of the Holy Spirit, he looked earnestly up into heaven, and
saw the glory of God, and Jesus standing at the right hand of
God; [56] and he said: Behold, I see the heavens opened, and the
Son of man standing at the right hand of God.

[57] And they cried out with a loud voice, and stopped their ears,
and, with one consent, rushed upon him, [58] and drove him out
of the city, and stoned him. And the witnesses laid down their
clothes at the feet of a young man called Saul. [59] And they
stoned Stephen while he was calling on *the Lord*, and saying:
Lord Jesus, receive my spirit. [60] And he kneeled down and cried
with a loud voice: Lord, let not this sin stand against them.
And when he had said this, he fell asleep. And Saul was well
pleased with his death.

VIII. [1] And at that time there was a great persecution
against the church that was in Jerusalem; and they were all

dispersed throughout the regions of Judea and Samaria, except
the apostles. [2] But devout men carried Stephen to his burial,
and made great lamentation over him. [3] But Saul attempted to
destroy the church; entering every house, and dragging men
and women, he delivered them up to prison.

[4] Then they that were dispersed went every-where preaching
the word. [5] And Philip went down to the city of Samaria, and
preached the Christ to them. [6] And the multitudes with one
mind gave heed to the things which were spoken by Philip,
when they heard, and saw the signs which he did. [7] For unclean spirits, crying with a loud voice, came out of many that
were possessed with them, and many paralytics and lame persons were cured. [8] And there was great joy in that city.

[9] But there was a certain man, named Simon, who had, before
this time, been practicing magic in the city, and astonishing the
people of Samaria, saying that he was some great one; [10] to
whom they all gave heed, from the least to the greatest, saying:
This man is the great power of God. [11] And they gave heed to
him because he had, for a long time, astonished them with his
magic arts. [12] But when they believed Philip, who preached the
good news concerning the kingdom of God and the name of Jesus
Christ, they were immersed, both men and women. [13] And Simon himself also believed; and after he was immersed, he continued with Philip; and, seeing the mighty deeds and the signs
which were done, he was astonished.

[14] Now when the apostles, who were in Jerusalem, heard that
Samaria had received the word of God, they sent to them Peter
and John; [15] who, when they had gone down, prayed for them,
that they might receive the Holy Spirit. [16] For he had not yet
fallen on any of them; only they had been immersed into the
name of the Lord Jesus. [17] Then they laid their hands on them,
and they received the Holy Spirit.

[18] And when Simon saw that the Holy Spirit was given through
the laying on of the hands of the apostles, he offered them money,
[19] saying: Give me, also, this authority, that whoever I shall lay
my hands on, may receive the Holy Spirit. [20] But Peter said to
him: Your money perish with you, because you thought that
the gift of God might be purchased with money. [21] You have
neither part nor share in this matter; for your heart is not
right in the sight of God. [22] Repent, therefore, of this your
wickedness, and pray God, if perhaps the purpose of your heart
may be forgiven you. [23] For I perceive that you are in the gall

of bitterness, and in the bond of iniquity. 24 But Simon answered and said: Pray you both to the Lord for me, that none
of the things which you have spoken come upon me.

25 Then, when they had given their testimony, and preached
the word of the Lord, they returned to Jerusalem, and preached
the gospel in many villages of the Samaritans.

26 And an angel of the Lord spoke to Philip, saying: Arise,
and go toward the south, to the road that leads from Jerusalem
to Gaza; this is desert. 27 And he arose and went. And behold,
a man of Ethiopia, a eunuch of great authority under Candace,
the queen of the Ethiopians, who had charge of all her treasure,
and had come to Jerusalem to worship, 28 was returning, and,
sitting in his chariot, read the prophet Isaiah.

29 And the spirit said to Philip: Go forward and join yourself
to this chariot. 30 And Philip ran forward, and heard him reading the prophet Isaiah; and he said: Do you understand what
you are reading? 31 He answered: How can I, unless some one
instruct me? And he invited Philip to come up and sit with
him. 32 The passage of the Scripture which he was reading,
was this: As a sheep for the slaughter was he led; and as a
lamb before his shearer is dumb, so opened he not his mouth
33 in his humiliation. The sentence against him was taken
away; but who shall describe the men of his generation? For
his life was taken from the earth. 34 And the eunuch answered
Philip, and said: I pray you, of whom speaks the prophet this?
Of himself, or of some other man? 35 And Philip opened his
mouth, and began at the same Scripture, and preached to him
Jesus.

36 And as they went along the road, they came to some water;
and the eunuch said: See, here is water; what hinders me from
being immersed? 38 And he commanded the chariot to stand
still; and they both went down into the water, both Philip and
the eunuch, and he immersed him. 39 And when they came up
out of the water, the Spirit of the Lord caught away Philip;
and the eunuch saw him no more, for he went on his way rejoicing. 40 But Philip was found at Azotus, and, passing
through, he preached the gospel in all the cities, till he came
to Cæsarea.

IX. 1 And Saul, still breathing out threatening and slaughter
against the disciples of the Lord, went to the chief priest, 2 and
asked of him letters to Damascus, for the synagogues, that, if

he should find any who were of this persuasion, either men or
women, he might bring them bound to Jerusalem.

3 And as he journeyed, he came near Damascus; and suddenly
there shone round about him a light from heaven. 4 And when
he had fallen to the earth, he heard a voice saying to him: Saul,
Saul, why do you persecute me? 5 He answered: Who art thou,
Lord? And the Lord said: I am Jesus, whom you persecute.
6 But rise, and go into the city, and it shall be told you what
you must do. 7 The men who journeyed with him stood amazed;
for they heard a voice, but saw no one. 8 And Saul arose from
the earth, and when his eyes were opened, he saw no one; but
they led him by the hand, and brought him into Damascus.
9 And he was three days without sight, and neither ate nor
drank.

10 Now there was a certain disciple in Damascus, named Ananias;
and the Lord said to him in a vision: Ananias. He answered:
Behold me, Lord. 11 And the Lord said to him: Arise,
and go into the street that is called Straight, and inquire at the
house of Judas for one called Saul of Tarsus: for behold, he is
praying; 12 and he has seen in a vision a man named Ananias,
coming in and laying his hand on him, that he may receive his
sight. 13 But Ananias answered: Lord, I have heard from many
of this man, how much evil he has done to thy saints in Jerusalem;
14 and here he has authority from the chief priests to bind
all that call upon thy name. 15 But the Lord said to him: Go;
for he is a vessel chosen by me to bear my name before nations
and kings, and the sons of Israel. 16 For I will show him what
great things he must suffer for my name.

17 And Ananias went, and entered the house, and laying
his hands on him, said: Brother Saul, the Lord, even Jesus,
who appeared to you on the road by which you came, has
sent me, that you may receive your sight, and be filled with
the Holy Spirit. 18 And immediately there fell from his eyes
something like scales, and he instantly received his sight; and
he arose, and was immersed. 19 And, having taken food, he
was strengthened.

And he was with the disciples in Damascus for some days;
20 and immediately he preached Jesus in the synagogues, that
he is the Son of God. 21 And all that heard him were astonished,
and said: Is not this he who destroyed in Jerusalem those that
call on this name, and who has come hither for this purpose,
that he might carry them bound to the chief priests? 22 But

Saul increased the more in strength, and confuted the Jews that
dwelt in Damascus, proving that this is the Christ. [23] And,
after many days had passed, the Jews determined to kill him.
[24] And their plot was made known to Saul; and they watched
the gates day and night, that they might kill him. [25] But the
disciples took him by night, and let him down through the wall
in a basket.

[26] And having come to Jerusalem, he attempted to associate
with the disciples: and they were all afraid of him, for they did
not believe that he was a disciple. [27] But Barnabas took him,
and brought him to the apostles, and told them how he had seen
the Lord on the road, and that he had spoken to him, and how
he had boldly preached in Damascus in the name of Jesus.
[28] And he was with them in Jerusalem, coming in and going out;
and, speaking boldly in the name of the Lord Jesus, [29] he conversed and reasoned with the Hellenists; but they undertook to
kill him. [30] And when the brethren learned this, they brought
him down to Cæsarea, and sent him out to Tarsus.

[31] Then the churches throughout the whole of Judea and Galilee and Samaria had peace, and were edified; and, walking in
the fear of the Lord, and in the comfort of the Holy Spirit, they
were multiplied.

[32] And it came to pass that Peter, passing through all the
places, came down also to the saints that dwelt in Lydda.
[33] And he found there a certain man named Æneas, who was a
paralytic, and had kept his bed for eight years. [34] And Peter
said to him: Æneas, Jesus the Christ restores you to health;
arise, and spread your bed for yourself. And he immediately
arose; [35] and all that dwelt in Lydda and Saron saw him; and
they turned to the Lord.

[36] Now there was in Joppa a certain disciple named Tabitha,
which name, when translated, is Dorcas. She was full of good
works and deeds of charity which she did. [37] And it came to
pass, in those days, that she was taken sick, and died. And
when they had washed her, they laid her in an upper room.
[38] And as Lydda was near to Joppa, the disciples, having heard
that Peter was there, sent two men to him, requesting him to
make no delay in coming to them.

[39] Then Peter arose, and went with them; and when he had
come, they brought him into the upper room; and all the widows
stood by him weeping, and showing the coats and garments that
Dorcas made while she was with them. [40] But Peter put them

all out, and kneeled down and prayed; and turning to the body,
he said: Tabitha, arise. And she opened her eyes; and when
she saw Peter, she sat up. 41 And he gave her his hand, and
raised her up. And when he had called in the saints and the
widows, he presented her alive. 42 And it was known throughout all Joppa, and many believed on the Lord. 43 And it came
to pass, that he remained many days in Joppa with one Simon,
a tanner.

X. 1 Now there was a certain man in Cæsarea, named Cornelius, a centurion of the band called the Italian band, 2 a devout man, and one that feared God with all his house, who did
many acts of charity to the people, and prayed to God always.
3 He distinctly saw, in a vision, about the ninth hour of the
day, an angel of God coming in to him, and saying to him, Cornelius.

4 And having looked steadily on him, he was afraid, and said:
What is it, Lord? He said to him: Your prayers and your
charitable deeds have come up for a memorial before God. 5 And
now send men to Joppa, and call for Simon, who is surnamed
Peter; 6 he lodges with one Simon a tanner, whose house is by
the sea. 7 When the angel who spoke to him had departed, he
called two of his household servants, and a devout soldier, one
of those who waited on him, 8 and having made known all things
to them, he sent them to Joppa.

9 And on the morrow, as they were going on their journey,
and were drawing near to the city, Peter went up on the house-
top to pray, about the sixth hour. 10 And he became very hungry, and desired to eat; but while they were making ready, he
fell into a trance; 11 and he saw heaven opened, and some vessel,
like a great sheet, descending, bound by the four corners, and
let down to the earth. 12 In this were all kinds of four-footed
beasts of the earth, and wild beasts and creeping things and
birds of the air. 13 And there came a voice to him: Rise, Peter,
kill and eat. 14 But Peter said: By no means, Lord; for I have
never eaten any thing common or unclean. 15 And the voice
came to him again a second time: What God has cleansed, you
must not call common. 16 This was done the third time; and
the vessel was taken up again into heaven.

17 Now, while Peter was perplexed within himself about the
meaning of the vision which he had seen, behold, the men who
had been sent from Cornelius, having made inquiry for the

house of Simon, stood before the gate. 18 And they called and
asked whether Simon, who was surnamed Peter, lodged there.
19 While Peter was thinking of the vision, the Spirit said to him:
Behold, three men ask for you: 20 arise then, and go down, and
go with them without hesitation, for I have sent them.

21 And Peter came down to the men, and said: Behold, I am
he whom you seek; what is the cause of your coming? 22 They
replied: Cornelius the centurion, a just man, and one that
fears God, and of good report among the whole nation of the
Jews, was instructed by a holy angel to call you to his house,
and to hear words from you. 23 Then he called them in, and
lodged them.

On the morrow he arose, and went with them; and some of
the brethren from Joppa accompanied him. 24 And on the next
day, they entered Cæsarea. And Cornelius was expecting them,
and had called together his relatives and near friends. 25 And as
Peter was coming in, Cornelius met him, and fell down at his
feet, and did him homage. 26 But Peter raised him up, saying:
Stand up; I also am a man. 27 And, conversing with him, he
went in, and found many that had come together.

28 And he said to them: You know that it is unlawful for a Jew
to associate with one of another nation, or to go into his house.
But God has showed me that I must not call any man common
or unclean. 29 For this reason, when I was sent for, I came
without making objection. I ask, therefore, for what purpose
have you sent for me? 30 And Cornelius replied: Four days ago,
I was fasting till this hour; and, at the ninth hour, I was praying in my house; and behold, a man stood before me in bright
clothing, 31 and said: Cornelius, your prayer is heard, and
your deeds of charity are remembered before God. 32 Send,
therefore, to Joppa, and call for Simon, who is surnamed Peter:
he lodges in the house of Simon a tanner, by the sea; who, when
he comes, will speak to you. 33 Therefore, I immediately sent
to you; and you have done well in coming. Now, therefore,
we are all here present before God, to hear all things that are
given in charge to you by God.

34 And Peter opened his mouth, and said: In truth, I perceive
that God is no respecter of persons; 35 but, in every nation, he
that fears him and works righteousness is accepted by him.
36 The word which he sent to the sons of Israel, preaching peace
by Jesus Christ, (he is Lord of all,) 37 that word, you know,
which was published through the whole of Judea, beginning

from Galilee, after the immersion that John preached; 38 how
God anointed Jesus of Nazareth with the Holy Spirit, and with
power; who went about doing good, and healing all that were
oppressed by the devil; for God was with him. 39 And we are
witnesses of all that he did, both in the country of the Jews,
and in Jerusalem; whom they slew by hanging him on a tree.
40 Him God raised up the third day, and caused him to appear,
41 not to all the people, but to witnesses who were before appointed by God, even to us, who did eat and drink with him,
after he rose from the dead.

42 And he commanded us to preach to the people, and to testify that this is he who has been appointed by God as the judge
of the living and the dead. 43 To him all the prophets bear testimony, that whoever believes on him shall receive remission of
sins through his name.

44 While Peter was speaking these things, the Holy Spirit fell
on all that heard the word. 45 And the believers that were of
the circumcision, as many as had come with Peter, were astonished, because on the Gentiles also was poured out the gift of
the Holy Spirit: 46 for they heard them speaking with tongues,
and magnifying God. Then Peter answered: 47 Can any one
forbid the water, that these should not be immersed, who have
received the Holy Spirit as well as we? 48 And he commanded
them to be immersed in the name of the Lord. Then they besought him to remain some days.

XI. 1 And the apostles and brethren that were in Judea,
heard that the Gentiles also had received the word of God.
2 And when Peter went up to Jerusalem, those who were of the
circumcision contended with him, 3 saying: You went in to uncircumcised men, and ate with them.

4 And Peter began, and laid the matter before them in order,
saying: 5 I was in the city of Joppa, praying; and, while in a
trance, I saw a vision, some vessel, like a great sheet, descending, let down from heaven by the four corners; and it came
even to me. 6 When I had looked attentively into it, I observed
and saw four-footed beasts of the earth, and wild beasts and
creeping things and birds of the air. 7 And I heard a voice
saying to me, Rise, Peter, kill and eat. 8 But I said, By no
means, Lord; for nothing common or unclean has ever entered
my mouth. 9 But the voice answered me a second time from
heaven, What God has cleansed, you must not call common.

10 This was done the third time, and all was drawn up again
into heaven.

11 And behold, three men who had been sent to me from Cæsarea, immediately came to the house where I was. 12 And the
Spirit commanded me to go with them without hesitation.
And these six brethren accompanied me. And we entered the
man's house: 13 and he told us how he had seen an angel in his
house, standing and saying to him, Send to Joppa and call for
Simon, who is surnamed Peter; 14 he will tell you words by
which you and all your house shall be saved.

15 And as I began to speak, the Holy Spirit fell on them, as
on us at the beginning. 16 Then I remembered the word of the
Lord, as he said, John immersed in water, but you shall be immersed in the Holy Spirit. 17 If, then, God gave them the like
gift that he gave to us who believed on the Lord Jesus Christ,
what was I, that I could withstand God? 18 And when they
heard these things, they ceased to contend; and they glorified
God, saying: Then, indeed, has God given to the Gentiles also
repentance in order to life.

19 Now those who had been dispersed by the persecution that
arose after the death of Stephen, traveled as far as Phenicia
and Cyprus and Antioch, speaking the word to none but Jews.
20 But some of them were men of Cyprus and Cyrene, who, when
they had come to Antioch, spoke to the Grecians, preaching the
Lord Jesus. 21 And the hand of the Lord was with them, and a
great number believed, and turned to the Lord.

22 And the report concerning them came to the ears of the
church that was in Jerusalem; and they sent out Barnabas to
go as far as Antioch. 23 When he had come, and had seen the
grace of God, he rejoiced; and he exhorted them all to remain,
with purpose of heart, faithful to the Lord. 24 For he was a
good man, and full of the Holy Spirit and of faith. And a great
multitude was added to the Lord.

25 And Barnabas went to Tarsus, to seek for Saul; 26 and when
he had found him, he brought him to Antioch. And it came to
pass, that they met together in the church for a whole year,
and taught a great multitude; and the disciples were called
Christians first at Antioch.

27 In those days prophets came from Jerusalem to Antioch.
28 And one of them, named Agabus, rose and made known, by
the Spirit, that a great famine was about to come on the whole
habitable land; which took place in the days of Claudius.

29 And every one of the disciples determined, as he had the
means, to send relief to the brethren that dwelt in Judea;
30 which also they did; and they sent it to the elders by the
hands of Barnabas and Saul.

XII. 1 At that time Herod the king undertook to afflict some
of the church. 2 And he slew with the sword James the brother
of John.
3 And when he saw that it pleased the Jews, he apprehended
Peter also. Those were the days of unleavened bread. 4 And
when he had apprehended him, he put him in prison, and delivered him to four tetrads of soldiers to guard him, intending
to bring him out to the people after the passover. 5 Therefore,
Peter was kept in prison; but fervent prayer to God was made
for him by the church.
6 When Herod was about to bring him out, on that night,
Peter was sleeping between two soldiers, bound with two chains;
and the keepers before the doors were guarding the prison.
7 And behold, an angel of the Lord stood by him, and a light
shone in the prison. And he gently struck Peter on the side,
and awoke him, saying: Arise quickly; and his chains fell from
his hands. 8 And the angel said to him: Gird yourself, and bind
on your sandals; and he did so. And he said to him: Throw
your mantle around you, and follow me. 9 And he went out,
and followed him; and he knew not that what was done by the
angel was real, but thought that he saw a vision.
10 And when they had passed through the first and the second
guard, they came to the iron gate that leads to the city, which
opened to them of its own accord. And they went out, and
passed on through one street; and the angel immediately departed from him. 11 And when Peter came to himself, he said:
Now I know, in truth, that the Lord has sent his angel, and
has delivered me from the hand of Herod, and from all that was
expected by the Jewish people.
12 And being aware of his condition, he came to the house of
Mary the mother of John, who is surnamed Mark, where many
had met together, and were praying. 13 And when he knocked
at the door of the entrance, a maid-servant, named Rhoda,
came to listen. 14 And recognizing Peter's voice, she did not
open the entrance for joy, but ran in and told that Peter was
standing before the entrance. 15 And they said to her: You are
mad. But she confidently affirmed that it was even so. Then

said they: It is his angel. 16 But Peter continued to knock;
and when they had opened the door, they saw him, and were
astonished. 17 But, having made a sign to them with his hand,
that they should keep silence, he made known to them how the
Lord had brought him out of the prison, and he said: Tell this
to James, and to the brethren. And he went out, and departed
to another place.

18 And when it was day, there was no little confusion among
the soldiers as to what had become of Peter. 19 But Herod,
when he had sought for him, and found him not, examined the
keepers, and commanded them to be put to death. And he went
down from Judea to Cæsarea, and there he remained.

20 And he was intending to make war upon the Tyrians and
Sidonians; but they came with one consent to him; and having made Blastus, who had charge of the king's bed-chamber,
their friend, they asked for peace, because their country was
supported by that of the king. 21 And on an appointed day,
Herod, having arrayed himself in royal apparel, and seated
himself on his throne, delivered an oration to them. 22 And the
people shouted: It is the voice of God, and not of man. 23 And
immediately an angel of the Lord smote him, because he did
not give God the glory. And having been eaten by worms, he
expired.

24 But the word of the Lord increased and multiplied. 25 And
Barnabas and Saul, after they had fulfilled their ministry, returned from Jerusalem, taking with them John, whose surname
was Mark.

XIII. 1 Now there were certain prophets and teachers in the
church that was at Antioch; Barnabas, and Simeon, who is
called Niger, and Lucius of Cyrene, and Manaen, who was
brought up with Herod the tetrarch, and Saul. 2 And while
they were ministering to the Lord, and fasting, the Holy Spirit
said: Set apart for me Barnabas and Saul, to the work to which
I have called them. 3 Then, after they had fasted and prayed,
and laid their hands on them, they sent them away.

4 Therefore, having been sent forth by the Holy Spirit, they
went down to Seleucia, and thence sailed to Cyprus. 5 And while
they were in Salamis, they preached the word of God in the synagogue of the Jews; and they had John as their attendant.

6 And having gone through the island as far as Paphos, they
found a certain magician, a Jewish false prophet, whose name

was Bar-jesus; [7] and he was with the proconsul, Sergius Paulus,
who was a man of intelligence. This man called for Barnabas
and Saul, and expressed an earnest wish to hear the word of
God. [8] But the magician, Elymas (for this is his name, when
translated) withstood them, desiring to turn away the proconsul from the faith. [9] Then Saul, who is also called Paul, filled
with the Holy Spirit, and looking earnestly upon him, [10] said:
O full of all deceit and all wickedness, child of the devil, enemy
of all righteousness, will you not cease to pervert the right
ways of the Lord? [11] And now, behold, the hand of the Lord is
upon you, and you shall be blind, not seeing the sun for a season.
And immediately there fell on him a mist and a darkness, and
he went about and sought some to lead him by the hand. [12] Then
the proconsul, seeing what was done, believed, being amazed at
the teaching of the Lord.

[13] And Paul and his companions put to sea from Paphos, and
went to Perga in Pamphylia. But John withdrew from them,
and returned to Jerusalem. [14] But having passed through from
Perga, they came to Antioch in Pisidia; and on the Sabbath-
day they went into the synagogue, and sat down. [15] After the
reading of the law and the prophets, the rulers of the synagogue sent to them, saying: Brethren, if you have a word of
exhortation for the people, speak.

[16] Then Paul arose, and waving his hand, said: Men of Israel,
and you who fear God, give audience. [17] The God of this people
chose our fathers, and exalted the people when they sojourned
in the land of Egypt, and with an uplifted arm he brought
them out from it. [18] And for about forty years, he cherished
them in the wilderness. [19] And when he had destroyed seven
nations in the land of Chanaan, he divided their land among
them by lot. [20] And after that he gave them judges, for about
four hundred and fifty years, till Samuel the prophet.

[21] And afterward they asked for a king, and God gave them
Saul the son of Kis, a man of the tribe of Benjamin, for forty
years. [22] And when he had removed him, he raised up David
to be their king; to whom he gave this testimony: I have found
David the son of Jesse a man after my own heart, who will do
all my will. [23] From the posterity of this man, God, according
to his promise, raised up for Israel a Savior, Jesus; [24] John
having first preached, before his coming, the immersion of
repentance to all the people of Israel.

[25] And as John was finishing his course, he said: Who do you

suppose that I am? I am not he; but behold, there is coming
after me one, the sandals of whose feet I am not worthy to loose.
26 Brethren, sons of the family of Abraham, and those among
you who fear God, to you is the word of this salvation sent.
27 For those who dwell in Jerusalem, and their rulers, because
they did not know him, nor the words of the prophets, which
are read every Sabbath-day, have fulfilled them in condemning
him. 28 And though they found no cause of death, yet they demanded of Pilate that he should be slain. 29 And when they
had fulfilled all that was written of him, they took him down
from the tree, and laid him in a sepulcher. 30 But God raised
him from the dead. 31 And he was seen for many days by those
who came up with him from Galilee to Jerusalem, who are his
witnesses to the people.

32 And we preach to you good news concerning the promise
made to our fathers, 33 that God has fulfilled the same to us,
their children, by raising up Jesus, as it is written in the second Psalm: Thou art my Son, this day have I begotten thee.
34 But that he raised him from the dead, no more to return to
corruption, he has spoken thus: I will give you the sure mercies
of David. 35 For which reason he says also in another Psalm:
Thou wilt not suffer thy Holy One to see corruption. 36 For
David, after serving the purpose of God in his own generation,
fell asleep, and was laid with his fathers, and saw corruption.
37 But he whom God raised up did not see corruption.

38 Be it known to you, therefore, brethren, that through this
man is preached to you the remission of sins: 39 and by him,
every one that believes is justified from all things, from which
you could not be justified by the law of Moses. 40 Take heed,
therefore, lest that which is spoken in the prophets come upon
you: 41 Behold, you despisers, and wonder, and perish. For I
work a work in your days, a work which you will not believe,
though one fully declare it to you.

42 And as they were departing from the synagogue, they were
requested to speak these things to them on the next Sabbath.
43 Now, after the congregation was dismissed, many of the Jews
and religious proselytes followed Paul and Barnabas, who spoke
to them, and persuaded them to continue faithful to the grace
of God. 44 And on the next Sabbath-day, almost the whole city
met together to hear the word of God.

45 But when the Jews saw the multitudes, they were filled with
envy, and spoke against those things which were spoken by Paul,

contradicting and reviling. 46 But Paul and Barnabas, speaking boldly, said: It was necessary that the word of God should
be spoken to you first: but since you reject it, and judge yourselves unworthy of eternal life, lo! we turn to the Gentiles.
47 For thus has the Lord given us commandment: I have placed
thee for a light to the Gentiles, that thou mayest be for salvation
to the most distant part of the earth.

48 When the Gentiles heard this they rejoiced, and glorified the
word of the Lord; and as many as were disposed for eternal life,
believed. 49 And the word of the Lord was published throughout
the whole of that region. 50 But the Jews incited the devout and
influential women, and the first men of the city, and raised a
persecution against Paul and Barnabas, and expelled them from
their borders. 51 But they shook off the dust from their feet
against them, and went to Iconium. 52 And the disciples were
filled with joy and the Holy Spirit.

XIV. 1 And it came to pass in Iconium, that they went together into the synagogue of the Jews, and so spoke that a
great multitude of the Jews and Greeks believed. 2 But the unbelieving Jews excited and embittered the minds of the Gentiles
against the brethren. 3 Therefore, they continued a long time,
and spoke boldly in the Lord, who gave testimony to the word
of his grace, by granting signs and wonders to be done by their
hands.

4 But the multitude of the city were divided; and some were
with the Jews, and some with the apostles. 5 But when there
was a violent purpose on the part of the Gentiles and of the
Jews, with their rulers, to outrage and to stone them, 6 being
aware of it, they fled to the cities of Lycaonia, Lystra, and
Derbe, and to the regions round about, 7 and there they preached
the gospel.

8 And there was a certain man in Lystra, without strength in
his feet, who sat, for he was a cripple from his mother's womb,
and had never walked. 9 This man heard Paul speak, who,
looking earnestly on him, and seeing that he had faith to be
saved, 10 said, with a loud voice: Stand erect upon your feet.
And he leaped and walked. 11 When the multitude saw what
Paul had done, they lifted up their voice, and said, in the Lyca-
onian language: The Gods have come down to us in the likeness
of men. 12 And they called Barnabas, Jupiter, and Paul, Mer-
cury, for he was the chief speaker.

13 Then the priest of Jupiter, whose temple was before the city,
having brought bulls and garlands to the entrance, intended to
offer sacrifice, with the multitudes. 14 But when the apostles,
Barnabas and Paul, heard of it, they rent their clothes, and ran
in among the multitude, crying out, 15 and saying: Men, why
are you doing these things? We also are human beings, with
passions like your own, and we preach the gospel to you, that
you may turn from these vanities to the living God, who made
the heaven, and the earth, and the sea, and all things that are
in them; 16 who, in past generations, permitted all the nations
to walk in their own ways; 17 and yet he did not leave himself
without testimony, doing good, and giving you rain from heaven,
and fruitful seasons, filling your hearts with food and gladness.
18 And with these words they hardly restrained the multitudes
from offering sacrifice to them.

19 Then came thither, from Antioch and Iconium, Jews, who
persuaded the multitudes; and having stoned Paul, they dragged
him out of the city, supposing that he was dead. 20 But while
the disciples were standing around him, he arose, and went into
the city.

And on the next day, he departed with Barnabas to Derbe;
21 and when they had preached the gospel to that city, and had
made many disciples, they returned to Lystra, and to Iconium,
and to Antioch, 22 strengthening the souls of the disciples, exhorting them to continue in the faith, and saying, that through
many afflictions we must enter the kingdom of God. 23 And
when they had appointed elders for them in every church, with
prayer and fasting, they commended them to the Lord, on whom
they believed. 24 And having passed through Pisidia, they came
into Pamphylia; 25 and when they had preached the word in
Perga, they went down to Attalia: 26 thence they sailed to Antioch, from which place they had been commended to the grace
of God, for the work which they had accomplished.

27 And having come and called together the church, they reported all that God had done with them, and that he had opened
the door of faith to the Gentiles. 28 And they continued a long
time with the disciples.

XV. 1 And certain men came down from Judea, and taught
the brethren, saying: Unless you be circumcised, according to
the custom of Moses, you can not be saved. 2 Therefore, after
Paul and Barnabas had no little dissension and disputation

with them, they determined that Paul and Barnabas, and certain others from among them, should go up to Jerusalem, to the apostles and elders, about this question. 3 Being, therefore, conducted on their journey by the church, they passed through Phenicia and Samaria, making known the conversion of the Gentiles; and they gave great joy to all the brethren. 4 When they arrived at Jerusalem, they were received by the church, and the apostles and elders, and they declared all that God had done with them. 5 But some of the sect of the Pharisees, who believed, arose, saying, that it was necessary to circumcise them, and to command them to keep the law of Moses.

6 And the apostles and elders came together to deliberate about this matter. 7 And after there had been much disputing, Peter arose, and said to them: Brethren, you know that, at the beginning, God made choice among us, that, by my mouth, the Gentiles should hear the word of the Gospel, and believe. 8 And God, who knows the heart, became a witness for them, by giving them the Holy Spirit, as he gave it also to us; 9 and he made no distinction between us and them, purifying their hearts by faith. 10 Now, therefore, why do you put God to the proof, by placing a yoke upon the neck of the disciples, which neither our fathers, nor we ourselves, were able to bear? 11 But we believe that we shall be saved, even as they, through the grace of our Lord Jesus Christ.

12 Then all the multitude kept silence, and listened to Barnabas and Paul, while they made known what signs and wonders God had done by them among the Gentiles.

13 And after they were silent, James answered and said: Brethren, hear me; 14 Simeon has declared how God, at the first, did visit the Gentiles, in order to take out from among them a people for his name. 15 And with this agree the words of the prophets; as it is written, 16 After this I will return, and build again the tabernacle of David which has fallen down; and I will build again its ruins, and I will set it up; 17 that the rest of men may seek after the Lord, and all the Gentiles, upon whom my name has been called, says the Lord, who does all these things. 18 Known to God from eternity are all his works. 19 For these reasons, my judgment is, that we give no trouble to those who, from among the Gentiles, have turned to God; 20 but that we write to them to abstain from pollutions of idols, and from lewdness, and from what is strangled, and from blood. 21 For, from ancient times, Moses has, in every

city, those who preach him, being read in the synagogue every
Sabbath-day.

22 Then it pleased the apostles and the elders, with the whole
church, to send to Antioch, with Paul and Barnabas, chosen
men from among themselves; Judas, who was surnamed Barsabas, and Silas, chief men among the brethren; 23 and they wrote
by their hands as follows:

The apostles, and the elders, and the brethren, to the brethren of the Gentiles in Antioch and Syria and Cilicia, greeting:
24 Inasmuch as we have heard that certain persons went out
from us and troubled you with words, subverting your souls,
saying, That you must be circumcised, and keep the law, to
whom we gave no commandment, 25 it has seemed good to us,
having come together with one mind, to send chosen men to
you, with our beloved Barnabas and Paul, 26 men who have en-
dangered their lives for the name of our Lord Jesus Christ.
27 We have sent, therefore, Judas and Silas, who will tell you the
same things in word. 28 For it has seemed good to the Holy
Spirit, and to us, to lay upon you no greater burden than these
necessary things: 29 That you abstain from things sacrificed to
idols, and from blood, and from what is strangled, and from
lewdness; from which if you keep yourselves carefully, you will
do well. Farewell.

30 So when these men were dismissed, they came to Antioch:
and having assembled the multitude, they delivered this letter.
31 When they had read it, they rejoiced for the consolation which
it gave. 32 And Judas and Silas, who were also prophets, exhorted the brethren with many words, and strengthened them.
33 And after spending some time, they were dismissed in peace
from the brethren, to those who had sent them. 34 But it pleased
Silas to remain there. 35 Paul also and Barnabas continued in
Antioch, teaching and preaching, with many others, the word
of the Lord.

36 And, after some days, Paul said to Barnabas, let us return,
and visit our brethren in every city in which we have preached
the word of the Lord, and see how they do. 37 And Barnabas
determined to take with him John, whose surname was Mark.
38 But Paul did not think it proper to take with them him who
had departed from them from Pamphylia, and did not go with
them to the work. 39 There was, therefore, a sharp contention,
so that they separated from each other: and Barnabas took
Mark, and sailed to Cyprus. 40 But Paul chose Silas, and de-

parted, having been commended to the grace of God by the
brethren. [41] And he passed through Syria and Cilicia, strengthening the churches.

XVI. [1] And he came to Derbe and Lystra; and behold, a
certain disciple was there, named Timothy, the son of a Jewess,
who was a believer; but his father was a Greek. [2] A good report was given of him by the brethren in Lystra and Iconium.
[3] This man Paul wished to go with him: and he took him and
circumcised him, on account of the Jews that were in those
places: for they all knew that his father was a Greek. [4] And
as they went through the cities, they delivered to them the
decrees that had been resolved on by the apostles and elders
at Jerusalem, that they might keep them. [5] Therefore, the
churches were established in the faith, and they increased in
number daily.

[6] When they had gone throughout Phrygia and the region of
Galatia, being forbidden by the Holy Spirit to preach the word
in Asia, [7] and had come to Mysia, they attempted to go into
Bithynia; and the Spirit did not permit them. [8] But having
passed by Mysia, they came down to Troas. [9] And, during the
night, a vision appeared to Paul. A certain man of Macedonia
stood and besought him, saying: Come over to Macedonia and
help us. [10] After he had seen the vision, we immediately endeavored to go into Macedonia, concluding that the Lord had
called us to preach the gospel to them.

[11] Therefore, setting sail from Troas, we came by a straight
course to Samothracia, and, on the following day, to Neapolis,
[12] and thence to Philippi, which is the first city of that part of
Macedonia, and a colony. We remained in that city some days:
[13] and on the Sabbath-day we went out of the city to the side
of a river, where, as usual, was the house of prayer; and we
sat down and spoke to the women who had come together.
[14] And a certain woman, named Lydia, a seller of purple, of the
city of Thyatira, who worshiped God, heard; whose heart the
Lord opened to attend to the things that were spoken by Paul.
[15] And when she and her household had been immersed, she besought us, saying: If you judge me to be faithful to the Lord,
come into my house, and make it your home. And she constrained us.

[16] And it came to pass, that as we were going to the house of
prayer, there met us a certain maid-servant that had a spirit

of Python, who brought much gain to her masters, by giving
responses. 17 She followed Paul and us, and cried out, saying:
These men are the servants of the most High God, who show
us the way of salvation. 18 And this she continued to do for
many days. But Paul, being grieved, turned and said to the
spirit: I command you, in the name of Jesus Christ, to come
out of her. And it came out that very hour.

19 And when her masters saw that the hope of their gain was
gone, they seized Paul and Silas, and dragged them into the
market to the rulers. 20 And having brought them to the magistrates, they said: These men, who are Jews, do greatly trouble
our city; 21 and they teach customs which it is not lawful for
us, who are Romans, to receive or to observe. 22 And the multitude rose up together against them; and the magistrates
stripped off their clothes, and gave command to beat them with
rods. 23 And when they had laid many stripes on them, they
threw them into prison, and charged the jailer to keep them
securely. 24 And having received such a charge, he put them
into the inner prison, and made their feet fast in the stocks.

25 And at midnight Paul and Silas prayed, and sung a hymn
to God; and the prisoners were listening to them. 26 And suddenly there was a great earthquake, so that the foundations of
the prison were shaken; and immediately all the doors were
opened, and every one's bonds were loosed. 27 And the jailer,
being aroused from sleep, and seeing the doors of the prison
open, drew his sword, and was about to kill himself, supposing
that the prisoners had fled. 28 But Paul called out with a loud
voice, saying: Do yourself no harm, for we are all here.

29 Then he called for a light, and sprang in, and trembling, he
fell down before Paul and Silas; 30 and, having brought them
out, he said: Sirs, what must I do to be saved? 31 They replied:
Believe on the Lord Jesus Christ, and you and your house shall
be saved. 32 And they spoke the word of the Lord to him, and
to all that were in his house. 33 And he took them at that hour
of the night, and washed the blood from their stripes; and he
was immersed, himself and all his, immediately. 34 And he
brought them into his house, and set food before them, and rejoiced, believing in God, with all his house.

35 But when it was day, the magistrates sent the lictors, saying: Release those men. 36 And the jailer told these words to
Paul: The magistrates have sent to release you. Now, therefore, come out, and go in peace. 37 But Paul said to them:

Having publicly scourged us uncondemned, us who are Romans,
they threw us into prison: and do they now put us out secretly?
No, verily: but let them come and lead us out. 38 And the lictors told these words to the magistrates: and they were alarmed
when they heard that they were Romans; 39 and they came, and
entreated them, and led them out, and requested them to depart
from the city. 40 And having come out of the prison, they went
into the house of Lydia; and when they had seen the brethren,
they comforted them, and departed.

XVII. 1 And when they had passed through Amphipolis
and Apollonia, they came to Thessalonica, where there was a
synagogue of the Jews. 2 And Paul, according to his custom,
went in to them, and, for three Sabbath-days, he reasoned with
them from the Scriptures, 3 explaining and affirming that it was
necessary for the Christ to suffer and to rise from the dead; and
that this Jesus whom I preach to you is the Christ. 4 And some
of them believed, and associated themselves with Paul and Silas;
of the devout Greeks, a great multitude, and of the chief women,
not a few.

5 But the unbelieving Jews, taking with them some evil men,
who were loungers about the markets, and collecting a mob, set
the city in an uproar; and having assaulted the house of Jason,
they sought to bring them out to the people. 6 But not finding
them, they dragged Jason and certain brethren before the rulers
of the city, crying out: These men, who have thrown the world
into confusion, have come hither also; 7 whom Jason has received into his house: and they all act in opposition to the decrees
of Cæsar, saying, That there is another king, Jesus. 8 And the
multitude, and the rulers of the city, were troubled when they
heard these things. 9 And they took security of Jason, and of
the others, and let them go.

10 And the brethren immediately sent away Paul and Silas by
night to Berea; and when they had come, they went into the
synagogue of the Jews. 11 These were of a better disposition
than those in Thessalonica, for they received the word with
all readiness of mind, examining the Scriptures daily, whether
these things were so. 12 Therefore, many of them believed; both
of influential women, who were Greeks, and of men, not a few.
13 But when the Jews of Thessalonica learned that the word of
God was preached by Paul in Berea also, they came thither,
and excited the multitude. 14 Then the brethren immediately

sent Paul away, to go as if to the sea; but Silas and Timothy
remained there. 15 And those who conducted Paul brought him
to Athens: and having received a commandment for Silas and
Timothy, that they should come to him as soon as possible,
they departed.

16 Now while Paul was waiting for them at Athens, his spirit
was stirred within him, when he saw the city full of idols
17 Accordingly, he reasoned in the synagogue with the Jews and
devout persons, and in the market daily, with those who chanced
to meet him. 18 And some of the Epicurean and Stoic philoso-
phers disputed with him; and some said: What can this babbler
possibly wish to say? Others said: He seems to be a pro-
claimer of strange demons: for he preached to them Jesus and
the Resurrection. 19 And they took him, and brought him to
Mars' hill, saying: Are we able to understand what this new
teaching is, which is announced by you? 20 For you bring some
strange things to our ears: we wish to understand then what
these things mean. 21 For all the Athenians and resident
strangers have leisure for nothing else than to tell or to hear
some new thing.

22 Then Paul stood in the midst of Mars' hill, and said: Men
of Athens, I perceive that in all respects your reverence for demons excels that of other men. 23 For as I was passing through,
and looking attentively at the objects of your worship, I dis-
covered also an altar with this inscription: TO THE UN-
KNOWN GOD. Whom therefore you ignorantly worship, him
I make known to you. 24 God, who made the world, and all
things that are in it, being Lord of heaven and earth, dwells
not in temples made with hands; 25 nor is he ministered to by
the hands of men, as if he needed any thing: for he himself
gives to all life, and breath, and all things: 26 and he has made
from one blood every nation of men, that they might dwell on
all the face of the earth, having marked out their appointed
times, and the bounds of their dwelling: 27 that they might seek
for God, if perhaps they would feel after him, and find him,
although, indeed, he is not far from every one of us. 28 For in
him we live, and move, and have our being: as also some of
your own poets have said: For we his offspring are.

29 Therefore, being the offspring of God, we ought not to think
that the Godhood is like gold, or silver, or stone, sculptured
by art and the device of man. 30 Yet the times of this ignorance
God overlooked; but now, he commands all men every-where

to repent: 31 because he has appointed a day in which he will
judge the world in righteousness, by the man whom he has
chosen, giving to all assurance of this, by having raised him
from the dead.

32 And when they heard of the resurrection of the dead, some
mocked; others said: We will hear you again concerning this
matter. 33 And so Paul departed from among them. 34 But certain men associated with him, and believed; among whom was
Dionysius the Areopagite, and a woman named Damăris, and
others with them.

XVIII. 1 After these things, Paul departed from Athens,
and came to Corinth; 2 and finding a certain Jew named Aquila,
born in Pontus, who had lately come from Italy, with Priscilla
his wife, because Claudius had commanded all Jews to depart
from Rome, he went to them; 3 and because he was of the same
trade, he made his home with them, and worked: for by trade
they were tent-makers. 4 But on every Sabbath, he reasoned
in the synagogue, and persuaded the Jews and the Greeks. 5 And
when Silas and Timothy came from Macedonia, Paul was roused
in spirit, and earnestly testified to the Jews, that the Christ
was Jesus.

6 But when they set themselves in opposition, and reviled, he
shook his clothing and said to them: Your blood be upon your
own head; I am clean. Henceforth I will go to the Gentiles
7 And he departed thence, and went into the house of a certain
man named Justus, who worshiped God, and whose house joined
the synagogue. 8 But Crispus, the ruler of the synagogue, believed on the Lord, with all his house; and many of the Corinthians hearing, believed, and were immersed. 9 And the Lord
spoke to Paul by a vision in the night: Fear not; but speak,
and be not silent; 10 for I am with you, and no one shall make
an assault upon you, to injure you; for I have many people in
this city. 11 And he remained there a year and six months,
teaching the word of God among them.

12 But while Gallio was proconsul of Achaia, the Jews, with
one mind, suddenly came upon Paul and brought him to the
judgment-seat, 13 saying: This man persuades men to worship
God contrary to the law. 14 But when Paul was about to open
his mouth, Gallio said to the Jews: If it were a matter of injustice, or of wicked mischief, O Jews, I would, with reason,
bear with you: 15 but if it is a question about a word, and

names, and your law, see to it yourselves: for I will not be a
judge of these things. [16]And he drove them from the judgment-seat. [17]And all the Greeks took Sosthenes, the ruler of
the synagogue, and beat him before the judgment-seat. And
Gallio cared for none of these things.

[18]And Paul, having remained many days longer, took leave
of the brethren, and sailed to Syria, and with him Priscilla and
Aquila, having shorn his head in Cenchrea; for he had a vow.
[19]And he came to Ephesus, and left them there; but he himself
went into the synagogue, and reasoned with the Jews. [20]And
though they besought him to remain with them a longer time,
he did not consent, [21]but took leave of them, saying: I must,
by all means, keep this coming feast in Jerusalem: but I will
return to you, if God be willing. And he sailed from Ephesus,
[22]and having landed at Cæsarea, and gone up and saluted the
church, he went down to Antioch. [23]And having spent some
time there, he departed, and went through the region of Galatia
and Phrygia in order, strengthening all the disciples.

[24]And a certain Jew, named Apollos, an Alexandrian by birth,
an eloquent man, and mighty in the Scriptures, came to Ephesus.
[25]He was instructed in the way of the Lord; and, being fervent
in spirit, he spoke and taught accurately the things of the Lord,
knowing only the immersion of John. [26]And he began to speak
boldly in the synagogue. But when Aquila and Priscilla heard
him, they took him, and taught him the way of God more accurately. [27]And when he wished to pass into Achaia, the brethren, exhorting him, wrote to the disciples to receive him. And
when he had come, he gave much help to the believers, through
the grace conferred on him. [28]For, with great strength, he
utterly confounded the Jews publicly, showing, by the Scriptures, that the Christ was Jesus.

XIX. [1]And it came to pass, while Apollos was at Corinth,
that Paul, after passing through the upper districts, came to
Ephesus, and finding certain disciples, [2]said to them: Have you
received the Holy Spirit since you believed? They said to him:
We have not only not received it, but we have not even heard
whether the Holy Spirit is given. [3]And he said to them: Into
what, then, were you immersed? They replied: Into John's
immersion. [4]And Paul said: John immersed with the immersion of repentance, saying to the people, that they must believe
on him who should come after him, that is, on the Christ, Jesus.

5 And when they heard this, they were immersed into the name
of the Lord Jesus. 6 And when Paul laid his hands on them,
the Holy Spirit came upon them, and they spoke with tongues,
and prophesied. 7 And all the men were about twelve.

8 And he entered the synagogue, and spoke boldly, reasoning,
and persuading them for three months, with respect to the
things of the kingdom of God. 9 But as some were hardened,
and did not believe, and spoke evil of that way before the multitude, he withdrew from them, and separated the disciples, and
discoursed daily in the school of one Tyrannus. 10 This continued for two years; so that all that dwelt in Asia heard the
word of the Lord, both Jews and Greeks. 11 Mighty deeds, also,
that were unusual, did God perform by the hands of Paul; 12 so
that handkerchiefs or aprons were carried from his body to the
sick, and diseases departed from them, and the evil spirits came
out of them.

13 And some of the roving Jews, who were exorcists, undertook to pronounce the name of the Lord Jesus over those who
had evil spirits, saying: I adjure you by the Jesus whom Paul
preaches. 14 And there were seven sons of Sceva, a Jewish
chief priest, who did this. 15 But the evil spirit answered and
said: Jesus I acknowledge, and Paul I know; but who are you?
16 And the man in whom the evil spirit was, leaped on them, and
overpowered them, and prevailed against them, so that they
fled from that house, naked and wounded. 17 And this became
known to all the Greeks and Jews that dwelt in Ephesus; and
fear fell upon them all, and the name of the Lord Jesus was
magnified. 18 And many of those who believed came and confessed, and made known their practices. 19 And many of those
who practiced magic, brought together their books, and burned
them, in the presence of all. And they computed their value,
and found it fifty thousand pieces of silver. 20 So mightily did
the word of the Lord grow and prevail.

21 When these things had been accomplished, Paul purposed
in spirit to go to Jerusalem, after he should pass through Macedonia and Achaia, saying: After I have been there, I must
see Rome also. 22 So, having sent into Macedonia two of those
who ministered to him, Timothy and Erastus, he remained for
a time in Asia.

23 And at that time there was no little excitement about that
way. 24 For a certain man, named Demetrius, a silversmith, by
making silver shrines for Diana, furnished no little trade to the

artists. 25 These he called together, with the workmen em-
ployed about such things, and said: Men, you know that our
wealth arises from this trade: 26 and you see and hear, that not
only at Ephesus, but throughout almost the whole of Asia, this
Paul, by his persuasions, has drawn away a great multitude,
saying, that they which are made with hands are not gods.
27 Now there is danger, not only that this our calling will come
into disgrace, but that the temple of the great goddess Diana
will be despised, and that the majesty of her whom all Asia and
the world worships, will be destroyed.

28 When they heard this, they were full of anger, and cried
out, saying: Great is Diana of the Ephesians! 29 And the whole
city was filled with confusion. And they seized Gaius and Aristarchus, who were Macedonians, Paul's fellow-travelers, and,
with one consent, rushed into the theater. 30 And when Paul
wished to go in among the people, the disciples did not permit
him. 31 Some of the Asiarchs also, who were friendly to him,
sent to him, and besought him not to trust himself into the
theater. 32 Some, therefore, were crying one thing, and some
another: for the assembly was confused, and the greater part
knew not for what they had come together. 33 And some of
the multitude put Alexander forward, the Jews urging him on.
And Alexander waved his hand, and wished to make a defense
to the people. 34 But perceiving that he was a Jew, they all
cried out, with one voice, for about two hours: Great is Diana
of the Ephesians.

35 But the town-clerk quieted the multitude, and said: Men
of Ephesus, what man is there who does not know that the
city of the Ephesians is a worshiper of the great Diana, and
of the image that fell down from Jupiter? 36 As these things,
then, can not be contradicted, you ought to be quiet, and do
nothing rashly. 37 For you have brought these men here, who
are neither robbers of temples, nor revilers of your goddess.
38 Therefore, if Demetrius, and the artists who are with him,
have a charge against any one, the courts are in session, and
the proconsuls are there; let them accuse each other. 39 But
if you have any inquiries to make about other matters, it shall
be determined in a lawful assembly. 40 For we are in danger
of being called to answer for this day's tumult, since there is
no cause by which we shall be able to account for this concourse. 41 And when he had said these things, he dismissed the
assembly.

XX. 1 After the tumult had ceased, Paul called the disciples to him, and bade them farewell, and departed, in order to go into Macedonia. 2 And when he had gone through those regions, and had exhorted them with many words, he came into Greece. 3 And having remained there three months, he determined to return through Macedonia, because a plot had been laid for him by the Jews, as he was about to sail to Syria. 4 And Sopater of Berea, and Aristarchus and Secundus of Thessalonica, and Gaius of Derbe, and Timothy and Tychicus and Trophimus, who were Asiatics, accompanied him to Asia. 5 These went before, and waited for us at Troas. 6 But we sailed from Philippi, after the days of unleavened bread, and came to them at Troas in five days, where we remained seven days.

7 And on the first day of the week, when the disciples came together to break bread, Paul discoursed to them, intending to depart on the morrow; and he continued his speech till midnight. 8 And there were many lamps in the upper room, in which they had met together. 9 And a certain young man, named Eutychus, was sitting in the window, overpowered with deep sleep: and, as Paul was discoursing a long time, being oppressed with sleep, he fell from the third story, and was taken up dead. 10 But Paul went down, and fell upon him, and embracing him, said: Be not troubled, for his life is in him. 11 And he went up again, and broke bread, and ate; and having conversed a long time, till daylight, he thus departed. 12 And they brought the young man alive, and were not a little comforted.

13 And we went on before to the ship, and put to sea for Assos, intending to take Paul on board at that place; for he had so directed, intending to go himself on foot. 14 And when he met us at Assos, we took him on board, and came to Mitylene; 15 and sailing from that place, we came, on the following day, opposite to Chios; and, on the next day, we arrived at Samos: and after stopping at Trogyllium, we came, on the next day, to Miletus. 16 For Paul had determined to sail past Ephesus, that he might not spend time in Asia; for he hastened, that, if it were possible for him, he might be in Jerusalem on the day of Pentecost.

17 From Miletus he sent to Ephesus, and called the elders of the church. 18 And when they had come to him, he said to them: You know, from the first day on which I came into Asia, how I was with you during the whole time, 19 serving the Lord with all lowliness of mind, and with tears, and with trials,

which came upon me through the plots of the Jews; 20 and
that I kept back nothing that was profitable, but preached
to you, and taught you both publicly, and from house to house,
21 bearing full testimony both to Jews and to Greeks, of the
repentance toward God, and of the faith toward our Lord
Jesus Christ.

22 And now, behold, I am going, bound in spirit, to Jerusalem,
not knowing what shall befall me there, 23 except that in every
city the Holy Spirit testifies to me, saying, That bonds and
afflictions await me. 24 But I esteem this a matter of no importance, nor do I hold my life dear to myself, so that I may
finish my course with joy, and the ministry that I have received
from the Lord Jesus, to bear full testimony to the gospel of the
grace of God. 25 And now, behold, I know that you all, among
whom I have gone preaching the kingdom of God, will see my
face no more. 26 For this reason I solemnly affirm to you this
day, that I am clean from the blood of all men. 27 For I did not
shun to declare to you the whole counsel of God.

28 Therefore, take heed to yourselves, and to all the flock over
which the Holy Spirit has made you overseers, that you be shepherds to the church of God, which he has purchased with his
own blood. 29 For I know this, that, after my departure, rapa-
cious wolves will enter in among you, who will not spare the
flock; 30 and men will arise from among yourselves, speaking
perverse things, that they may draw off disciples after them.
31 Therefore watch, remembering that for three years, by day
and by night, I ceased not to warn every one of you with tears.
32 And now, brethren, I commend you to God, and to the word
of his grace; to him who is able to build you up, and to give
you an inheritance among all the sanctified. 33 I have coveted
no man's silver, or gold, or apparel. 34 You yourselves know
that these hands ministered to my necessities, and to those
who were with me. 35 In all things I taught you by example,
that by thus laboring, you ought to support the weak, and to
remember the words of the Lord Jesus; for he himself said, It
is more blessed to give, than to receive.

36 And when he had thus spoken, he kneeled down and prayed
with them all. 37 And they all wept much, and fell on Paul's
neck, and kissed him, 38 grieving most of all for the word he had
spoken, that they would see his face no more. And they conducted him to the ship.

XXI. 1 And it came to pass that, after we had separated from
them, we put to sea, and came by a straight course to Cos, and
on the following day, to Rhodes, and thence to Patara. 2 And
finding a ship that was going to Phenicia, we embarked, and
put to sea. 3 And we came in view of Cyprus; and, leaving it
to the left, we sailed to Syria, and landed at Tyre: for there the
ship was to put off her lading. 4 And we remained there seven
days, after finding the disciples. These urged Paul, by the
Spirit, not to go up to Jerusalem. 5 And when these days were
completed, we went forth, and continued our journey, they all,
with their wives and children, conducting us out of the city: and
we kneeled down on the shore, and prayed. 6 And when we had
bid each other farewell, we embarked, and they returned home.

7 And completing the voyage from Tyre, we arrived at Ptole-
mais: and having saluted the brethren, we remained with them
one day. 8 On the following day we departed, and came to Cæsarea, and went into the house of Philip the evangelist, who was
one of the seven; and we remained with him. 9 This man had
four virgin daughters, who had the gift of prophecy.

10 And as we remained there many days, there came down,
from Judea, a certain prophet, named Agabus; 11 and he came
to us, and taking Paul's girdle, he bound his own hands and
feet, and said: Thus says the Holy Spirit; the Jews that are in
Jerusalem will so bind the man to whom this girdle belongs;
and they will deliver him into the hands of the Gentiles. 12 And
when we heard these things, we, and those of that place also,
besought him not to go up to Jerusalem. 13 But Paul answered:
What do you effect by weeping, and breaking my heart? For
I am ready, not only to be bound, but also to suffer death in
Jerusalem, for the name of the Lord Jesus. 14 And as he would
not be persuaded, we kept silence, and said: The will of the
Lord be done.

15 And after these days we prepared for our journey, and went
up to Jerusalem. 16 There went with us also some of the disciples from Cæsarea, who took with them Mnason of Cyprus, an
old disciple, with whom we should lodge.

17 And when we came to Jerusalem, the brethren received us
gladly. 18 And, on the following day, Paul went in with us to
James, and all the elders were present. 19 And when he had
saluted them, he related, in every particular, the things which
God had done among the Gentiles by his ministry.

20 And when they heard it, they glorified the Lord, and said

to him: You see, brother, how many myriads of the Jews there
are that believe, and they are all zealous for the law. 21 And
they have heard it reported of you, that you teach all the Jews
that are among the Gentiles to apostatize from Moses; commanding them not to circumcise their children, nor to walk
according to the customs. 22 What, then, is to be done? A multitude must certainly come together; for they will hear that
you have come. 23 Do, therefore, this which we advise you.
We have four men who have a vow on them. 24 Take them, and
join with them in their vow of abstinence, and pay their ex-
penses, in order that they may shave their heads; and all will
know that the things which they have heard reported of you
are nothing; but that you yourself also walk orderly, and keep
the law. 25 But with respect to the Gentiles that believe, we
have written; having decided that they should observe no such
thing; but that they keep themselves from things sacrificed to
idols, and from blood, and from what is strangled, and from
lewdness.

26 Then Paul took the men, and, on the following day, joining
in their vow of abstinence, he entered the temple, and gave
notice when the days of abstinence would be completed, at
which time an offering should be made for each of them.

27 And when the seven days were about to be completed, the
Jews from Asia, seeing him in the temple, threw all the multitude into confusion, and laid their hands on him, 28 crying out:
Men of Israel, help! this is the man who teaches all men every-
where against this people, and the law, and this place: and
besides, he has even brought Greeks into the temple, and defiled
this holy place. 29 For, before this time, they had seen Trophimus, the Ephesian, with him in the city, whom they supposed
Paul had brought into the temple. 30 And the whole city was
moved; and the people ran together, and, seizing Paul, they
dragged him out of the temple, and the gates were immediately
closed.

31 And while they were seeking to kill him, report was brought
to the officer of the band, that the whole of Jerusalem was in
an uproar. 32 And he immediately took soldiers and centurions,
and ran down to them. When they saw the officer and the
soldiers, they ceased beating Paul. 33 Then the officer came
near and took him, and commanded him to be bound with two
chains, and demanded who he was, and what he had done.
34 And some in the multitude cried out one thing, and some an-

other. But not being able to obtain any certain knowledge on
account of the tumult, he commanded him to be led into the
fortress. 35 And when he was on the steps, it happened that he
was carried by the soldiers, on account of the violence of the
multitude. 36 For the greater part of the people followed, crying out: Away with him!

37 But as Paul was about to be led into the fortress, he said to
the officer: May I speak to you? He replied: Do you understand Greek? 38 Are you not that Egyptian, who, before these
days, made an insurrection, and led out into the wilderness
four thousand men of the Assassins? 39 But Paul replied: I
am a Jew of Tarsus of Cilicia, a citizen of no unknown city;
and I beseech you, permit me to speak to the people. 40 And
when he had given him permission, Paul, standing upon
the steps, waved his hand to the people. And when there was
great silence, he addressed them in the Hebrew language,
saying:

XXII. 1 Brethren and fathers, hear my defense, which I now
make before you. 2 When they heard that he spoke to them in
the Hebrew language, they kept the greater silence. And he
said: 3 I am a Jew, born in Tarsus of Cilicia, yet educated in
this city, at the feet of Gamaliel, and instructed according to
the strict discipline of the law of our fathers, being zealous for
God, as you all are this day. 4 And I persecuted this way to
the death, binding and delivering into prison both men and
women, 5 as the chief priest and the whole body of elders will
testify for me. From them I also received letters to the brethren, and went to Damascus, to bring those, also, who were
there, bound to Jerusalem, that they might be punished.

6 But it came to pass, that, as I was on my journey, and was
drawing near to Damascus, about midday, there suddenly shone
from heaven a great light round about me; 7 and I fell to the
ground, and heard a voice saying to me, Saul, Saul, why do you
persecute me? 8 And I answered, Who art thou Lord? And he
said to me, I am Jesus the Nazarene, whom you persecute.
9 They who were with me saw the light, and were afraid, but
did not understand the voice of him who spoke to me. 10 And
I said, What shall I do, Lord? And the Lord said to me, Arise,
and go into Damascus, and there you shall be told of all things
that are appointed for you to do.

11 And as I could not see for the glory of that light, I was led

by the hand by those who were with me, and went into Damascus. 12 And one Ananias, a devout man according to the law,
who had a good report from all the Jews that dwelt there,
13 came to me, and standing by me, said, Brother Saul, receive
your sight. And the same hour I looked upon him. 14 And he
said, The God of our Fathers has chosen you, that you should
know his will, and see the Just One, and hear the voice of his
mouth; 15 for you shall be his witness to all men of what you
have seen and heard. 16 And now, why do you delay? Arise,
and be immersed, and wash away your sins, calling on the name
of the Lord.

17 And it came to pass, after I had returned to Jerusalem,
and while I was praying in the temple, that I was in a trance,
18 and saw him saying to me, Make haste, and depart quickly
from Jerusalem, for they will not receive your testimony concerning me. 19 And I said, Lord, they themselves know that I
threw into prison, and scourged, in every synagogue, those who
believed on thee; 20 and that when the blood of Stephen, thy
witness, was shed, I also stood by and approved, and kept the
clothing of those who slew him. 21 And he said to me, Depart,
for I will send you far off to the Gentiles.

22 And they heard him to this word, and lifted up their voice,
saying: Away with such a man from the earth! for it is not fit
that he should live. 23 And as they were crying out, and toss-
ing off their clothes, and throwing dust into the air, 24 the officer commanded him to be led into the fortress, and gave orders
that he should be examined by scourging, that he might know
for what cause they so cried out against him. 25 But Paul said
to the centurion who stood by, as he caused him to be bent forward to the straps: Is it lawful for you to scourge a man who
is a Roman, and uncondemned? 26 And when the centurion
heard that, he went out and told it to the officer, saying: What
are you about to do? for this man is a Roman. 27 And the officer came and said to him: Tell me, are you a Roman? He answered: Yes. 28 And the officer answered: With a great sum
did I purchase this citizenship. And Paul replied: But I was
born a citizen. 29 Then, those who were about to examine him,
immediately departed from him. And the officer was afraid,
when he learned that he was a Roman, and because he had
bound him.

30 And, on the next day, wishing to know certainly why he
was accused by the Jews, he loosed him, and commanded the

chief priests and all the Sanhedrim to meet together. And he
brought Paul down, and placed him before them.

XXIII. 1 And Paul, looking earnestly upon the Sanhedrim,
said: Brethren, I have lived in all good conscience toward God
to this day. 2 And the chief priest, Ananias, commanded those
who stood by to smite him on the mouth. 3 Then Paul said to
him: God will smite you, you whitened wall! for do you sit to
judge me according to the law, and yet violate the law by
commanding me to be smitten? 4 And those who stood by said:
Do you revile God's chief priest? 5 And Paul replied: I did
not know, brethren, that he was the chief priest: for it is written, You shall not speak evil of the ruler of your people.

6 But when Paul perceived that one part belonged to the Sadducees, and the other to the Pharisees, he cried out, in the Sanhedrim: Brethren, I am a Pharisee, the son of a Pharisee; for
the hope of the resurrection of the dead am I judged. 7 And
when he had said this, there arose a dissension between the
Pharisees and the Sadducees, and the multitude was divided.
8 For the Sadducees say that there is no resurrection; neither
angel nor spirit: but the Pharisees acknowledge both. 9 And
there arose a great clamor. And the scribes, on the part of the
Pharisees, arose and contended, saying: We find no evil in this
man; but if a spirit or an angel has spoken to him, let us not
fight against God. 10 And when there arose a great dissension,
the officer, fearing that Paul would be torn to pieces by them,
commanded the soldiers to go down, and to take him by force
from among them, and to bring him into the fortress.

11 And on the following night, the Lord stood by him, and
said: Take courage; for as you have testified of me in Jerusalem, so must you testify also in Rome.

12 And when it was day, the Jews combined together, and
bound themselves under a curse, saying, that they would neither
eat nor drink till they had killed Paul. 13 And there were more
than forty who formed this conspiracy. 14 And they went to
the chief priests and elders, and said: We have surely bound
ourselves under a curse, that we will taste nothing till we have
killed Paul. 15 Now therefore, do you, together with the Sanhedrim, give notice to the officer, that he bring him down to you
to-morrow, as if you intended to inquire more accurately into
the matters concerning him: and before he comes near, we are
ready to kill him.

16 But the son of Paul's sister heard of the plot, and he went
and entered the fortress, and told Paul. 17 And Paul called one
of the centurions to him, and said: Conduct this young man to
the officer, for he has something to tell him. 18 So he took him,
and led him to the officer, and said: The prisoner Paul called
me to him, and requested me to conduct this young man to you;
for he has something to tell you. 19 And the officer took him by
the hand, and went aside with him privately, and inquired:
What is it that you have to tell me? 20 He answered: The Jews
have agreed to request you to bring Paul down into the Sanhedrim to-morrow, as if they intended to inquire something more
accurately concerning him. 21 Do not, however, be persuaded
by them; for more than forty men of them are lying in wait
for him; and they have bound themselves under a curse, that
they will neither eat nor drink till they have killed him. And
now they are ready, waiting for a promise from you. 22 Then
the officer sent the young man away, with this charge: Tell no
one that you have made these things known to me.

23 And he called to him two centurions, and said: Make ready
two hundred soldiers, and seventy horsemen, and two hundred
spearmen, that they may depart to Cæsarea at the third hour
of the night. 24 And provide beasts on which they may set Paul,
and take him in safety to Felix the governor. 25 And he wrote
a letter in this form: 26 Claudius Lysias to the most excellent
governor, Felix, greeting: 27 This man was taken by the Jews,
and was about to be killed by them. Then I went with soldiers,
and rescued him, having learned that he was a Roman. 28 But
wishing to know the cause for which they accused him, I
brought him down into their Sanhedrim. 29 And I found that
he was accused about questions of their law, but had nothing
worthy of death or of bonds charged against him. 30 And as I
was informed that a plot was about to be laid against the man
by the Jews, I immediately sent him to you, and commanded
his accusers to say in your presence what they had against him.
Farewell.

31 Then the soldiers took Paul, as they were commanded, and
brought him by night to Antipatris. 32 And, on the morrow,
they left the horsemen to go with him, and returned to the fortress. 33 When they came to Cæsarea, and delivered the letter
to the governor, they presented Paul also before him. 34 And
when he had read the letter, he inquired to what province he
belonged. And learning that he was from Cilicia he said: I

will hear you when your accusers also have come. And he ordered him to be kept under guard in Herod's palace.

XXIV. [1] And after five days, Ananias the chief priest came
down with the elders and a certain orator, Tertullus; and they
informed the governor against Paul. [2] And when he was called
forth, Tertullus began to accuse him, saying: [3] Since through
you we enjoy great quietness, and since whatever has been undertaken for this nation has been conducted to a successful issue by your foresight at all times and in all places, we accept it,
most excellent Felix, with all thankfulness. [4] But that I may
not detain you longer, I beseech you to hear us, in your clemency, a few words. [5] For we have found this man a pest and
a mover of sedition among all the Jews throughout the world,
a ringleader also of the sect of the Nazarenes. [6] He also attempted to profane the temple; and we took him, and wished to judge
him according to our law. [7] But Lysias the officer came, and,
with much violence, took him out of our hands, [8] and commanded his accusers to come before you. From him you may be able yourself, by examination, to gain a knowledge of all these things of which we accuse him.

[9] And the Jews united in accusing him, saying that these things were so.

[10] Then Paul, after the governor had nodded to him to speak,
answered: Knowing that you have been for many years a judge
of this nation, I do the more cheerfully offer a defense for myself; [11] for you can understand that there are not more than
twelve days since I went up to Jerusalem to worship. [12] And
they found me neither disputing with any one in the temple,
nor exciting the multitude in the synagogue, or in the city:
[13] nor are they able to prove the things of which they now accuse me. [14] But this I confess to you, that after the way which
they call sect, so do I worship the God of my fathers; believing
all things that are written in the law and in the prophets;
[15] having hope in God, which they themselves also admit, that
there will be a resurrection of the dead, both of the just and of
the unjust. [16] And I do exercise myself in this, always to have
a conscience void of offense toward God and man.

[17] But, after many years, I came to bring charitable gifts to
my nation, and offerings. [18] While engaged in these things, certain Jews from Asia found me fulfilling my vow of abstinence
in the temple, not with a multitude, nor with tumult. [19] These

ought to be here before you, and bring their charge, if they have
any, against me. 20 Or let these persons here say, what offensive
conduct they found in me when I stood before the Sanhedrim,
21 except in this one expression, which I uttered while standing
among them: With respect to the resurrection of the dead, I
am judged by you this day.

22 But Felix, having a more accurate knowledge of this way,
put them off, and said: When Lysias the officer comes down, I
will inquire fully into your matters. 23 And he commanded the
centurion to keep him under guard, and to relax the rigor of his
confinement, and to forbid no one of his friends to minister or
to come to him.

24 And, after some days, Felix came with his wife Drusilla,
who was a Jewess; and he sent for Paul, and heard him concerning the faith in Christ. 25 And as he reasoned of righteousness, temperance, and the judgment to come, Felix trembled,
and answered: For the present withdraw; when I have a con-
venient season, I will call for you. 26 He hoped, at the same
time, that money would have been given him by Paul, to release
him. For this reason, he sent for him very frequently, and
conversed with him.

27 But, after two years, Felix received Portius Festus as his
successor; and Felix, wishing to confer a favor on the Jews,
left Paul bound.

XXV. 1 Then Festus, having entered upon his government,
after three days went up from Cæsarea to Jerusalem. 2 And the
chief priest and first men of the Jews informed him against
Paul, 3 and, asking a favor against him, besought him that he
would send and have him brought to Jerusalem, laying a plot
to kill him on the road. 4 Then Festus answered, that Paul was
under guard in Cæsarea, and that he himself would soon depart
thither. 5 Therefore, said he, let those among you who are men
of influence, go down with me, and accuse this man, if there is
any wickedness in him.

6 And he remained among them not more than eight or ten
days, and then went down to Cæsarea. And, on the next day
he sat upon the judgment-seat, and commanded Paul to be
brought. 7 And when he had come, the Jews who had come
down from Jerusalem stood around, and brought many and
heavy accusations against Paul, which they were not able to
prove, 8 he answering for himself: Neither against the law of

the Jews, nor against the temple, nor against Cæsar, have I
committed any offense. 9 But Festus, willing to confer a favor
on the Jews, answered Paul, and said: Are you willing to go
up to Jerusalem, and there be judged before me concerning
these things? 10 And Paul answered: I am standing at the
judgment-seat of Cæsar, where I ought to be judged. To the
Jews I have done no wrong, as you very well know. 11 If,
however, I be an offender, and have done any thing worthy of
death, I refuse not to die. But if the things of which these
men accuse me are nothing, no one can deliver me to them.
I appeal to Cæsar. 12 Then Festus, after conferring with the
council, answered: To Cæsar have you appealed? To Cæsar
you shall go.

13 And after some days, King Agrippa and Bernice came down
to Cæsarea, to salute Festus. 14 And as they remained there
many days, Festus made known to the king the facts concerning
Paul, saying: There is a certain man, who was left in bonds by
Felix, 15 concerning whom, when I was in Jerusalem, the chief
priests and elders of the Jews informed me, asking for judgment
against him. 16 I replied to them, that it is not the custom of
the Romans to deliver any man up to death, before the accused
has had his accusers face to face, and has had an opportunity to
answer concerning the charge that is against him. 17 Therefore, when they had come hither with me, I made no delay;
but, on the next day, sat on the judgment-seat, and commanded
the man to be brought forth. 18 And when his accusers stood
up, they brought no such charge against him as I expected;
19 but they had certain questions against him, about their own
religion, and about a certain Jesus that had died, who, Paul
affirmed, was alive. 20 But, being in doubt about the question
concerning this man, I asked him if he would go up to Jerusalem, and there be judged with respect to these matters. 21 But
when Paul made his appeal, that he should be kept for the judgment of Augustus, I commanded him to be kept, till I could
send him to Cæsar.

22 And Agrippa said to Festus: I could wish to have heard the
man myself. He replied: To-morrow you shall hear him.

23 Therefore, on the morrow, when Agrippa and Bernice came
with great pomp, and entered the place of audience, with the
officers and principal men of the city, Paul, at the command of
Festus, was brought forth. 24 And Festus said: King Agrippa,
and all men here present, you see this man, about whom all the

multitude of the Jews, both in Jerusalem and in this place, have entreated me, crying out, that he ought to live no longer.
25 But finding that he had done nothing worthy of death, and as he himself has appealed to Augustus, I have determined to send him.
26 Concerning him I have nothing certain to write to my Lord. For this reason, I have brought him before you all, and especially before you, King Agrippa, that, after the examination has been held, I may have something to write.
27 For it seems to me unreasonable to send a prisoner, and not to make known the charges that are against him.

XXVI.
1 Then Agrippa said to Paul: You are permitted to speak for yourself. Then Paul stretched forth his hand, and answered for himself.

2 I think myself happy, King Agrippa, because I shall this day make my defense before you, concerning all things of which I am accused by the Jews;
3 especially, since you are acquainted with all the customs and questions that are among the Jews. For this reason, I beseech you to hear me patiently.

4 My course of life from my youth, which, from the beginning, was among my own nation in Jerusalem, know all the Jews;
5 who, knowing me from the first, could testify, if they would, that, according to the strictest sect of our religion, I lived a Pharisee.
6 And now I stand and am judged for the hope of the promise made by God to our fathers;
7 to which promise our twelve tribes, zealously serving night and day, hope to come: on account of which hope, King Agrippa, I am accused by the Jews.
8 What? Is it thought a thing incredible among you, that God raises the dead?

9 I verily thought with myself, that I ought to do many things against the name of Jesus the Nazarene.
10 And this I did in Jerusalem; and many of the saints did I shut up in prison, having received authority from the chief priests: and when they were put to death, I gave my vote against them.
11 And I punished them often in every synagogue, and compelled them to speak impiously; and, being exceedingly mad against them, I persecuted them even to foreign cities.

12 While I was engaged in these things, and was going to Damascus with authority and commission from the chief priests,
13 at midday, while I was on the road, I saw, O King, a light from heaven, above the brightness of the sun, shining round about me and those who journeyed with me.
14 And when we

had all fallen to the earth, I heard a voice speaking to me, and
saying, in the Hebrew language, Saul, Saul, why do you persecute me? It is hard for you to kick against the goads. 15 And
I said, Who art thou, Lord? He replied, I am Jesus, whom
you persecute. 16 But arise, and stand upon your feet; for I
have appeared to you for this purpose, to make you a minister
and a witness of the things which you have seen, and of those
in which I will appear to you, 17 delivering you from the people,
and from the Gentiles, to whom now I send you, 18 in order to
open their eyes, and to turn them from darkness to light, and
from the authority of Satan to God, that they may receive remission of sins, and an inheritance among the sanctified, by
faith in me.

19 Wherefore, King Agrippa, I was not disobedient to the
heavenly vision; 20 but announced first to those in Damascus
and Jerusalem, and throughout all the region of Judea, and
then to the Gentiles, that they should repent and turn to God,
and do works worthy of repentance. 21 For these reasons the
Jews seized me in the temple, and endeavored to kill me.
22 Having, therefore, obtained help from God, I have stood till
this day, testifying both to small and to great, saying nothing
else than the things which the prophets and Moses did say
should come to pass: 23 that Christ should suffer, and that he
first, by his resurrection from the dead, should show light to
the people, and to the Gentiles.

24 And as he spoke these things in his defense, Festus said, with
a loud voice: Paul, you are mad; much learning drives you to
madness. 25 But he replied: I am not mad, most excellent Festus, but speak forth the words of truth and soberness. 26 For
the king has knowledge of these things, before whom, also, I
speak with boldness; for I am persuaded that none of these
things have escaped his notice; for this was not done in a corner. 27 King Agrippa, do you believe the prophets? I know
that you believe. 28 Then Agrippa said to Paul: You almost
persuade me to be a Christian. 29 And Paul replied: I could
pray to God, that not only you, but also all that hear me to-
day, were both almost and altogether such as I am, except these
bonds.

30 And the king arose, and the governor, and Bernice, and
those who sat with them. 31 And when they had withdrawn,
they conversed with one another, saying: This man does nothing
worthy of death or of bonds. 32 And Agrippa said to Festus:

This man could have been set at liberty, if he had not appealed
to Cæsar.

XXVII. [1]And as it was determined that we should sail to
Italy, they delivered Paul and some other prisoners to a centurion of the Augustan band, named Julius. [2]And going on
board a ship of Adramyttium, we put to sea, intending to sail
by the coast of Asia, Aristarchus, a Macedonian of Thessalonica,
being with us. [3]On the next day, we touched at Sidon; and
Julius treated Paul with kindness, and permitted him to go to
his friends, and receive their attentions. [4]And thence we put
to sea, and sailed under the lee of Cyprus, because the winds
were adverse. [5]And when we had sailed across the sea opposite
Cilicia and Pamphylia, we came to Myra, a city of Lycia.
[6]And there the centurion found a ship of Alexandria, sailing
to Italy; and he put us on board. [7]For many days we sailed
slowly; and having with difficulty come off Cnidus, the wind
not permitting us to go further, we sailed under the lee of Crete,
off Salmone: [8]and coasting along it with difficulty, we came to
a place called Fair Havens, near which is the city of Lasea.
[9]But, after much time had been spent, and sailing was now
dangerous, for the fast was already past, Paul admonished them,
[10]saying: Men, I perceive that this voyage will be with damage
and much loss, not only to the cargo and the ship, but also to
our lives. [11]But the centurion had more confidence in the
pilot, and in the owner of the ship, than in the things which
were spoken by Paul. [12]And as the harbor was not commo-
dious to winter in, the majority advised that they should put
to sea from that place also, if, by any means, they might reach
Phœnix, and winter there, which is a harbor of Crete, lying
toward the south-west and north-west.
[13]And when the south wind blew gently, supposing that they
had gained their object, they launched the ship, and ran along
close to the shore of Crete. [14]But in a little time a tempestuous
wind, called Euroclydon, blew against it. [15]And the ship being
caught and unable to bear up against the wind, we committed
it to the gale, and were driven along. [16]And running under
the lee of a certain island called Clauda, we with difficulty se-
cured the boat. [17]When they had taken it up, they used helps,
undergirding the ship. And fearing lest they should fall into
the quicksand, they lowered the mast, and thus were driven
along. [18]And as we were greatly tossed by the tempest, on the

next day they threw overboard the cargo; 19 and on the third
day, with our own hands, we threw out the tackling of the ship.
20 And as neither sun nor stars appeared for many days, and no
small tempest lay upon us, all hope of our being saved was at
length taken away.

21 But, after long abstinence from food, Paul stood up in the
midst of them, and said: O men, you ought to have been persuaded by me, and not to have put to sea from Crete; and you
would have avoided this damage and loss. 22 And now I exhort
you to be of good cheer; for there shall be no loss of life among
you, but only of the ship. 23 For there stood by me this night
an angel of God, whose I am, and whom I serve, 24 and said, Fear
not, Paul; you must stand in the presence of Cæsar; and behold, God has given you all that are sailing with you. 25 For
this reason, O men, be cheerful; for I believe God, that it shall
be even as it was told to me. 26 But we must be thrown upon a
certain island.

27 But when the fourteenth night had come, and we were drift-
ing up and down in the Adriatic Sea, about midnight the sailors
supposed that they were drawing near some land. 28 And they
sounded, and found twenty fathoms: and when they had gone
a little further, and sounded again, they found fifteen fathoms.
29 And fearing that we would fall upon rocks, they threw out four
anchors from the stern, and wished for day.

30 And as the sailors were attempting to flee from the ship, and
were letting down the boat into the sea, under the pretext that
they were about to let down anchors from the prow, 31 Paul said
to the centurion and the soldiers: Unless these remain in the
ship, you can not be saved. 32 Then the soldiers cut away the
ropes of the boat, and let it fall off.

33 And while the day was coming on, Paul exhorted them all
to take food, saying: This is the fourteenth day that you have
been in suspense, and continued without food, having taken
nothing. 34 Wherefore, I exhort you to take food; for this will
promote your safety. For not a hair shall fall from the head of
any of you. 35 And when he had said this, he took bread, and
gave thanks to God before them all, and broke, and began to eat.
36 And all became cheerful, and also partook of food. 37 And all
of us that were in the ship were two hundred and seventy-six
souls. 38 When they were satisfied with food, they lightened the
ship by throwing the provisions into the sea.

39 And when it was day, they did not recognize the land; but

they perceived an inlet, that had an accessible shore, into which
they desired, if they could, to thrust the ship. 40 And, after cutting away the anchors, they committed the ship to the sea, at
the same time loosing the lashings of the rudders: and they set
up the front sail to the wind, and kept the ship firmly toward
the shore. 41 And falling into a place where two currents met,
they ran the ship aground, and the prow stuck fast, and remained immovable; but the stern was broken by the violence
of the waves. 42 The soldiers' counsel was to kill the prisoners,
lest some of them should swim out and escape. 43 But the centurion, wishing to save Paul, kept them from their purpose,
and commanded those who were able to swim, to throw themselves into the sea first, and get to land; 44 and then the rest,
some on planks, and others on what could be taken from the
ship. And thus it came to pass, that all got safe to land.

XXVIII. 1 And when they had saved themselves, they then
learned that the island was called Melita. 2 And the barbarians
showed us no ordinary kindness; for they kindled a fire, and received us all, because of the rain which was falling, and because
of the cold.

3 And when Paul had brought together a heap of brushwood,
and laid it on the fire, a viper came out, by reason of the heat,
and fastened itself on his hand. 4 And when the barbarians
saw the reptile hanging from his hand, they said to one another:
This man is certainly a murderer, whom, although he has saved
himself from the sea, justice does not permit to live. 5 Then
he shook the reptile from him into the fire, and suffered no
harm. 6 But they were expecting that he would become in-
flamed and swollen, or would suddenly fall down dead; yet,
after expecting it for a long time, and seeing no harm befall
him, they changed their mind, and said he was a god.

7 Among the estates about that place were those of the chief
man of the island, whose name was Publius, who took us to his
house, and, for three days, entertained us kindly. 8 And it happened that the father of Publius was lying sick with fever and
dysentery. And Paul went in to him, and prayed, and laid his
hands on him, and restored him to health. 9 Therefore, after
this had been done, the rest also in the island who had diseases,
came and were cured. 10 And they also honored us with many
honors; and, when we put to sea they supplied us with such
things as we needed.

11 After three months we put to sea in a ship of Alexandria,
which had wintered in the island, whose sign was the Dioscuri.
12 And we landed at Syracuse, and remained there three days:
13 from which place, by coasting about, we came to Rhegium;
and one day afterward, the south wind arose; and we came, on
the next day, to Puteoli, 14 where we found brethren, and were
persuaded to remain with them seven days. And thus we went
toward Rome. 15 And from this place, the brethren, having
heard of us, came out as far as Apii Forum and the Three
Taverns, to meet us. When Paul saw the brethren, he thanked
God, and took courage.

16 When we came to Rome, the centurion delivered the prisoners to the captain of the guard; but Paul was permitted to
dwell by himself, with a soldier that guarded him.

17 And it came to pass, after three days, that he called together
the chief men of the Jews; and when they had come, he said
to them: Brethren, though I have done nothing against the
people, or the customs of our fathers, yet I was delivered as a
prisoner from Jerusalem into the hands of the Romans. 18 They,
after examination, would have released me, for they found no
cause of death in me. 19 But because the Jews spoke against it,
I was compelled to appeal to Cæsar: not that I have any accusation to bring against my own nation. 20 For this reason, I called
for you, that I might see you and speak to you; for on account
of the hope of Israel, I am bound with this chain.

21 And they said to him: We have neither received letters from
Judea concerning you, nor has any one of the brethren come,
and reported or spoken any evil of you. 22 But we think it right
to hear from you what you think: for, as it respects this sect,
we know that it is every-where spoken against.

23 And when they had appointed him a day, many came to
him at his lodgings; to whom, from morning till evening, he
earnestly testified, and set forth the kingdom of God, persuading
them concerning Jesus, both from the law of Moses, and from
the prophets. 24 And some believed the things that were spoken,
and some believed not. 25 And not agreeing among themselves,
they departed, after Paul had spoken one word: Well did the
Holy Spirit speak to our fathers by Isaiah the prophet, 26 saying:
Go to this people and say, You shall surely hear, but you will
not understand; and you shall surely see, but you will not
perceive. 27 For the heart of this people has become fat, and
with their ears they hear heavily, and their eyes they have

closed, lest they should see with their eyes, and hear with their
ears, and understand with their heart, and should turn to me,
and I should restore them to health. 28 Therefore, be it known
to you that the salvation of God is sent to the Gentiles, and
they will hear. 29 And when he had said these things, the Jews
departed, and had great disputation among themselves. 30 And
Paul dwelt two whole years in his own rented house, and received all that came to him, 31 preaching the kingdom of God,
and teaching the things concerning the Lord Jesus Christ, with
all boldness and without hinderance.

PAUL TO THE ROMANS.

PART I.—*Introduction.*

I. 1 PAUL, a servant of Jesus Christ, a called apostle, set
apart for the gospel of God, 2 which he formerly promised through his prophets in the Holy Scriptures, 3 concerning
his Son Jesus Christ our Lord, who was born of the posterity
of David according to the flesh, 4 but declared to be the Son of
God with power, according to his holy spiritual nature, by his
resurrection from the dead, 5 through whom we have received
grace and apostleship, in order to the obedience of faith among
all nations, for the honor of his name, 6 among whom are you
also the called of Jesus Christ, 7 to all that are in Rome, beloved of God, called saints: Grace be to you, and peace from
God our Father, and the Lord Jesus Christ.

8 First, I thank my God, through Jesus Christ, on account of
you all, because your faith is spoken of throughout the whole
world. 9 For God is my witness, whom I serve with my spirit
in the gospel of his Son, that, without ceasing, I make mention
of you, 10 always in my prayers making request, that, if possible, I may at length have a prosperous journey, by the will of
God, to come to you. 11 For I greatly desire to see you, that I
may impart to you some spiritual gift, in order that you may
be established; 12 that is, that I may both give and receive comfort, while I am among you, through our common faith.

13 But, brethren, I do not wish you to be ignorant that I often
purposed to come to you, though I have been hindered to the
present time, that I might have some fruit among you also,

even as among other Gentiles. 14 I am a debtor both to the
Greeks and to the barbarians; both to the wise and to the unwise. 15 So that, as far as I am able, I am ready to preach the
gospel to you also, who are in Rome.

PART II.—*The Thesis.*

16 For I am not ashamed of the gospel: for it is the power of
God in order to salvation, to every one that believes, to the Jew
first, and also to the Greek. 17 For in it the righteousness of
God by faith is revealed, in order to faith: as it is written, He
that is justified by faith, shall live.

THE ARGUMENT.

SECTION FIRST.

Of Justification.

18 For the wrath of God is revealed from heaven against all
ungodliness and unrighteousness of men, who, by unrighteousness, restrain the truth. 19 Because that which may be known
of God, is manifest among them; for God has made it manifest
to them, 20 (for, since the creation of the world, his attributes,
which are invisible, are clearly seen, being perceived through
the things that are made, both his eternal power and divinity,)
that they may be without excuse; 21 because, when they knew
God, they did not glorify him as God, nor were they thankful;
but they became perverse in their reasonings, and their wicked
heart was darkened; 22 professing to be wise, they became foolish, 23 and exchanged the glory of the incorruptible God for an
image like corruptible man, and birds, and four-footed beasts,
and creeping things.

24 For which reason God delivered them up, in the desires of
their hearts, to uncleanness, that they might dishonor their
bodies among themselves; 25 who exchanged the truth of God
for a lie, and worshiped and served the creature more than the
Creator, who is blessed forever. Amen. 26 For this reason,
God delivered them over to vile passions: for their females
exchanged their natural use for that which is against nature:
27 and in like manner also the males, leaving the natural use of
the females, burned in their lusts one toward another, males
with males practicing infamous lewdness, and receiving in themselves the due reward of their error.

28 And as they refused to acknowledge God, God delivered them

up to an undiscerning mind, to do detestable things; [29] as they
were filled with all unrighteousness, lewdness, wickedness,
covetousness, malice; full of envy, murder, contention, deceit,
malignity; [30] whisperers, evil-speakers, haters of God, insolent,
proud, boasters, inventors of evil things, disobedient to parents;
[31] without understanding, covenant-breakers, without natural
affection, implacable, unmerciful; [32] who, acknowledging the
judgment of God, that those who practice such things are
worthy of death, not only do them, but approve those who
practice them.

II. [1] For which reason, you are without excuse, O man, whoever you are, that judge; for in that in which you judge another, you condemn yourself; for you who judge, practice the
same things. [2] But we know that the judgment of God against
those who practice such things, is according to truth. [3] But do
you, O man, who judge those that practice such things, and
yet do the same, conclude that you will escape the judgment of
God? [4] Or, do you despise the riches of his goodness, and his
forbearance, and his long suffering, not knowing that the goodness of God leads you to repentance?

[5] But, according to your hard and impenitent heart, you
treasure up to yourself wrath for a day of wrath, and of the
revelation of the righteous judgment of God, [6] who will render
to every man according to his works; [7] to those who, by patient
continuance in good works, seek for glory and honor and incorruptibility, eternal life: [8] but to those who are contentious, and
obey not the truth, but obey unrighteousness, anger and wrath,
[9] affliction and distress, upon every soul of man that practices
what is evil, of the Jew first, and also of the Greek: [10] but
glory and honor and peace to every one that practices what is
good, to the Jew first, and also to the Greek: [11] for there is no
respect of persons with God.

[12] For as many as have sinned without law, shall also perish
without law; and as many as have sinned under law, shall be
judged by law, [13] in the day when God shall judge the secret
works of men by Jesus Christ, according to my gospel. [14] For
not the hearers of the law are just before God, but the doers of
the law shall be justified. [15] For when the Gentiles, who have
not a law, do, by nature, the things of the law, these who have
not a law, are a law to themselves, [16] who show that the work
which the law requires, is written in their hearts, their con-

science bearing testimony, and their reasonings with each other
accusing, or making excuse.
17 But if you are named Jew, and rest in the law, and make
your boast in God, 18 and know his will, and approve what is
excellent, being instructed by the law: 19 if you are also confident that you yourself are a guide for the blind, a light to
those who are in darkness, 20 an instructor of the simple, a
teacher of the unlearned, because you have the form of true
knowledge in the law; 21 you, then, who teach another, do you
not teach yourself? You who preach that a man should not
steal, do you steal? 22 You who say that a man should not
commit adultery, do you commit adultery? You who detest
idols, do you rob temples? 23 You who make your boast in the
law, do you, by transgressing the law, dishonor God? 24 For
the name of God is reviled among the Gentiles, on account of
you, as it is written.
25 Now, circumcision is indeed profitable, if you keep the law:
but, if you transgress the law, your circumcision becomes uncircumcision. 26 If, then, he who is uncircumcised keeps the
righteousness of the law, shall not his uncircumcision be counted
for circumcision? 27 And shall not he whose want of circumcision is owing to his birth, if he keeps the law, condemn you,
who, by the literal circumcision, transgress the law? 28 For he
is not a Jew who is one outwardly, nor is that circumcision
which is outward in the flesh: 29 but he is a Jew who is one
inwardly; and circumcision is that of the heart, in the spirit,
not in the letter, whose praise is not of men, but of God.

III. 1 What advantage then has the Jew, or what profit has
circumcision? 2 Much in every respect; but chiefly that the
oracles of God were intrusted to them. 3 What, indeed, if some
have been unfaithful? Will their unfaithfulness overthrow the
faithfulness of God? 5 It can not be. But let God be true,
though every man be a liar, as it is written: That thou mightest be justified in thy words, and mightest overcome when thou
art judged.
5 But if our unrighteousness causes the righteousness of God to
be better known, what shall we say? Is God unrighteous, who
inflicts punishment? I speak as a man. 6 It can not be: for if
so, how shall God judge the world?
7 Yet, if the truth of God has, through my lie, been greatly
advanced to his glory, why am I still judged as a sinner?

8 Then, why not say, (as we are slanderously reported as
saying, and, as some affirm, that we do say,) Let us do evil,
that good may come? Of such persons the condemnation is
just.

9 What then? Do we, Jews, excel? Not at all: for we have
already convicted all, both Jews and Greeks, of being under sin,
10 as it is written: There is none righteous, no, not one; 11 there
is none that understands; there is none that seeks after God;
12 they have all turned out of the way; they have alike become
unprofitable; there is none that does good, not even one; 13 their
throat is an open sepulcher; with their tongues they have used
deceit; the poison of asps is under their lips; 14 their mouth is
full of cursing and bitterness; 15 their feet are swift to shed
blood; 16 destruction and misery are in their ways; 17 and the
way of peace they have not known; 18 there is no fear of God
before their eyes.

19 Now we know that what the law says, it speaks to those
who are under the law, that every mouth may be stopped, and
all the world become guilty before God. 20 Wherefore, by works
of law, no flesh shall be justified in his sight; for by law is the
knowledge of sin.

21 But now, the righteousness of God without law is revealed, being attested by the law and the prophets; 22 I repeat
it, the righteousness of God through faith in Jesus Christ,
which is for all, and on all that believe; for there is no difference; 23 for all have sinned, and come short of the glory of God,
24 yet may be justified freely by his grace, through the redemption that is in Christ Jesus; 25 whom God has set forth as a
propitiatory sacrifice, through faith in his blood, in order to
manifest his righteousness, in passing by the sins that were
formerly committed through the forbearance of God; 26 in order
to manifest his righteousness at the present time, that he might
be just, while he justifies him who believes in Jesus.

27 Where, then, is boasting? It is excluded. By what law?
Of works? No; but by the law of faith. 28 For we conclude
that a man is justified by faith, without deeds of law. 29 Is
he the God of the Jews only? Is he not also the God of the
Gentiles? Yes, of the Gentiles also: 30 since there is one God,
who will justify the circumcision by faith, and the uncircumcision through the faith. 31 Do we, then, make law void
through the faith? It can not be. On the other hand, we
establish law.

IV. 1 What, then, shall we say that Abraham our father has
found, as it respects the flesh? 2 For if Abraham was justified
by works, he has cause for boasting, but not before God. 3 For
what says the Scripture? Abraham believed God, and it was
counted to him for righteousness. 4 Now to him that works,
the reward is not counted as a favor, but as a debt: 5 but to him
that works not, but believes on him that justifies the ungodly,
his faith is counted for righteousness.

6 Even as David also speaks of the blessedness of the man
to whom God counts righteousness without works, saying:
7 Blessed are they whose iniquities are forgiven, and whose sins
are covered. 8 Blessed is the man to whom the Lord will not
charge sin.

9 Comes this blessedness then on those who are circumcised
only, or on those who are uncircumcised also? For we say that
faith was counted to Abraham for righteousness.

10 Under what circumstances, then, was it counted? After he
was circumcised? Or, while he was uncircumcised? Not after
he was circumcised, but while he was uncircumcised. 11 And he
received the sign of circumcision, as a seal of the righteousness
of the faith that he had while he was uncircumcised, in order
that he might be the father of all that believe, even in a state
of uncircumcision, so that righteousness might be counted to
them also; 12 and the father of circumcision to those who are
not only circumcised, but who, also, walk in the steps of that
faith which our father Abraham had while he was yet uncircumcised.

13 For the promise that he should be the heir of the world,
was not to Abraham, nor to his posterity, through law, but
through the righteousness of faith. 14 For if they that are of
the law be heirs, the faith is made powerless, and the promise
is unmeaning; 15 for the law inflicts punishment; for where no
law is, there is no transgression. 16 Therefore, the inheritance
is by faith, that it may be according to grace, in order that the
promise may be sure to all his posterity, not to those only who
are of the law, but to those, also, who are of the faith of Abraham, who is the father of us all, 17 (as it is written: I have made
you a father of many nations,) in the sight of him in whom he
believed, even God, who makes the dead alive, and calls those
things which are not, as though they were.

18 He, against hope, confidently believed that he would become
the father of many nations, according to that which was spoken:

So shall your posterity be. 19 And not being weak in faith, he
considered not his own body, which was already dead, (for he
was about a hundred years old,) nor the deadness of Sarah's
womb; 20 and he doubted not, through unbelief, with respect to
the promise of God, but was strong in faith, giving glory to
God, 21 and being fully persuaded that what he had promised
he was able also to perform. 22 For this reason, it was counted
to him for righteousness.

23 But that it was counted to him, was not written for his
sake alone, 24 but for our sakes also, to whom it shall be counted,
if we believe on him that raised Jesus our Lord from the dead,
25 who was delivered up for our offenses, and raised again for
our justification.

V. 1 Therefore, being justified by faith, we have peace with
God through our Lord Jesus Christ, 2 through whom we have
had access, by faith, into this grace in which we stand; and we
rejoice in hope of the glory of God.

3 And not only so, but we rejoice in afflictions also; because
we know that affliction produces patience, 4 and patience, an
approved character, and an approved character, hope; 5 and this
hope disappoints us not; because the love of God is poured
abundantly into our hearts through the Holy Spirit that is
given to us. 6 For when we were yet without strength, at the
appointed time, Christ died for the ungodly. 7 For hardly, indeed, will one die for a just man; yet, perhaps, for the good
man some one would even dare to die. 8 But God makes known
his love to us in this, that while we were yet sinners, Christ
died for us: 9 much more, then, since we are now justified by his
blood, we shall be saved from the wrath through him. 10 For if,
while we were enemies, we were reconciled to God by the death
of his Son, much more, having been reconciled, shall we be
saved by his life.

11 And not only so, but we rejoice in God through our Lord
Jesus Christ, by whom we have now received the reconciliation.

12 For this reason, as by one man sin entered into the world,
and by his sin, death; and so death passed through to all men,
because all have sinned: 13 for till the law, sin was in the world;
but sin is not charged where there is no law. 14 Yet death
reigned from Adam to Moses, even over them that did not sin
in the likeness of Adam's transgression, who is the type of him
that was to come. 15 But the favor bestowed is not, in all re-

spects, like the offense: for if, by the offense of one, the many have died, much more have the grace of God and the gift which is by the grace of the one man Jesus Christ, been made abundant for the many.
[16] And the gift is not like the sentence that came through one who sinned: for the sentence to condemnation was because of one offense; but the favor bestowed in order to justification, is because of many offenses.
[17] For if, by one man's offense, death has reigned through that one, much more shall those who receive the abundance of the grace, and of the gift of righteousness, reign in life through the one, who is Jesus Christ.
[18] Therefore, as, by one offense, sentence came on all men to condemnation, so, also, by one act of righteousness, the gift has come on all men to justification of life.
[19] For as by the disobedience of the one man the many have been made sinners, so, also, by the obedience of the one, the many shall be made righteous.

[20] But, law came in beside, in order that the offense might abound: but where sin abounded, grace did much more abound:
[21] that as sin has reigned, ending in death, so might grace reign by righteousness, ending in life eternal, through Jesus Christ our Lord.

SECTION SECOND.

Of Sanctification, Redemption, and Glorification.

VI. [1] What, then, shall we say? Shall we continue in sin that grace may abound?
[2] It can not be. How shall we that are dead to sin, live any longer in it?
[3] Know you not that as many of us as were immersed into Christ Jesus, were immersed into his death?
[4] Therefore, we were buried with him, by immersion, into death, that as Christ was raised from the dead by the glory of the Father, so also we should walk in a new life.
[5] For if we have become united to him by the likeness of his death, we shall certainly be united to him by the likeness of his resurrection;
[6] knowing this, that our former man has been crucified with him, in order that the sinful body may be deprived of its power, so that we should no longer serve sin:
[7] for he that is dead is freed from sin.

[8] Now if we have died with Christ, we believe that we shall also live with him;
[9] because we know that Christ, having been raised from the dead, dies no more; death has dominion over him no longer;
[10] for, as it regards his dying, he, once for all,

died to sin; but as it regards his living, he lives to God. [11] So
also do you count yourselves as dead indeed to sin, but as living
to God, in Christ Jesus our Lord.

[12] Therefore, let not sin reign in your mortal body so that you
obey it; [13] and present not your members to sin, as instruments
of unrighteousness, but present yourselves to God as alive from
the dead; and your members to God, as instruments of righteousness. [14] For sin shall not have dominion over you; for you
are not under law, but under grace.

[15] What then? Shall we sin, because we are not under law,
but under grace? It can not be. [16] Know you not, that to
whom you present yourselves as servants to obey, his servants
you are whom you obey, whether of sin that leads to death, or
of obedience that leads to righteousness? [17] But thanks be to
God, that though you were the servants of sin, yet you have
obeyed from the heart the form of teaching, in which you have
been instructed; [18] and being made free from sin, you have become the servants of righteousness. [19] I speak of what is common among men, on account of the weakness of your flesh: for
as you have presented your members as servants to uncleanness,
and to lawlessness, in order to lawlessness, so now present your
members as servants to righteousness, in order to holiness.
[20] For when you were the servants of sin, you were free with
respect to righteousness. [21] What fruit, therefore, had you at
that time, in those things of which you are now ashamed? For
the end of those things is death. [22] But now, since you have
been made free from sin, and have become servants to God, you
have your fruit to holiness, and the end, eternal life. [23] For the
wages of sin is death; but the gift of God is eternal life in
Christ Jesus our Lord.

VII. [1] Know you not, brethren, for I speak to you that are
acquainted with law, that the law has dominion over a man as
long as he lives? [2] For the woman that has a husband, is bound
by the law to her husband as long as he lives: but if her husband die, she is loosed from the law of her husband. [3] So then,
if, while her husband lives, she be married to another man, she
shall be called an adulteress. But if her husband die, she is
free from the law; so that she is not an adulteress, though she
be married to another man.

[4] So then, my brethren, you, also, died to the law, by the body
of the Christ, in order that you might be married to another,

to him who was raised from the dead—that we should bring
forth fruit to God. [5] For when we were in the flesh, the sinful
passions which were excited by the law, were active in our
members, so as to bring forth fruit to death: [6] but now we are
made free from the law, being dead to that by which we were
bound, so that we may serve in newness of spirit, and not in the
oldness of the letter.

[7] What, then, shall we say? Is the law sin? It can not be.
Indeed, I had not known sin, except through law. For I had
not known evil desire, unless the law had said: You shall not
have any evil desire. [8] But sin, taking occasion through the
commandment, rendered active within me every evil desire.
For without the law, sin was dead. [9] Indeed, I was alive without the law, once; but when the commandment came, sin became alive, and I died: [10] and the commandment, which was
given for life, I found to be for death. [11] For sin, taking occasion by the commandment, deceived me, and by it slew me.
[12] Therefore, the law is holy, and the commandment, holy and
just and good.

[13] Has, then, that which is good become death to me? It can
not be. But sin, that it might appear sin, was causing death
to me through that which is good, in order that sin, through
the commandment, might become exceedingly sinful. [14] For we
know that the law is spiritual; but I am carnal, sold into
bondage to sin. [15] For what I do, I know not: for that which
I wish to do, this I do not; but that which I hate, this I do.
[16] If, then, I do that which I wish not to do, I give assent to
the law, that it is good, [17] Now, then, it is no longer I that do
it, but sin that dwells in me. [18] For I know that in me, that is,
in my flesh, dwells no good; for to will is present with me; but
to perform that which is good, I find not. [19] For the good that
I wish to do, I do not; but the evil that I wish not to do, this I
do. [20] Now, if I do that which I wish not to do, it is no longer
I that do it, but sin that dwells in me.

[21] I find, then, this law: That, when I wish to do good, evil is
present with me. [22] For, in the inward man, I delight in the law
of God: [23] but I perceive another law in my members, at war
with the law of my mind, and making me a captive to the law
of sin, which is in my members.

[24] Wretched man that I am! Who will deliver me from this
body that subjects me to death? [25] I thank God that I shall be
delivered through Jesus Christ our Lord. Therefore, I myself,

with the mind, serve the law of God, but with the flesh, the law
of sin.

VIII. [1] There is now, therefore, no condemnation to those
who are in Christ Jesus. [2] For the law of the spirit of life in
Christ Jesus has freed me from the law of sin, and of death.
[3] For what the law could not do, because it was weak through
the flesh, God has done, who, sending his own son in the likeness of sinful flesh, and for a sin-offering, condemned sin in the
flesh, [4] that the righteousness of the law might be fulfilled in
us, who walk not according to the flesh, but according to the
Spirit.

[5] For those who are according to the flesh, mind the things of
the flesh; but those who are according to the Spirit, the things
of the Spirit. [6] For the mind of the flesh is death; but the mind
of the Spirit is life and peace. [7] Because the mind of the flesh
is enmity against God; for it is not subject to the law of God,
nor indeed can it be. [8] Those, then, who are in the flesh, can
not please God.

[9] But you are not in the flesh, but in the Spirit, if indeed the
Spirit of God dwells in you. Now, if any one has not the Spirit
of Christ, he is not his. [10] But if Christ is in you, the body is
dead, on account of sin, but the Spirit is life, on account of
righteousness. [11] And if the Spirit of him who raised Jesus
from the dead dwells in you, he that raised the Christ from the
dead will give life to your mortal bodies, because of his Spirit
that dwells in you.

[12] Therefore, brethren, we are debtors, not to the flesh, to live
according to the flesh; [13] for if you live according to the flesh,
you shall die: but if, through the Spirit, you put to death the
deeds of the body, you shall live. [14] For as many as are led by
the Spirit of God, they are the sons of God. [15] For you have
not again received the spirit of bondage, that you may fear; but
you have received the spirit of adoption, by which we cry, Abba,
Father. [16] The spirit itself testifies with our spirit, that we are
the children of God; [17] and, if children, then heirs; heirs of
God, and joint-heirs with Christ, if indeed we suffer with him,
that we may also be glorified together.

[18] For I consider the sufferings of the present time not worthy
to be compared with the glory that shall be revealed for us.
[19] For the earnest expectation of the creature waits for the revelation of the sons of God. [20] For the creature was subject to

frailty, (not by its own will, but for his sake who subjected it,)
21 in hope, that even the creature itself shall be made free from
the bondage of corruption, and introduced into the glorious
liberty of the children of God. 22 For we know that every
creature groans, and is in pain together, till now: 23 and not
only they, but ourselves also, who have the first fruits of the
Spirit, even we ourselves groan within ourselves, waiting for
the adoption, the redemption of our body. 24 For we are saved
by this hope; but hope that is seen is not hope; for, what any
one sees, why does he also hope for it? 25 But if we hope for
that which we see not, we wait for it with patience.

26 In like manner, also, the Spirit helps our infirmities; for
we know not what we should pray for as we ought, but the
Spirit itself intercedes for us, with groanings unutterable.
27 And he that searches the hearts knows what is the mind
of the Spirit, that he intercedes for the saints according to
the will of God.

28 And we know that all things work together for good, to
those who love God, to those who are called according to his
purpose. 29 For those whom he foreknew, he predestinated to
be conformed to the image of his Son, that he might be the
first-born among many brethren: 30 and those whom he predestinated he also called, and those whom he called he also
justified, and those whom he justified he also glorified.

31 What, then, shall we say to these things? If God is for
us, who can be against us? 32 He that spared not his own Son,
but delivered him up for us all, how will he not with him also
freely give us all things? 33 Who shall lay any thing to the
charge of God's elect? It is God that justifies. 34 Who is he
that condemns? It is Christ that died: rather, indeed, that
has risen, who is at the right hand of God, who also intercedes
for us. 35 Who shall separate us from the love of the Christ?
Shall affliction, or distress, or persecution, or famine, or nakedness, or danger, or the sword? 36 As it is written: For thy
sake, we are killed all the day long; we are counted as sheep
for the slaughter. 37 Yet, in all these things, we are more
than conquerors, through him that loved us. 38 For I am
persuaded that neither death, nor life, nor angels, nor principalities, nor powers, nor things present, nor things to come,
39 nor hight, nor depth, nor any other creature, will be able
to separate us from the love of God which is in Christ Jesus
our Lord.

SECTION THIRD.

God's Dealings with Israel as a People.

IX. 1 I speak the truth in Christ, I lie not, my conscience
bearing me testimony in the Holy Spirit, 2 that I have great
sorrow and unceasing grief in my heart; 3 for I could wish myself to be accursed from Christ, for my brethren, my kinsmen
according to the flesh; 4 who are Israelites, to whom belong the
adoption, and the glory, and the covenants, and the giving of
the law, and the service, and the promises; 5 to whom belong
the fathers, and of whom is the Christ, as it respects the flesh,
who is over all, God blessed forever. Amen.

6 It is not possible that the word of God has failed; for they
are not all Israel who are of Israel. 7 Nor, because they are
the posterity of Abraham, are they all children: but in Isaac
shall your posterity be called. 8 That is, the children of the
flesh are not the children of God; but the children of the
promise are counted for the posterity. 9 For the word of the
promise is this: At this time will I come, and Sarah shall have
a son. 10 Not only so, but when Rebecca had conceived by one,
even our father Isaac, (11 the children, indeed, having not yet
been born, and having done neither good nor evil, that the
purpose of God according to election might stand, not of
works, but of him that calls,) 12 it was said to her: The elder
shall serve the younger; 13 as it is written: Jacob have I loved,
but Esau have I hated.

14 What, then, shall we say? Is there unrighteousness with
God? It can not be. 15 For he says to Moses: I will show
mercy to whom I will show mercy; and I will show compassion
to whom I will show compassion. 16 Therefore, it is not of him
that wills, nor of him that runs, but of God that shows mercy.
17 For the Scripture says to Pharaoh: For this very purpose
have I raised you up, that I may show in you my power, and
that my name may be published in all the earth. 18 Therefore,
he has mercy on whom he wills to have mercy: and whom he
wills to harden, he hardens.

19 You will then say to me, Why does he yet find fault? For
who has resisted his will? 20 No, but rather, O man, who are
you that dispute with God? Shall the thing formed say to
him that formed it, Why have you made me thus? 21 Has not
the potter power over the clay, to make from the same mass one
vessel for honor, and another for dishonor? 22 What, then, if

God, intending to show his wrath, and to make his power
known, yet, in much long-suffering bore with the vessels of
wrath fitted for destruction: 23 and, that he might make known
the riches of his glory on the vessels of mercy which he before
prepared for glory, showed mercy to us, 24 whom he has called,
not only from among the Jews, but also from the Gentiles?
25 As he says also in Hosea: I will call that my people which is
not my people, and her beloved, who was not beloved. 26 And
it shall come to pass, that, in the place where it was said to
them: You are not my people, there shall they be called the
sons of the living God. 27 But Isaiah cries concerning Israel:
Though the number of the sons of Israel be as the sand of the
sea, a remnant shall be saved: 28 for his word he fulfills, and he
decrees in righteousness; for his word that is decreed, will the
Lord execute upon the land. 29 And as Isaiah said before: Unless the Lord of hosts had left us a posterity, we should have
been like Sodom, and been made like Gomorrah.

30 What, then, shall we say? That the Gentiles, who did not
seek after righteousness, have obtained righteousness, even the
righteousness which is by faith: 31 but Israel, who sought after
a law of righteousness, has not attained to a law of righteousness. 32 And why? Because they sought it not by faith, but
as if by works of law: for they stumbled against that stone
of stumbling, 33 as it is written: Behold, I lay in Zion a stone
of stumbling, and a rock of offense: and whoever believes on
him, shall not be ashamed.

X. 1 Brethren, my heart's desire and prayer to God for Israel
is, that they may be saved. 2 For I testify for them, that they
have a zeal for God, but not according to knowledge. 3 For
being ignorant of God's righteousness, and seeking to establish
their own righteousness, they have not submitted to the righteousness of God. 4 For Christ is the end of the law for righteousness, to every one that believes.

5 For Moses describes the righteousness which is by the law:
That the man who does these things shall live by them. 6 But
the righteousness by faith speaks thus: Say not in your heart,
Who shall ascend into heaven? that is, to bring Christ down;
7 or, Who shall descend into the abyss? that is, to bring Christ
again from the dead. 8 But what says it? The word is near
you, in your mouth and in your heart; that is, the word of
faith which we preach; 9 that if you will confess with your

mouth, that Jesus is Lord, and will believe in your heart that
God has raised him from the dead, you shall be saved. 10 For
with the heart we believe, in order to righteousness; and with
the mouth we make confession, in order to salvation. 11 For the
Scripture says: He that believes on him shall not be ashamed.
12 For there is no difference between the Jew and the Greek; for
the same Lord of all is rich to all that call on him: 13 For every
one that calls on the name of the Lord shall be saved.

14 How, then, shall they call on him in whom they have not
believed? And how shall they believe in him of whom they
have not heard? And how shall they hear without a preacher?
15 And how shall they preach, unless they be sent? As it is
written: How beautiful are the feet of those who preach the
gospel of peace, who bring joyous news of good things! 16 But
they have not all obeyed the gospel; for Isaiah says: Lord, who
has believed our report? 17 So, then, faith comes by hearing,
and hearing by the word of God. 18 But I say: Have they not
heard? Yes, verily; their voice has gone forth into all the
earth: and their words to the ends of the world. 19 But I say:
Did not Israel know? First, Moses says: I will excite you to
jealousy by that which is no nation; and by a foolish nation I
will provoke you to wrath. 20 But Isaiah is very bold, and
says: I was found by them that sought me not: I was made
manifest to them that asked not after me. 21 But with respect
to Israel, he says: All day long have I stretched out my hands
to a disobedient and contradicting people.

XI. 1 I say, then, has God rejected his people? It can not
be. For I am an Israelite, of the posterity of Abraham, of the
tribe of Benjamin. 2 God has not rejected his people whom he
foreknew. Know you not what the Scripture says in regard to
Elijah? how he intercedes with God against Israel, saying:
3 Lord, they have killed thy prophets, and digged down thy
altars, and I am left alone, and they seek my life. 4 But what
says the answer of God to him? I have reserved for myself
seven thousand men, who have not bowed the knee to Baal.
5 Thus, then, at the present time also, there is a remnant according to the election of grace. 6 And if the election is by
grace, it is no longer by works; otherwise grace is no longer
grace.

7 What then? Israel has not obtained that which he seeks;
but the chosen have obtained it, and the rest have been hardened

to this day, 8 as it is written: God has given them a spirit of
stupor, eyes with which they can not see, and ears with which
they can not hear. 9 And David says: Let their table become a
trap, and a net, and a snare, and a recompense to them; 10 let
their eyes be darkened, so that they may not see, and let them
bow down their back always.

11 I say, then, Have they stumbled, in order that they may
fall? It can not be. But rather, through their fall, salvation
has come to the Gentiles, to excite them to jealousy. 12 Now,
if their fall be the riches of the world, and their loss be the
riches of the Gentiles, how much more shall their full accept-
ance *be the riches of the world?* 13 For I speak to you, Gentiles;
inasmuch as I am the apostle of the Gentiles, I do honor to my
ministry, 14 if, by any means, I may excite to jealousy those who
are my flesh, and save some of them. 15 For, if the casting
away of them be the reconciling of the world, what shall the
reception of them be, but life from the dead?

16 Now, if the first fruit is holy, the mass is holy also: and if
the root is holy, the branches are holy also. 17 And if some of
the branches were broken off, and you, being a wild olive, have
been grafted in among them, and partake with them of the root
and fatness of the olive, 18 boast not against the branches; but
if you boast, boast not that you bear the root, but that the root
bears you. 19 You will say then: The branches were broken off,
that I might be grafted in. 20 Well; on account of unbelief
they were broken off; but you stand by faith. Be not high-
minded, but fear. 21 For if God spared not the natural branches,
take heed, lest he spare not you.

22 Behold, then, the goodness and severity of God: toward
them that fell, severity; but toward you, goodness, if you continue in his goodness; otherwise, you also shall be cut off.
23 And they, also, if they continue not in unbelief, shall be
grafted in; for God is able to graft them in again. 24 For if
you were cut out from an olive tree that is wild by nature, and
were grafted, against nature, into a good olive, how much more
shall these, which are the natural branches, be grafted into their
own olive?

25 For I do not wish you, brethren, to be ignorant of this mystery—lest you be wise in your own conceit—that blindness has
happened to Israel in part, till the full number of the Gentiles
shall have come in. 26 And so all Israel shall be saved, as it is
written: There shall come out of Zion the Deliverer, and he

shall turn away ungodliness from Jacob. 27 And this is my
covenant with them, when I shall take away their sins. 28 As
it respects the gospel, they are enemies of God for your sakes;
but as it respects their election, they are beloved for the fathers'
sakes: 29 for God's gifts and calling are irrevocable. 30 For as
you formerly did not believe God, but now have obtained mercy
through their unbelief; 31 so, also, these have not now believed,
that through the mercy shown to you, they also may obtain
mercy. 32 For God has delivered them all over to unbelief, that
he may have mercy on them all.

33 O the depth of the riches, both of the wisdom and of the
knowledge of God! How unsearchable are his judgments, and
his ways past finding out! 34 For who has known the mind of
the Lord? Or, who has been his counselor? 35 Or, who has
first given to him, and received from him a recompense? 36 For
from him, and by him, and for him, are all things. To him be
glory through the ages! Amen.

PART III.—*Hortatory and Practical.*

XII. 1 I beseech you, therefore, brethren, by the mercies of
God, that you present your bodies a living sacrifice, holy, acceptable to God, which is your reasonable service. 2 And be not
conformed to this age, but be transformed by the renewing of
your mind, that you may learn what the will of God is—the
good, and the acceptable, and the perfect.

3 For I say, through the grace given to me, to every one that
is among you, that he must not think of himself more highly
than he ought to think; but that he be disposed to think mod-
estly, as God has distributed to each a measure of faith. 4 For
as we have many members in one body, and all the members
have not the same office, 5 so we, the many, are one body in
Christ, and members one of another. 6 Since, then, we have
gifts which differ according to the grace that is given to us,
whether we have the gift of prophecy, let us prophesy according
to the proportion of our faith; 7 or, if we have a ministry, let
us be active in our ministry; if any one teaches, let him attend
to his teaching; 8 or, if any exhorts, let him attend to exhortation; if any one gives, let him do it with sincerity; he that
rules, with diligence: he that shows mercy, with cheerfulness.

9 Let love be without hypocrisy. Abhor that which is evil;
cleave to that which is good; 10 in love to the brotherhood, be
kindly affectionate one to another; in showing honor, be exam-

ples one to another; 11 in what requires diligence, be not slothful; in spirit, be fervent; in service, be devoted to the Lord;
12 in hope, be joyful; in affliction, be patient; in prayer, be
persevering; 13 administer to the necessities of the saints; be
careful to entertain strangers; 14 bless them that persecute
you; bless, and curse not; 15 rejoice with them that rejoice,
and weep with them that weep; 16 cultivate the same disposition, one toward another: mind not high things, but conform
yourselves to things that are lowly.

Be not wise in your own conceits; 17 repay to no one evil for
evil; practice that which is honorable in the sight of all men.
18 If possible, as far as may be in your power, be at peace with
all men. 19 Beloved, avenge not yourselves, but give place to the
wrath *of God;* for it is written: Vengeance is mine, I will repay,
says the Lord. 20 If, therefore, your enemy is hungry, feed him;
if he is thirsty, give him drink; for by doing this, you will heap
coals of fire on his head. 21 Be not overcome by evil; but overcome evil with good.

XIII. 1 Let every soul be subject to the higher authorities.
For there is no authority but from God: the authorities that
are, have been appointed by God. 2 Therefore, he that resists
the authority, resists the appointment of God; and those who
resist shall receive to themselves condemnation. 3 For rulers
are not a terror to works that are good, but to those which are
evil. Will you, then, not be afraid of the authority? Do that
which is good, and you shall receive praise from the same. 4 For
he is the minister of God to you for that which is good. But if
you do what is evil, be afraid; for he bears not the sword in
vain. For he is the minister of God to inflict punishment on
him that does evil.

5 Wherefore, it is necessary to be subject, not only because of
punishment, but also for conscience' sake. 6 On this very account, too, pay tribute also: for they are the public servants
of God, attending continually to this very thing. 7 Render,
therefore, to all their dues; tribute, to whom tribute is due;
custom, to whom custom; fear, to whom fear; honor, to whom
honor is due.

8 Owe no one any thing, except to love one another; for he
that loves another, has fulfilled the law. 9 For these commandments: You shall not commit adultery, you shall not kill, you
shall not steal, you shall not indulge evil desire; and if there

is any other commandment, all are summed up in this saying,
namely: You shall love your neighbor as yourself. 10 Love
works no evil to our neighbor; therefore, love is the fulfilling
of the law.

11 And do this, because you know the time, that the hour has
already come when we should awake out of sleep; for now is
our salvation nearer than when we believed: 12 the night is far
advanced, the day draws near. Let us, therefore, put off the
works of darkness, and let us put on the armor of light. 13 Let
us walk in a becoming manner, as in the day; not in riotings
and in drunkenness, not in lewdness and in wantonness, not in
contention and in envy: 14 but put on the Lord Jesus Christ,
and make no provision for the desires of the flesh.

XIV. 1 Him that is weak in the faith, receive kindly, but not
to judge his reasonings. 2 One believes that he may eat all
things; another, who is weak, eats herbs. 3 Let not him that
eats, despise him that eats not; and let not him that eats not,
judge him that eats: for God has received him. 4 Who are you
that judge another man's servant? To his own master he
stands or falls; indeed, he shall stand, for God is able to make
him stand.

5 One man thinks that one day is better than another; another
thinks that every day is alike. Let each be fully assured in
his own mind. 6 He that regards the day, to the Lord he regards it; and he that does not regard the day, to the Lord he
does not regard it. He that eats, eats to the Lord; for he gives
God thanks: and he that eats not, to the Lord he eats not, and
gives God thanks. 7 For no one lives to himself, and no one dies
to himself. 8 For if we live, we live to the Lord; or if we die, we
die to the Lord. Whether, therefore, we live or die, we are the
Lord's. 9 For this very purpose, Christ both died and rose, and
lived again, that he might have dominion over the dead and the
living.

10 But why do you judge your brother? Or why do you despise your brother? For we all shall stand before the judgment-seat of the Christ. 11 For it is written: As I live, says the
Lord, to me every knee shall bow, and every tongue shall confess to God. 12 Therefore, every one of us shall give an account
of himself to God.

13 Let us, therefore, no longer judge one another: but rather
decide to put no stumbling-block or snare in your brother's

way. 14 I know and am persuaded in the Lord Jesus, that there
is nothing unclean of itself; but if any one thinks that any
thing is unclean, to him it is unclean. 15 But if your brother is
grieved on account of your food, you no longer walk according
to love. Do not, with your food, destroy him, for whom Christ
died. 16 Therefore, let not that which is your good be evil spoken
of. 17 For the kingdom of God is not food and drink, but righteousness and peace and joy in the Holy Spirit.
18 For he who serves the Christ in these things is acceptable
to God, and approved by men. 19 Therefore, let us seek those
things which belong to peace, and those which tend to mutual
edification. 20 Destroy not the work of God on account of food.
All meats, indeed, are clean; but meat is an evil to that man
who, by eating, causes another to stumble. 21 It is good neither
to eat flesh, nor to drink wine, nor to do any thing by which
your brother stumbles, or is ensnared, or is made weak. 22 Have
you faith? Have it to yourself before God. Blessed is he who
condemns not himself in that which he approves. 23 But he
that doubts is condemned, if he eat, because he eats not with
faith. Every thing that is not of faith, is sin.

XV. 1 But we that are strong ought to bear the infirmities
of those who are not strong, and not to please ourselves. 2 Let
each one of us please his neighbor in that which is good for his
edification. 3 For the Christ did not please himself; but as it is
written: The reproaches of them that reproached thee, fell on
me. 4 For the things which were formerly written, were written
for our instruction, that we, through the patience and the comfort which the Scriptures give, might have hope. 5 Now, may
the God of patience and comfort make you of the same mind
one toward another, according to Christ Jesus; 6 that with one
mind and with one voice you may glorify God, even the Father of
our Lord Jesus Christ. 7 Wherefore, receive one another with
kindness, as the Christ has received you, to the glory of God.
8 Now, I say, that Jesus Christ, as a minister, was of the
circumcision for the sake of the truth of God, in order to confirm the promises made to the fathers, 9 and that the Gentiles
might glorify God for his mercy, as it is written: For this
cause I will give praise to thee among the Gentiles, and to thy
name will I sing. 10 And again he says: Rejoice, you Gentiles,
with his people. 11 And again: Praise the Lord, all you Gentiles, and applaud him, all you peoples. 12 And again, Isaiah

says: There shall be a root of Jesse, and he that shall rise to
rule the Gentiles, in him shall the Gentiles trust. 13 Now may
the God of hope fill you with all joy and peace in believing,
that you may abound in the hope, by the power of the Holy
Spirit.

Part IV.—*Conclusion.*

14 And I myself am persuaded concerning you, my brethren,
that you yourselves are full of all goodness, having been filled
with all knowledge, able also to instruct one another. 15 Yet I
have written to you more boldly in part, my brethren, as if I
would put you in remembrance, on account of the grace which
is given to me by God, 16 that I may be the public servant of
Jesus Christ to the Gentiles, officiating as a priest with respect
to the gospel of God, that the offering up of the Gentiles may
be acceptable, having been sanctified by the Holy Spirit. 17 I
have, therefore, cause to glory in Christ Jesus in things that
pertain to God.

18 For I will not dare to speak of any of those things which
Christ has not accomplished through me, by word and deed, in
order to make the Gentiles obedient, 19 by the power of signs
and wonders by the power of the Holy Spirit. So that from
Jerusalem, and round about as far as Illyricum, I have fully
preached the gospel of the Christ; 20 so earnestly desirous have
I been to preach the gospel, not where Christ had been named,
lest I should build on another man's foundation; 21 but, as it is
written: They to whom he was not preached, shall see; and
they who have not heard, shall understand.

22 For which reason, also, I have been often hindered from
coming to you. 23 But now, having no longer a place in these
regions, and having had for many years a strong desire to come
to you, 24 when I make my journey into Spain, I hope, in passing through, to see you, and to be conducted by you on my
journey thither, after I am first partly satisfied with your company. 25 But now I am going to Jerusalem, to minister to the
saints. 26 For Macedonia and Achaia have been pleased to make
a contribution for the poor saints who are in Jerusalem: 27 they
have been pleased to do so, and they are their debtors. For if
the Gentiles have become partakers of their spiritual things,
they ought to minister to them in things pertaining to the flesh.
28 When, therefore, I shall have performed this, and have delivered to them this fruit, I will go by you into Spain. 29 And

I know that in coming to you, I shall come in the fullness of
the blessing of Christ.
30 Now I beseech you, brethren, by our Lord Jesus Christ, and
by the love of the Spirit, that you strive together with me, in
your prayers to God for me, 31 that I may be delivered from the
unbelievers in Judea, and that this service of mine, which is for
Jerusalem, may be acceptable to the saints; 32 that I may come
to you with joy, by the will of God, and may be refreshed among
you. 33 The God of peace be with you all. Amen.

XVI. 1 I commend to you Phœbe our sister, who is a dea-
coness of the church that is in Cenchrea, 2 that you receive her
in the Lord in a manner worthy of saints, and that you aid her
in whatever matter she may have need of you; for she has
aided many, and myself also.
3 Salute Priscilla and Aquila, my fellow-laborers in Christ
Jesus; 4 who, for my life, laid down their own necks; to whom
not only do I give thanks, but all the churches of the Gentiles:
5 and salute the church that is in their house. Salute Epene-
tus my beloved, who is the first fruits of Asia to Christ. 6 Salute Mary, who bestowed much labor on us. 7 Salute Androni-
cus and Junia, my kinsmen, and my fellow-prisoners, who are
noted among the apostles, who, also, were in Christ before me.
8 Salute Amplias, my beloved in the Lord. 9 Salute Urbanus,
our fellow-workman in Christ, and Stachys my beloved. 10 Salute Apelles, approved in Christ. Salute those who are of the
household of Aristobulus. 11 Salute Herodion, my kinsman.
Salute those of the household of Narcissus, who are in the Lord.
12 Salute Tryphena and Tryphosa, who labored in the Lord.
Salute Persis the beloved, who labored much in the Lord. 13 Salute Rufus, the chosen in the Lord, and his mother and mine.
14 Salute Asyncritus, Phlegon, Hermas, Patrobas, Hermes, and
the brethren with them. 15 Salute Philologus and Julia, Ne-
reus and his sister, and Olympas, and all the saints that are
with them. 16 Salute one another with a holy kiss. The
churches of the Christ salute you.
17 Now I beseech you, brethren, to mark those who make divisions and cause offenses in opposition to the teaching which
you have learned, and avoid them. 18 For such serve not our
Lord Christ, but their own appetites; and, by good words and
fair speeches, they deceive the hearts of the simple. 19 For your
obedience has gone abroad to all men: I rejoice, therefore, on

your account. But I desire you to be wise in respect to that
which is good, and guileless in respect to that which is evil.
20 The God of peace will soon bruise Satan under your feet.
The grace of our Lord Jesus Christ be with you.
21 Timothy, my fellow-workman, and Lucius and Jason and
Sosipater, my kinsmen, salute you.
22 I, Tertius, who wrote this letter, salute you in the Lord.
23 Gaius, my host, and the host of the whole church, salutes
you. Erastus, the treasurer of the city, and Quartus, my
brother, salute you. 24 The grace of our Lord Jesus Christ be
with you all. Amen.
25 Now to him who is able to strengthen you according to my
gospel, even the preaching of Jesus Christ, according to the
revelation of the mystery which was concealed during the times
of the ages, 26 but is now made manifest, and through the Scriptures of the prophets, according to the commandment of the
eternal God, made known among all nations for the obedience
of faith, 27 to the only wise God, through Jesus Christ, be glory
throughout the ages. Amen.

PAUL TO THE CORINTHIANS.

FIRST LETTER.

I. 1 PAUL, a called apostle of Jesus Christ, by the will of
God, and Sosthenes my brother, 2 to the church of God
which is in Corinth, to the sanctified in Christ Jesus, called
saints, with all that in every place call on the name of Jesus
Christ our Lord, both theirs and ours: 3 grace be to you, and
peace from God our Father, and from the Lord Jesus Christ.
4 I thank my God always on your account, for the grace of
God which is given to you in Christ Jesus; 5 that you are enriched by him in every thing, in all speech, and in all knowledge, 6 even as the testimony concerning the Christ was confirmed among you, 7 so that you are deficient in no gift, while
waiting for the revelation of our Lord Jesus Christ. 8 He also
will establish you even to the end, and make you blameless in
the day of our Lord Jesus Christ. 9 God is faithful, by whom
you have been called into the fellowship of his Son Jesus Christ
our Lord.
10 Now, I beseech you, brethren, by the name of our Lord

Jesus Christ, that you all speak the same thing, and that there
be no schisms among you, but that you be perfectly united in
the same mind, and in the same judgment. [11] For it has been
made known to me concerning you, my brethren, by the family
of Cloe, that there are contentions among you. [12] I mean this:
that each one of you says, I am of Paul, and I of Apollos, and
I of Cephas, and I of Christ.

[13] Is the Christ divided? Was Paul crucified for you? or were
you immersed into the name of Paul? [14] I thank God that I
immersed none of you, but Crispus and Gaius; [15] that no one
may say that I immersed into my own name. [16] I did, indeed,
immerse the household of Stephanas; besides, I know not
whether I immersed any other. [17] For Christ sent me not to
immerse, but to preach the gospel: not with wisdom of speech,
lest the cross of the Christ should be deprived of its power.
[18] For the preaching of the cross is to those who perish, foolishness; but to us who are saved, it is the power of God. [19] For
it is written: I will destroy the wisdom of the wise; and I will
set aside the understanding of the prudent. [20] Where is the
wise man? Where is the scribe? Where is the disputer of this
age? Has not God made foolish the wisdom of this world?
[21] For, since in the wisdom of God, the world, by its wisdom,
knew not God, it has pleased God, through the foolishness of
what is preached, to save those who believe. [22] For the Jews ask
for a sign, and the Greeks seek for wisdom; [23] but we preach
Christ crucified; to the Jews, indeed, a stumbling-block, and to
the Greeks, foolishness: [24] but to those who are called, both
Jews and Greeks, Christ, the power of God, and the wisdom of
God. [25] For the foolishness of God is wiser than men; and the
weakness of God is stronger than men.

[26] For you see your calling, brethren, that not many wise
men according to the flesh, not many mighty, not many noble
call you; [27] but God has chosen the foolish things of the world,
that he may bring to shame the wise; and the weak things of
the world has God chosen, that he may put to shame the strong;
[28] and the ignoble things of the world, and the things that are
despised, has God chosen, and the things that are not, that he
might bring to naught things that are; [29] that no flesh should
glory in his presence. [30] But of him are you in Christ Jesus,
who has become to us, from God, wisdom and righteousness and
sanctification and redemption; [31] that, as it is written: He that
glories, let him glory in the Lord.

II. 1 And I, brethren, when I came to you, came not with
excellence of speech or of wisdom, declaring to you the testimony of God. 2 For I determined not to know any thing among
you but Jesus Christ, and him crucified. 3 And I was with you
in weakness, and in fear, and in much trembling: 4 and my
speech and my preaching were not in persuasive words of man's
wisdom, but in demonstration of the Spirit and of power, 5 that
your faith might not be in the wisdom of men, but in the power
of God.

6 Yet we speak wisdom among the perfect; but not the wisdom
of this age, nor of the rulers of this age, who are brought to
naught: 7 but we speak God's wisdom in a mystery, even that
which had been hidden, which God predestined before the ages,
for our glory, 8 which none of the rulers of this age knew; for,
had they known it, they would not have crucified the Lord of
Glory. 9 But, as it is written: Eye has not seen, and ear has
not heard, and into the heart of man have not entered the
things which God has prepared for them that love him. 10 But
God has revealed them to us through his Spirit; for the Spirit
searches all things, even the deep things of God. 11 For what man
knows the things of man, but the spirit of man which is in him?
Even so, the things of God no one knows, but the Spirit of God.

12 And we have received, not the spirit of the world, but the
Spirit which is from God, that we may know the things that
are freely given to us by God: 13 which things also we speak, not
in words taught by man's wisdom, but in words taught by the
Spirit, comparing spiritual things with spiritual things. 14 But
an animal man receives not the things of the Spirit of God, for
they are foolishness to him, and he can not know them, because
they are spiritually discerned. 15 But the spiritual man discerns
all things; yet he himself is discerned by no one. 16 For who
has known the mind of the Lord, that he may instruct him?
But we have the mind of Christ.

III. 1 And I, brethren, was not able to speak to you, as to
spiritual men, but as to those who are carnal, as to babes in
Christ. 2 I fed you with milk, not with meat; for you were not
then able *to bear it;* indeed, not even now are you able; 3 for you
are yet carnal. For, since envy and strife and divisions are
among you, are you not carnal, and do you not walk as men?
4 For when one says, I am of Paul, and another, I of Apollos,
are you not carnal?

5 Who, then, is Paul? and who is Apollos? Ministers by whom
you have believed, even as the Lord gave to each one. 6 I planted,
Apollos watered: but God made to grow. 7 So, neither he that
plants nor he that waters is any thing: but God that makes to
grow. 8 But he that plants and he that waters are one; and
each one shall receive his own reward, according to his own
labor. 9 For we are fellow-laborers for God: you are God's
field, you are God's building.

10 According to the grace of God that is given to me, as a wise
master-builder, I have laid the foundation, and another builds
on this. But let every one take heed how he builds on this.
11 For other foundation can no man lay than that which is laid,
which is Jesus Christ. 12 If any man builds on this foundation,
gold, silver, precious stones, wood, hay, stubble, 13 each man's
work shall be made manifest; for the day shall make it manifest,
for it is revealed with fire: and the fire shall try each man's
work, what sort it is. 14 If any man's work abide, which he
builds on this, he shall receive a reward; 15 if any man's work
be burned, he shall suffer loss: but he himself shall be saved,
yet so, as through fire.

16 Know you not that you are the temple of God, and that the
Spirit of God dwells in you? 17 If any man defile the temple of
God, him shall God destroy: for the temple of God is holy, which
temple you are. 18 Let no one deceive himself: if any one among
you is considered as wise in this age, let him become a fool, that
he may be wise. 19 For the wisdom of this world is foolishness
with God; for it is written: He takes the wise in their own
craftiness. 20 And again: The Lord knows the thoughts of the
wise, that they are vain.

21 Therefore, let no one glory in men; for all things are yours,
22 whether Paul, or Apollos, or Cephas, or the world, or life, or
death, or things present, or things to come, all are yours; 23 and
you are Christ's: and Christ is God's.

IV. 1 Let each one so think of us as ministers of Christ, and
stewards of the mysteries of God. 2 Now it is required in stewards, that each one be found faithful. 3 But with me, it matters
very little, that I should be judged by you, or by the judgment
of men: indeed, I do not judge myself. 4 For, though I am conscious of no wrong, yet by this I am not justified: but he that
judges me is the Lord. 5 So, then, judge nothing before the
time, till the Lord comes, who will bring to light the secret

works of darkness, and will also make manifest the counsels of
the hearts: and then shall each have his praise from God.

6 And these things, brethren, I have, in figure, applied to myself and Apollos, for your sakes, that you may learn in us not
to think more of *teachers* than what has been written; and that
no one of you be vain of one to the injury of another. 7 For
who gave you distinction, *as a teacher?* And what have you
as a teacher, that you did not receive? And if you received it,
why do you boast, as if you had not received it?

8 You, Corinthians, are already full; you are already rich;
you have reigned as kings independently of us. And O that
you did indeed reign, that we also might reign with you! 9 For
I think that God has appointed us the apostles, to the lowest
place, as under sentence of death; for we have become a spectacle to the world, both to angels and to men. 10 We are fools
for Christ's sake, but you are wise in Christ; we are weak, but
you are strong; you are honored, but we are despised. 11 Even
to this present hour we both hunger and thirst, and are poorly
clothed, and are maltreated, and wander about without a home,
12 and labor, working with our own hands. When reviled, we
bless; when persecuted, we endure; 13 when defamed, we entreat;
we have become like the outcasts of the world, the offscouring
of all things to this day.

14 I do not write these things that I may make you ashamed;
but as my beloved children I admonish you. 15 For though
you have ten thousand tutors in Christ, yet you have not many
fathers: for in Christ Jesus I have begotten you through the
gospel. 16 I exhort you, therefore, be imitators of me.

17 For this reason have I sent to you Timothy, who is my son,
beloved and faithful in the Lord, that he may remind you of my
ways that are in Christ, as I teach every-where, in every church.
18 Now, some have become arrogant, as if I were not coming to
you; 19 but I will come to you quickly, if the Lord will; and I
will know, not the speech of those who have become arrogant,
but the power. 20 For the kingdom of God is not in speech, but
in power. 21 What do you wish? Shall I come to you with a
rod, or in love, and in the spirit of gentleness?

V. 1 It is generally reported that there is lewdness among
you; and such lewdness as is not even mentioned among the
Gentiles—that a certain one has his father's wife. 2 And you
are puffed up, and have not rather mourned, that he that has

done this deed might be taken from among you. [3] For I, indeed,
as absent in body, but present in spirit, have already, as if I
were present, judged him that has so done this thing; [4] in the
name of our Lord Jesus Christ, when you and my spirit have
come together, with the power of our Lord Jesus Christ, [5] that
we deliver such a one over to Satan, for the destruction of the
flesh, that the spirit may be saved in the day of the Lord Jesus.
[6] Your boasting is not good; know you not that a little leaven
leavens the whole mass? [7] Purge out the old leaven, that you
may be a new mass, as you are without leaven; for Christ, our
passover, has been sacrificed for us. [8] Therefore, let us keep the
feast, not with old leaven, nor with the leaven of malice and
wickedness, but with the unleavened bread of purity and truth.
[9] I have written to you in the letter not to associate with
lewd persons; [10] yet without the least allusion to the lewd, or
the covetous, or the extortioners, or the idolaters of this world;
for then you must go out of the world; [11] but now I write to
you, not to associate with any one professing to be a brother, if
he is lewd, or covetous, or an idolater, or a reviler, or a drunk-
ard, or an extortioner: with such a one not even to eat. [12] For
what right have I to judge those who are without? Do you not
judge those who are within? [13] But God will judge those who
are without. *So then judge*, and put away that wicked man from
among you.

VI. [1] Does any one of you that has a matter of dispute with
another, presume to be judged before the unrighteous, and not
before the saints? [2] Know you not that the saints shall judge
the world? And if the world is to be judged by you, are you
unworthy to decide concerning the smallest matters? [3] Know
you not that we shall judge angels? Much more then, things
pertaining to this life. [4] If, then, you have controversies pertaining to things of this life, do you set them to judge who are
the least esteemed in the church?
[5] I speak to your shame. Is it so, that there is not among
you a wise man, not even one, who shall be able to arbitrate
between his brethren? [6] But brother goes to law with brother,
and this before the unbelievers? [7] Now certainly, you are altogether in fault, that you have lawsuits with one another.
Why do you not rather suffer injustice? Why do you not
rather suffer yourselves to be defrauded? [8] But you act unjustly, and you defraud, and that, too, your brethren. [9] Know

you not that the unrighteous shall not inherit the kingdom of
God? Be not deceived; neither lewd persons, nor idolaters, nor
adulterers, nor catamites, nor sodomites, 10 nor thieves, nor de-
frauders, nor drunkards, nor revilers, nor extortioners, shall
inherit the kingdom of God. 11 And such were some of you:
but you are washed, but you are sanctified, but you are justified, in the name of the Lord Jesus, and by the Spirit of our God.
12 All meats are lawful for me: but all are not profitable. All
are lawful for me; but I will not be brought under subjection by
any. 13 Meats for the stomach, and the stomach for meats; but
God will destroy both it and them. But the body is not for
lewdness, but for the Lord, and the Lord for the body: 14 and
God has raised up the Lord, and will also raise us up by his
power. 15 Know you not that your bodies are the members of
Christ? Shall I, then, take the members of the Christ, and
make them the members of a harlot? It must not be.
16 Know you not that he that is joined to a harlot, is one
body? For the two, says the Scripture, shall be one flesh.
17 But he that is joined to the Lord, is one spirit. 18 Shun lewdness. Every sin that a man commits, is without the body; but
he that is guilty of lewdness sins against his own body. 19 Know
you not that your body is the temple of the Holy Spirit, which
you have from God, and that you are not your own? 20 For you
have been bought with a price: therefore glorify God in your
body.

VII. 1 Now concerning the things of which you wrote to me,
it is good for a man not to touch a woman. 2 But, to avoid lewd
practices, let every man have his own wife, and every woman
her own husband. 3 Let the husband render to the wife that
which is due, and likewise, also, the wife to the husband. 4 The
wife has not power over her own body, but the husband; likewise, also, the husband has not power over his own body, but
the wife. 5 Debar not one another, unless by agreement for a
time, that you may have leisure for prayer; and come together
again, lest Satan tempt you through your incontinence. 6 But
this I say by permission, not by commandment: 7 for I could
wish that all men were even as I am myself. But each one has
his own gift from God, one in this way, another in that.
8 But I say to the unmarried and to the widows: It would be
good for them, if they remain as I myself. 9 But if they can
not be continent, let them marry; for it is better to marry than

to burn. [10] But to the married I give commandment, not I, but
the Lord: Let not the wife leave her husband: [11] but if she
leave him, let her remain unmarried, or be reconciled to her
husband: and, let not the husband put away his wife.

[12] But to the rest, I, and not the Lord, say: If any brother
has a wife that believes not, and she is well pleased to dwell
with him, let him not put her away. [13] And if any woman has
a husband that believes not, and he is well pleased to dwell with
her, let her not put him away. [14] For the unbelieving husband
is sanctified by the wife, and the unbelieving wife is sanctified
by the husband; for if not, then are your children unclean; but
now they are holy. [15] But if the unbelieving depart, let him
depart; the brother or sister is not bound in such cases. But
God has called us to live in peace. [16] For how do you know, O
wife, but that you may save your husband? Or how do you
know, O husband, but that you may save your wife? [17] But as
God has assigned a place to every one, as the Lord has called
every one, so let him continue to live: and so do I command in
all the churches.

[18] Has any one been called that had been circumcised? Let
him not seek to remove the mark of circumcision. Has any
one been called that had not been circumcised? Let him not be
circumcised. [19] Circumcision is nothing, and uncircumcision is
nothing; but the keeping of the commandments of God is *our
aim*. [20] Let every one remain in that condition in which he was,
when called. [21] Were you a servant when you were called?
Care not for it. But if you can become free, rather enjoy your
freedom. [22] For he that is in the Lord, having been called when
a servant, is the Lord's freedman. Likewise, also, the freeman
who has been called, is Christ's servant. [23] You have been
bought with a price; become not the servants of men. [24] Brethren, let every one, in whatever condition he is called, abide in
this with God.

[25] But with respect to virgins, I have no commandment of the
Lord: yet I give my judgment as one that is enabled, by the
mercy of the Lord, to be faithful. [26] I think, then, that this is
good for the present affliction—that it is good for a man to be
as he is. [27] Are you bound to a wife? Seek not a separation.
Are you loosed from a wife? Seek not a wife. [28] But if you
should marry, you would not sin. And if a virgin should marry,
she would not sin. But such will have affliction in the flesh.
But I spare you.

29 Now, this I say, brethren, the time is fraught with trials.
It remains that those who have wives be as though they had
them not; 30 and those who weep, as though they wept not; and
those who rejoice, as though they rejoiced not; and those who
buy, as though they possessed not: 31 and those who use this
world, as not abusing it; for the outward show of this world
passes away. 32 But I would have you to be without anxiety.
The unmarried man is concerned about the things of the Lord,
how he may please the Lord: 33 but he that is married, is concerned about the things of the world, how he may please his
wife. 34 There is a difference also between a wife and a virgin.
The unmarried woman is concerned about the things of the
Lord, that she may be holy in body and in spirit; but she that
is married, is concerned about the things of the world, how she
may please her husband. 35 I speak this for your own profit;
not that I would entangle you, but that you may decorously
and devotedly wait upon the Lord, without distraction.

36 But if any man thinks he would treat his virgin daughter
amiss, should she pass the bloom of life, and it is necessary that
it should be so, let him do as he pleases, he does not sin; let
them (*the suitor and the daughter*) marry. 37 But he that stands
firm in his purpose, having no necessity *to give his daughter in
marriage*, but has liberty with respect to his own will, and has
thus decided in his own heart, that he will keep his daughter
a virgin, does well. 38 So then, even he that gives her in marriage, does well; but he that gives her not in marriage, does
better.

39 The wife is bound as long as her husband lives; but if her
husband die, she is free to be married to whom she will, only
in the Lord. 40 But she is happier, in my judgment, if she
remains as she is; and I think that I have, also, the Spirit of
God.

VIII. 1 Now, with respect to meats offered to idols, we know,
(for we all have knowledge: knowledge puffs up with pride, but
love edifies. 2 If any one thinks that he knows any thing, he
knows nothing yet, as he ought to know it: 3 but if any one
loves God, he is taught by him). 4 With respect, then, to the
eating of meats offered to idols, we know that an idol is nothing in the world, and that there is no other God but one. 5 For
though there are those which are called gods, whether in heaven
or on earth, (as there are many gods, and many lords,) 6 yet to

us there is one God, the Father, from whom are all things, and
we for him; and one Lord, Jesus Christ, by whom are all things,
and we by him. 7 But all have not this knowledge; for some,
under the persuasion that an idol is a reality, even yet eat meat,
as if it were offered to an idol, and their conscience being weak,
is defiled.

8 But meat commends us not to God; for, neither if we eat
are we better, nor, if we eat not, are we worse. 9 But take heed,
lest, by any means, this right of yours become a stumbling-
block to those who are weak. 10 For, if any one see you, who
have knowledge, reclining at table in an idol's temple, will not
the conscience of him who is weak be emboldened, so that he
will eat meats offered to idols? 11 and will not the weak brother,
for whom Christ died, perish through your knowledge? 12 But
if you sin in this way against the brethren, and wound their
weak conscience, you sin against Christ. 13 For which reason,
if meat cause my brother to fall, I will never eat meat, lest I
cause my brother to fall.

IX. 1 Am I not free? Am I not an apostle? Have I not seen
Jesus Christ our Lord? Are you not my work in the Lord?
2 If I am not an apostle to others, yet certainly I am to you;
for the seal of my apostleship are you in the Lord. 3 My
answer to those who examine me is this: 4 Have we not the
right to eat and drink? 5 Have we not the right to lead about
a sister wife, as the other apostles, and the brothers of the
Lord, and Cephas? 6 Or, have I only, and Barnabas, no right
to leave off working?

7 What man ever serves as a soldier, at his own expense?
Who plants a vineyard, and eats not of its fruit? Or who tends
a flock, and eats not of the milk of the flock? 8 Do I speak
these things as a man? Or does not the law, also, say the
same? 9 For it is written in the law of Moses: You shall not
muzzle the ox that treads out the grain? Has God a care for
oxen? 10 or does he say it wholly for our sakes? For our sakes,
no doubt, it was written: that he that plows should plow in
hope, and that he that thrashes should thrash in hope of par-
taking. 11 If we have sown, for your benefit, things that are
spiritual, is it a great thing that we reap your carnal things?
12 If others partake of this right over you, should not we rather?
But we have not used this right: but we endure all things, lest
we should hinder the gospel of the Christ.

13 Do you not know that those who are engaged about sacred
rites have their living from the temple? and that those who
attend upon the altar are partakers with the altar? 14 So, also,
the Lord has ordained that those who preach the gospel should
live by the gospel.

15 But I have availed myself of none of these things; nor do
I write these things that it should be so done to me. For it
would be better for me to die, than that any one should make
my boasting vain. 16 For though I preach the gospel, I have
no cause for boasting; for a necesssity is laid upon me; yes,
alas for me, if I preach not the gospel. 17 For if I do this willingly, I have a reward; but if unwillingly, an apostolic stewardship has been intrusted to me. 18 What, then, is my reward?
That, while I preach, I may make the gospel of Christ to be
without charge, in order that I may not abuse my authority in
the gospel.

19 For, though I am free from all men, yet have I made myself
a servant to all, that I may gain the more. 20 And to the Jews,
I became as a Jew, that I might gain the Jews: to those who
are under law, as under law, (not being myself under law,) that
I might gain those who are under law; 21 to those who are without law, as without law, (not being myself without law to God,
but under law to Christ,) that I might gain those who are without law: 22 to the weak I became like one who was weak, that
I might gain the weak: I have become all things to all men,
that I may, by all means, save some. 23 And this I do for the
gospel's sake, that I may share its benefits with *you*.

24 Know you not that all the runners in the race-course run
the race, but that one receives the prize. So run, that you may
obtain the prize. 25 Every combatant in the public games is
temperate in all things: they, indeed, that they may obtain a
corruptible, but we, that we may obtain an incorruptible crown.
26 I, therefore, so run, not as with uncertainty; I so aim my
blows, not as one that beats the air; 27 but I put my body under
severe discipline, and bring it into subjection, lest, after I have
preached to others, I myself should be rejected.

X. 1 Now, brethren, I do not wish you to be ignorant, that
all our fathers were under the cloud, and that all passed through
the sea, 2 and were all immersed into Moses, in the cloud and
in the sea; 3 and did all eat the same spiritual food, 4 and did all
drink the same spiritual drink: for they drank of that spiritual

Rock that followed them, and that Rock was the Christ. [5] But
with the most of them God was not well pleased, for they were
overthrown in the wilderness.

[6] Now these things took place as examples for us, that we
should not desire evil things, as they, also, desired. [7] Neither
be you idolaters, as some of them were, as it is written: The
people sat down to eat and to drink, and rose up to engage in
idolatrous sport. [8] Nor let us be guilty of lewdness, as some of
them were guilty, and fell, in one day, twenty-three thousand.
[9] Nor let us tempt the Christ, as some of them also tempted,
and were destroyed by serpents. [10] Nor do you murmur, as
some of them also murmured, and were destroyed by the de-
stroyer. [11] Now all these things happened to them as examples,
and they are written for the instruction of us, upon whom the
ends of the ages have come. [12] Wherefore, let him that thinks
he stands, take heed lest he fall.

[13] No trial has come upon you but such as is common to man:
but God is faithful, who will not suffer you to be tried more than
you are able *to bear;* but he will, with the trial, make a way to
escape, so that you be able to bear up under it.

[14] Wherefore, my beloved, flee from idolatry. [15] I speak as to
wise men; judge you what I say. [16] The cup of blessing which
we bless, is it not the participation of the blood of the Christ?
The bread which we break, is it not the participation of the
body of the Christ? [17] Because the loaf is one, we, the many,
are one body, for we are all partakers of the one loaf. [18] Look
at Israel according to the flesh: are not those who eat the sacrifices partakers with the altar? [19] What, then, do I say? That
an idol is any thing? or, that what is sacrificed to an idol is
any thing? [20] But *I say,* that the things which the Gentiles
sacrifice, they sacrifice to demons, and not to God. I do not
wish you to be partakers with demons. [21] You can not drink
the cup of the Lord, and the cup of demons: you can not be
partakers of the table of the Lord, and of the table of demons.
[22] Do we provoke the Lord to jealousy? Are we stronger
than he?

[23] All meats are lawful *for me;* but all are not profitable; all
are lawful, but all do not edify. [24] Let no one seek his own, but
each the welfare of the other. [25] Any thing that is sold in the
market, eat, asking no questions on account of conscience: [26] for
the earth and its fullness are the Lord's.

[27] If any one of the unbelievers invites you *to a feast,* and you

are disposed to go, eat any thing that is set before you, asking
no questions for conscience' sake. 28 But if any one say to you:
This is sacrificed to idols; eat not, for the sake of him that
pointed it out, and for conscience' sake: 29 conscience, I say,
not your own, but that of the other. Why, then, is my liberty
judged by the conscience of another? 30 If I partake with
thanksgiving, why am I evil spoken of on account of that for
which I give thanks? 31 Whether, therefore, you eat or drink,
or whatever you do, do all to the glory of God. 32 Give no occasion for stumbling, either to the Jews, or to the Greeks, or to
the church of God; 33 even as I please all men in all things, not
seeking my own good, but that of the many, in order that they
may be saved.

XI. 1 Be imitators of me, as I am of Christ. 2 Now, I praise
you, brethren, because you remember me in all things, and keep
the traditions as I delivered them to you. 3 But I wish you to
know, that the head of every man is the Christ, and the head
of the woman is the man; and the head of Christ is God.
4 Every man that prays or prophesies, having his head covered,
dishonors his head. 5 But every woman that prays or prophesies
with her head uncovered, dishonors her head: for it is one and
the same as if she was shaved. 6 For if a woman has no vail
on, let her also be shaved. But if it is a shame to a woman to
be shorn or shaven, let her have a vail.

7 For a man ought not to vail his head, because he is the image
and glory of God; but the woman is the glory of the man. 8 For
the man is not of the woman, but the woman of the man: 9 for
the man was not created for the woman, but the woman for the
man. 10 For this reason ought the woman to have a token of
subjection on her head, on account of the angels. 11 But neither
is the woman without the man, nor the man without the woman,
in the Lord. 12 For as the woman is of the man, so also is the
man by the woman; but all things are of God.

13 Judge in yourselves, whether it is becoming that a woman
pray to God unvailed. 14 Does not nature itself teach you, that,
if a man has long hair, it is a dishonor to him? 15 But if a
woman has long hair, it is a glory to her; for her hair is given
to her for a vail. 16 But if any one seems to be contentious, we
have no such custom, nor have the churches of God.

17 But I praise you not in this, which I now mention, that you
come together, not for the better, but for the worse. 18 For, in

the first place, when you come together in the church, I hear
that there are schisms among you, and I partly believe it: 19 for
there must be sects among you, that the approved may be made
known among you.

20 When, therefore, you come together in one place, it is not
to eat the Lord's supper; 21 for each one, in eating, takes before
another, his own supper; and one is hungry, and another is
drunken. 22 What, have you not houses in which to eat and
drink? or do you despise the church of God, and put those to
shame who have nothing to eat? What shall I say to you?
Shall I praise you in this? I praise you not.

23 For I received from the Lord that which I also delivered to
you: That the Lord Jesus, on the night in which he was delivered up, took bread; 24 and when he had given thanks, he
broke it, and said: Take, eat; this is my body, which is broken
for you; do this in remembrance of me. 25 In like manner also,
the cup, after he had supped, saying: This cup is the new covenant in my blood: do this, as often as you drink it, in remembrance of me. 26 For as often as you eat this bread, and drink
this cup, you do show the Lord's death till he come.

27 Wherefore he that eats this bread, or drinks this cup of the
Lord, in an improper manner, shall be guilty of the body and
the blood of the Lord. 28 But let a man examine himself, and
so let him eat of this bread, and drink of this cup: 29 for he
that eats and drinks, not discerning the body, eats and drinks
condemnation to himself. 30 For this reason, many among you
are weak and sick, and many sleep. 31 For if we would judge
ourselves, we should not be judged; 32 but being judged, we are
chastened by the Lord, that we may not be condemned with the
world. 33 Wherefore, my brethren, when you come together to
eat, wait for one another: 34 and if any one is hungry, let him
eat at home, that you come not together for condemnation.
35 But other things I will set in order when I come.

XII. 1 But concerning spiritual gifts, brethren, I do not wish
you to be ignorant. 2 You know that you were Gentiles, carried away to those dumb idols, as you might be led. 3 For this
reason, I make known to you, that no one, speaking by the
Spirit of God, calls Jesus accursed: and no one can say that
Jesus is Lord, but by the Holy Spirit.

4 Now there are diversities of gifts, but the same Spirit; 5 and
there are diversities of ministries, but the same Lord; 6 and

there are diversities of operations, but the same God, who makes
them all effectual in all. 7 But the manifestation of the Spirit
is given to each one, for the good of all. 8 For to one is given,
by the Spirit, the word of wisdom; to another, the word of
knowledge, by the same Spirit; 9 to another, faith, by the same
Spirit; to another, gifts of healing, by the same Spirit; 10 to
another, the working of mighty deeds; to another, prophecy;
to another, the discerning of spirits; to another, different kinds
of tongues; to another, the interpretation of tongues. 11 But all
these, the one and the same Spirit makes effectual, distributing
to each, respectively, as he wills.

12 For as the body is one, and has many members, and all the
members of the body, being many, are one body, so also is the
Christ. 13 For by one Spirit we all were immersed into one body,
whether Jews or Greeks, whether bond or free; and we all have
been made to drink of one Spirit.

14 For the body is not one member, but many. 15 If the foot
shall say: Because I am not the hand, I am not of the body, is
it, for this reason, no part of the body? 16 And if the ear shall
say: Because I am not the eye, I am not of the body, is it, for
this reason, no part of the body? 17 If the whole body were an
eye, where were the hearing? If the whole were hearing, where
were the smelling? 18 But now God has placed the members,
each of them, in the body, as it has pleased him. 19 And if they
were all one member, where were the body? 20 But now there
are many members, but one body. 21 The eye can not say to the
hand: I have no need of you; or again, the head to the feet: I
have no need of you.

22 But much more are those members of the body necessary,
which seem to be more feeble. 23 And those members of the
body, which, we think, are less honorable, around these we place
the more abundant honor; and our uncomely members have the
more abundant comeliness: 24 for our comely members have no
need. But God has so arranged the body, giving more abundant
honor to that part which is deficient, 25 that there may be no
schism in the body; but that the members should have the same
anxious care, one for another; 26 and if one member suffer, all
the members suffer with it; or if one member is honored, all the
members rejoice with it. 27 Now, you are the body of Christ, and,
as individuals, you are members.

28 And God has placed some in the church, first, apostles; sec-
ondly, prophets; thirdly, teachers; then mighty deeds; then

gifts of healing; helps, governments, kinds of tongues. 29 Are
all apostles? Are all prophets? Are all teachers? Are all
workers of mighty deeds? 30 Have all the gifts of healing? Do
all speak with tongues? Do all interpret? 31 But seek earnestly the best gifts; and yet I show you a more excellent
way.

XIII. 1 Though I speak with the tongues of men and of angels, but have not love, I have become as sounding brass, or a
clanging cymbal. 2 And though I have the gift of prophecy,
and understand all mysteries, and all knowledge; and though I
have all faith, so that I could remove mountains, and have not
love, I am nothing. 3 And though I give all my goods to feed
the poor, and though I deliver up my body to be burned, and
have not love, I am profited nothing.

4 Love suffers long, and is kind; love envies not; love boasts
not; is not vain, 5 does nothing unbecoming, seeks not her own,
is not easily provoked, thinks no evil, 6 rejoices not in iniquity,
but rejoices in the truth; 7 bears all things, believes all things,
hopes all things, endures all things.

8 Love never fails; but whether there be gifts of prophecy,
they shall have an end; or tongues, they shall cease; or knowledge, it shall have an end. 9 For we know in part, and we
prophesy in part; 10 but when that which is perfect has come,
then that which is in part shall have an end. 11 When I was a
child, I spoke as a child, I had the mind of a child, I thought
as a child; but when I became a man, I put away childish
things. 12 Now we see through a mirror, obscurely; but then
face to face; now I know in part, but then shall I know, even
as I am known.

13 And now abide faith, hope, love, these three; but the greatest
of these is love.

XIV. 1 Cultivate love, and earnestly desire spiritual gifts,
but rather that you may prophesy. 2 For he that speaks in an
unknown tongue, speaks not to men, but to God; for no one
understands him: but yet in spirit he speaks mysteries. 3 But
he that prophesies speaks to men so as to build them up, to exhort and comfort them. 4 He that speaks in an unknown tongue,
edifies himself; but he that prophesies, edifies the church. 5 I
am willing, indeed, that you should all speak in tongues, but
rather that you should prophesy; for greater is he that proph-

esies than he that speaks in tongues, unless he interprets, in
order that the church may receive instruction.

6 Now, brethren, if I come to you, speaking in tongues, in
what will I profit you, unless I speak to you by revelation, or
by knowledge, or by prophecy, or by teaching? 7 And even life-
less instruments, which produce sound, whether pipe or harp,
unless they give a distinction in the notes, how shall that which
is piped or harped be known? 8 For if the trumpet give an uncertain sound, who will prepare himself for battle? 9 So, also,
unless you, with the tongue, utter words that are intelligible,
how shall that which is spoken be known? for you will speak
into the air. 10 There are, it may be, so many kinds of voices
in the world, and none of them is without meaning. 11 If, then,
I know not the meaning of the voice, I shall be to him that
speaks a barbarian; and he that speaks will be a barbarian to
me.

12 So, also, do you, since you greatly desire spiritual gifts,
seek to excel to the building up of the church. 13 For which
reason, let him that speaks in an unknown tongue pray that he
may interpret. 14 For if I pray in an unknown tongue, the
spirit which I have prays, but my understanding is unfruitful.
15 What, then, is it? I will pray with the spirit which is given
to me, and I will pray with my understanding also. I will sing
with the spirit that is given to me, and I will sing with my
understanding also. 16 Otherwise, if you bless with the spirit
that is given to you, how will he that occupies the place of the
unlearned man say Amen, when you give thanks, since he understands not what you say? 17 For you give thanks well, but
the other is not edified. 18 I thank God that I speak in tongues
more than you all. 19 Yet in the church I would rather speak
five words with my understanding, that I may instruct others,
than ten thousand words in an unknown tongue.

20 Brethren, be not children in understanding: yet, in malice,
be child-like; but, in understanding, be full-grown men. 21 In
the law it is written: Through men of other tongues and other
lips will I speak to this people; and not even thus will they
hear me, says the Lord. 22 Therefore, tongues are for a sign,
not to those who believe, but to those who believe not: but
prophecy is not for those who believe not, but for those who
believe.

23 If, then, the whole church come together into the same
place, and all speak in tongues, and there came in unlearned

men, or unbelievers, will they not say that you are mad? 24 But
if all prophesy, and there comes in an unbeliever, or an unlearned man, he is convinced by all, he is examined by all, 25 and
the secrets of his heart are made manifest; and so, falling down
on his face, he will worship God, and report that God is really
among you.

26 What, then, is it, brethren? When you come together, each
one of you has a psalm, has something to teach, has an unknown tongue, has a revelation, has an interpretation. Let all
things be done for edification. 27 If any speak in an unknown
tongue, let two, or, at most, three, speak at each meeting, and
in succession: and let one interpret. 28 But if there be no in-
terpreter, let him keep silence in the church: but let him speak
to himself, and to God. 29 Let two or three prophets speak, and
let the others judge: 30 and if any thing be revealed to one who
is sitting by, let the first be silent. 31 For you can all prophesy,
one by one, that all may learn, and all may be encouraged;
32 and the spirits of the prophets are subject to the prophets;
33 for God is not the author of confusion, but of peace, as in all
the assemblies of the saints.

34 Let your women keep silence in the assemblies; for they
are not permitted to speak; but they must be in subjection, as
also says the law. 35 But if they wish to learn any thing, let
them ask their own husbands at home; for it is a shame for
women to speak in an assembly. 36 Has the word of God come
forth from you? or did it come to you only?

37 If any one has the reputation of being a prophet, or spiritual man, let him acknowledge that the things which I write
to you are the commandments of the Lord. 38 But if any one
be ignorant, let him be ignorant. 39 Wherefore, brethren, earnestly desire to prophesy, and forbid not to speak with tongues.
40 Let all things be done with propriety, and in good order.

XV. 1 But I make known to you, brethren, the gospel that I
preached to you, which also you received, in which also you
stand, 2 by which also you are saved, if you hold fast the word
which I preached to you, unless you believed in vain.

3 For I delivered to you among the first things, that which I
also received: That Christ died for our sins, according to the
Scriptures; 4 and that he was buried; and that he rose again
the third day, according to the Scriptures; 5 and that he was
seen by Cephas, then by the twelve; 6 after that, he was seen by

more than five hundred brethren at once, of whom the greater
part remain till this day; but some have fallen asleep. 7 After
that, he was seen by James, then by all the apostles. 8 Last of
all, he was seen by me also, as one untimely born. 9 For I am
the least of the apostles, and I am not worthy to be called an
apostle, because I persecuted the church of God. 10 But, by the
grace of God, I am what I am; and his grace, which was bestowed on me, has not been bestowed in vain: but I have labored
more abundantly than they all; not I, however, but the grace
of God which was with me. 11 Whether, therefore, I or they, so
we preached, and so you believed.

12 But if Christ is preached that he rose from the dead, how
say some among you, that a resurrection of the dead is impossible? 13 But if a resurrection of the dead is impossible, Christ
has not been raised. 14 And if Christ has not been raised, then
vain is our preaching, and vain also your faith. 15 We are, indeed, also found false witnesses of God; for we have testified
against God, that he raised the Christ, whom he did not raise,
if, indeed, the dead are not raised. 16 For if the dead are not
raised, Christ has not been raised; 17 and if Christ has not been
raised, your faith is vain; you are yet in your sins. 18 Then,
also, those who have fallen asleep in Christ have perished. 19 If
in this life only we have hope in Christ, we are of all men the
most miserable.

20 But now, Christ has risen from the dead, the first-fruits of
those who slept. 21 For, since through man came death, through
man comes also the resurrection of the dead. 22 For, as in Adam
all die, so, also, in Christ shall all be made alive: 23 but each in
his own order; Christ the first-fruit, afterward, those who are
Christ's at his coming. 24 Then comes the end, when he shall
have delivered up the kingdom to God, even the Father; when
he shall have put down every principality and authority and
power: 25 for he must reign till he has put all enemies under
his feet. 26 The last enemy, Death, shall be destroyed. 27 For
he has put all things under his feet. But when the Scripture
says, that all things are put under him, it is evident that he is
excepted, who did put all things under him. 28 And when all
things shall have been put under him, then, also, shall the Son
himself be subjected to him that did put all things under him,
that God may be the all in all.

29 For else, what shall those do, who are immersed for the dead,
if the dead rise not at all? Why, then, are they immersed for

the dead? 30 And why are we in danger every hour? 31 I pro-
test, by the joy which I have over you in Christ Jesus our Lord,
I die daily. 32 If, to speak as a man, I have fought with wild
beasts at Ephesus, what advantage is it to me, if the dead rise
not? Let us eat and drink, for to-morrow we die. 33 Be not deceived: Evil communications corrupt good manners. 34 Awake,
as you should, to soberness, and sin not; for some have not the
knowledge of God. I speak this to your shame.

35 But some one will say: How are the dead raised up? and
with what body do they come? 36 Thoughtless man! That
which you sow is not made alive, unless it die; 37 and as to that
which you sow, you sow not the body that shall be produced,
but the naked grain, it may be of wheat, or of some other grain:
38 But God gives it a body, as it pleases him; and to every seed,
its proper body. 39 All flesh is not the same flesh; but there is
one flesh of men, another of beasts, another of fishes, and
another of birds. 40 There are also bodies celestial, and bodies
terrestrial: but the glory of the celestial is one, and that of the
terrestrial is another. 41 There is one glory of the sun, and
another glory of the moon, and another glory of the stars; for
star differs from star in glory.

42 So, also, is the resurrection of the dead. It is sown in corruption, it is raised in incorruption: 43 it is sown in dishonor,
it is raised in glory: it is sown in weakness, it is raised in power:
44 it is sown an animal body, it is raised a spiritual body.
There is an animal body, and there is a spiritual body. 45 So,
also, it is written: The first man Adam became a living soul,
the last Adam a life-giving spirit. 46 But that was not first
which is spiritual, but that which is animal; and afterward that
which is spiritual. 47 The first man is of the earth, earthy; the
second man, the Lord from heaven. 48 As the earthy man was,
such also are the earthy; and as the heavenly man is, such also
shall the heavenly be. 49 And as we have borne the image of
the earthy, we shall also bear the image of the heavenly. 50 But
this I say, brethren, that flesh and blood can not inherit the
kingdom of God, nor does corruption inherit incorruption.

51 Behold, I declare to you a mystery. We shall not all sleep,
but we shall all be changed 52 in a moment, in the twinkling of
an eye, at the last trumpet: For the trumpet shall sound, and
the dead shall be raised incorruptible, and we shall be changed.
53 For this corruptible body must put on incorruptibility; and
this mortal body must put on immortality. 54 And when this

corruptible body shall have put on incorruptibility, and this
mortal body shall have put on immortality, then shall come to
pass the word that is written: Death is swallowed up in victory. 55 O Death, where is thy sting? O Hades, where is thy
victory? 56 The sting of death is sin; and the strength of sin
is the law. 57 But thanks be to God, who gives us the victory
through our Lord Jesus Christ. 58 Therefore, my beloved brethren, be firm, immovable, always abounding in the work of the
Lord; for you know that your labor is not in vain in the Lord.

XVI. 1 As it respects the collection which is for the saints,
as I have given orders to the churches of Galatia, so also do
you. 2 On the first day of the week, let each of you lay by him,
and treasure up as he has prospered, that there may be no
collections when I come. 3 And when I come, whatever persons
you approve, I will send with letters to carry your favor to
Jerusalem. 4 And if it be proper that I also should go, they
shall go with me.

5 Now I will come to you, when I have passed through Macedonia, for I intend to go through Macedonia; 6 and perhaps I
may abide with you, or even spend the winter, that you may
conduct me on my way to whatever place I may go. 7 For I do
not wish to see you now in passing; for I hope to spend some
time with you, if the Lord permit. 8 But I will continue in
Ephesus till Pentecost: 9 for a great and effective door is opened
to me, and there are many adversaries.

10 If Timothy come, see that he be with you without fear: for
he works the work of the Lord, as I also do. 11 Therefore, let
no one despise him; but conduct him forth in peace, that he
may come to me: for I look for him with the brethren.

12 As it respects Apollos my brother, I urged him much to go
to you with the brethren, yet he was not at all inclined to go
now; but he will go when he has a suitable time.

13 Be watchful, stand fast in the faith, be men, be resolute.
14 Let every thing be done by you in love.

15 I beseech you, brethren, (you know the house of Stephanas,
that they are the first-fruits of Achaia, and that they have devoted themselves to the ministry of the saints,) 16 that you
submit yourselves to such, and to every one that works and
labors with us.

17 I rejoice at the coming of Stephanas and Fortuuatus and
Achaicus; for they have supplied what was wanting on your

part: 18 for they have refreshed my spirit, and yours. Therefore, acknowledge such.
19 The churches of Asia salute you: Aquila and Priscilla, with
the church that is in their house, send you many salutations in
the Lord. 20 All the brethren salute you. Salute one another
with a holy kiss.
21 The salutation of me, Paul, with my own hand. 22 If any
one loves not the Lord Jesus Christ, let him be accursed. The
Lord comes.
23 The grace of our Lord Jesus Christ be with you. 24 My love
be with you all in Christ Jesus. Amen.

PAUL TO THE CORINTHIANS.

SECOND LETTER.

I. 1 PAUL, an apostle of Jesus Christ, by the will of God,
and Timothy my brother, to the church of God which
is in Corinth, with all the saints that are in all Achaia: 2 grace
be to you, and peace from God our Father, and from the Lord
Jesus Christ.
3 Blessed be the God and Father of our Lord Jesus Christ, the
Father of mercies, and the God of all comfort, 4 who consoles us
in all our afflictions, so that we are able to comfort those who
are in any affliction, with the comfort with which we ourselves
are comforted by God. 5 For as the sufferings for the Christ
abound in us, so also through Christ abounds our consolation.
6 And if we are afflicted, it is for your consolation and salvation, which salvation is effected by your patient endurance of
the same sufferings that we also suffer; (and our hope in you is
steadfast;) or if we are consoled, it is for your comfort and salvation; 7 because we know, that as you are partakers of the
sufferings, so also you shall be partakers of the comfort.
8 For we do not wish you to be ignorant, brethren, concerning
our affliction which came upon us in Asia, that we were exceedingly oppressed, beyond our strength, so that we despaired even
of life. 9 But we have in ourselves the sentence of death, that
we may not trust in ourselves, but in God, who raises the dead;
10 who delivered us from so great a death, and does still deliver
us: in whom we have confidence, that he will continue to deliver us, 11 if you also unite in prayer for our aid, that the favor

bestowed on us, through the intercession of many persons, may
cause thanks to be given by many for us.

12 For the ground of our rejoicing is this: the testimony of
our conscience that we have lived in the world—more abundantly, indeed, for you—in sincerity and godly purity, not in
carnal wisdom, but in the grace of God. 13 For we write to you
nothing else than what you recognize, or even acknowledge;
and which I hope you will acknowledge to the end; 14 as some
of you also acknowledge us, that we are the cause of your rejoicing, even as you, also, are of ours, in the day of the Lord
Jesus.

15 And in this confidence I intended to go to you before, that
you might have a second benefit; 16 and by you, to pass through
into Macedonia, and to come again to you from Macedonia, and
be conducted by you into Judea. 17 In forming this purpose,
did I, therefore, behave with levity? or do I purpose what I
purpose, according to the flesh, that there may be with me, yes,
yes, and no, no?

18 But God is true; for our preaching to you was not yes and
no: 19 for the Son of God, Jesus Christ, who was preached among
you by us, by me and Sylvanus and Timothy, was not yes and
no, but in him was yes. 20 For whatever promises of God there
are, are in him yes, and in him amen, to the glory of God by
us. 21 For he who establishes us with you in Christ, and has
anointed us, is God, 22 who has also set his seal upon us, and
given us the earnest of the Spirit in our hearts.

23 But I call on God as a witness against my soul, that wishing
to spare you, I did not go to Corinth; 24 not that we are lords
over your faith, but fellow-workers for your joy: for by faith
you stand.

II. 1 But I determined this in myself, that with sorrow I
would not again come to you: 2 for if I cause you to grieve, who
is he that makes me glad, but he that is made sorry by me?
3 And I wrote to you this very thing, that, on coming to you, I
might not have sorrow from those from whom I ought to receive
joy; because I have confidence in you all, that my joy is the joy
of you all. 4 For out of much affliction and distress of heart, I
wrote to you with many tears: not that you might be grieved,
but that you might know the love which I have more abundantly
for you.

5 But if any one has caused grief, he has grieved, not me only,

but, in some measure—not to speak harshly—all of you 6 Sufficient for such a one is the punishment, which was inflicted by
the greater number: 7 so that, on the other hand, you should
rather forgive and comfort him, lest such a one should be swallowed up in too much sorrow. 8 Wherefore, I exhort you to give
him an assurance of your love. 9 For I wrote to you for this
purpose also, that I might have a sure proof from you, whether
you are obedient in all things. 10 Whom you forgive any thing,
I forgive it also: for what I have forgiven, if I have forgiven
any thing, I have forgiven for your sake, in the person of Christ,
11 lest an advantage should be taken of us by Satan; for we are
not ignorant of his devices.

12 And when I came to Troas to preach the gospel of the Christ,
and a door was opened to me in the Lord, 13 I had no rest in my
spirit, because I did not find Titus my brother; but I took leave
of them, and went into Macedonia.

14 Now, thanks be to God, who always causes us to triumph in
the Christ, and sheds in every place, by us, the fragrance of the
knowledge of himself. 15 For, through God, we are a sweet odor
of Christ, among the saved, and among the lost: 16 to the one,
we are the odor of death ending in death; to the other, the odor
of life ending in life: and who is sufficient for these things?
17 For we do not, as the many, adulterate the word of God; but,
as from sincerity, but, as from God, in the sight of God speak
we in Christ.

III. 1 Do we begin again to commend ourselves? or do we
need, as some do, letters of commendation to you, or letters of
commendation from you? 2 You are our letter, written in our
hearts, known and read by all men; 3 you are well known to be
a letter of Christ, written by us as his ministers, not with ink,
but with the Spirit of the living God, not in tables of stone, but
in fleshy tables of the heart.

4 Now, confidence such as this we have, through the Christ,
toward God; 5 not that we are able, of ourselves, to devise any
thing as from ourselves; but our ability is from God, 6 who has
made us able ministers of the new covenant, not of letter, but
of spirit: for the letter kills, but the spirit makes alive. 7 For
if the ministering of death, *by means of a covenant* that was written and engraven in stones, was glorious, so that the sons of
Israel could not look steadily at the face of Moses, on account
of the glory of his face, which glory was to come to an end:

8 how shall not the ministering of the spirit be more glorious?
9 For if the ministering of condemnation be glory, much more
does the ministering of righteousness surpass in glory. 10 For
that which was made glorious had no glory in this respect, because of the glory that surpasses. 11 For if that which was to
come to an end was glorious, much more that which is to remain
is glorious.

12 Since then we have such hope, we use great plainness of
speech, 13 and do not as Moses did, who put a vail over his face,
so that the sons of Israel could not steadily look to the end of
that which was to come to an end. 14 But their minds were
blinded: for till this day, in the reading of the old covenant,
the same vail remains not taken away, which vail is removed
in Christ. 15 But to this day, when Moses is read, the vail is
upon their heart: 16 but whenever their heart shall turn to the
Lord, the vail shall be taken away. 17 Now the Lord is the
Spirit; and where the Spirit of the Lord is, there is liberty.
18 And we all, with unvailed face, reflecting the glory of the
Lord, are changed into the same image, from glory to glory,
even as by the Lord the Spirit.

IV. 1 Wherefore, having this ministry, inasmuch as we have
received mercy, we faint not; 2 but we have renounced the
secret works of shame, not walking in craftiness, nor adulter-
ating the word of God; but, by the manifestation of the truth,
commending ourselves to every man's conscience in the sight
of God.

3 But if our gospel is vailed, it is vailed among the lost,
4 whose unbelieving minds the god of this age has darkened, so
that the light of the glorious gospel of Christ, who is the image
of God, should not shine to them. 5 For we preach not ourselves, but Christ Jesus the Lord, and ourselves your servants, for Jesus' sake. 6 Because God, who commanded the light
to shine out of darkness, has shined in our hearts, to give the
light of the glorious knowledge of God in the person of Jesus
Christ.

7 But we have this treasure in earthen vessels, that the exceeding greatness of the power may be God's and not our own.
8 We are pressed on all sides, yet not restrained; perplexed, but
not in despair; 9 persecuted, but not forsaken; cast down, but
not destroyed; 10 always bearing about in our body the violent
death of the Lord Jesus, that the life also of Jesus may be made

manifest in our body. 11 For we who live are continually delivered up to death for Jesus' sake, that the life also of Jesus may
be made manifest in our mortal flesh.
12 So, then, death is active in us, but life in you. 13 But, having
the same spirit of faith, according to that which is written, I
believed, and for this reason I have spoken; we also believe, and
for this reason we speak, 14 knowing that he who raised up the
Lord Jesus will raise us up also by Jesus, and present us together with you. 15 For all these afflictions are for your sakes,
that the favor which abounds *to me*, may, through the thanksgiving of the many, abound richly to the glory of God.
16 For this reason we faint not: but though our outward
man perish, yet the inward man is renewed day by day. 17 For
our present light affliction works out for us an eternal fullness
of glory, excelling all excellence, 18 while we look not at the
things that are seen, but at the things that are not seen: for
the things seen are temporal; but the things not seen are
eternal.

V. 1 For we know that if our earthly house, which is but a
tent, should be destroyed, we have a building from God, a house
not made with hands, eternal in the heavens. 2 For in this we
groan, earnestly desiring to be clothed upon with our house
that is from heaven, 3 since, having been clothed, we shall not
be found naked. 4 For we who are in this tabernacle do groan,
being burdened, not because we wish to be unclothed, but clothed
upon, that what is mortal may be swallowed up by life.
5 Now, he that has formed us for this very thing is God, who
also has given us the earnest of the Spirit. 6 Therefore, we are
always confident, especially since we know that, while living in
the body, we are absent from the Lord: 7 for we walk by faith,
not by sight: 8 we are confident, indeed, and would be pleased
rather to depart from the body, and to dwell with the Lord.
9 For this reason we also endeavor, whether we remain in the
body or depart from it, to be acceptable to him. 10 For we must
all appear before the judgment-seat of Christ, that each may
receive his reward for the things done in his body, according to
what he has done, whether good or evil.
11 Knowing, then, the fearful judgment of the Lord, we persuade men; but we are made manifest to God. I hope, indeed,
that we are also made manifest in your consciences. 12 We do
not again commend ourselves to you, but give you an occasion

to boast of us, that you may be able to answer those who glory
in appearance, and not in heart. 13 For if we be beside ourselves,
it is for God; or, if we be of sound mind, it is for you. 14 For
the love of Christ constrains us, because we have this judgment—that if one died for all, then have all died: 15 and he died
for all, that those who live should no more live for themselves,
but for him who died for them, and rose again.

16 So, then, we henceforth know no man according to the flesh;
if, indeed, we have known Christ according to the flesh, yet now
we no longer thus know him. 17 So, then, if any man is in Christ,
he is a new creature; the old things have passed away; behold,
all things have become new. 18 And all these things are from
God, who has reconciled us to himself through Jesus Christ, and
has given to us the ministry of reconciliation; 19 that is, that
God was in Christ, reconciling the world to himself, not charging their offenses to them, and he has committed to us the word
of reconciliation.

20 Therefore, we act as embassadors for Christ, as though God
entreated through us; we beseech in Christ's stead, be reconciled to God: 21 for he has made him, who knew no sin, a sin-
offering for us, that we might become the righteousness of God
in him.

VI. 1 As co-workers with him, we beseech you, that you receive not the grace of God in vain: (2 for he says: I have heard
thee in an acceptable time, and in the day of salvation I have
helped thee. Behold, now is the acceptable time; behold, now
is the day of salvation:) 3 for we put no stumbling-block in any
man's way, in order that this ministry may not be blamed; 4 but
in all things we commend ourselves as the ministers of God, in
much suffering, in afflictions, in distresses, in straits, 5 in stripes,
in prisons, in commotions, in labors, in watchings, in fastings;
6 by purity, by knowledge, by long forbearance, by kindness, by
the Holy Spirit, by love unfeigned, 7 by the word of truth, by
the power of God, by the armor of righteousness on the right
hand and on the left, 8 by honor and dishonor, by evil report,
and good report; as impostors, yet truthful; 9 as unknown, yet
well-known; as dying, and behold, we live; as chastened, and
yet not put to death; 10 as sorrowful, yet always rejoicing; as
poor, yet making many rich; as having nothing, yet possessing
all things.

11 Corinthians, our mouth is opened to you, our heart is en-

larged: 12 you are not straitened in us, but you are straitened
in your own affections. 13 That you may repay me in like manner, (I speak as to children,) be you also enlarged.

14 Be not unequally yoked together with unbelievers: for what
fellowship has righteousness with lawlessness? What communion has light with darkness? 15 What agreement has
Christ with Belial? What connection has a believer with an
unbeliever? 16 What has a temple of God in common with one
of idols? For you are the temple of the living God, as God has
said: I will dwell in them, and walk among them; and I will
be their God, and they shall be my people. 17 For this reason,
come out from among them, and separate yourselves, says the
Lord, and touch not an unclean person, and I will receive you;
18 and I will be to you a father, and you shall be to me sons and
daughters, says the Lord Almighty.

VII. 1 Therefore, having these promises, beloved, let us
cleanse ourselves from every pollution of the flesh and spirit,
perfecting holiness in the fear of God. 2 Regard us cordially;
we have wronged no one, we have corrupted no one, we have
made gain by no one. 3 I do not say this to condemn you; for
I have said before, that you are in our hearts, so that we could
die with you, and live with you. 4 Great is my plainness of
speech to you, great is my boasting of you; I am filled with
comfort, I am exceedingly joyful in all our affliction.

5 For when we came into Macedonia, our flesh had no rest;
but we were oppressed on every side: without were battles,
within were fears. 6 But God, who comforts those who are cast
down, comforted us by the coming of Titus; 7 and not only by
his coming, but also by the consolation with which he was comforted in you when he told us of your strong affection, your
grief, your zeal for me; so that I rejoiced the more. 8 For although I caused you sorrow by my letter, I do not regret it,
though I did regret it. For I see that the same letter gave you
sorrow, though but for a short time. 9 Now I rejoice not that
you were made sorry, but that you sorrowed in order to repentance. For you sorrowed in a way acceptable to God, that you
might in nothing receive injury from us. 10 For godly sorrow
works repentance not to be regretted, which leads to salvation:
but the sorrow of the world works death. 11 For behold this
very thing, that you sorrowed in a godly manner; what ear-
nestness it produced in you; what defense of yourselves; what

indignation; what fear; what strong affection; what zeal;
what assertion of right. In all respects you have shown yourselves to be blameless in this matter. 12 Therefore, though I
wrote to you, it was not on account of him who did the wrong,
nor on account of him who received the wrong; but that our
diligent care for you, in the sight of God, might be made manifest
to you.
13 For this reason, we have been comforted by means of your
comfort: and we rejoiced exceedingly more indeed, on account
of the joy of Titus, for his spirit was refreshed by you all.
14 For if I boasted of you to him, in any respect, I am not made
ashamed; but as I have spoken all things to you in truth, so
also has our boasting to Titus been found to be truth: 15 and
his affection for you is the more abundant, as he remembers
the obedience of you all, how you received him with fear and
trembling. 16 I rejoice that I have confidence in you in all
things.

VIII. 1 We make known to you, brethren, God's gracious gift,
which has been given in the churches of Macedonia; 2 that
under an afflicting trial, their averflowing joy, and their deep
poverty, abounded to the riches of their liberality; 3 for I testify
that according to their power, and beyond their power, they
gave voluntarily, 4 beseeching us, with much entreaty, that they
might give, and take part in the ministering to the saints; 5 and
they did this, not only as we had hoped, but they gave themselves first to the Lord, and then to us, through the will of God;
6 so that we exhorted Titus, that, as he had previously begun,
so he would bring to an end this gift among you also.
7 Now as you excel in every thing, in faith, and in speech,
and in knowledge, and in all diligence, and in your love for us,
see that you excel in this gift also. 8 I do not speak this as a
commandment, but on account of the zeal of others, and to
prove the sincerity of your love. 9 For you know the grace of
our Lord Jesus Christ, that, though he was rich, yet, for your
sakes, he became poor, that you, through his poverty, might become rich. 10 And I give my judgment in this matter; for this
is profitable for you, who began not only to do, but to show a
willing mind, a year ago. 11 Now, therefore, perfect also the
doing of this; that as there was a readiness of mind to be willing, so also there may be an accomplishment *of the doing*, out
of that which you have. 12 For if there is a readiness of mind,

one is accepted according to what he has, not according to what
he has not. [13] For I do not intend that there shall be relief to
others, and affliction to you; but that, according to equality,
your abundance, at the present time, may supply their wants;
[14] and that, *at a future time*, their abundance may supply your
wants; that there may be equality, [15] as it is written: He that
gathered much had nothing over; and he that gathered little
did not lack.

[16] But thanks be to God, who put the same earnest care for
you in the heart of Titus: [17] for he accepted my exhortation,
and, being more earnest, he went to you of his own accord.
[18] And we have sent with him the brother whose praise in the
gospel is in all the churches; [19] and who, moreover, was chosen
by the churches as our fellow-traveler with this gift, which is
to be distributed by us to the glory of the Lord himself, and as
a declaration of your readiness of mind; [20] being careful for
this—that no one shall blame us in this abundance, which is
ministered by us; [21] for we provide what is honorable, not only
in the sight of the Lord, but also in the sight of men. [22] And
we have sent with them our brother, whom we have often
proved to be diligent in many things, but now much more diligent on account of the strong confidence which he has in you.
[23] If it is necessary to speak of Titus, he is my partner and fel-
low-worker for you; if our brethren are spoken of, they are the
apostles of the churches, the glory of Christ. [24] Therefore, give
to them, in the presence of the churches, a proof of your love,
and of our boasting of you.

IX. [1] For of the relief which is for the saints, it is needless
for me to write to you. [2] For I know your readiness of mind,
on account of which I boasted of you to the Macedonians, that
Achaia was ready a year ago: and your zeal has incited very
many. [3] But I have sent the brethren, that our boasting of you
in this respect may not be in vain; that you may be ready, as
I said: [4] lest, possibly, should the Macedonians come with me,
and find you unprepared, we (not to say you) might be made
ashamed by this same confident boasting. [5] Therefore, I thought
it necessary to exhort the brethren to go before to you, and make
ready beforehand your bounty, which has been so much talked
of before, that this might be ready as a bounty, and not as a
gift extorted from you.

[6] But remember this, that he who sows sparingly, shall also

reap sparingly; and he who sows bountifully, shall also reap
bountifully. 7 Let each one give, as he purposes in his heart;
not with grief, nor from necessity: for God loves a cheerful
giver. 8 And God is able to confer every gift upon you abundantly, that you, always having all sufficiency in every thing,
may have enough for every good work; 9 as it is written: He
has scattered abroad; he has given to the poor; his righteousness remains forever. 10 Now, he that furnishes seed to the
sower will both furnish bread for food, and multiply your seed
sown, and increase the fruits of your righteousness; 11 that you
may be enriched in every thing, for all liberality which produces through us thanksgiving to God; 12 because the adminis-
tration of this service not only supplies the wants of the saints,
but also abounds in many thanksgivings to God; (13 since
through the proof which this service gives, they glorify God for
your acknowledged subjection to the gospel of Christ, and for
the liberality of your contribution for them, and for all;) 14 and
in their prayer for you, since they have strong affection for you
on account of the eminent grace of God that is in you. 15 Thanks
be to God for his unspeakable gift.

X. 1 Now I, the same Paul, who, when present among you,
am timid, but when absent, am bold toward you, entreat you,
by the mildness and gentleness of Christ; 2 I, indeed, beseech
you, that I may not, when present, be bold with that confidence
with which I think I shall be bold against some, who think of
us as if we walked according to the flesh. 3 For though we
walk in the flesh, we do not war according to the flesh, (4 for the
weapons of our warfare are not carnal, but mighty, through
God, for the overthrowing of strongholds,) 5 overthrowing reasonings and every high thing that exalts itself against the
knowledge of God, and leading captive every thought to the
obedience of the Christ, 6 and being ready to take vengeance on
all disobedience, when your obedience shall have been fully
established.

7 Do you look on things according to the outward appearance?
If any one trusts in himself, that he is Christ's, let him again
reason thus of himself: that as he is Christ's, so also are we.
8 For though I should boast even somewhat more abundantly of
our authority, which the Lord has given us for edification, and
not for your destruction, I would not be ashamed: 9 that I may
not seem as if I would terrify you by letters. 10 For his letters,

says one, are weighty and powerful, but his bodily presence is
weak, and his style of speech contemptible. 11 Let such a one
conclude thus—that such as we are in word, by letters, while
absent, such also will we be in deed, when present.
12 For we do not presume to rank or compare ourselves with
some of those who commend themselves: but they; measuring
themselves by themselves, and comparing themselves with themselves, have no understanding. 13 But we will not boast ourselves with respect to regions not measured to us; but according to the measure of the line which God, who measures, has
appointed for us to reach even to you. 14 For we do not stretch
ourselves too far, as if we did not come to you: for even as far
as to you, have we already come in the gospel of the Christ,
15 not boasting ourselves in the labors of others in regions not
measured off to us, but having hope that, when your faith is
increased, we shall be magnified among you abundantly, according to our line, 16 so as to preach the gospel in regions beyond
you, and not to boast in regions made ready under another
man's line. 17 But let him that boasts, boast in the Lord: 18 for
he that commends himself is not approved; but he whom the
Lord commends.

XI. 1 I wish you could bear with me a little in my folly; but
yet bear with me: 2 for I am jealous over you with a godly
jealousy: for I have betrothed you to one husband, that I may
present you a chaste virgin to Christ. 3 But I fear lest, as the
serpent deceived Eve by his cunning, so your minds should be
corrupted from the simplicity which pertains to Christ. 4 For
if he that comes should preach another Jesus, whom we did not
preach, or, if you receive another Spirit, which you did not receive, or another gospel, which you have not accepted, you
would well bear with him.
5 I count myself indeed to be in no respect inferior to the very
greatest of the apostles. 6 But if I am unpolished in my style
of speech, yet I am not so in knowledge. But we have been
fully manifested among you in all things. 7 Have I committed
a sin, in making myself lowly, that you might be exalted, because I preached the gospel to you without cost? 8 I robbed
other churches, taking wages to do you service: and when I
was present with you, and wanted, I was not a burden to any
one; 9 for the brethren who came from Macedonia supplied my
wants; and in every thing I have kept myself from being bur-

densome to you, and will continue to keep myself. [10] As the
truth of Christ is in me, this boasting shall not be silenced,
in my case, in the regions of Achaia. [11] Why? Because I do
not love you? God knows. [12] But what I am doing I will also
continue to do, that I may cut off occasion from those who
desire an occasion, that in what they boast, they may be found
even as we.

[13] For such men are false apostles, deceitful workers, trans-
forming themselves into the apostles of Christ; [14] and no wonder, for Satan himself is transformed into an angel of light.
[15] Therefore, it is no great thing if his ministers also transform
themselves so as to be like the ministers of righteousness; of
such, the end shall be according to their works.

[16] I say again, let no one think that I am without understanding; but if so, even as one without understanding bear with
me, that I also may boast a little. [17] What I say, I say not
according to the Lord, but as in folly, in this same confidence
of boasting. [18] Since many boast according to the flesh, I also
will boast. [19] For it is a pleasure to you to bear with men of no
understanding, since you yourselves are wise. [20] For you bear
it, if one enslave you, if one devour you, if one take from you,
if one exalt himself, if one smite you on the face.

[21] I speak of *their* reproaches, as if we were weak. In whatever matter any one is bold, (I speak foolishly,) I also am bold.
[22] Are they Hebrews? So am I. Are they Israelites? So am I.
Are they of the posterity of Abraham? So am I. [23] Are they
ministers of Christ? (I say it foolishly,) I am above them. In
labors more abundant, in stripes above measure, in prisons
more frequent, in deaths often. [24] From the Jews, five times I
received forty stripes, save one; [25] three times I was beaten with
rods; once I was stoned; three times I have been shipwrecked;
a night and a day I spent in the deep. [26] In journeyings often,
in perils from rivers, in perils from robbers, in perils from my
own race, in perils from the Gentiles, in perils in the city, in
perils in the desert, in perils in the sea, in perils among false
brethren; [27] in weariness and in toil, in watchings often, in
hunger and thirst, in fastings often, in cold and nakedness:
[28] besides those things which come upon me from other sources,
I have a daily concourse of troubles—my anxiety for all the
churches.

[29] Who is weak, and I am not weak? Who is led into sin,
and I am not incensed? [30] If I must boast, I will boast in my

infirmities. [31] The God and Father of our Lord Jesus Christ,
who is blessed for ever, knows that I do not lie. [32] In Damascus, the governor under Aretas the king, guarded the city of
the Damascenes, desiring to apprehend me: [33] and through a
window I was let down in a basket through the wall, and escaped his hands.

XII. [1] To boast is not suitable for me; I will come to visions
and revelations from the Lord. [2] I knew a man in Christ fourteen years ago; that such a one (whether in the body, I know
not, or out of the body, I know not: God knows;) was caught
away to the third heaven. [3] I also know that such a man
(whether in the body, or out of the body, I know not: God
knows,) [4] was caught away to Paradise, and heard words not to
be spoken, which it is not lawful for a man to utter.

[5] Of such a one I will boast; but of myself I will not boast,
unless in my infirmities. [6] For though I should choose to boast,
I would not be void of understanding: for I will speak the
truth. But I forbear, lest any one should think of me more
than what he sees me to be, or what he hears of me.

[7] And, lest I should be too much exalted by the excellence of
the revelations, there was given to me a thorn in the flesh, a
messenger of Satan to buffet me, that I might not be too much
exalted. [8] With regard to this, I three times entreated the Lord
that it might leave me; [9] and he said to me: My grace is sufficient for you; for my power is made perfect in weakness.
Most gladly, therefore, will I boast in my infirmities, that the
power of the Christ may abide upon me. [10] For this reason, I
take pleasure in infirmities, in outrages, in necessities, in persecutions, in straits, for Christ's sake. For when I am weak,
then am I strong.

[11] I have become of no understanding; you have compelled
me. For I ought to have been commended by you: I am in no
respect inferior to the very greatest of the apostles, although
I am nothing. [12] Truly, the signs of an apostle were worked
among you in all patience, in signs and wonders and mighty
deeds. [13] For what is it in which you were inferior to other
churches, unless in this—that I did not burden you? Forgive
me this wrong.

[14] Behold, I am ready the third time to come to you, and I
will not burden you: for I seek not yours, but you. For the
children ought not to lay up treasure for the parents, but the

parents for the children. 15 I, indeed, will most gladly spend
and be spent for your souls; though the more abundantly I love
you, the less I be loved.

16 Be it so, indeed; I did not burden you; but being crafty, I
caught you by deceit. 17 Did I overreach you by any of those
whom I sent to you? 18 I exhorted Titus, and with him sent
the brother. Did Titus overreach you? Did we not walk in the
same spirit? Did we not walk in the same steps?

19 Do you think again that we offer you a defense of ourselves?
We speak all these things before God in Christ, beloved, for your
edification. 20 For I fear, lest when I come I shall find you not
such as I wish, and I shall be found by you not such as you
wish: lest there shall be contentions, envies, excitements, strife,
evil speaking, whisperings, party spirit, disorderly conduct:
21 lest, when I come again, my God will humble me among you,
and I shall mourn over many of those who have already sinned,
and have not repented of the uncleanness and lewdness and
wantonness which they have committed.

XIII. 1 The third time am I coming to you. By the mouth
of two or three witnesses, every matter shall be established.
2 I have foretold, and now the second time, as if I was present,
though being absent, I foretell to those who have sinned, and
to all others, that, if I come again, I will not spare; 3 since you
seek a proof of Christ's speaking in me, who toward you is not
weak, but who is mighty in you: 4 for though he was crucified
in weakness, yet he lives by the power of God. For we also
are weak in him, but we shall live with him by the power of
God toward you. 5 Make trial of yourselves, whether you are
in the faith; put yourselves to the proof. Do you not know
your own selves, that Christ Jesus is in you? unless you be
without proof.

6 But I hope that you will know that we are not without
proof. 7 Yet I pray to God that you may do no evil; not that
we may appear as having proof, but that you may do what is
good, though we be as without proof. 8 For we can do nothing
against the truth, but *we can do something* for the truth. 9 For
we rejoice when we are weak, and you are strong. And we pray
also for this—your perfection. 10 For this reason, I write these
things, while absent, that I may not, when present, use severity,
according to the authority which the Lord has given me for
edification, and not for destruction.

11 Finally, brethren, farewell; be perfect, be comforted, be of
the same mind, be at peace; and the God of love and of peace
will be with you. 12 Salute one another with a holy kiss. All
the saints salute you.
13 The grace of the Lord Jesus Christ, and the love of God,
and the communion of the Holy Spirit, be with you all.

PAUL TO THE GALATIANS.

I. 1 PAUL, an apostle, (not from men, nor by man, but by
Jesus Christ, and God the Father, who raised him
from the dead,) 2 and all the brethren that are with me, to the
churches of Galatia: 3 grace be to you, and peace from God the
Father, and from our Lord Jesus Christ, 4 who gave himself for
our sins, that he might deliver us from this present evil age,
according to the will of our God and Father, 5 to whom be glory
from age to age. Amen.
6 I am astonished that you are so soon turning away from
him that called you into the grace of Christ, to another gospel:
7 which is nothing else than that there are some who trouble
you, and are determined to pervert the gospel of the Christ.
8 But though we, or an angel from heaven, preach to you any
other gospel than that which we have preached, let him be
accursed. 9 As we said before, so even now I say again, if any
one preaches to you any other gospel than that which you have
received, let him be accursed. 10 For, do I now seek the favor
of men, or of God? or do I strive to please men? If, indeed, I
would still please men, I should not be the servant of Christ.
11 But I make known to you, brethren, that the gospel which
is preached by me, is not according to man: 12 for neither did I
receive it from man, nor was it taught me, but by the revelation
of Jesus Christ. 13 For you have heard of my former mode of
life in Judaism, that I greatly persecuted the Church of God,
and laid it waste; 14 and I surpassed in Judaism many of my
own age and nation, being more exceedingly zealous for the tradition of my fathers.
15 But when God, who chose me from my mother's womb, and
called me by his grace, was pleased 16 to reveal his Son in me,
that I might preach him among the Gentiles, I at once declined
all conference with flesh and blood: 17 nor did I go up to Jeru-

salem, to those who were apostles before me; but I went away
into Arabia, and then returned to Damascus.
18 Then, after three years, I went up to Jerusalem, in order to
become personally acquainted with Peter; and I remained with
him fifteen days: 19 but of the apostles I saw no other, but
James the brother of the Lord. 20 With respect to the things
which I now write to you, behold, before God I lie not.
21 Then, I went into the regions of Syria and Cilicia: 22 but I
was not known, in person, to the churches of Judea which are
in Christ. 23 They had heard only that he who formerly persecuted us was now preaching the faith which he once destroyed.
24 And they glorified God in me.

II. 1 Then, fourteen years after, I went up again to Jerusalem
with Barnabas, and I took Titus also with me. 2 And I went
up because of a revelation, and communicated to them the gospel that I preach among the Gentiles, but privately to those
who are of reputation, lest, by any means, I should run or had
run in vain. 3 But not even Titus, who was with me, though
he was a Greek, was compelled to be circumcised. 4 *I acted thus*
indeed on account of false brethren, stealthily brought in, who
stole in to spy out our freedom, which we have in Christ Jesus,
that they might bring us into bondage, 5 to whom we yielded in
submission, not even for an hour, in order that the truth of the
gospel might remain with you.
6 But from those who were supposed to be something; (what
they were is a matter of no importance to me: God does not
accept the person of man;) they, indeed, who were supposed to
be something, communicated no additional truth to me; 7 but,
on the other hand, seeing that I was intrusted with the gospel
of the uncircumcision, as Peter was with that of the circumcision, (8 for he who gave efficiency to Peter, for the apostleship
of the circumcision, gave efficiency to me also, *as an apostle* for
the Gentiles,) 9 and knowing the grace that was given to me,
James and Cephas and John, who seemed to be pillars, gave to
me and Barnabas the right hand of fellowship, that we should
go to the Gentiles, but they to the circumcision, 10 *requesting* only
that we would remember the poor, which same thing I have
been diligent in doing.
11 But when Peter came to Antioch, I openly opposed him,
because he had incurred blame. 12 For, before certain persons
came from James, he ate with the Gentiles: but, when they had

come, he withdrew, and separated himself, because he feared
those who were of the circumcision. 13 And the other Jews,
also, acted hypocritically with him, so that even Barnabas was
led away by their hypocrisy.
14 But when I saw that they did not walk uprightly according
to the truth of the gospel, I said to Peter, before them all: If
you, being a Jew, live after the manner of the Gentiles, and not
after the manner of the Jews, why do you compel the Gentiles
to observe Jewish customs? 15 We, who are Jews by birth, and
not Gentile sinners, 16 knowing that a man is not justified by
works of law, but by faith in Jesus Christ, even we have believed on Christ Jesus, that we may be justified by faith in
Christ, and not by works of law: because, by works of law no
flesh shall be justified. 17 But if, while we seek to be justified
in Christ, we ourselves are also found sinners, is Christ, therefore, the minister of sin? It can not be. 18 For if I build
again those things which I have destroyed, I make myself a
transgressor. 19 For, through law, I have died to law, that I
might live to God. 20 I have been crucified with Christ, yet I
live; no longer I, but Christ lives in me. And the life which I
now live in the flesh, I live by the faith of the Son of God, who
loved me, and gave himself for me. 21 I do not set aside the
grace of God: for if righteousness be through law, then Christ
has died in vain.

III. 1 O thoughtless Galatians, who has bewitched you, before
whose eyes Jesus Christ has been plainly set forth crucified?
2 This only I wish to learn of you: Did you receive the Spirit
by works of law, or by the hearing of faith? 3 Are you so
thoughtless? After having begun in Spirit, do you make an
end in flesh? 4 Have you suffered so many things in vain? if,
indeed, it be in vain. 5 He that supplies to you the Spirit, and
works mighty deeds among you, does he this by works of law
or by the hearing of faith? 6 even as Abraham believed God,
and it was counted to him for righteousness.
7 Know, therefore, that those who are of faith are the sons of
Abraham. 8 For the Scripture, foreseeing that God would justify the Gentiles by faith, preached beforehand the gospel to
Abraham, *saying:* In you shall all the nations be blessed. 9 So,
then, those who are of faith are blessed with faithful Abraham.
10 For as many as are of the works of the law are under the

curse: for it is written, Cursed is every one that does not continue in all things written in the book of the law to do them.
11 But that no one is justified by law in the sight of God, is evident: for the just by faith shall live. 12 The law, indeed, is not
of faith; but he that does these things shall live by them.
13 Christ has bought us off from the curse of the law by becoming a curse for us: (for it is written, Cursed is every one that
hangs on a tree:) 14 in order that the blessing of Abraham may
come upon the Gentiles in Christ Jesus, that we may receive the
promise of the Spirit through the faith.

15 Brethren, I speak of things common among men: No one
sets a covenant aside, or enjoins any thing additional after it is
confirmed, though it be a man's covenant. 16 Now the promises
were spoken to Abraham and to his offspring; he does not say:
And to offsprings, as *if he spoke* of many; but as of one, And to
your offspring, which is Christ. 17 And this I affirm, that the
covenant which had been before confirmed by God with respect
to Christ, the law, which was four hundred and thirty years
after, could not annul so as to make the promise of no effect.
18 For if the inheritance be by law, it is no longer by promise:
but God bestowed it on Abraham by promise.

19 What, then, was the purpose of the law? It was added on
account of transgressions, (till the offspring should come, to
whom the promise was made,) having been appointed through
the service of angels, in the hand of a mediator. 20 Now, a mediator for one is impossible; but God is one.

21 Is the law, then, against the promises of God? It can not
be. For if a law had been given which could have given life,
surely righteousness would have been by law. 22 But the Scripture has shut up all under sin, that the promise by faith in
Christ Jesus may be given to those who believe. 23 But before
the faith came, we were kept under law, being shut up to the
faith which was to be revealed.

24 So, then, the law was our pedagogue that *led us* to Christ,
that we might be justified by faith. 25 But since the faith has
come, we are no longer under a pedagogue: 26 for you are all the
sons of God, by faith in Christ Jesus: 27 for as many of you as
have been immersed into Christ, have put on Christ. 28 There
is neither Jew nor Greek, there is neither bondman nor freeman,
there is neither male nor female: for you are all one in Christ
Jesus. 29 And if you are Christ's, then you are Abraham's posterity, and heirs according to the promise.

IV. 1 But I say, that the heir, as long as he is a minor, differs
in no respect from a servant, though he is owner of all; 2 but is
under guardians and managers till the time appointed by the
father. 3 So, also, we, when we were minors, were in bondage
under the rudiments of the world. 4 But when the fullness of
the time came, God sent forth his Son, born of a woman, born
under the law, 5 that he might buy off those who were under
the law, that we might receive the adoption. 6 And because
you are sons, God has sent forth the Spirit of his Son into your
hearts, crying, Abba, Father. 7 So, then, you are no longer
a servant, but a son; and if a son, an heir also of God, through
Christ.

8 But, then, because you knew not God, you were enslaved to
those who, by nature, are not gods: 9 now, however, after having known God, rather indeed having been known by God, how
is it that you are turning back to the weak and beggarly rudiments, to which you desire again to be in bondage, as at first?
10 You observe days and months and times and years. 11 I fear
for you, lest I have bestowed labor upon you in vain.

12 Brethren, I beseech you, be as I am; because I was as you
are. You have injured me in nothing. 13 You know that through
weakness of the flesh I preached the gospel to you at the first:
14 And my trial, which was in my flesh, you did not despise or
loathe; but you received me as an angel of God, as Christ Jesus.
15 How great, then, was your blessedness! For I testify for you,
that, if possible, you would have torn out your eyes, and have
given them to me. 16 Have I then become your enemy, because
I tell you the truth?

17 They are ardently attached to you, but not honorably; indeed, they desire to exclude us, that you may be ardently attached to them. 18 It is honorable to be ardently attached
always, in what is honorable, and not only when I am present
with you. 19 My little children, for whom I again suffer the
pains of gestation, till Christ be formed in you, 20 I desire to be
present with you now, and to change my tone, for I am in doubt
concerning you.

21 Tell me, you that desire to be under the law, do you not understand the law? 22 For it is written, that Abraham had two
sons: one by a bondmaid, and one by a free woman. 23 But the
one by the bondmaid was born according to the flesh; the other,
by the free woman, was by promise. 24 These things are alle-
gorized: for these women are the two covenants; the one from

the Mount Sinai that brings forth for bondage, which is Hagar.
25 For Hagar represents Mount Sinai in Arabia, and corresponds
to the present Jerusalem, for she is in bondage with her children. 26 But Jerusalem which is above is free; and she is the
mother of us all. 27 For it is written: Rejoice you barren, that
do not bear: break forth and cry aloud, you that travail not:
for many more are the children of the deserted, than of her that
had the husband *of the deserted*. 28 We, indeed, brethren, like
Isaac, are children of promise. 29 But as then, he that was born
according to the flesh persecuted him that was born according
to the Spirit, so even now. 30 But what says the Scripture?
Cast out the bondwoman and her son; for the son of the bondwoman shall not be heir with the son of the free woman.
31 Therefore, brethren, we are not children of the bondwoman,
but of the free woman.

V. 1 Stand firm, therefore, in the freedom with which Christ
has made us free, and be not held fast again in the yoke of
bondage.

2 Behold, I Paul say to you, that if you be circumcised, Christ
will profit you nothing. 3 I testify indeed again to every man
that is circumcised, that he is bound to do the whole law.
4 You that are justified by law, have withdrawn from Christ:
you have fallen from grace. 5 For we, through the Spirit which
we obtain by faith, wait for the hope of righteousness. 6 For,
in Christ Jesus, neither circumcision avails any thing, nor uncircumcision, but faith that works by love.

7 You were running well; who kept you back from obedience
to the truth? 8 This readiness to be persuaded is not from him
that calls you. 9 A little leaven leavens the whole mass. 10 I
have confidence in you through the Lord, that you will cultivate
no other disposition: but he that troubles you, who ever he
may be, shall bear his condemnation. 11 But, brethren, if I yet
preach circumcision, why am I yet persecuted? Then, the
offense of the cross has ceased. 12 O that those who trouble
you would even cut themselves off!

13 For you have been called to freedom, brethren: only use not
your freedom as an occasion for the flesh, but become servants
to one another, through love. 14 For all the law is fulfilled in
one commandment, in this: You shall love your neighbor as
yourself. 15 But if you bite and devour one another, take heed
lest you be utterly destroyed by one another.

16 I say this: Walk in the Spirit, and you will not fulfill the
desires of the flesh. 17 For the desire of the flesh is against the
Spirit, and the desire of the Spirit is against the flesh; and these
are opposed, the one to the other, so that you can not do what
you would. 18 But if you are led by the Spirit, you are not
under law. 19 Now the works of the flesh are well known, and
they are these—lewdness, uncleanness, wantonness, 20 idolatry,
sorcery, enmities, strifes, jealousies, anger, party-spirit, divisions, sects, 21 envyings, murders, drunkenness, revelings, and
such like; with respect to which, I tell you now, as I also told
you in times past, that those who practice such things shall not
inherit the kingdom of God.

22 But the fruit of the Spirit is love, joy, peace, long-suffering, gentleness, goodness, faithfulness, 23 meekness, self-control.
Against such there is no law. 24 Now those who are Christ's
have crucified the flesh with its passions and desires. 25 If we
live in the Spirit, let us also walk in the Spirit. 26 Let us not
be vainglorious, provoking one another, envying one another.

VI. 1 Brethren, if a man be overtaken in any fault, do you,
who are spiritual, restore such a one in the spirit of meekness,
considering yourself, lest you also be tempted. 2 Bear with the
weaknesses of one another, and so fulfill the law of Christ.
3 For if any one think himself to be something when he is
nothing, he deceives himself: 4 but let each one prove his own
work, and then he will have cause to boast with respect to himself only, and not with respect to another: 5 for each one shall
bear his own burden.

6 Let him that is instructed in the word share with his instructor in all good things. 7 Be not deceived; God is not
mocked. For whatever a man sows, that also shall he reap.
8 For he that sows for his flesh shall from the flesh reap corruption; but he that sows for his spirit shall from the Spirit reap
life eternal. 9 Let us not become weary in well doing: for in
in due season we shall reap, if we faint not. 10 Therefore, as we
have opportunity, let us do good to all, but especially to those
who are the household of the faith.

11 You see how long a letter I have written to you with my
own hand. 12 As many as wish to make a fair show in the flesh,
these compel you to be circumcised, only that they may not
suffer persecution for the cross of the Christ. 13 For not even
do those very men, who are circumcised, keep the law: but they

wish you to be circumcised, that they may boast in your flesh.
[14] But may I never boast save in the cross of our Lord Jesus Christ, by whom the world has been crucified to me, and I to
the world. [15] For in Christ Jesus neither circumcision is any
thing, nor uncircumcision, but a new creature. [16] And as many
as walk by this rule, peace and mercy be upon them, and upon the Israel of God.

[17] Henceforward let no one give me trouble: for I bear in my body the wounds which I received on account of the Lord Jesus.

[18] Brethren, the grace of our Lord Jesus Christ be with your spirit. Amen.

PAUL TO THE EPHESIANS.

I. [1] PAUL, an apostle of Jesus Christ by the will of God,
to the saints that are in Ephesus, and the faithful in
Christ Jesus: [2] grace be to you, and peace from God our Father,
and from the Lord Jesus Christ.

[3] Praised be the God and Father of our Lord Jesus Christ,
who has blessed us with every spiritual blessing in heavenly
things in Christ, [4] according as he chose us in him before the
foundation of the world, that we should be holy and blameless
before him in love, [5] having predestinated us for adoption to
himself through Jesus Christ, according to the good pleasure of
his will, [6] for the praise of the glory of his grace, by which he
has shown us favor in the Beloved, [7] in whom we have redemption through his blood, *even* the remission of sins, according to
the riches of his grace, [8] which he has made to abound to us in
all wisdom and understanding, [9] by making known to us the
mystery of his will according to his good purpose which he had
before established in himself, [10] for a dispensation at the fullness
of the times, in order that he might bring together for himself
all things in the Christ, both those which are in the heavens,
and those which are on earth; [11] in him in whom we have obtained our portion, having been predestinated according to the
purpose of him who works all things according to the counsel
of his will, [12] that we should be for the praise of his glory; *even
we*, who before had hope in the Christ: [13] in whom you also
hoped after you heard the word of truth, the gospel of your salvation: in whom, after you also believed, you were sealed with
the Holy Spirit of promise, [14] which is the earnest of our in-

heritance, *given* for the redemption of his possession to the
praise of his glory.

15 For this reason I also, since I have heard of your faith in
the Lord Jesus, and your love to all the saints, 16 do not cease
to give thanks for you, making mention of you in my prayers,
17 that the God of our Lord Jesus Christ, the Father of glory,
may give you the spirit of wisdom and of revelation in the acknowledgment of him, 18 that, the eyes of your understanding being enlightened, you may know what is the hope of his
calling, and what are the glorious riches of his inheritance in
the saints, 19 and what is the exceeding greatness of his power
toward us who believe in accordance with the energy of his
mighty power, 20 which he made active in the Christ when he
raised him from the dead, and caused him to sit at his right hand
in the heavenly places, 21 high above every principality and authority and power and dominion, and every name that is named,
not only in this age, but also in that which is to come; 22 and
subjected all things under his feet, and made him head over all
things for the church, 23 which is his body, the fullness of him
who fills all his members with all things,

II. 1 Even you, being dead to offenses and sins, 2 in which you
formerly walked according to the course of this world, according to the prince of the power of the air, the spirit that is ac-
tively at work in the sons of disobedience: 3 among whom also
we all formerly lived in the desires of our flesh, doing the will
of the flesh and of the feelings, and were by nature children of
wrath, even as others: 4 but God, being rich in mercy, on account of his great love with which he loved us, 5 made alive
with Christ even us, being dead to our offenses, (by grace you
are saved,) 6 and raised us up, and made us sit together in
heavenly places, in Christ Jesus; 7 that he might show, in the
ages to come, the exceeding riches of his grace by his kindness
to us in Christ Jesus.

8 For by grace you have been saved through the faith; and
this matter is not of yourselves; it is the gift of God: 9 not by
works, lest any one should boast. 10 For we are his workman-
ship, created in Christ Jesus for good works, which God before
prepared, that we should walk in them.

11 For which reason, remember that you were formerly Gentiles, by natural descent, and that you are called Uncircumcision
by the Circumcision; so called, from a mark made in the flesh

by hands; 12 that you were at that time without Christ, being
aliens from the community of Israel, and strangers to the covenants of promise, having no hope, and having no God in the
world: 13 but now, in Christ Jesus, you, who were formerly far
off, have become near, by the blood of the Christ. 14 For he is
our peace, who has made both parties one, and broken down the
partition wall that separated us, 15 having abolished, in his flesh,
the cause of enmity, the law of commandments in ordinances,
that he might, by himself, form the two into one new man, thus
making peace; 16 and that he might reconcile both, in one body,
to God, through the cross, having by it put to death the cause
of enmity; 17 and having come, he preached peace to you who
were far off, and to those who were near: 18 for, through him,
we both have access in one Spirit to the Father.

19 Now, therefore, you are no longer strangers and sojourners,
but fellow-citizens with the saints, and of the household of God,
20 having been builded upon the foundation of the apostles and
prophets, Jesus Christ himself being the chief corner-stone,
21 in whom the whole building, compactly fitted together, grows
into a holy temple in the Lord; 22 in whom you also are builded
together, for a dwelling-place of God by his Spirit.

III. 1 For this reason, I Paul, the prisoner of the Christ Jesus
on account of you Gentiles, 2 if, indeed, you have heard of the
stewardship of the grace of God, which was given to me for
your benefit, 3 that by revelation was made known to me the
mystery, (as I briefly wrote above, 4 so that, when you read, you
can see my understanding in the mystery of the Christ,) 5 which,
in other generations, was not made known to the sons of men,
as it is now revealed to his holy apostles and prophets by the
Spirit; 6 that the Gentiles should be fellow-heirs, and of the
same body, and partakers of his promise in the Christ, through
the gospel, 7 of which I was made a minister according to the
gift of the grace of God which was given to me, in proportion
to the energy of his power: 8 to me, who am by far the least of
all the saints, has this grace been given, that I might preach
among the Gentiles the unsearchable riches of the Christ, 9 and
enlighten all men with respect to the plan of the mystery, which
was concealed from the ages in God, who created all things;
10 to the end that the manifold wisdom of God might now be
made known, through the church, to the principalities and
authorities in the heavenly regions, 11 according to the arrange-

ment of the ages, which he established by Christ Jesus our
Lord, 12 in whom we have boldness and access with confidence,
through our faith in him. 13 For which cause I beseech you
not to grow faint on account of my afflictions for you, which
are your glory.

14 For this reason I bow my knees to the Father of our Lord
Jesus Christ, 15 from whom the whole family in heaven and on
earth is named, 16 that he may grant to you, according to the
riches of his glory, to be mightily strengthened by his Spirit in
the inner man, 17 that Christ may dwell in your hearts through
the faith; 18 that, being rooted and founded in love, you may be
fully able to comprehend with all the saints what is the breadth
and length and depth and hight, 19 and to know the love of the
Christ which passes our knowledge, that you may be filled with
all the fullness of God.

20 Now to him that is able to do exceeding abundantly above
all that we ask or think according to his power which works in
us, 21 to him be glory in the church by Christ Jesus, throughout
all the generations of the age of ages. Amen.

IV. 1 I therefore, the prisoner in the Lord, exhort you to
walk in a manner worthy of the calling with which you have
been called; 2 with all lowliness and meekness, with long-suffering, bearing with one another in love, 3 earnestly endeavoring
to keep the unity of the Spirit in the bond of peace. 4 There is
one body and one Spirit, even as you have been called in one
hope of your calling; 5 one Lord, one faith, one immersion;
6 one God and Father of all, who is over all, and through all,
and in you all.

7 But grace has been given to each one of us, according to the
measure of the gift of the Christ. 8 For which reason, the
Scripture says: When he ascended on high, he led captive a
multitude of captives, and gave gifts to men. 9 But this—He
ascended—what does it mean, but that he also descended into the
lower earthly regions? 10 He that descended is also he that ascended high above all the heavens, that he might fill all things.

11 And he himself gave some *to be* apostles, and some, prophets;
and some, evangelists; and some, pastors and teachers; 12 for
the complete instruction of the saints, for the work of the ministry, for the building up of the body of the Christ, 13 till we all
come to the unity of the faith, and of the knowledge of the Son
of God, to a perfect man, to a measure of stature that fully

develops the Christ; 14 that we might no longer be children, tossed
and carried about by every wind of teaching, through the arti-
fice of men, through craftiness used by them for the deliberate
planning of deceit; 15 but speaking truthfully in love, we might
grow up in all things, into him who is the head, *even* the Christ,
16 from whom the whole body, compactly fitted together, and
united by every helping joint, according to the energy in the
measure of each part, makes increase of the body, for the building up of itself in love.

17 This I say, therefore, and appeal to you solemnly in the
Lord, that you no longer walk as the other Gentiles walk, in
the error of their minds, 18 darkened in their understanding,
alienated from the life of God through the ignorance that is in
them, because of the hardness of their heart; 19 who, being past
feeling, have given themselves up to licentiousness, that they
may work all manner of uncleanness with greediness.

20 But you have not so learned the Christ, 21 if, indeed, you
have heard of him, and been taught by him, as the truth is in
Jesus: 22 that, as to your former life, you put off the old man,
which is corrupt, according to its deceitful desires, 23 and that
you be renewed in the spirit of your mind, 24 and put on the
new man, which, according to the will of God, is created in
righteousness and true holiness. 25 For which reason, putting
away lying, speak, every one, truth with his neighbor: for we
are members one of another.

26 Be angry, and yet do not sin: let not the sun go down on
your wrath, 27 nor give place to the devil.

28 Let him that steals, steal no more: but rather let him
labor, working with his hands that which is good, that he may
have something to give to him that has need.

29 Let no impure speech come out of your mouth, but whatever is good for needful edification, that it may give grace to
the hearers: 30 and grieve not the Holy Spirit of God, with
which you have been sealed for the day of redemption.

31 Let all bitterness and anger and wrath and clamor and impious speaking be put away from you, with all malice: 32 and
be kind to one another, compassionate, forgiving one another, as
God in Christ has forgiven you.

V. 1 Be you, therefore, imitators of God, as beloved children;
2 and walk in love, as the Christ also loved us, and gave himself
for us as an offering and a sacrifice to God for a sweet odor.

3 But lewdness, and all manner of uncleanness, or covetousness, let them not be named among you, as it becomes saints;
4 nor obscene language, nor foolish talking, nor jesting, which
are not becoming; but rather the giving of thanks. 5 For you
know this, that no lewd nor unclean person, nor covetous
man, who is an idolater, has any inheritance in the kingdom
of the Christ and of God. 6 Let no one deceive you with
vain words: for on account of these things, the wrath of
God comes upon the sons of disobedience. 7 Therefore, be not
partakers with them. 8 For you were formerly darkness; but
now you are light in the Lord: walk as children of light; (9 for
the fruit of the Spirit is in all goodness and righteousness and
truth;) 10 learning what is acceptable to the Lord; 11 and do not
participate in the unfruitful works of darkness, but rather even
reprove them; 12 for it is a shame even to speak of the things
that are done by them in secret. 13 But all these works, when
reproved, are made manifest by the light: for every thing that
makes manifest is light. 14 Wherefore, the Scripture says:
Awake you that sleep, and arise from the dead, and Christ will
give you light.

15 See, then, that you walk circumspectly, not as unwise, but
as wise men, 16 redeeming the time, because the days are evil.
17 Wherefore, be not ignorant, but understand what the will of
the Lord is. 18 And be not drunk with wine, in which is debauchery; but be filled with the Spirit; 19 speaking to yourselves
in psalms and hymns and spiritual songs, singing and making
melody in your heart to the Lord, 20 giving thanks to our God
and Father always for all things in the name of our Lord Jesus
Christ; 21 being subject one to another in the fear of God.

22 Wives, be subject to your own husbands as to the Lord:
23 for the husband is the head of the wife, as the Christ also is
the head of the church; and he is the savior of the body. 24 But
as the church is subject to the Christ, so, also, let the wives be
subject to their own husbands in every thing.

25 Husbands, love your wives, as the Christ also loved the
church, and delivered himself up for it, 26 that he might sanctify it, having cleansed it by the bath of water through the
word, 27 in order that he might present it to himself a glorious
church, having neither stain, nor wrinkle, nor any such thing;
but that it should be holy and without blemish. 28 So ought
men to love their own wives as their own bodies. He that loves
his wife loves himself; 29 for no one ever yet hated his own flesh,

but nourishes and cherishes it, even as the Christ the church:
30 because we are members of his body, being of his flesh, and
of his bones. 31 For this cause a man shall leave his father and
his mother, and shall cleave to his wife, and the two shall be
one flesh. 32 Great is this mystery; but I speak of Christ and
of the church. 33 But yet, let each one of you so love his wife as
himself; and let the wife see that she reverence her husband.

VI. 1 Children, obey your parents in the Lord: for this is
right. 2 Honor your father and your mother, which is the first
commandment with a promise, 3 that it may be well with you,
and that you may live long on the earth.

4 And you fathers, do not provoke your children to anger: but
bring them up in the instruction and discipline of the Lord.

5 Servants, be subject to your masters according to the flesh,
with fear and trembling, in the simplicity of your heart, as to
the Christ; 6 not with eye-service, as pleasing men, but as the
servants of Christ, doing the will of God from the soul; 7 with
good will doing service as to the Lord, and not as to men;
8 knowing that whatever good any one does, the same shall he
receive from the Lord, whether he is a servant or a freeman.

9 And you masters, do the same things to them, leaving off
threatening, knowing that you yourselves have a master in
heaven, and there is no respect of persons with him.

10 Finally, my brethren, be strong in the Lord, and in his
mighty power. 11 Put on the whole armor of God, that you
may be able to stand firm against the wiles of the devil: 12 for
our conflict is not with flesh and blood, but with the principalities, with the authorities, with the rulers of the darkness of
this world, with the wicked spirits in the heavenly regions.
13 Therefore, take up the whole armor of God, that you may be
able to withstand *them* in the evil day, and having overcome
them all, to stand firm.

14 Stand, therefore, having your loins girded about with truth,
and wearing the breastplate of righteousness, 15 and having
your feet shod with readiness in behalf of the gospel of peace;
16 taking up, over all, the shield of faith, with which you
shall be able to quench all the fiery darts of the wicked one;
17 and take the helmet of salvation, and the sword of the
Spirit, which is the word of God: 18 praying with all prayer
and supplication, at all times, in the Spirit; and to this end
being watchful in all perseverance, and supplication for all

the saints: 19 and for me, that speech may be given me, in open-
ing my mouth with boldness, that I may make known the mystery of the gospel, 20 for which I am an embassador in chains,
that in it I may speak boldly, as I ought to speak.
21 But that you, also, may know my affairs, how I do, Tychicus, my beloved brother and faithful minister in the Lord, will
make known all things to you; 22 him I have sent to you for
this very purpose, that you may know our affairs, and that he
may comfort your hearts.
23 Peace be to the brethren, and love with faith from God the
Father and the Lord Jesus Christ.
24 Grace be with all those who love our Lord Jesus Christ in
sincerity.

PAUL TO THE PHILIPPIANS.

I. 1 PAUL and Timothy, servants of Jesus Christ, to all the
saints in Christ Jesus that are in Philippi, with the
bishops and deacons: 2 grace be to you, and peace from God our
Father, and from the Lord Jesus Christ.
3 I thank my God on every remembrance of you—4 always in
every supplication of mine for you all, making my supplication
with joy—5 for your fellowship in the gospel from the first day
till now: 6 being confident of this very thing, that he who has
begun a good work in you, will carry it on till the day of Jesus
Christ; 7 as it is right for me to think this of you all, because
I have you in my heart; both in my bonds and in my defense
and confirmation of the gospel, *I say I have* you all in my heart
as being joint partakers of my grace. 8 For God is my witness
how ardently I love you with the affection of Christ Jesus.
9 I also pray for this, that your love may abound yet more
and more in knowledge and all understanding, 10 in order that
you may distinguish things that differ, to the end that you may
be pure and blameless till the day of Christ, 11 being filled with
the fruit of righteousness, which fruit is by Jesus Christ, to the
glory and praise of God.
12 But I wish you to know, brethren, that the things which
have befallen me have turned out rather to the advancement of
the gospel; 13 so that my bonds, which are for Christ have become known to be such in all the palace, and in all other places;

14 and most of the brethren in the Lord, having confidence in
my bonds, are more bold to speak the word without fear.

15 Some, indeed, preach the Christ, because of envy and a contentious disposition, and some because of good-will. 16 These do
it from love, because they know that I am set for the defense of
the gospel; 17 those preach Christ from a contentious disposition, not sincerely, thinking that they will add affliction to my
bonds. 18 What difference does this make? Christ is, never-
theless, preached in every way, whether in pretense or in truth;
and in this I rejoice, yes, and I will rejoice: 19 for I know that
this will result in my benefit through your supplication, and the
supply of the Spirit of Jesus Christ, 20 according to my earnest
expectation and hope, that in nothing shall I be ashamed, but
with all boldness, as at all times, so even now, Christ will be
magnified in my body, whether by life or by death.

21 For to me to live is Christ, and to die is gain. 22 But if this,
my life in the flesh, would be profitable for my work *in the ministry*, verily, what I should choose I know not. 23 I am in a strait
between the two, having the desire to depart and be with Christ,
which is far better: 24 yet to abide in the flesh is more needful
for you. 25 And of this I feel assured, that I shall remain and
continue among you all for your advancement and joy in the
faith, 26 that your rejoicing in Christ Jesus may become more
abundant through me by my being present among you again.

27 Only conduct yourselves in a manner worthy of the gospel
of the Christ, that, whether I come and see you, or be absent, I
may hear of your affairs, that you stand fast in one spirit, with
one soul striving together for the faith of the gospel, 28 and in
nothing terrified by your adversaries: which is to them an evident token of destruction, but to you of salvation, and that
from God. 29 For to you it is given in behalf of Christ, not
only to believe on him, but, also, to suffer for him, 30 since you
have the same conflict that you saw in me, and now hear to be
in me.

II. 1 If, therefore, there is any consolation in Christ, if any
comfort arising from love, if any participation of the Spirit, if
any affections and mercies, 2 fulfill my joy, that you be of the
same mind, having the same love, of one soul, of one mind;
3 doing nothing in strife and vain glory, but in lowliness of
mind let each esteem others better than himself. 4 Consider not
each one his own gifts, but each one also the gifts of others.

5 Let this mind be in you, which was also in Christ Jesus,
6 who, being in the form of God, did not think it an act of rob-
bery to be equal with God; 7 but he divested himself by taking
the form of a servant, and being made in the likeness of men:
8 and being found in appearance as a man, he humbled himself
by becoming obedient even to death, the death, indeed, of the
cross. 9 For which reason God has highly exalted him, and, also,
bestowed on him a name that is above every name; 10 that in
the name of Jesus every knee should bow of those who are in
heaven, and those who are on earth, and those who are under the
earth; 11 and that every tongue should confess that Jesus Christ
is Lord, to the glory of God the Father.

12 So, then, my beloved, as you have always obeyed, not as in
my presence only, but now much more in my absence, work out
your own salvation with fear and trembling; 13 for it is God,
who, of his good pleasure, works in you both the will and the
power to perform. 14 Do all things without murmurings and
disputings, 15 that you may be without reproach and harmless,
the children of God, without blame, in the midst of a wicked
and perverse generation, among whom you shine as luminaries
in the world, 16 holding forth the word of life, that I may rejoice
in the day of Christ, that I did not run in vain, nor labor in
vain.

17 But if I am poured out on the sacrifice and service of your
faith, I rejoice, and rejoice with you all. 18 In like manner do
you also rejoice, and rejoice with me. 19 But I trust in the Lord
Jesus, to send Timothy shortly to you, that I also may be refreshed by knowing your condition; 20 for I have no one of a
kindred spirit who will sincerely care for your condition: 21 for
all seek their own, not the things of Jesus Christ. 22 But you
know his approved character, that as a son with a father he has
served with me in the gospel. 23 Him, therefore, I hope to send
immediately, as soon as I know how it may go with me. 24 But
I trust in the Lord that I myself also will come shortly.

25 Yet I thought it necessary to send to you Epaphroditus, my
brother and companion in labor and fellow-soldier, but your
apostle, who also ministered to my want, 26 because he longed
after you all, and was much distressed, because you had heard
that he was sick. 27 And, indeed, he was sick near to death;
but God had mercy on him, and not on him only, but on me
also, that I might not have sorrow upon sorrow. 28 I sent him,
therefore, the sooner, that, by seeing him again, you might

rejoice, and that I might be the less sorrowful. [29] Receive him,
therefore, in the Lord with all joy, and regard such as worthy
of honor; [30] because for the work of the Christ he was near to
death, not regarding his life, that he might supply that which
was lacking in your service to me.

III. [1] Finally, my brethren, rejoice in the Lord. To write
the same things to you is to me indeed not burdensome; but for
you it is safe.

[2] Beware of the dogs, beware of the evil workers, beware of
the concision. [3] For we are the circumcision, who worship God
in spirit, and rejoice in Christ Jesus, and have no confidence in
the flesh; [4] though, indeed, I have a ground of confidence in
the flesh. If any other thinks he has a ground of confidence in
the flesh, I more; [5] circumcised the eighth day, of the race of
Israel, of the tribe of Benjamin, a Hebrew of the Hebrews; as
it respects law, a Pharisee; [6] as it respects zeal, persecuting the
church; as it respects righteousness which is by law, blameless.
[7] But the things which were gain to me, these I counted loss for
Christ.

[8] Yes, verily, I also count all things to be loss, for the excellence of the knowledge of Christ Jesus my Lord, on account of
whom I have suffered the loss of all things, and do count them
to be refuse, that I may gain Christ, [9] and be found in him, not
having my own righteousness which was by law, but the righteousness which is by faith in Christ, the righteousness which is
of God by faith, [10] that I may know him, and the power of his
resurrection, and the fellowship of his sufferings, by conforming
myself to his death, [11] if, by any means, I may attain to the
resurrection from the dead.

[12] Not that I have already attained, or have already reached
the goal; but I am pressing forward, that I may lay hold on
that for which I was laid hold on by Christ Jesus. [13] Brethren,
I do not conclude that I have already laid hold: [14] but one thing
I do; forgetting the things which are behind, and reaching forward to those which are before, I press toward the goal, for the
prize of the high calling of God in Christ Jesus.

[15] Let us, therefore, as many as are fully enlightened, be of
this mind: and if you are of another mind with respect to any
thing, God will reveal even this to you. [16] But as far as we have
attained, let us walk by the same rule, let us have the same
mind. [17] Be imitators of me, brethren, and observe those who

thus walk as you have us for an example. [18] For many walk, of
whom I often said to you, and now say even weeping, that they
are enemies of the cross of the Christ, [19] whose end is destruction,
whose god is their appetite, and whose glory is in their shame,
who mind earthly things. [20] But our citizenship is in heaven,
whence also we look for the Savior, the Lord Jesus Christ, [21] who
will transform our humbled body, and make it like his glorious
body, according to that power by which he is able to subdue all
things to himself.

IV. [1] So, then, my brethren, beloved and ardently desired, my
joy and my crown, so stand fast in the Lord, my beloved.
[2] I beseech Euodia, and I beseech Syntyche, that they be of the
same mind in the Lord. [3] Now I beseech you also, true yoke-
fellow, to assist those women who labored with me in the gospel,
with Clement also, and my other fellow-laborers, whose names
are in the book of life.
[4] Rejoice in the Lord always; and again I say, Rejoice. [5] Let
your gentleness be known to all men: the Lord is at hand.
[6] Be anxious about nothing, but in every thing, by prayer and
supplication with thanksgiving, let your requests be made known
to God: [7] and the peace of God, which passes all understanding,
will keep your hearts and minds in Christ Jesus.
[8] Finally, brethren, whatever things are true, whatever things
are honorable, whatever things are just, whatever things are
pure, whatever things are lovely, whatever things are of good
report, if there is any virtue, or any praise, think of these
things. [9] Do those things which you have learned and received,
and heard and seen in me, and the God of peace will be with you.
[10] I rejoiced in the Lord greatly, that now at length your care
for me has revived again; in this, indeed, you had me in mind,
but you lacked opportunity. [11] I do not speak in respect to
want: for I have learned, in whatever condition I am, to be
content. [12] I know what it is to be in want, and what it is to
have abundance. Every-where and in all things, I have been
fully instructed in being full and in being hungry, in having
abundance and in being in want. [13] I am able to do all things
through Christ who strengthens me.
[14] Yet you have done well in contributing to the relief of my
affliction. [15] Now you Philippians know also, that in the beginning of the gospel, when I departed from Macedonia, no church
contributed to me so that I kept an account of giving and

receiving, but you only. [16] For even when I was in Thessalonica,
you sent once and again to aid me in my need. [17] Not that I
seek a gift; but I desire fruit that may abound to your account.
[18] But I have all, and abound. I am full, having received from
Epaphroditus your gifts, a sweet odor, a sacrifice acceptable,
well-pleasing to God. [19] But my God will supply all your need,
according to his riches in glory in Christ Jesus. [20] Now to God,
even our Father, be glory from age to age. Amen.

[21] Salute every saint in Christ Jesus. The brethren that are
with me salute you. [22] All the saints salute you, especially those
who are of Cæsar's household.

[23] The grace of our Lord Jesus Christ be with you all. Amen.

PAUL TO THE COLOSSIANS.

I. [1] PAUL, an apostle, of Jesus Christ, by the will of God,
and Timothy my brother, [2] to the saints and faithful
brethren in Christ that are in Colosse: grace be to you, and
peace from God our Father, and our Lord Jesus Christ.

[3] We give thanks to the God and Father of our Lord Jesus
Christ, praying always for you, [4] since we heard of your faithfulness in Christ Jesus, and your love for all the saints, [5] in
consequence of the hope which is laid up for you in the heavens.
of which you heard before in the word of the truth of the gospel, [6] which is present among you, as it is also in all the world,
and is producing fruit, even as it has been doing also among you,
since the day you heard and knew the grace of God in truth, [7] as
you learned from Epaphras, our dear fellow-servant, who is a
faithful servant of Christ for you, [8] and who also made known
to us your love in spirit.

[9] For this reason, we, also, from the day in which we heard it,
do not cease to pray for you, and to request that you may be
filled with the knowledge of his will, in all wisdom and spiritual
understanding, [10] so that you may walk in a manner worthy of
the Lord, in order to please him in all things, by means of every
good work bringing forth fruit, and increasing in the knowledge
of God, [11] strengthened with all power, according to his glorious
might, in order to all patience and long-suffering with joyfulness,
[12] giving thanks to the Father, who has made us fit for a portion
of the inheritance of the saints in light: [13] who has delivered us

from the authority of darkness, and has translated us into the
kingdom of his beloved Son, [14] in whom we have redemption, the
forgiveness of sins; [15] who is the image of the invisible God, the
first-born of every creature; [16] for by him were all things created, things in heaven and things in earth, visible and invisible,
whether thrones, or lordships, or principalities, or authorities;
all things have been created by him, and for him: [17] and he is
before all things, and by him all things consist: [18] and he is the
head of the body, the church: and he is the beginning, the first
born from the dead, that in all things he might be pre-eminent;
[19] for it pleased *the Father* that all his fullness should dwell in
him, [20] and by him to reconcile all things to himself, having
made peace by the blood of his cross; by him, I say, whether
things on earth or things in heaven.

[21] And you, who were formerly alienated and enemies in your
mind by wicked works, yet now has he reconciled [22] by means of
death in his fleshly body, that he may present you holy, and
without spot, and blameless in his sight; [23] if you continue in
the faith, founded and settled, and be not moved away from the
hope of the gospel that you have heard, which has been preached
to every creature under heaven, of which I, Paul, have been
made a minister.

[24] Now I rejoice in my sufferings for you, and fill up what remains of my sufferings for Christ in my flesh for the sake of his
body, which is the church, [25] of which I was made a minister
according to the commission from God, which was given to me
for you, that I might fully preach the word of God, [26] the mystery which was concealed from the ages and the generations, but
is now made manifest to his saints, [27] to whom God would make
known what is the glorious riches of this mystery among the
Gentiles, which is Christ in you, the hope of glory, [28] whom we
preach, warning every man, and teaching every man in all wisdom, that we may present every man perfect in Christ Jesus:
[29] to which end I also labor, striving according to his energy,
which works in me mightily.

II. [1] For I wish you to know how great a conflict I have for
you, and for those in Laodicea, and for as many as have not seen
my face in the flesh; [2] that their hearts may be comforted, they
being firmly united in love in order to gain all the riches of the
full assurance of understanding, that they may acknowledge the
mystery of God, even the Father, and of Christ, [3] in whom are

stored up all the treasures of wisdom and of knowledge. [4] Now
I say this, that no one may deceive you by persuasive words.
[5] For, though I am absent in flesh, yet I am present with you in
spirit, rejoicing to behold your order, and the firmness of your
faith in Christ. [6] As, therefore, you received Christ Jesus our
Lord, so walk in him, [7] rooted, and built up in him, and strengthened in the faith, as you have been taught, abounding in it with
thanksgiving.

[8] See that no one make you the victims of imposture by means
of philosophy and vain deceit, according to the tradition of men,
according to the rudiments of the world, and not according to
Christ: [9] for in him dwells all the fullness of the Godhood bodily.
[10] And you are complete in him who is the head of all principality and authority: [11] in whom you have been also circumcised
with the circumcision made without hands, in the putting off
the body of the sins of the flesh, by the circumcision of Christ,
[12] having been buried with him in immersion, in which you
were also raised with him by your faith in the energy of God,
who raised him from the dead. [13] And you, being dead to your
offenses and the uncircumcision of your flesh, he has made alive
together with him, having forgiven you all your offenses; [14] having blotted out the handwriting in ordinances which was against
us, which was opposed to us, he also took it out of the way,
driving a nail through it by means of his cross; [15] and having
spoiled the principalities and authorities, he made a show of
them openly by triumphing over them through it.

[16] Let no one judge you, therefore, in meat or in drink, or in
respect to a feast, or the new moon, or Sabbaths, [17] which things
are a shadow of things to come, but the substance is in Christ.
[18] Let no one gain his purpose in depriving you of the palm by
an affected humility and worship of angels, prying into things
which he has not seen, vainly puffed up by his fleshly mind,
[19] and not holding the head, from which the whole body gathering vigor, and firmly united by joints and bands, increases with
the increase of God.

[20] If, then, you have died with Christ from the elements of the
world, why, as though living in the world, do you submit to
ordinances? [21] Touch not, taste not, handle not, [22] (all of which
are for the destruction of those who use them,) according to the
commandments and teachings of men; [23] and these have a show
of wisdom in will-worship and affected humility and neglect of
the body, and in no regard for the gratification of the flesh.

III. 1 If, then, you have been raised with Christ, seek the things
that are above, where the Christ sits at the right hand of God;
2 mind the things that are above, not the things that are on the
earth: 3 for you are dead, and your life is hid with the Christ in
God. 4 When the Christ, who is our life, shall appear, then shall
you also appear with him in glory.

5 Put to death, therefore, your members that are on the earth,
lewdness, uncleanness, passion, evil desire, and covetousness,
which is idolatry; 6 on account of these things the wrath of
God comes on the children of disobedience, 7 in which things you
also formerly walked when you lived in them. 8 But now do you
also put away all these—anger, wrath, malice, reviling, obscene
language from your mouth. 9 Lie not one to another, seeing
that you have put off the old man with his deeds, 10 and have
put on the new man, which is renewed for knowledge, according to the image of him that created him; 11 in which new creation there is neither Greek nor Jew, circumcision nor uncircumcision, Barbarian, Scythian, bond nor free: but Christ is all
and in all.

12 Put on, therefore, as the elect of God, holy and beloved, a
merciful disposition, kindness, humbleness of mind, meekness,
long-suffering: 13 bearing with one another, and forgiving one
another, if any one have a complaint against any; even as
Christ forgave you, so also do you: 14 and over all these put on
love, which is the bond of perfectness. 15 And let the peace of
God, to which you are called in one body, rule in your hearts,
and be thankful.

16 Let the word of the Christ dwell in you richly in all wisdom,
by teaching and admonishing one another in psalms, hymns,
and spiritual songs, singing with gratitude in your hearts to
the Lord. 17 And whatever you do in word or deed, do all in
the name of the Lord Jesus, giving thanks to God and the Father
by him.

18 Wives, be subject to your husbands, as it is becoming in
the Lord. 19 Husbands, love your wives, and be not bitter
against them.

20 Children, obey your parents in all things: for this is well-
pleasing to the Lord. 21 Fathers, provoke not your children to
anger, lest they be disheartened.

22 Servants, obey in all things your masters according to the
flesh, not with eye-service, as pleasing men, but with simplicity
of heart, fearing God. 23 And whatever you do, do from the

soul, as to the Lord, and not to men; 24 knowing that from the
Lord you will receive the reward of the inheritance: for you
serve the Lord Christ. 25 But he that does wrong shall receive
for the wrong which he has done; and there is no respect of
persons.

IV. 1 Masters, give to your servants what is just and equal,
for you know that you have a master in heaven.
2 Persevere in prayer, and be watchful in the same with thanksgiving; 3 praying at the same time also for us, that God may
open for us a door of utterance to speak the mystery of the
Christ, for which I am in bonds, 4 that I may make it manifest,
as I ought to speak.
5 Walk in wisdom toward those who are without, redeeming the
time. 6 Let your speech be always with grace, seasoned with
salt, that you may know how you ought to answer every one.
7 All that relates to me, Tychicus, my beloved brother and
faithful minister and fellow-servant in the Lord, will make
known to you. 8 I have sent him to you for this very purpose,
that he may know your condition, and comfort your hearts; 9 I
have sent him with Onesimus, my faithful and beloved brother,
who is one of you. They will make known all things that are
done here.
10 Aristarchus, my fellow-prisoner, salutes you, and so does
Marcus the nephew of Barnabas, concerning whom you received
commandments; if he come to you, receive him; 11 Jesus also,
who is called Justus, salutes you: these are of the circumcision:
and these only are my fellow-workers for the kingdom of God,
who have been a comfort to me. 12 Epaphras, who is one of you,
a servant of Christ, salutes you; he always strives earnestly for
you in his prayers, that you may stand perfect and complete in
all the will of God. 13 For I testify for him, that he has a great
zeal for you and those in Laodicea and those in Hierapolis.
14 Luke, the beloved physician, and Demas, salute you.
15 Salute the brethren in Laodicea, and Nymphas, and the
church that is in his house. 16 And when this letter has been
read among you, cause that it be read in the church of the Lao-
diceans also; and see that you also read the letter from Laodicea; 17 and say to Archippus: Take heed to the ministry which
you have received in the Lord, that you fulfill it.
18 The salutation of me, Paul, with my own hand. Remember
my bonds. Grace be with you. Amen.

PAUL TO THE THESSALONIANS.

FIRST LETTER.

I. 1 PAUL and Sylvanus and Timothy to the church of the Thessalonians, which is in God the Father and in the Lord Jesus Christ: grace be to you, and peace from God our Father, and the Lord Jesus Christ.

2 We give thanks to God always for you all, making mention of you in our prayers, 3 remembering unceasingly your work of faith, and your labor of love, and your patience of hope in our Lord Jesus Christ, in the sight of our God and Father: 4 because we know, brethren beloved of God, your election. 5 For our gospel came not to you in word only, but also in power, and in the Holy Spirit, and in full assurance, as you know what sort of persons we were among you for your sakes. 6 And you became imitators of us and of the Lord, having received the word in much affliction with joy of the Holy Spirit, 7 so that you were examples to all that believe, in Macedonia and Achaia. 8 For from you, the word of the Lord sounded out, not only in Macedonia and Achaia, but also your faith in God has gone abroad in every place, so that we have no need to speak any thing. 9 For they themselves declare concerning us what kind of entrance we had to you, and how you turned to God from idols, to serve the living and true God, 10 and to wait for his Son from heaven, even Jesus, whom he raised from the dead, and who delivers us from the coming wrath.

II. 1 For you yourselves know, brethren, our entrance among you, that it was not in vain. 2 But having suffered before, and having been outraged, as you know, in Philippi, we were bold in our God to speak to you the gospel of God in the midst of great peril. 3 For our exhortation arose not from deception, nor from uncleanness, nor was it with guile; 4 but as God had judged us worthy to be intrusted with the gospel, so we speak, not as pleasing men, but God, who tries our hearts. 5 For neither flattering words did we at any time use, as you know, nor a pretext for covetousness; God is witness: 6 nor did we seek glory from men, neither from you nor from others; though we could have been burdensome as the apostles of Christ. 7 But we were gentle among you. As a nurse nourishes her children,

[8]so, having a strong affection for you, we were well pleased to impart to you not only the gospel of God, but our own lives also, because you had become dear to us. [9]For you remember, brethren, our labor and toil; for, laboring night and day, that we might not be burdensome to any one of you, we preached to you the gospel of God. [10]You are witnesses, and God also, in how holy and just and blameless a manner we conducted ourselves among you that believe, [11]as indeed you know how we exhorted and comforted and charged every one of you, as a father his children, [12]that you should walk in a manner worthy of God, who has called you to his own kingdom and glory.

[13]For this reason, also, we thank God without ceasing; because, when you received the word of God, as preached by us, you embraced it, not as the word of men, but, as it is in truth, the word of God, which effectually works in you that believe. [14]For you, brethren, became imitators of the churches of God in Judea which are in Christ Jesus; for you, also, have suffered the same things from your own countrymen, that they have suffered from the Jews, [15]who both killed the Lord Jesus and the prophets, and have persecuted us, and do not please God, and are opposed to all men, [16]forbidding us to speak to the Gentiles that they may be saved, in order that they may fill up their sins at all times: but the wrath is coming upon them to the full.

[17]But we, brethren, having been taken from you for a short time, in person, not in heart, did, with great desire, endeavor the more earnestly to see your face. [18]For this reason, we intended to go to you, (I Paul) both once and again, but Satan hindered us. [19]For what is our hope, or joy, or crown of rejoicing? Are not even you, in the presence of our Lord Jesus Christ at his coming? [20]You indeed are our glory and joy.

III. [1]Wherefore, being no longer able to contain ourselves, we thought it good to be left at Athens alone; [2]and we sent Timothy our brother and minister of God in the gospel of the Christ, in order that he might strengthen and comfort you with respect to your faith, [3]that no one be moved by these afflictions; for you yourselves know that we are appointed to this: [4]for even when we were with you, we told you beforehand that we were about to be afflicted, as it also came to pass, and as you know. [5]For this reason, when I could no longer contain myself, I sent to know your faith, lest by any means the tempter had tempted you, and our labor should be in vain.

6 But now, since Timothy has come to us from you, and has
told us the good news of your faith and love, and that you have
a good remembrance of us at all times, greatly desiring to see
us, as indeed we desire to see you, 7 for this reason we are comforted concerning you, brethren, in all our distress and affliction, by your faith: 8 for now we live, if you stand firm in the
Lord. 9 For what thanks can we render to God for you, for the
great joy with which we rejoice on your account before our God,
10 night and day praying exceedingly that we may see your face,
and perfect that which is lacking in your faith?

11 Now, may God himself, even our Father, and the Lord Jesus
Christ, direct our way to you. 12 And may the Lord cause you
to increase and abound in love to one another and to all, even
as we toward you, 13 in order that he may establish your hearts
blameless in holiness, in the presence of our God and Father, at
the coming of our Lord Jesus Christ with all his saints.

IV. 1 Finally, then, brethren, we beseech and exhort you, by
our Lord Jesus, that as you learned from us how you ought to
walk and please God, you would abound more and more. 2 For
you know what commandments we gave you by our Lord Jesus.
3 For this is the will of God, your sanctification, that you keep
yourselves from lewdness; 4 that each one of you know how to
keep his vessel in sanctification and in honor, 5 not in passionate
desire, as the Gentiles do, who know not God; 6 that no one take
advantage of or injure his brother in this matter; because the
Lord takes vengeance for all such things, as we also told you
before, and fully testified: 7 for God has not called us for uncleanness, but for holiness. 8 Therefore, he that despises, despises not man, but God, who has given us his Holy Spirit.

9 But with respect to brotherly love, you have no need that I
write to you: for you yourselves are taught of God to love one
another; 10 and indeed you do this to all the brethren that are
in all Macedonia. But we exhort you, brethren, that you abound
in love more and more, 11 and that you earnestly endeavor to live
quietly, and that you attend to your own business, and work
with your own hands, as we commanded you; 12 in order that
you may walk with propriety toward those who are without,
and may have need of nothing.

13 But concerning those who have fallen asleep, I would not
have you ignorant, brethren, that you may not grieve, as others
who have no hope. 14 For if we believe that Jesus died and rose

again, so also *should we believe that* God will, through Jesus, bring
with him those who sleep. [15] For this we say to you by the word
of the Lord, that we, the living, who remain till the coming of
the Lord, shall not precede those who are asleep: [16] for the Lord
himself will descend from heaven with a shout, with the voice
of the archangel, and with the trump of God; and the dead in
Christ shall arise first; [17] then we, the living who remain, shall,
together with them, be caught up in clouds into the air to meet
the Lord, and so shall we be ever with the Lord. [18] So, then,
comfort one another with these words.

V. [1] But, brethren, you have no need that I write to you of
the times and seasons; [2] for you yourselves know perfectly that
the day of the Lord so comes as a thief in the night: [3] for when
they shall say, Peace and safety, then sudden destruction comes
upon them, as the pains of birth upon a woman with child, and
they shall not escape.

[4] But you, brethren, are not in darkness, that that day should
overtake you as a thief. [5] You are all sons of light, and sons of
day: we are not of night, nor of darkness. [6] Therefore, let us
not sleep, as do others, but let us watch and be sober. [7] For
those who sleep, sleep in the night; and those who are drunken,
are drunken in the night. [8] But let us, who are of the day, be
sober, having on the breastplate of faith and love, and for a
helmet, the hope of salvation: [9] for God has not appointed us to
wrath, but to the obtaining of salvation through our Lord Jesus
Christ, [10] who died for us, that, whether we wake or sleep, we
might live together with him. [11] Wherefore, exhort one another,
and edify one another, as you also do.

[12] Now we beseech you, brethren, to have regard for those who
labor among you, and preside over you in the Lord, and admonish you, [13] and that you esteem them very highly in love on account of their work. Be at peace among yourselves. [14] We
exhort you, brethren, admonish the unruly, comfort the faint-
hearted, earnestly care for the weak-minded, be of a long-suffering disposition toward all.

[15] See that no one render evil for evil to any, but always pursue that which is good toward one another and toward all.

[16] Rejoice always; [17] pray without ceasing; [18] in every thing
give thanks; for this is the will of God in Christ Jesus concerning you.

[19] Quench not the Spirit. [20] Despise not prophesyings. [21] Prove

all things; hold fast that which is good. 22 Abstain from every
appearance of evil.
23 Now the God of peace himself sanctify you wholly; and may
your whole spirit and soul and body be preserved blameless at
the coming of our Lord Jesus Christ. 24 Faithful is he that
calls you; and he will do *what he has promised.*
25 Brethren, pray for us. 26 Salute all the brethren with a
holy kiss. 27 I adjure you by the Lord, that this letter be read
to all the holy brethren.
28 The grace of our Lord Jesus Christ be with you.

PAUL TO THE THESSALONIANS.

SECOND LETTER.

I. 1 PAUL and Sylvanus and Timothy to the church of the
Thessalonians in God our Father and in the Lord Jesus
Christ: 2 grace be to you, and peace from God our Father, and
the Lord Jesus Christ.
3 We are bound to give thanks to God always for you, brethren, as it is right, because your faith grows exceedingly, and the
love of every one of you all toward each other abounds: 4 so
that we ourselves glory in you, among the churches of God, for
your patience and faith in all your persecutions and afflictions
which you endure; 5 *which endurance of yours* is a proof of the
righteous judgment of God, in order that you may be counted
worthy of the kingdom of God, for which you suffer: 6 since,
indeed, it is a righteous thing with God, to repay affliction to
those who afflict you, 7 and to you who are afflicted, rest with
us, at the revelation of our Lord Jesus from heaven with his
mighty angels, 8 in flaming fire, to take vengeance on those who
know not God, and who obey not the gospel of our Lord Jesus
Christ; 9 these shall suffer punishment in that day, even eternal
destruction, far from the presence of the Lord, and from the
glory of his power, 10 when he shall come to be glorified in his
saints, and to be admired in all those who believe, and in you
also, because our testimony among you was believed.
11 In order to which, we also pray always for you, that our
God may count you worthy of this calling, and may fulfill all
the good pleasure of his goodness, and the work of faith with
power, 12 that the name of our Lord Jesus Christ may be glorified

in you, and you in him, according to the grace of our God, and
the Lord Jesus Christ.

II. [1] But, we beseech you, brethren, concerning the coming of
our Lord Jesus Christ, and our coming together to him, [2] that
you be not hastily shaken from the persuasion of your mind,
nor be troubled, neither by spirit, nor by report, nor by letter
as *written* by us, as though the day of the Lord is at hand. [3] Let
no one deceive you by any means; for that day will not come,
unless the apostasy come first, and the man of sin be revealed, the
son of perdition, [4] who opposes and exalts himself above every
one that is called God, or that is worshiped, so that he sits as God
in the temple of God, openly showing himself that he is God.
[5] Do you not remember that, while I was with you, I told you
these things? [6] And now you know what restrains, in order
that he may be revealed in his own proper time. [7] For the mystery of iniquity is already at work; only he that now restrains
will restrain, till he be taken out of the way: [8] and then shall
that lawless one be revealed, whom the Lord Jesus will destroy
by the spirit of his mouth, and will utterly overthrow by the
brightness of his coming: [9] he will destroy him, whose coming
is, according to the energy of Satan, with all power and signs
and wonders of falsehood, [10] and with all the delusion of unrighteousness in those who perish, because they did not receive
the love of the truth, in order that they might be saved. [11] And
for this reason God will send them strong delusion, in order that
they may believe a lie, [12] that all may be condemned who believe
not the truth, but have pleasure in unrighteousness.
[13] But we are bound to give thanks to God always for you,
brethren, beloved of the Lord, because God did, from the beginning, choose you to salvation, by sanctification of the Spirit and
belief of the truth, [14] to which he called you by our gospel, in
order that you might obtain the glory of our Lord Jesus Christ.
[15] Therefore, brethren, stand fast, and hold the traditions
which you have been taught, whether by word or by our letter.
[16] Now may our Lord Jesus Christ himself, and God, even our
Father, who has loved us, and given us eternal consolation and
good hope through grace, [17] comfort your hearts, and strengthen
you in every good word and work.

III. [1] Finally, brethren, pray for us, that the word of the
Lord may run and be glorified even as among you; [2] and that

we may be delivered from wicked and evil men; for all have not
the disposition for faith. 3 But the Lord is faithful, and he will
strengthen you, and keep you from the evil one. 4 And we have
confidence in the Lord with respect to you, that you both do,
and will continue to do, the things which we command you.
5 And the Lord direct your hearts to the love of God, and to the
patience of the Christ.

6 Now we command you, brethren, in the name of our Lord
Jesus Christ, that you withdraw from every brother that walks
disorderly, and not according to the tradition which he received
from us. 7 For you yourselves know how you ought to imitate
us: for we did not behave in a disorderly manner among you,
8 nor did we eat any one's bread for nothing: but worked with
labor and toil, night and day, that we might not burden any one
of you; 9 this we did, not because we have not authority, but
that we might give ourselves to you as an example, in order
that you might imitate us. 10 For when we were with you, we
gave you this commandment, that if any one will not work,
neither let him eat.

11 For we hear that some walk about among you in a disorderly manner, doing no work, but being busybodies. 12 Now we
command such, and exhort them by our Lord Jesus Christ, that
they work with quietness, and eat their own bread. 13 And you,
brethren, should not be weary in well-doing. 14 And if any one
obey not our word by this letter, note that man, and do not
keep company with him, that he may be ashamed; 15 and yet do
not regard him as an enemy, but admonish him as a brother.
16 Now the Lord of peace himself give you peace always by all
means. The Lord be with you all.

17 The salutation of Paul with my own hand, which is the
token in every letter: so I write.

18 The grace of our Lord Jesus Christ be with you all. Amen.

PAUL TO TIMOTHY.

FIRST LETTER.

I. 1 PAUL, an apostle of Jesus Christ, according to the appointment of God our Savior, and the Lord Jesus Christ
our hope, 2 to Timothy, my true son in the faith; grace, mercy,
peace from God our Father, and Christ Jesus our Lord.

[3] As, on going into Macedonia, I besought you to remain in
Ephesus, that you might charge some that they teach no other
thing, [4] nor give heed to fables and endless genealogies, which
produce disputes rather than godly edification, which is in faith;
([5] Now the end of the commandment is love out of a pure
heart, and out of a good conscience, and out of faith unfeigned:
[6] which things some not having aimed at, have turned aside to
idle disputation, [7] desiring to be teachers of law, though understanding neither what they say nor of what they boldly affirm.
[8] But we know that the law is good, if any one use it lawfully;
[9] knowing this, that law is not made for a righteous man, but
for the lawless and disobedient, for the ungodly and for sinners,
for the unholy and for scorners, for murderers of fathers and
murderers of mothers, for man-slayers, [10] for lewd persons, for
sodomites, for men-stealers, for liars, for perjured persons, and
for whatever other thing is opposed to sound teaching, [11] according to the glorious gospel of the blessed God, which has been
intrusted to me.
[12] And I thank Christ Jesus our Lord, who has given me
power, because he counted me faithful, and put me into the
ministry; [13] me, *I say*, who before was a reviler and a persecu-
tor and an overbearing man. But I obtained mercy, because I
did it ignorantly in unbelief: [14] and the grace of our Lord was
very abundant with faith, and love which is in Christ Jesus.
[15] Assuredly true and worthy of all acceptation is this saying:
that Christ Jesus came into the world to save sinners, of whom
I am chief. [16] But for this reason I obtained mercy, that in me
first Jesus Christ might show all long-suffering, for an example
to those who might afterward believe on him in order to life
eternal. [17] Now to the King of the ages, the incorruptible,
invisible, only wise God, be honor and glory from age to age.
Amen.)
[18] This charge I commit to you, son Timothy, in accordance
with the preceding prophecies concerning you, that by them
you may war the good warfare, [19] holding faith and a good conscience, which some having thrust from them, as it respects faith
have made shipwreck; of whom are Hymenæus and Alexander,
[20] whom I have delivered to Satan, that they may learn not to
revile.

II. [1] I exhort, therefore, first of all, that supplications,
prayers, intercessions, and giving of thanks be made for all

men, [2] for kings, and for all that are in authority, that we may
lead a quiet and peaceable life in all godliness and gravity.
[3] For this is good and acceptable in the sight of God our Savior,
[4] who is willing that all men should be saved, and come to the
knowledge of the truth. [5] For there is one God, and one mediator between God and man, the man Christ Jesus, [6] who gave
himself a ransom for all, *of which* the testimony *has been given* in
its proper times, [7] to give which testimony I have been appointed
a preacher and an apostle; (I speak the truth, and lie not;) a
teacher of the Gentiles in faithfulness and in truth.

[8] I will, therefore, that the men pray every-where, lifting up
holy hands without wrath and disputation. [9] In like manner,
also, *I will* that the women adorn themselves with decorous
dress, with modesty and sobriety, not with plaited hair, or gold,
or pearls, or costly raiment, [10] but with good works; since this
becomes women who profess godliness.

[11] Let the women learn in silence with all subjection. [12] I
suffer not a woman to teach, nor to usurp authority over the
man, but to be in silence. [13] For Adam was first formed, then
Eve. [14] And Adam was not deceived: but the woman being deceived, was in transgression; [15] but they shall be saved by the
bearing of children, if they continue in faith and love and holiness with sobriety.

III. [1] This is a true saying: If any desires the office of a
bishop, he desires a good work. [2] A bishop, then, must be blameless, the husband of one wife, watchful, sober-minded, modest,
hospitable, able to teach, [3] not fond of wine, not quarrelsome,
not one who makes money by base means; but gentle, not contentious, not covetous; [4] one that rules his own house well,
having his children in subjection with all gravity: [5] for if a man
knows not how to rule his own house, how will he take care of
the church of God? [6] Not a new convert, lest, having become
conceited, he fall into the condemnation of the devil. [7] Further,
he must have a good reputation from those who are without, lest
he fall into reproach and the snare of the devil.

[8] The deacons, likewise, must be grave, not double-tongued,
not given to much wine, not makers of money by base means,
[9] holding the mystery of the faith in a pure concience. [10] And
let these also be first proved, then let them become deacons,
being blameless. [11] Their wives likewise must be grave, not
slanderous, watchful, faithful in all things. [12] Let the deacons

be the husbands of one wife, ruling their children and their own houses well. 13 For those who have filled the office of a deacon well, gain for themselves a good degree, and great boldness in the faith that is in Christ Jesus.

14 I write these things to you, hoping to come to you shortly; 15 but if I delay, that you may know how you ought to conduct yourself in the house of God, which is the church of the living God, the pillar and support of the truth. 16 And confessedly great is the mystery of godliness: God was manifest in flesh, justified in spirit, seen by angels, preached among the Gentiles, believed on in the world, received up in glory.

IV. 1 Now the Spirit says expressly, that, in the last times, some shall depart from the faith, giving heed to seducing spirits, and teachings suggested by demons, 2 through the hypocrisy of liars, who are seared in their conscience, 3 who forbid to marry, and command to abstain from meats, which God has created to be received with thanksgiving by those who believe, and know the truth. 4 For every creature of God is good, and nothing is to be rejected, if it be received with thanksgiving; 5 for it is sanctified by the word of God, and by prayer.

6 By recommending these things to the attention of the brethren, you will be a good minister of Jesus Christ, being nourished with the words of the faith, and of good teaching, which you have fully known. 7 But reject those profane and old-womanish fables, and exercise yourself for godliness. 8 For the exercise of the body is profitable for little; but godliness is profitable for all things, and has the promise of the life that now is, and also of that which is to come. 9 This is a true saying, and worthy of all acceptation: 10 for to this end we both labor, and suffer reproach, because we trust in the living God, who is the Savior of all men, especially of those who believe. 11 These things command and teach.

12 Let no one despise your youth; but be an example to the believers, in word, in behavior, in love, in spirit, in faithfulness, in purity. 13 Till I come, give attention to reading, to exhortation, to teaching. 14 Neglect not the gift that is in you, which was given you according to prophecy, with the laying on of the the hands of the eldership. 15 Meditate upon these things; give yourself wholly to them, that your advancement may be manifest in all things. 16 Take heed to yourself, and to your teach-

ing; continue in them; for by doing this, you will save both
yourself, and those who hear you.

V. [1] Do not rebuke an elderly man, but entreat him as a
father; the younger men, as brothers: [2] the elder women,
as mothers; the younger women, as sisters, with all purity.
[3] Honor widows that are widows indeed. [4] But if any widow has
children or grand-children, let them learn first to be dutiful to
their own family, and to requite their parents; for that is good
and acceptable in the sight of God. [5] But she that is a widow
indeed, and left alone, trusts in God, and continues in supplications and prayers night and day. [6] But she that lives voluptuously, is dead while she lives. [7] These things also give in charge,
that they may be blameless. [8] And if any one provides not for
his own, and especially for those of his own household, he has
denied the faith, and is worse than an unbeliever.

[9] Let a widow be put on the list, if she is not under sixty
years, having been the wife of one man, [10] having a good reputation for good works; if she has borne children, if she has entertained strangers, if she has washed the saints' feet, if she has
relieved the afflicted, if she has diligently followed every good
work. [11] But the younger widows reject: for when they become
wanton against the Christ, they desire to marry, [12] incurring
condemnation, because they have set aside their former obliga-
tion. [13] At the same time, also, they learn to be idle, wandering
about from house to house; and not only idle, but tattlers also,
and busybodies, speaking things which are not proper. [14] I will,
therefore, that the younger widows marry, bear children, man-
age the house, and *thus* give no occasion to the adversaries to
speak reproachfully. [15] For some have already turned aside
after Satan. [16] If any believing man or woman has widows, let
him or her relieve them, and let not the church be burdened,
that it may relieve those who are widows indeed.

[17] Let the elders who rule well, be counted worthy of double
honor, especially those who labor in word and teaching. [18] For
the Scripture says: You shall not muzzle the ox that treads out
the grain; and, The laborer is worthy of his hire.

[19] Receive not an accusation against an old man, unless before
two or three witnesses. [20] Those who sin rebuke before all, that
the rest also may fear. [21] I charge you before God and the Lord
Jesus Christ, and the elect angels, that you observe these things
without prejudice, and that you do nothing by partiality.

22 Lay hands hastily on no man, nor be partaker of other men's sins: keep yourself pure.

23 Drink water no longer, but use a little wine for your stomach's sake, and your frequent infirmities.

24 Some men's sins are manifest beforehand, going before to
judgment. Some persons, however, they follow after. 25 Like-
wise, also, the good works *of some* are manifest beforehand; and those which are otherwise can not be concealed.

VI. 1 Let as many servants as are under the yoke count their
own masters worthy of all honor, that the name of God, and
his teaching, be not reviled. 2 And those who have believing
masters, let them not despise them, because they are brethren: but rather let them serve them, because they who partake of the benefit *of their service*, are believers and beloved *brethren*. These things enforce in your teaching and exhortation.

3 If any one teaches other things, and does not assent to the
sound words of our Lord Jesus Christ, and to the teaching which
is according to godliness, 4 he is mad with conceit, knowing
nothing, but has a morbid fondness for questions and contentions about words, out of which come envy, strife, railing, evil
suspicions, 5 and wranglings, on the part of men who are corrupt
in mind, and destitute of the truth, who suppose that godliness is a source of gain. From such withdraw yourself.

6 But godliness, with a contented disposition, is great gain.
7 For we brought nothing into this world, and it is certain that
we can carry nothing out. 8 And having food and raiment,
with these let us be content. 9 But those who will be rich fall
into temptation and a snare, and many foolish and hurtful desires, which drown men in destruction and perdition. 10 For the
love of money is the root of all evil; through the desire of which, some have erred from the faith, and pierced themselves through with many sorrows.

11 But do you, O man of God, shun these things, and pursue
righteousness, godliness, faithfulness, love, patience, meekness.
12 Fight the good fight of the faith; lay hold on eternal life, to
which you have been called, and for which you confessed the
good confession before many witnesses. 13 I charge you, in the
sight of God, who makes all things alive, and before Christ
Jesus, who, before Pontius Pilate, confessed a good confession,
14 that you keep this commandment, *so that you may be* spotless
and blameless till the appearing of our Lord Jesus Christ,

15 which, in his own times, he will show, who is the blessed and
only Potentate, the King of kings, and Lord of lords; 16 who
alone has immortality, dwelling in light unapproachable, whom
no man has seen, or can see, to whom be honor and power eternal.
Amen.

17 Charge those who are rich in this age, that they be not
proud, nor trust in uncertain riches, but in the living God, who
gives us all things richly for our enjoyment, 18 that they do
good, that they be rich in good works, that they be ready to distribute, liberal, 19 treasuring up for themselves a good foundation for the time to come, that they may lay hold on eternal life.

20 O Timothy, keep that which is committed to your charge,
avoiding those profane and empty babblings, and disputations
about knowledge falsely so called; 21 by making a profession of
this knowledge, some have erred as it respects the faith. Grace
be with you. Amen.

PAUL TO TIMOTHY.

SECOND LETTER.

I. 1 PAUL, an apostle, of Jesus Christ, by the will of God,
according to the promise of life, which is in Christ
Jesus, 2 to Timothy my beloved son; grace, mercy, and peace
from God our Father, and Christ Jesus our Lord.

3 I thank God, whom I serve with a pure conscience, after the
custom of my forefathers, that, without ceasing, I have remembrance of you in my prayers night and day, 4 greatly desiring
to see you, being mindful of your tears, that I may be filled
with joy; 5 for I remember the unfeigned faith that is in you,
which dwelt first in your grandmother Lois, and in your mother
Eunice; and I am persuaded that it dwells in you also.

6 Wherefore I exhort you to kindle up the gift of God that is
in you by the laying on of my hands. 7 For God has not given
us the spirit of fear, but of power, and of love, and of a sound
mind.

8 Be not, therefore, ashamed of the testimony of our Lord, nor
of me, his prisoner: but jointly suffer evil in the gospel according to the power of God, 9 who has saved us, and called us with
a holy calling, not according to our works, but according to his
own purpose and grace, which was given us in Christ Jesus before the times of the ages, 10 but is now made manifest by the

appearing of our Savior Jesus Christ, who has deprived death of
its power, and brought life and incorruptibility to light through
the gospel; 11 to which I have been appointed a preacher, and
an apostle, and a teacher of the Gentiles; 12 for which cause I
also suffer these things; yet I am not ashamed: for I know in
whom I have believed, and I am persuaded that he is able to
keep that which I have intrusted to him till that day.

13 Hold fast the form of sound words which you have heard
from me, in faithfulness and in love which is in Christ Jesus.
14 That good thing which was intrusted to you, keep by the Holy
Spirit that dwells in us.

15 You know this, that all those who are in Asia have turned
away from me; *all those, I say*, of whom are Phygellus and Her-
mŏgenes. 16 May the Lord give mercy to the house of Onesiphorus, for he often refreshed me, and was not ashamed of my chain:
17 but when he was in Rome, he sought for me very diligently,
and found me. 18 The Lord grant to him, that he may find
mercy from the Lord in that day. And in how many things he
ministered to me in Ephesus, you know very well.

II. 1 Do you, therefore, my son, be strong in the grace that is
in Christ Jesus; 2 and the things which you heard from me
through many witnesses, these do you commit to faithful men,
who shall be able to teach others also. 3 Do you, therefore,
suffer evil, as a good soldier of Jesus Christ. 4 Every one that
serves as a soldier keeps himself free from the business of this
life, that he may please him that has chosen him to be a soldier.
5 And if any one also contend in the public games, he is not
crowned, unless he contend according to the laws. 6 It is necessary that the farmer should labor, before he partakes of the
fruits. 7 Consider what I say, for *I pray that* the Lord may give
you understanding in all things.

8 Remember that Jesus Christ, of the posterity of David, was
raised from the dead, according to my gospel; 9 in which I suffer evil, as an evil-doer, even to bonds: but the word of God is
not bound. 10 For this reason I endure all things for the sake
of the elect, that they also may obtain the salvation that is in
Christ Jesus, with eternal glory. 11 Assuredly true is the saying: If indeed we have died with him, we shall also live with
him; 12 if we are patient, we shall also reign with him; if we
deny him, he will also deny us; 13 if we are unfaithful, he remains faithful: he can not deny himself.

[14] Put them in mind of these things, charging them before the
Lord that they dispute not about words to no profit, *which disputes end* in the overthrow of the hearers. [15] Strive to present
yourself to God as approved, a workman that has no cause to
be ashamed, rightly setting forth the word of truth. [16] But shun
profane and vain babblings; for they will make further advance
to ungodliness, [17] and their word will eat as a gangrene: of whom
are Hymenæus and Philetus, [18] who, as it respects the truth, have
erred, saying that the resurrection has already taken place;
and they overthrow the faith of some.
[19] But the foundation of God stands firm, having this inscription: The Lord knows those who are his; and, Let every one
that names the name of Christ depart from iniquity. [20] In a
great house, however, there are not only vessels of gold and of
silver, but also of wood and of earth, and some for honor, and
some for dishonor. [21] If, therefore, any one will cleanse himself
from these strifes about words, he will be a vessel for honor, sanctified, highly useful to the master, prepared for every good work.
[22] Shun youthful desires, and follow righteousness, faithfulness, love, peace, with those who call on the Lord out of a pure
heart. [23] But avoid foolish and unprofitable questions, because
you know that they produce contentions: [24] and the servant of
the Lord must not be contentious, but gentle toward all men,
able to teach, patient under evils, [25] in meekness instructing those
who oppose themselves, if, possibly, God may give them repentance in order to the acknowledgment of the truth, [26] and that
they may awake to sobriety out of the snare of the devil, after
having been taken captive by him according to his will.

III. [1] But know this, that in the last days trying times will
come. [2] For men will be lovers of themselves, lovers of money,
boasters, proud, revilers, disobedient to parents, unthankful,
unholy, [3] without natural affection, implacable, false accusers,
intemperate, fierce, haters of those who are good, [4] traitors, rash,
conceited, lovers of pleasures more than lovers of God, [5] having
a form of godliness, but denying its power: from these also
turn away. [6] For of this sort are those who worm themselves
into houses, and lead captive silly women that are laden with
sins, and influenced by various desires, [7] that are always learning, and never able to come to the knowledge of the truth.
[8] Now as Janes and Jambres withstood Moses, so these also
will withstand the truth; men corrupt in mind, rejected as it

respects the faith. 9 But they shall proceed no further; for
their madness shall be manifest to all, as was the madness of
those men.

10 But you have fully known my teaching, my course of life,
my purpose, my faithfulness, my long-suffering, my love, my
patience, 11 my persecutions, my sufferings which came upon me
in Antioch, in Iconium, in Lystra; you well know what persecutions I endured: and yet out of them all, the Lord delivered
me. 12 And all that will live godly in Christ Jesus, shall suffer
persecution. 13 But evil men and impostors will become worse
and worse, deceiving, and being deceived.

14 But do you continue in the things which you have learned
and well understood, knowing from whom you learned them,
15 and that from a child you have known the Holy Scriptures,
which are able to make you wise in order to salvation, through
faith that is in Christ Jesus. 16 All Scripture is given by in-
spiration of God, and is profitable for teaching, for reproof, for
correction, for instruction in righteousness, that the man of God
may be perfect, thoroughly furnished for every good work.

IV. 1 I charge you, therefore, before God and the Lord Jesus
Christ, who will judge the living and the dead at his appearing
and his kingdom, 2 preach the word, be urgent in season and out
of season, reprove, rebuke, exhort with all long-suffering and
teaching. 3 For the time will come when they will not endure
sound teaching, but according to their own desires they will
procure for themselves an abundance of teachers to gratify
their itching ears: 4 and they will turn away their ears from the
truth, and be turned to fables. 5 But do you be watchful in all
things, endure evil, do the work of an evangelist, fulfill your
ministry.

6 For I am now ready to be poured out, and the time of my
departure is at hand. 7 I have fought the good fight, I have
finished the race, I have kept the faith: 8 henceforth there is
laid up for me the crown of righteousness, which the Lord, the
righteous judge, will give me at that day; and not to me only,
but to all those who love his appearing.

9 Endeavor to come to me shortly; 10 for Demas has forsaken
me, having loved the present age; and he has gone to Thessalonica, Crescens to Galatia, Titus to Dalmatia. 11 Only Luke is
with me. Take Mark, and bring him with you, for he is useful
to me for the ministry. 12 I have sent Tychicus to Ephesus.

13 When you come, bring the cloak that I left in Troas with Car-
pus, and the books, especially the parchments.
14 Alexander the coppersmith did me much evil: the Lord repay him according to his works. 15 Do you, also, beware of him,
for he has greatly withstood our words.
16 At my first defense no one stood by me, but all forsook me;
may it not be laid to their charge: 17 but the Lord stood by me,
and gave me strength, that through me that which is preached
might be fully known, and that all the Gentiles might hear:
and I was delivered out of the mouth of the lion. 18 And the
Lord will deliver me from every evil work, and bring me safe to
his heavenly kingdom. To him be glory from age to age. Amen.
19 Salute Prisca and Aquila, and the household of Onesiphorus.
20 Erastus remained at Corinth. I left Trophimus sick at
Miletus. 21 Endeavor to come to me before winter. Eubulus
and Pudens and Linus and Claudia and all the brethren salute
you. 22 The Lord Jesus Christ be with your spirit. Grace be
with you all. Amen.

PAUL TO TITUS.

I. 1 PAUL, a servant of God, and an apostle of Jesus Christ,
according to the faith of God's elect, and the acknowledgment of the truth, which is according to godliness; 2 in hope
of eternal life, which God, who can not lie, promised before the
times of the ages, 3 but he has in his own times manifested his
word by preaching, which was committed to me according to
the commandment of God our Savior; 4 to Titus, my true son,
according to the common faith: grace, mercy, and peace from
God the Father, and the Lord Jesus Christ our Savior.
5 I left you in Crete for this purpose, that you might set in
order the things that are wanting, and ordain elders in every
city, as I commanded you: 6 if any one is blameless, the husband
of one wife, if he has faithful children that are not accused of
riotous living, or disobedient. 7 For the bishop must be blameless, as the steward of God; not self-willed, not passionate, not
fond of wine, not quarrelsome, not one who makes money by
base means; 8 but hospitable, a lover of goodness, sober-minded,
just, holy, temperate, 9 holding fast the sure word as it is taught,
that he may be able, by sound teaching, both to exhort and to
convince the opposers.

10 For there are many unruly and vain talkers and deceivers,
especially those of the circumcision, 11 whose mouths must be
stopped: these subvert whole houses by teaching, for the sake
of base gain, things which they ought not to teach. 12 One of
themselves, a prophet of their own, has said: The Cretans are
always liars, evil wild beasts, lazy gluttons. 13 This testimony
is true; wherefore rebuke them severely, that they may be sound
in the faith, 14 and not give heed to Jewish fables, and commandments of men that turn away from the truth. 15 To the pure,
all things are pure: but to the defiled and unbelieving, nothing
is pure; but their mind and their conscience are defiled. 16 They
profess that they know God, but in their works they deny him,
being detestable and disobedient, and, as it respects every good
work, rejected.

II. 1 But do you speak the things that become sound teaching;
2 that the aged men be vigilant, grave, sober-minded, sound in
faith, in love, in patience; 3 that the aged women likewise be,
in deportment, as it becomes holy women, not slanderers, not
enslaved to much wine, teachers of good things, 4 that they may
teach the young women to be sober-minded, to love their husbands, to love their children, 5 to be discreet, chaste, fond of home,
good, obedient to their own husbands, that the word of God be
not reviled.

6 Exhort the young men likewise to be sober-minded, 7 in all
things showing yourself an example of good works; in teaching,
showing incorruptness, gravity, 8 sound speech that can not be
condemned; that he that is opposed may be ashamed, seeing he
has no evil thing to say of us.

9 Exhort servants to be subject to their own masters, and to
please them well in all things, not contradicting, 10 not stealing,
but showing all good faithfulness, that they may adorn the
teaching of God our Savior in all things.

11 For the grace of God, which brings salvation to all men, has
appeared, 12 teaching us, that denying ungodliness and worldly
desires, we should live soberly and righteously and godly in the
present age; 13 looking for the blessed hope, and the glorious appearing of our great God and Savior Jesus Christ, 14 who gave
himself for us, that he might redeem us from all iniquity, and
purify for himself a peculiar people, zealous of good works.
15 Speak these things, and exhort and rebuke with all strictness.
Let no one despise you.

III. 1 Put them in mind to be subject to principalities and
authorities, to obey rulers, to be ready for every good work, 2 to
revile no one, not to be contentious, but gentle, showing all
meekness to all men. 3 For we ourselves also were formerly
foolish, disobedient, deceived, serving various desires and pleasures, living in malice and envy, hateful, and hating one another.
4 But when the kindness and philanthropy of God our Savior
appeared, he saved us, 5 not by works of righteousness which
we had done, but according to his own mercy, by the washing
of regeneration, and renewing of the Holy Spirit, 6 which he
poured out on us richly, through Jesus Christ our Savior; 7 that,
being justified by his grace, we might become heirs according
to the hope of eternal life.
8 This saying is true, and in respect to these things, I will that
you affirm strongly, in order that those who have believed in
God may be careful to practice good works: these are the things
that are honorable and profitable for men. 9 But foolish questions and genealogies and strifes and contentions about the law,
avoid; for they are unprofitable and vain. 10 A man that is a
sectary, reject, after the first and second admonition, 11 knowing that such a one is perverted, and sins, being self-condemned.
12 When I send Artemas to you, or Tychicus, hasten to come
to me at Nicopolis; for I have determined to spend the winter
there. 13 Conduct Zenas the lawyer, and Apollos on their journey with care, that nothing may be wanting to them. 14 Let
our people also learn to practice good works for necessary uses,
that they may not be unfruitful.
15 All that are with me salute you. Salute those who love us
in faithfulness. Grace be with you all. Amen.

PAUL TO PHILEMON.

1 PAUL, a prisoner of Jesus Christ, and Timothy my brother,
to Philemon my beloved, and our fellow-laborer, 2 and to
our beloved Apphia, and to Archippus our fellow-soldier, and to
the church that is in your house: 3 grace be to you all, and peace
from God our Father, and the Lord Jesus Christ.
4 I thank my God, making mention of you always in my
prayers, 5 hearing of your love and your faith, which you have
in the Lord Jesus, and toward all the saints, 6 that your par-

ticipation in the faith may be active in the acknowledgment of
every good thing that is in us, to *the honor of* Christ Jesus. 7 For
we have great joy and comfort in your love, because the hearts
of the saints have been refreshed by you, brother.

8 Wherefore, though I have great boldness in Christ to command you to do that which is becoming, 9 yet, on account of my
love, I rather exhort you, being such a one as Paul the aged,
and now also a prisoner on account of Jesus Christ. 10 I beseech
you for my son Onesimus, whom I have begotten in my bonds,
11 who, for some time, has been unprofitable to you, but now is
very profitable to you and to me: 12 I send him back, and do
you receive him, that is, my son. 13 I did wish to keep him with
me, that, in your stead, he might serve me in my bonds for the
gospel; 14 but, without your consent, I was not willing to do
any thing, that your good deed might not be as a matter of
necessity, but one of free-will.

15 Perhaps, indeed, he departed for a short time for this reason,
that you might receive him forever; 16 no longer as a servant,
but above a servant, a brother beloved, especially by me, and
how much more by you, both in the flesh and in the Lord. 17 If,
then, you regard me as a partner, receive him as myself. 18 But
if he has done you any wrong, or owes you any thing, put that
to my account. 19 I, Paul, do write it with my own hand, I will
repay it; that I may not say to you, that you owe to me even
yourself besides. 20 Yes, brother, let me have joy of you in the
Lord: refresh my heart in the Lord. 21 Having confidence in
your obedience, I write to you, knowing that you will do even
more than I say. 22 At the same time, also, prepare me a lodg-
ing: for I hope that through the prayers of you all, I may be
given to you. 23 Epaphras, my fellow-prisoner in Christ Jesus,
salutes you: 24 so also do Marcus, Aristarchus, Demas, Lucas,
my fellow-laborers. 25 The grace of our Lord Jesus Christ be
with your spirits. Amen.

PAUL TO THE HEBREWS.

I. 1 GOD, who in many parts and in many ways spoke in
ancient times to the fathers by the prophets, has in
these last days spoken to us by his Son, 2 whom he has appointed
heir of all things, by whom, also, he made the ages; 3 who,

being the effulgence of his glory and the exact representation of
his essence, and upholding all things by his own powerful word,
when he had by himself made expiation for our sins, sat down
at the right hand of the Majesty on high, [4] having become so
far superior to the angels, as the name which he has inherited
is more excellent than theirs.

[5] For to which of the angels did he at any time say: Thou art
my Son, this day have I begotten thee? And again: I will be
to him a Father, and he shall be to me a Son? [6] And again,
when he brings the first-begotten into the world, he says: And
let all the angels of God worship him. [7] And of the angels he
says: Who makes his angels winds, and his ministers a flame of
fire. [8] But to the Son: Thy throne, O God, is from age to age:
a scepter of rectitude is the scepter of thy kingdom. [9] Thou
hast loved righteousness, and hated iniquity; therefore, God,
thy God, has anointed thee with the oil of gladness above thy
fellows. [10] And, Thou, Lord, in the beginning, didst lay the
foundation of the earth, and the heavens are the works of thy
hands. [11] They shall perish; but thou remainest: and they all
shall grow old as a garment; [12] and as a mantle thou shalt fold
them up, and they shall be changed; but thou art the same, and
thy years shall not fail.

[13] But to which of the angels has he said at any time: Sit on
my right hand, till I make thy enemies thy footstool? [14] Are
they not all ministering spirits, sent forth to minister to those
who shall inherit salvation?

II. [1] Therefore, we ought to give the more earnest heed to
the things which we have heard, lest we let them glide away.
[2] For if the word spoken by angels was steadfast, and every
transgression and disobedience received a just punishment,
[3] how shall we escape, if we neglect so great salvation? which
at first began to be spoken by the Lord, and was confirmed to us
by those who heard him; [4] God also bearing testimony with them
by signs and wonders, and by various mighty deeds, and by dis-
tributions of the Holy Spirit, according to his own will.

[5] For not to angels has he subjected the world to come of
which we speak. [6] But one in a certain place testified, saying:
What is man, that thou art mindful of him; or the son of man,
that thou dost visit him? [7] Thou hast made him a little lower
than the angels; thou hast crowned him with glory and honor;
[8] thou hast put all things under his feet. For, in putting all

things under him, he left nothing that is not put under him:
but now we do not yet see all things put under him. [9] But we
see Jesus, who was made a little lower than the angels, that he
might, by the grace of God, taste death for every man—we see
him, on account of his having suffered death, crowned with
glory and honor. [10] For it became him, for whom are all things,
and by whom are all things, in bringing many sons to glory, to
make the author of their salvation perfect through sufferings.
[11] For both he that sanctifies, and those who are sanctified,
are all of one Father: for which reason, he is not ashamed to
call them brethren, saying: [12] I will declare thy name among
my brethren; in the midst of the assembly, will I sing hymns
to thee. [13] And again: I will put my trust in him. And again:
Behold, I, and the children that God has given me. [14] Since,
then, the children are partakers of flesh and blood, he also, in
like manner, partook of the same, that, through his death, he
might deprive of power him that has the power of death, that
is, the devil; [15] and might set free those who, through fear of
death, were all their lifetime subject to bondage. [16] For, verily,
he does not take hold of angels, but he takes hold of the posterity of Abraham. [17] Wherefore, it behooved him to be made
like his brethren in all things, that he might be a merciful and
faithful high-priest in things pertaining to God, in order to
make expiation for the sins of the people. [18] For, inasmuch as
he himself has suffered in being tempted, he is able to help those
who are tempted.

III. [1] Wherefore, holy brethren, partakers of the heavenly
calling, consider the apostle and high-priest of our confession,
Christ Jesus, [2] who is faithful to him that appointed him, as
Moses also was faithful in all his house. [3] For this man is
counted worthy of more glory than Moses, inasmuch as he who
has builded the house, has more honor than the house. [4] For
every house is builded by some one; but he that built all things
is God. [5] And Moses indeed was faithful in all his house as a
servant, to bear testimony to those things which were to be
spoken afterward; [6] but Christ, as a Son over his own house;
whose house we are, if we hold the confidence and the joy of
our hope firm to the end.
[7] Wherefore, as the Holy Spirit says: To-day, if you will hear
his voice, [8] harden not your hearts, as in the bitter provocation,
in the day of trial in the wilderness, [9] where your fathers tried

me, proved me, and saw my works forty years. [10] Wherefore,
I was angry with that generation, and said, They do always err
in their heart, and they have not known my ways: [11] so that I
swore in my anger, They shall not enter into my rest. [12] Take
heed, brethren, lest there be in any of you an evil heart of unbelief in apostatizing from the living God. [13] But exhort one
another daily, while it is called To-day, lest any of you be hardened by the deceitfulness of sin. [14] For we are partakers of
the Christ, if we hold our begun confidence firm to the end;
[15] while it is said, To-day, if you will hear his voice, harden not
your hearts, as in the bitter provocation. [16] For some, when
they had heard, did bitterly provoke; yet, not all that came out
of Egypt by Moses. [17] But with whom was he angry forty years?
Was it not with those who sinned, whose carcasses fell in the
wilderness? [18] But to whom did he swear that they should not
enter into his rest, but to those who believed not? [19] And so
we see that they could not enter in because of unbelief.

IV. [1] Let us fear, therefore, lest, as a promise of entering
into his rest still remains, any of you should seem to come
short of it. [2] For we have had the good news preached to us,
even as they had: but the word preached did not profit them,
for it was not mixed with faith in those who heard it. [3] For we
who have believed are to enter into rest, as he said: So I swore
in my anger, they shall not enter into my rest; namely, *that
rest from* his works which had been finished from the foundation
of the world. [4] For he spoke in a certain place of the seventh
day, thus: And God did rest on the seventh day from all his
works; [5] and in this place again: They shall not enter into my
rest.

[6] Since, then, it remains that some must enter into it, and
they, to whom the good news was first preached, did not enter in
on account of unbelief, [7] again, he determines a certain day, saying in David, after so long a time, To-day, as it is said, To-day,
if you will hear his voice, harden not your hearts. [8] For, if
Joshua had given them rest, he would not, after this, have
spoken of another day. [9] There remains, therefore, a Sabbath-
state for the people of God. [10] For he that has entered into his
rest, he also has ceased from his own works, as God did from his.

[11] Let us earnestly strive, therefore, to enter into that rest,
lest any one fall after the same example of unbelief. [12] For the
word of God is living and powerful, and sharper than any two-

edged sword, and pierces even to the dividing asunder of soul
and spirit, and of the joints and marrow, and is a discerner of
the thoughts and intents of the heart. 13 And there is no creature which is not manifest in his sight: but all things are naked,
and exposed to the eyes of him to whom we must give an account.

14 Seeing, then, that we have a great high-priest, who has
passed through the heavens, Jesus the Son of God, let us hold
fast our confession. 15 For we have not a high-priest that can
not sympathize with our infirmities; but he was tempted in all
things like ourselves, yet without sin. 16 Let us come, therefore,
with boldness, to the throne of grace, that we may receive
mercy, and find grace to help in every time of need.

V. 1 For every high-priest chosen from among men, is appointed for men, in things pertaining to God, that he may offer
gifts and sacrifices for sin: 2 being able to have compassion on
the ignorant and erring, because he himself is beset with infirmity: 3 and on account of this, he ought, as for the people,
so also for himself, to make offering for sins. 4 And no one
takes this honor to himself, but he that is called by God, as
Aaron also was called. 5 So, also, the Christ did not take upon
himself the honor of becoming a high-priest: but he *gave him
this honor*, who said to him, Thou art my Son, this day have I
begotten thee: 6 as he says also in another place, Thou art a priest
forever, after the order of Melchisedec.

7 In the days of his flesh, having offered up prayers and supplications, with strong crying and tears, to him that was able
to save him from death, and having been heard with respect to
that which he feared, 8 although he was a Son, he yet learned
obedience from the things which he suffered; 9 and, having been
made perfect, he became the author of eternal salvation to all
that obey him, 10 being called by God a high-priest after the
order of Melchisedec.

11 Of him we have many things to say, and difficult to be explained, if we do say them, since you are slow in understanding.
12 For though you ought to be teachers, considering the time,
yet you have need that some one teach you again what are the
first elements of the oracles of God; and you have become such
as have need of milk, and not of strong food. 13 For every one
that partakes of milk is unskillful in the word of righteousness:
for he is a babe. 14 But strong food belongs to those who are of

mature age, who, by use, have their internal senses exercised to
the discerning of both good and evil.

VI. [1] Therefore, omitting the elementary Christian teaching,
let us go on to the perfection *of Christian instruction*, not laying
again the foundation of repentance from dead works, and of
faith toward God, [2] of the teaching with respect to immersions,
and of the laying on of hands, of the resurrection of the dead,
and of eternal condemnation. [3] And this we will do, if God
permit. [4] For it is impossible to renew again to repentance
those who have once been enlightened, and have tasted of the
heavenly gift, and have been made partakers of the Holy Spirit,
[5] and have tasted the good word of God, and the powers of the
coming age, [6] if they fall away; since they again crucify in
themselves the Son of God, and put him to an open shame.

[7] For the land which drinks up the rain that comes often upon
it, and produces herbs suitable for those for whom it is culti-
vated, receives blessing from God. [8] But that which produces
thorns and thistles is rejected, and is near the curse, the end of
which is to be burned.

[9] But, beloved, we are confident of better things concerning
you, and of things that tend to salvation, though we thus speak.
[10] For God is not unjust, that he should forget your work, and
the love which you have shown for his name by having ministered to the saints, and by continuing to minister.

[11] But we desire every one of you to show the same diligence,
in order to have your hope fully assured to the end: [12] that you
may not become slothful, but imitators of those who, through
faith and patience, inherit the promises. [13] For when God made
promise to Abraham, because he could swear by no greater, he
swore by himself, [14] saying: Most surely will I abundantly bless
you, and abundantly multiply you. [15] And so, when he had
waited patiently, he received the promises. [16] For, verily, men
swear by the greater, and an oath for confirmation is to them
an end of all contradiction.

[17] Wherefore, God, being more abundantly willing to show to
the heirs of his promise the immutability of his purpose, inter-
posed an oath, [18] that by two immutable things, in which it was
impossible for God to lie, we might have strong consolation, who
have fled to lay hold on the hope set before us; [19] which hope
we have as an anchor for the soul, both sure and steadfast, and
which enters in beyond the vail, [20] whither a forerunner for us

has gone, even Jesus, who is made a high-priest forever after
the order of Melchisedec.

VII. [1] For this Melchisedec, king of Salem, priest of the most
high God, who met Abraham returning from the slaughter of the
kings, and blessed him, [2] to whom also Abraham gave a tenth of
all, being, first, by interpretation, King of righteousness, and
then, also, King of Salem, which means King of peace, [3] without father, without mother, without genealogy, having neither
beginning of days, nor end of life, but being made to resemble
the Son of God, remains a priest forever.

[4] Now consider how great this man was, to whom even the
patriarch Abraham gave a tenth of the spoils, [5] And those of
the sons of Levi, who receive the office of priesthood, have a
commandment to take tithes of the people according to the
law, that is, of their brethren, though they come out of the
loins of Abraham: [6] but he who does not count his genealogy
from them, received tithes from Abraham, and blessed him that
had the promises. [7] And, without any contradiction, the less is
blessed by the better.

[8] And in the one instance, men that die receive tithes; but in
the other, he receives them who has the testimony that he lives.
[9] And so to speak, even Levi, who receives tithes, paid tithes
through Abraham; [10] for he was yet in the loins of his father,
when Melchisedec met him.

[11] If, then, there had been a perfect expiation by means of the
Levitical priesthood, (for with reference to it, the people received
the law,) what further need was there that another priest should
be raised up after the order of Melchisedec, and not be called
after the order of Aaron? [12] It is evident that, when the priesthood is changed, there is of necessity a change also of the law.
[13] For he of whom these things are said, belongs to another tribe,
from which no one attended upon the altar. [14] For it is very clear
that our Lord sprung from Judah, of which tribe Moses spoke
nothing concerning priesthood.

[15] And it is yet far more evident, if, after the likeness of Melchisedec, there arises another priest, [16] who is made, not according to the law of a fleshly commandment, but according to the
power of an endless life; for he testifies, [17] Thou art a priest
forever after the order of Melchisedec.

[18] For, indeed, there is a setting aside of the preceding commandment, because it was weak and unprofitable, [19] (for the

law made no perfect expiation), and the introduction of a better
hope, by which we draw near to God. 20 And inasmuch as he
was made a priest, not without an oath, (21 for those priests
were made such without an oath, but this one with an oath, by
him that said to him, The Lord swore, and will not regret, Thou
art a priest forever after the order of Melchisedec;) 22 in so much
has Jesus become the surety of a better covenant.

23 And those priests, indeed, have been many, because they
were prevented by death from continuing *in office.* 24 But this
man, because he continues forever, has an unchangeable priesthood. 25 Wherefore, he is able also to save through all time
those who come to God by him, since he always lives to make
intercession for them.

26 For such a high-priest is suited to us, who is holy, harmless,
undefiled, separate from sinners, and exalted above the heavens;
27 who needs not daily, as those high-priests, to offer up sacrifices, first for his own sins, and then for the sins of the people:
for this he did once, when he offered up himself. 28 For the law
makes men high-priests, who have infirmity; but the word of
the oath, which was after the law, makes the Son, who is perfected forever.

VIII. 1 Now concerning the things that have been spoken, the
principal point is *this:* We have such a high-priest, who has
taken his seat at the right hand of the throne of the Majesty
in the heavens; 2 a minister of the holy places, and of the true
tabernacle, which the Lord pitched, and not man.

3 For every high-priest is appointed to offer gifts and sacrifices: wherefore, it is necessary that this one also have something
which he may offer. 4 For if he were on earth, he could not be
a priest; because there are priests that offer gifts according to
the law: 5 and these serve the copy and shadow of heavenly
things, as Moses was admonished of God when he was about to
make the tabernacle: See now, says he, that you make all things
according to the pattern shown you in the mount. 6 But now
he has obtained a more excellent ministry, inasmuch as he is
the mediator of a better covenant, which is established with
reference to better promises.

7 For if that first covenant had been faultless, no place would
have been sought for a second. 8 For, finding fault with them,
he says: Behold, the days are coming, says the Lord, when I
will ratify a new covenant for the house of Israel, and for the

house of Judah: 9 not like the covenant which I made with their
fathers, in the day when I took them by the hand to lead them
out of the land of Egypt: because they continued not in my
covenant, and I disregarded them, says the Lord. 10 For this
is the covenant that I will make with the house of Israel, after
those days, says the Lord; putting my laws into their understanding, I will also write them upon their hearts; and I will
be to them a God, and they shall be to me a people; 11 and they
shall not teach, every one his citizen, and every one his brother,
saying, Know the Lord: for all shall know me, from the least
of them to the greatest; 12 because I will be merciful to their
unrighteousness, and their sins and their iniquities I will remember no more.
13 In saying, A new covenant, he has regarded the first as out
of use. Now, that which is out of use, and has become old, is
ready to disappear.

IX. 1 Now, the first covenant also had ordinances of worship,
and the worldly sanctuary: 2 for a tabernacle was constructed,
the first, in which were the candlestick, and the table, and the
presence bread; and this tabernacle is called holy. 3 But after
the second vail, the tabernacle which is called the holy of holies;
4 which had the golden censer, and the ark of the covenant over-
laid on all sides with gold, in which were the golden pot that
held the manna, and the rod of Aaron that budded, and the
tables of the covenant; 5 and over the ark, the cherubim of glory
overshadowing the mercy-seat; of which things we can not now
speak particularly.
6 Now, when these things were thus arranged, the priests
went, at all times, into the first tabernacle, discharging the
service of God. 7 But into the second, the high-priest alone
went once during the year, not without blood, which he offered
for himself, and for the errors of the people: 8 the Holy Spirit
signifying this, that the way into the most holy was not yet
made manifest, while the first tabernacle was still standing,
9 which, as a symbol, *remains* to the present time, in which are
offered both gifts and sacrifices that can not make perfect, as it
respects the conscience, him that does the service; 10 since *he
relies* only on meats and drinks and various immersions, ordinances indeed of the flesh, which were imposed till the time of
reformation.
11 But Christ, having come a high-priest of the good things to

come, through the greater and more perfect tabernacle, not
made with hands, (that is, not of this building,) [12] entered, not
by the blood of goats and calves, but by his own blood, once
for all, into the most holy, having obtained eternal redemption.
[13] For if the blood of bulls and goats, and the ashes of a heifer
sprinkling the unclean, cleanses them as it respects the purity
of the flesh, [14] how much more will the blood of the Christ, who,
through the eternal Spirit, offered himself without spot to God,
cleanse your conscience from dead works, in order that you may
serve the living God?

[15] And for this reason, he is the mediator of the new covenant:
that, since his death has taken place for the redemption of
transgressions that were under the former covenant, those who
are called may receive the promise of the eternal inheritance.
[16] For where a testament is, it is necessary that there be brought
in the death of the testator: [17] for a testament goes into effect
after men are dead: seeing that it has no validity at all while
the testator lives.

[18] Wherefore, the first covenant was not instituted without
blood. [19] For when Moses had spoken to all the people every
commandment of the law, he took the blood of calves and of
goats, with water and scarlet wool and hyssop, and sprinkled
both the book itself and all the people, saying: [20] This is the
blood of the covenant which God enjoins on you: [21] and, in like
manner, he sprinkled with blood both the tabernacle, and all the
vessels of the service. [22] And, indeed, according to the law,
almost all things are cleansed by blood; and without the shed-
ding of blood there is no remission.

[23] It was necessary, therefore, that the copies of the things in
the heavens should be consecrated by these sacrifices; but that
the heavenly things themselves should be consecrated by better
sacrifices than these. [24] For the Christ has not entered the holy
places made with hands, the copies of the true; but he has entered heaven itself, now to present himself in the presence of
God for us. [25] Nor *has he entered*, that he should offer himself
often, as the high-priest enters the holy places every year with
the blood of another: [26] for then, he must have suffered often
since the foundation of the world. But now once in the end of
the ages, he has appeared in order to put away sin by the sacrifice of himself. [27] And, as it is appointed to men once to die,
and after this the judgment, [28] so the Christ was once offered to
bear the sins of many; and to those who look for him he will

appear the second time, without a sin-offering, in order to salvation.

X. 1 For the law, having a shadow of good things to come,
and not the very image of the things, can never, with the same
sacrifices, which they offer year by year continually, make a
perfect expiation for those who come to them: 2 for then, would
they not have ceased to be offered? because the worshipers, after
being once cleansed, would no longer have a consciousness of
sins. 3 There is, however, in these sacrifices, a remembrance of
sins every year.

4 For it is impossible that the blood of bulls and of goats
should take away sins. 5 Wherefore, when he comes into the
world, he says: Sacrifice and offering thou hast not desired, but
a body thou hast prepared me; 6 in whole burnt-offerings and
offerings for sin, thou hast had no pleasure. 7 Then, said I, Behold, I come, (in the roll of the book it is written of me,) to do
thy will, O God. 8 After saying above, Thou didst neither desire,
nor take pleasure in sacrifice and offering and whole burnt-offerings and offerings for sin, which are offered according to the
law, 9 then he said, Behold, I come to do thy will: he takes
away the first, that he may establish the second. 10 By which
will, we are sanctified through the offering of the body of Jesus
Christ, once for all time.

11 And every priest stands daily ministering, and offering often-
times the same sacrifices, which can never take away sins: 12 but
after offering one sacrifice for sins, he himself sits continually
at the right hand of God, 13 henceforth waiting till his enemies
be made his footstool. 14 For by one offering, he has made a
perfect and perpetual expiation for the sanctified.

15 And, indeed, the Holy Spirit is a witness for us. For after
he had said before, 16 This is the covenant that I will make with
them after those days, says the Lord; putting my laws in their
hearts, I will also write them in their understandings: 17 he
adds, And their sins and iniquities I will remember no more.
18 Now, where remission of these is, there is no more offering
for sin.

19 Having therefore, brethren, confidence to enter the holiest
by the blood of Jesus, 20 by a new and living way which he has
dedicated for us, through the vail, that is, his flesh; 21 and having a great high-priest over the house of God, 22 let us draw near
with a true heart, in full assurance of faith, having our hearts

sprinkled from an evil conscience, and our bodies washed with
pure water; 23 let us hold fast the unwavering confession of our
hope, for he is faithful who has promised: 24 and let us consider
one another that we may excite to love and good works, 25 not
forsaking the assembling of ourselves together, as is the custom
of some; but exhorting one another, and so much the more, as
you see the day approaching.

26 For if we sin willfully, after we have received the knowledge
of the truth, there remains no longer a sacrifice for sins; 27 but
a certain fearful looking for of judgment, and a fiery indignation which will devour the adversaries. 28 He that despised
Moses' law, died without mercy, on the testimony of two or
three witnesses: 29 of how much severer punishment do you think
he shall be thought worthy, who has trodden under foot the Son
of God, and has counted the blood of the covenant, with which
he was sanctified, a common thing, and has done despite to the
Spirit of grace? 30 For we know him who has said, Vengeance
is mine, I will repay, says the Lord. And again, The Lord will
judge his people. 31 It is a fearful thing to fall into the hands
of the living God.

32 But remember the former days, in which, after you were enlightened, you endured a great conflict of sufferings; 33 partly,
while you became a public spectacle, by reproaches and afflictions: partly, while you became partakers with those who were
so treated. 34 For you sympathized with me in my bonds, and
endured joyfully the seizure of your possessions, knowing that
you have for yourselves a better and abiding substance in the
heavens. 35 Cast not away, therefore, your confidence, which
has a great reward.

36 For you have need of patience, that, after you have done
the will of God, you may receive the promise. 37 For yet a very,
very little while, and He that comes will come, and will not
delay. 38 But the just by faith shall live; and if he draw back,
my soul will have no pleasure in him. 39 But we are not of those
who draw back to perdition; but of those who believe to the
saving of the soul.

XI. 1 Now, faith is confidence with respect to things hoped
for, persuasion with respect to things not seen: 2 for by this
the ancients obtained a good reputation.

3 By faith we understand that the ages were set in order by the

word of God, so that the things which are seen, have not come
into being from things that appear.
4 By faith Abel offered to God more sacrifice than Cain; on
account of which he received testimony that he was righteous, God testifying of his gifts; and by it he, though dead, yet
speaks.
5 By faith Enoch was translated that he should not see death,
and was not found, because God had translated him: for before
his translation he had the testimony that he pleased God. 6 But
without faith it is impossible to please him; for he that comes
to God must believe that he is, and that he is a rewarder of
those who diligently seek him.
7 By faith Noah, after being warned concerning things not yet
seen, moved with fear, prepared an ark for the salvation of his
house; by which faith he condemned the world, and became an
heir of the righteousness which is by faith.
8 By faith Abraham, when called to go out into a place that
he should afterward receive for an inheritance, obeyed; and he
went out, not knowing whither he went. 9 By faith he sojourned
in the land of promise, as in a strange land, dwelling in tents
with Isaac and Jacob, the heirs with him of the same promise:
10 for he looked for a city that has foundations, whose architect
and builder is God. 11 By faith also Sarah herself received
strength for the conception of seed, and brought forth a child
when past the time of life, because she counted him faithful
who had promised. 12 Therefore, there were born of one, who
was dead as it respects these things, a posterity like the stars
of heaven in multitude, and like the sand on the sea-shore, in-
numerable.
13 All these died in faith, not having received the promises, but
having seen them afar off, and having embraced them and confessed that they were strangers and sojourners in the land.
14 For those who say such things, declare plainly that they seek
a country. 15 And if indeed they had been mindful of that from
which they came, they could have had an opportunity to return.
16 But now they desire a better, that is, a heavenly country;
wherefore God is not ashamed of them, that he should be called
their God: for he has prepared for them a city.
17 By faith Abraham, when he was tried, offered up Isaac:
even his first-born, did he that had received the promises, offer
up, 18 of which first-born it was said: In Isaac shall your posterity be called: 19 for he concluded that God was able to raise

him up, even from the dead; wherefore he received him even in
a similitude.

20 By faith Isaac blessed Jacob and Esau concerning things to
come. 21 By faith Jacob, when he was dying, blessed each of
the sons of Joseph, and worshiped on the top of his staff.

22 By faith Joseph, when he was dying, made mention of the
departure of the sons of Israel, and gave commandment concerning his bones.

23 By faith Moses was concealed by his parents for three
months after his birth, because they saw that he was a beautiful
child: and they feared not the command of the king. 24 By faith
Moses, when he became a man, refused to be called the son of
Pharaoh's daughter, 25 choosing rather to suffer evil with the
people of God than to enjoy the pleasure of sin for a season;
26 esteeming the reproach on account of the Christ as greater
riches than the treasures of Egypt: for he earnestly looked to
the reward. 27 By faith he left Egypt, not fearing the anger of
the king: for he patiently endured, as seeing him that is invisible. 28 By faith he kept the passover, and the affusion
of blood, that he who destroyed the first-born might not touch
them.

29 By faith they passed through the Red Sea as by dry land,
which the Egyptians attempting to do, were drowned.

30 By faith the walls of Jericho fell down, after the people had
gone around them for seven days.

31 By faith Rahab the harlot perished not with the disobedient,
because she had received the spies with peace.

32 And what further shall I say? For the time would fail me,
were I to tell of Gideon, and of Barak, and of Samson, and of
Jephthah, of David also and Samuel, and of the prophets, 33 who,
through faith, subdued kingdoms, worked righteousness, obtained promises, closed the mouths of lions, 34 quenched the violence of fire, escaped the edge of the sword, out of weakness
were made strong, became valiant in battle, turned to flight the
armies of the aliens. 35 Women received their dead raised to
life again: but others were beat to death, not accepting deliv-
erance, that they might obtain a better resurrection; 36 others
had trial of mockings and scourgings, bonds also, and imprison-
ments. 37 They were stoned, they were sawn asunder, they were
tempted, they were slain with the sword: they went about in
sheep-skins, in goat-skins, being destitute, afflicted, oppressed
with evils, 38 (of whom the world was not worthy,) wandering

in deserts, and in mountains, and in caverns, and in dens of
the earth.

[39] And all these, having obtained a good reputation by faith,
received not the promise, [40] because God had provided some
better thing for us, that they, without us, should not be made
perfect.

XII. [1] Wherefore, since we also have so great a cloud of witnesses lying round about us, let us lay aside every weight, and
the sin that so easily besets us, and let us run with patience the
race that lies before us, [2] looking to Jesus the author and finisher
of the faith, who, for the joy that was set before him, endured
the cross, despising the shame, and has taken his seat at the
right hand of the throne of God. [3] For consider him that endured such opposition of sinners against himself, lest you become weary and despondent in your minds.

[4] You have not yet resisted to blood, in your contest with sin;
[5] and you have forgotten the exhortation which is addressed to
you as to sons: My son, despise not the chastening of the Lord,
nor faint when you are reproved by him. [6] For, whom the Lord
loves, he chastens, and scourges every son that he receives. [7] If
you endure chastening, God deals with you as with sons: for
what son is there whose father chastens him not? [8] But if you
are without chastisement, of which all are partakers, then are
you bastards, and not sons.

[9] So, then, we have had fathers of our flesh who corrected us,
and we reverenced them; shall we not much rather be in subjection to the Father of our spirits, and live? [10] For they, indeed, for a few days, chastened us as they thought it good; but he
chastens us for our profit, that we may be partakers of his holiness. [11] But no chastisement seems, at the time, to be a matter
of joy, but of grief: yet afterward, it yields the peaceable fruit
of righteousness to those who are exercised by it.

[12] Wherefore, lift up the hands that hang down, and strengthen
the feeble knees, [13] and make straight paths for your feet, lest
that which is lame be turned aside; but rather let it be restored
to health. [14] Follow peace with all, and holiness, without
which no man shall see the Lord; [15] taking care, lest any one
slight the grace of God; lest any root of bitterness spring up
and trouble you, and by this many be defiled; [16] lest there be
any lewd person, or profane man, as Esau, who, for a single
meal, sold his birthright. [17] For you know that afterward, when

he desired to inherit the blessing, he was rejected: for he found
no means to change *his father's* mind, though he sought it earnestly with tears.

18 For you have not come to a mountain that may be touched,
and that burns with fire, and to blackness and darkness and
tempest, 19 and to the sound of a trumpet, and to the utterance
of words, the hearing of which utterance caused the people to
entreat that the word might not be spoken to them again; 20 for
they could not endure that which was commanded, And if even
a beast touch the mountain, it shall be stoned: 21 and so terrible
was the sight, that even Moses said, I exceedingly fear and
tremble. 22 But you have come to Mount Zion, and the city of
the living God, the heavenly Jerusalem, and to myriads of
angels; 23 to the general assembly and church of the first-born,
who are enrolled in heaven, and to God, the judge of all, and to
the spirits of the just made perfect, 24 and to Jesus the mediator
of the new covenant, and to the blood of sprinkling that speaks
better things than the blood of Abel.

25 See that you reject not him that speaks: for if they escaped
not who rejected that earthly man who gave the oracles, much
more shall not we escape, if we turn away from him that is from
heaven, 26 whose voice then shook the earth; but now he has
promised, saying, Yet once more I will shake not the earth only,
but also the heaven. 27 And this *prophecy*, Yet once more, sig-
nifies the removing of the things that are shaken, as of things
that have been made, that the things which can not be shaken
may remain. 28 Wherefore, as we receive a kingdom that can
not be shaken, let us have gratitude, by which we may serve
God acceptably, with reverence and godly fear: 29 for our God
is a consuming fire.

XIII. 1 Let brotherly love continue. 2 Be not forgetful to
entertain strangers: for, by this means, some have unconsciously
entertained angels. 3 Remember those who are in bonds, as if
you yourselves had been bound, and those who suffer affliction,
since you yourselves are in the body.

4 Marriage is honorable among all men, and the bed undefiled;
but lewd men and adulterers God will judge. 5 Let there be no
money-loving disposition; be content with such things as you
have. For he has said: I will never leave you, nor will I ever
forsake you. 6 So, then, we may boldly say: The Lord is my
helper, and I will not fear what man will do to me.

7 Remember those who rule over you, who have spoken to you
the word of God: attentively consider the result of their conduct,
and imitate their faith. 8 Jesus Christ is the same yesterday,
and to-day, and forever. 9 Be not carried away by various and
strange teachings: for it is good that the heart be strengthened
with grace, not with meats, which have not profited those who
were occupied with them. 10 We have a sacrifice, of which those
who serve the tabernacle have no right to eat.

11 For the bodies of those animals whose blood, shed for sin,
is carried by the high-priest into the holiest, are burned without the camp. 12 Wherefore, Jesus also, that he might sanctify
the people by his own blood, suffered without the gate. 13 Therefore, let us go forth to him without the camp, bearing his reproach. 14 For here we have no abiding city, but we seek one
to come. 15 Through him, therefore, let us offer the sacrifice of
praise to God continually, that is, the fruit of our lips, giving
thanks to his name.

16 But forget not to do good, and to be liberal: for with such
sacrifices God is well pleased. 17 Obey those who rule over you,
and be submissive: for they watch for your souls, as those who
must give an account; that they may do this with joy, and not
with grief: for that would be fatal to you. 18 Pray for us: for
we trust that we have a good conscience, willing to live honorably in all things. 19 And I the more earnestly entreat you to
do this, that I may be restored to you the sooner.

20 Now may the God of peace, who brought again from the
dead our Lord Jesus Christ, the great Shepherd of the sheep,
through the blood of the eternal covenant, 21 perfect you in
every good work, in order that you may do his will, working in
you that which is acceptable in his sight, through Jesus Christ,
to whom be glory from age to age. Amen.

22 I beseech you, brethren, bear with my word of exhortation:
for I have written to you in few words.

23 Know that our brother Timothy is set at liberty, with whom,
if he come shortly, I will see you. 24 Salute all your rulers, and
all the saints. The saints of Italy salute you.

Grace be with you all. Amen.

THE LETTER OF JAMES.

I. 1 JAMES, a servant of God, and of the Lord Jesus Christ,
to the twelve tribes that are in the dispersion, greeting.
2 My brethren, count it all joy, when you fall into manifold
trials, 3 knowing that the trial of your faith produces patience.
4 But let patience have its work perfected, that you may be perfect and faultless, wanting in nothing.
5 Now, if any of you lack wisdom, let him ask of God, who
gives to all liberally, and upbraids not; and it shall be given
him. 6 But let him ask in faith, doubting not: for he that
doubts, is like a wave of the sea, driven by the wind, and
tossed. 7 For let not that man think that he shall receive any
thing from the Lord. 8 A double-minded man is unstable in all
his ways.
9 Let the brother that is in a lowly condition, glory in his ex-
altation: 10 but he that is rich, in his humiliation; because as
the flower of the grass he shall pass away. 11 For the sun rises
with its burning heat, and withers the grass, and its flower falls,
and the beauty of its form perishes. So, also, shall the rich
man fade away in his ways.
12 Blessed is the man that endures trial: for, being approved,
he shall receive the crown of life which the Lord has promised
to those who love him. 13 Let no one say, when he is tempted,
My temptation is from God; for God can not be tempted by evils,
and he himself tempts no man. 14 But every one is tempted
when he is drawn away by his own desire, and is deluded. 15 So,
then, desire, when it has conceived, brings forth sin; and sin,
when it is matured, brings forth death.
16 Be not deceived, my beloved brethren; 17 every good gift,
and every perfect gift is from above, and comes down from the
Father of lights, with whom there is no change, nor slightest
trace of turning. 18 Of his own will, he begot us with the word
of truth, in order that we might be, as it were, the first-fruits
of his creatures.
19 So, then, my beloved brethren, let every man be swift to
hear, slow to speak, slow to wrath. 20 For the wrath of man
produces not the righteousness of God. 21 Wherefore, laying
aside all filthiness, and every excess caused by malice, receive
with meekness the ingrafted word, which is able to save your
souls.

22 But be doers of the word, and not hearers only, deceiving yourselves. 23 For if any one is a hearer of the word, and not a doer, he is like a man that looks at his natural face in a mirror: 24 for he looks at himself, and goes away, and immediately forgets what sort of person he is. 25 But he that looks intently into the perfect law of liberty, and remains constant, being not a forgetful hearer, but a doer of the work, he shall be blessed in his deed.

26 If any one among you seems to be religious, and bridles not his tongue, but deceives his own heart, this man's religion is vain. 27 Religion, pure and undefiled before God and the Father, is this: To visit the fatherless and widows in their affliction, and to keep himself unspotted from the world.

II. 1 My brethren, do not hold the faith of our glorious Lord Jesus Christ, so as to show a partiality for persons. 2 For if there comes into your assembly a man in splendid apparel, and with gold rings on his fingers, and there comes in also a poor man, in mean clothing, 3 and you show regard to him that wears the splendid apparel, and say to him, Sit here in an honorable place; and you say to the poor man, Do you stand there, or sit here, under my footstool; 4 are you not partial in yourselves? and are you not judges having evil thoughts? 5 Hear, my beloved brethren: Has not God chosen the poor of this world, rich in faith, and heirs of the kingdom which God has promised to those who love him? 6 But you dishonor the poor man. Do not the rich oppress you, and do they not themselves drag you to the judgment-seats? 7 Do they not themselves revile that honorable name which is called upon you? 8 If, however, you fulfill the law of highest excellence according to the Scripture, You shall love your neighbor as yourself, you do well. 9 But if you show partiality for persons, you work sin, and are convicted by the law as transgressors.

10 For whoever shall keep the whole law, and yet fail in one, is an offender against all. 11 For he that said, Do not commit adultery, said also, Do not kill. Now, though you do not commit adultery, yet, if you kill, you are a transgressor of law.

12 So speak, and so act, as those who shall be judged by the law of liberty. 13 For he shall have judgment without mercy, who has shown no mercy. Mercy glories over judgment.

14 What profit is there, my brethren, if any one say he has faith, and have not works? Can faith save him? 15 If a brother

or sister be naked, and destitute of daily food, 16 and any of you
say to them, Go in peace, be warmed and be filled, and yet give
them not the things that are needful for the body, what does
this profit them? 17 So, also, faith, if it has not works, is dead,
being by itself. 18 But some one will say, You have faith, and
I have works; show me your faith by your works, and I will
show you my faith by my works. 19 You believe that there is
one God; you do well: the demons also believe and tremble.
20 But will you know, O vain man, that faith without works is
dead?

21 Was not Abraham our father justified by works, when he
offered his son Isaac on the altar? 22 Do you see that faith was
a co-worker in his works, and by works his faith was made
perfect? 23 And the Scripture was fulfilled, which says, Abraham believed God, and it was counted to him for righteousness:
and he was called the friend of God. 24 Do you see that a man
is justified by works, and not by faith only?

25 Likewise, was not Rahab the harlot justified by works, when
she had received the messengers, and sent them out another way?
26 For as the body without the spirit is dead, so faith without
works is dead also.

III. 1 My brethren, be not many teachers, knowing that we
shall receive the greater condemnation. 2 For in many things
we all offend. If any one offends not in word, he is a perfect
man, able also to bridle the whole body. 3 Behold, we put bits
into horses' mouths that they may obey us, and we turn about
their whole body. 4 Behold also the ships, which are very great,
and are driven by violent winds; yet they are turned about by
a very small helm, to whatever point the will of him that directs
it may determine. 5 So, also, the tongue is a little member, and
boasts great things. Behold, how great a forest does a little
fire set in a blaze. 6 And the tongue is a fire, the world of iniquity. So is the tongue placed among our members, defiling
the whole body, setting on fire the course of life, and being set
on fire by hell.

7 For every kind of beasts and of birds, of creeping things and
of things in the sea, is tamed, and has been tamed by man: 8 but
the tongue no man can tame; it is an unruly evil; it is full of
deadly poison. 9 With it we bless God, even the Father: and
with it we curse men who are made in the likeness of God.
10 Out of the same mouth come forth blessing and cursing.

These things, my brethren, ought not so to be. [11] Does a
fountain send forth from the same cavern sweet water and
bitter? [12] Can the fig-tree, my brethren, bear olives, or the
vine, figs? So no fountain can produce salt water and fresh.

[13] Who is wise and discreet among you? Let him show, by a
good behavior, his works, with the meekness of wisdom. [14] But
if you have bitter envying and strife in your hearts, glory not,
and lie not against the truth. [15] This wisdom comes not from
above, but is earthly, animal, demoniac. [16] For where envy and
strife are, there is commotion, and every evil work. [17] But the
wisdom that is from above is first pure, then peaceable, gentle,
easy to be entreated, full of mercy and good fruits, without partiality, and without hypocrisy. [18] And those who cultivate
peace, sow for themselves a harvest of righteousness in peace.

IV. [1] Whence come wars and strifes among you? Come they
not hence, even of your passions, which war in your members?
[2] You desire, and you have not; you kill, and are earnestly desirous of having, and yet you can not obtain; you fight and
war, and yet you have not, because you ask not. [3] You ask, and
receive not, because you ask amiss, that you may spend it on
your passions.

[4] Adulterers and adulteresses, know you not that the friend-
ship of the world is enmity to God? Whoever, therefore, will
be a friend of the world, is an enemy of God. [5] Do you suppose
that the Scripture speaks to no purpose? Does the Spirit that
dwells in us incline to envy? *No.* [6] But he gives more grace.
Wherefore he says: God sets himself against the proud, but
gives grace to the lowly. [7] Submit yourselves, therefore, to
God; resist the devil, and he will flee from you; [8] draw near to
God, and he will draw near to you. Cleanse your hands, you
sinners, and purify your hearts, you double-minded men. [9] Be
afflicted, and mourn, and weep: let your laughter be turned to
mourning, and your joy to sorrow. [10] Humble yourselves in the
sight of the Lord, and he will exalt you.

[11] Do not speak evil one of another, brethren. He that speaks
evil of his brother, and judges his brother, speaks evil of the
law, and judges the law: but if you judge the law, you are not
a doer of the law, but a judge. [12] There is one law-giver that
is able to save, and to destroy: who are you that judge another?

[13] Come, now, you that say, Let us go to-day, or to-morrow,
into this city, and remain there a year, and trade, and make

gain; [14] and yet you know not what will take place to-morrow.
For what is your life? Is it not, indeed, a vapor, that appears
for a little while, and then vanishes away? [15] Instead of that,
you ought to say, If the Lord will, we shall live, and do this, or
that. [16] But now you glory in your boastings: all such glory-
ing is evil. [17] Therefore, to him that knows how to do good, and
does it not, to him it is sin.

V. [1] Come, now, you rich men, weep and lament for your
miseries that are coming upon you. [2] Your wealth is corrupted,
and your garments are moth-eaten: [3] your gold and your silver
are covered with rust; and their rust will be a testimony against
you, and will eat your flesh as fire. You have heaped up treasures in the last days. [4] Behold, the hire of the laborers who
have reaped your fields, which has been unjustly withheld by you,
cries out: and the cries of those who have reaped, have entered
into the ears of the Lord of hosts. [5] You have lived in pleasure
on the earth, and been wanton; you have nourished your hearts,
as in a day of slaughter. [6] You have condemned and killed the
Just One: and he does not set himself against you.

[7] Be patient, therefore, brethren, till the coming of the Lord.
Behold, the farmer looks for the precious fruit of the earth, and
waits patiently for it, till he receives the early and the latter
rain. [8] Be you also patient, establish your hearts: for the coming of the Lord draws near.

[9] Indulge not in complaints against one another, brethren, lest
you be condemned: behold, the judge stands before the door.
[10] Take, my brethren, the prophets who spoke in the name of
the Lord, as an example of suffering evil, and of patience.
[11] Behold, we count those happy who endure. You have heard
of the patience of Job, and have seen the final dealing of the
Lord, that the Lord is very compassionate and merciful.

[12] But above all things, my brethren, swear not, either by
heaven, or by the earth, or with any other oath: but let your
yes, be yes, and your no, be no, lest you fall into condemnation.

[13] Is any one among you afflicted? let him pray. Is any one
cheerful? let him sing praise. [14] Is any one among you sick?
let him call for the elders of the church, and let them pray over
him, anointing him with oil, in the name of the Lord. [15] And
the prayer of faith shall save the sick; and the Lord will raise
him up. And if he have committed sins, they shall be forgiven
him.

16 Confess your faults one to another, and pray for one another,
that you may be restored to health: the fervent prayer of a
righteous man avails much. 17 Elijah was a man with passions
like our own; and he earnestly prayed that it might not rain;
and it did not rain on the land for three years and six months.
18 And he prayed again; and the heavens gave rain, and the
earth brought forth its fruit.

19 Brethren, if any among you should err from the truth, and
one should turn him back, 20 let him know that he who turns
back a sinner from the error of his way, will save a soul from
death, and cover a multitude of sins.

FIRST LETTER OF PETER.

I 1 PETER, an apostle of Jesus Christ, to the sojourners that
are dispersed through Pontus, Galatia, Cappadocia,
Asia, and Bithynia, 2 elect according to the foreknowledge of
God the Father, by the sanctification of the Spirit, in order to
obedience, and sprinkling of the blood of Jesus Christ: grace
be to you, and peace be multiplied.

3 Blessed be the God and Father of our Lord Jesus Christ, who,
according to his abundant mercy, has, by the resurrection of
Jesus Christ from the dead, regenerated us for a living hope 4 in
respect to an inheritance incorruptible, and undefiled, and that
fades not away, reserved in heaven for us, 5 who are kept secure
by the power of God through faith, to a salvation ready to be
revealed in the last time: 6 in which you rejoice, though now
for a little while, since it is needful, you are in sorrow under
various temptations; 7 that the trial of your faith, being much
more precious than gold, which perishes though it be tried by
fire, may be found to be for praise and honor and glory, at the
revelation of Jesus Christ; 8 whom, though you have not seen
him, yet you love; on whom not now looking, but believing, you
rejoice with joy unspeakable, and full of glory, 9 receiving the
end of your faith, the salvation of your souls.

10 Concerning which salvation the prophets that prophesied
of the grace that should be for you, did inquire, and search diligently, 11 inquiring what things, and what time, the Spirit of
Christ that was in them did signify, when it testified, beforehand, the sufferings of Christ, and the glories that should fol-

low them; 12 to whom it was revealed, that, not for themselves,
but for us, they ministered the things that are now preached to
you by those who have made known to you the gospel, through
the Holy Spirit sent down from heaven; into which things
angels desire to look.

13 Wherefore, gird up the loins of your mind; be watchful,
and hope constantly for the grace that is to be brought to you
at the revelation of Jesus Christ: 14 As obedient children, not
conforming yourselves to the desires which you formerly had in
your ignorance; 15 but as he who has called you is holy, so be
you holy in all your behavior: 16 because it is written, Be you
holy, for I am holy.

17 And since you call on the Father, who, without respect of
persons, judges according to every man's work, pass the time
of your sojourning in fear: 18 because you know that you were
not redeemed with corruptible things, as silver or gold, from
your vain mode of life received by tradition from your fathers,
19 but with the precious blood of Christ, as of a lamb without
spot and blemish, 20 who was indeed foreordained before the
foundation of the world, but manifested in these last times for
you, 21 who through him do believe in God who raised him from
the dead, and gave him glory, that your faith and hope might
be in God.

22 Having purified your souls in obeying the truth through
the Spirit, to unfeigned love of the brethren, love one another
with a pure heart fervently, 23 having been begotten again, not
with corruptible seed, but with incorruptible, by the word of
God, which lives and abides forever. 24 For all flesh is as grass,
and all the glory of man as the flower of grass; the grass withers,
and its flower falls away: but the word of the Lord abides forever: and this is the word which has been preached as gospel
to you.

II. 1 Therefore, laying aside all malice, and all guile, and
hypocricies, and envyings, and all evil speakings, 2 as new-born
babes, earnestly desire the pure spiritual milk, that you may
grow by it, 3 if, indeed, you have tasted that the Lord is gracious.

4 Coming to him as to a living stone, rejected indeed by man,
but in the sight of God, chosen and precious, 5 you, also, as living stones, are built up a spiritual house, a holy priesthood, that
you may offer up spiritual sacrifices, acceptable to God through

Jesus Christ. [6] For it is contained in the Scripture: Behold, I
lay in Zion a chief corner-stone, chosen, precious; and he that
believes on him shall not be ashamed. [7] To you, then, who believe, is this preciousness: but the stone which the builders
rejected, has become the head of the corner, [8] and a stone of
stumbling, and a rock of offense to the disobedient, who stumble
at the word because they are disobedient, to which stumbling
they were also appointed. [9] But you are a chosen race, a royal
priesthood, a holy nation, a purchased people, that you should
show forth the virtues of him who has called you out of darkness into his wonderful light: [10] who formerly were not a people,
but now are the people of God; who had not received mercy, but
now have received mercy.

[11] Beloved, I beseech you, as strangers and sojourners, that
you keep yourselves from fleshly desires, which war against the
soul, [12] maintaining an honorable mode of life among the Gentiles, that, inasmuch as they speak against you as evil-doers,
they may, on account of your good works which they witness,
glorify God in the day of visitation.

[13] Submit yourselves to every ordinance of man, for the Lord's
sake; whether it be to the king, as supreme ruler, [14] or to governors, as those sent by him for the punishment of evil-doers,
and for the praise of those who do well. [15] For such is the will
of God, that by doing good you may put to silence the ignorance
of foolish men; [16] as being free, and yet not using your freedom
as a cloak for malice, but as servants of God. [17] Honor all men;
love the brotherhood; reverence God; honor the king.

[18] Servants, be subject to your masters with all respect; not
only to the good and gentle, but also to the perverse. [19] For
this is praiseworthy, if any one, on account of conscience toward God, endure sorrows, suffering unjustly. [20] For what
praise is due, if, when you are punished for your faults, you
endure it patiently? But if, when you do well, and suffer for it,
you endure it patiently, this is praiseworthy in the sight of God.
[21] To this, indeed, you have been called; because even Christ suffered for us, leaving you an example, that you should follow his
footsteps. [22] He did no sin, nor was guile found in his mouth.
[23] When he was reviled, he did not revile again; when he suffered,
he did not threaten, but committed himself to him that judges
righteously. [24] He himself bore our sins in his own body on the
tree, that we, having died to sins, might live to righteousness.
By his stripes you were healed. [25] For you were like sheep that

had gone astray; but now you have returned to the shepherd
and bishop of your souls.

III. 1 Likewise, you wives, be in subjection to your own husbands; that, if any obey not the word, they may, without the
word, be won by the conduct of their wives, 2 by observing your
blameless and reverential conduct. 3 Let not your adorning be
that which is outward, which consists in plaiting the hair, and
wearing gold, and putting on apparel: 4 but let it be the hidden
man of the heart, adorned with the incorruptible ornament of
a meek and quiet spirit, which, in the sight of God, is of great
price. 5 For, in former times, the holy women also, who trusted
in God, thus adorned themselves, being in subjection to their
own husbands, 6 as Sarah obeyed Abraham, calling him lord:
and you are her children, if you do good, and fear no dismay.
7 Likewise, you husbands, dwell with them according to knowledge, bestowing honor on the wife as the weaker vessel, and as
being heirs together of the grace of life, in order that your
prayers may not be hindered.
8 Finally, be all of the same mind, be sympathizing, lovers of
the brethren, kind-hearted, humble-minded; 9 not repaying evil
for evil, nor reviling for reviling, but, on the other hand, blessing, since you know that for this end you were called, that you
might inherit blessing. 10 For he that will love life, and see
good days, let him keep his tongue from evil, and his lips from
speaking guile: 11 let him turn from evil and do good: let him
seek peace, and pursue it. 12 For the eyes of the Lord are upon
the righteous, and his ears are open to their cry: but the face
of the Lord is against those who do evil.
13 And who is he that will harm you, if you be followers of
that which is good? 14 But yet, if you even suffer for righteousness, happy are you. Yet fear not their terror, nor be
troubled: 15 but reverence the Lord God in your hearts, and be
always ready to answer every one that asks of you a reason for
the hope that is in you, with meekness and fear; 16 having a
good conscience, that, inasmuch as they speak against you as
evil-doers, they may be ashamed who traduce your good conduct in Christ.
17 For it is better, if such be the will of God, that you suffer
for doing good, than for doing evil. 18 For Christ also once suffered for sins, the Just for the unjust, that he might bring us to
God, having been put to death in flesh, but made alive in spirit;

19 in which also he went and preached to the spirits in prison,
20 who formerly were disobedient, when the long-suffering of
God waited in the days of Noah, while an ark was preparing,
in which few, that is, eight souls, were brought in safety through
the water; 21 the likeness of which, even immersion, (not the
putting away of the filth of the flesh, but the seeking of a good
conscience toward God,) does now also save us, through the
resurrection of Jesus Christ, 22 who has gone into heaven, and
is at the right hand of God, angels and authorities and powers
having become subject to him.

IV. 1 Since, then, Christ has suffered for us in the flesh, do
you also arm yourselves with the same determination; for he
that has suffered in the flesh has ceased from sin, 2 so that he no
longer lives the rest of his time in the flesh, according to the
desires of men, but according to the will of God. 3 For the time
past of our life should be enough for us to have worked the will
of the Gentiles, while we walked in licentiousness, lusts, drunkenness, revelings, drinkings, and unlawful idolatries. 4 They
are amazed at this—that you run not with them into the same
excess of debauchery, and they revile you. 5 These shall give
an account to him that is ready to judge the living and the dead.
6 For this cause, indeed, even those who have died had the gospel
preached to them, that though they might be judged according
to the will of men in the flesh, yet they might live according to
the will of God in the spirit.

7 But the end of all things is at hand; be sober-minded, therefore, and watchful, that you may pray. 8 But, above all things,
have fervent love one for another; for love will cover a multitude of sins. 9 Be hospitable, one to another, without murmuring. 10 As each has received a gift, minister the same one to
another, as good stewards of the manifold grace of God. 11 If
any man speaks, let him speak as the oracles of God: if any
man ministers, let him do this as from the strength which
God supplies; that in all things God may be glorified through
Jesus Christ, to whom be glory and strength from age to age.
Amen.

12 Beloved, be not amazed at the fiery trial that has come on
you to try you, as if some strange thing had happened to you.
13 But, inasmuch as you are partakers of the sufferings of the
Christ, rejoice, that, at the revelation of his glory, you may also
be exceedingly joyful. 14 If you are reproached on account of

Christ, happy are you: for the glorious Spirit of God rests upon
you. On their part he is reviled, but on your part he is glorified: 15 for no one of you should suffer as a murderer, or a thief,
or an evil-doer, or as a busybody in other men's matters. 16 But
if any one suffer as a Christian, let him not be ashamed, but let
him glorify God on this account. 17 For the time has come that
judgment must begin at the house of God; and if it begin first
at us, what shall be the end of those who obey not the gospel of
God? 18 And if the righteous man is hardly saved, where shall
the ungodly man and the sinner appear? 19 Wherefore, let those
also who suffer according to the will of God, by doing good,
commit their souls to him as to a faithful Creator.

V. 1 The elders that are among you I exhort, who am a fel-
low-elder, and a witness of the sufferings of the Christ, and a
sharer in the glory that is to be revealed. 2 Act as shepherds to
the flock of God which is among you, taking the oversight, not
by compulsion, but willingly; not for the sake of sordid gain,
but from readiness of mind: 3 neither as being lords over *God's*
possessions, but being examples to the flock. 4 And when the
chief shepherd shall appear, you shall receive the crown of glory
that fades not away.

5 Likewise, you younger, be in subjection to the older: do you
all indeed be subject one to another, and be clothed with humility: for God resists the proud, but gives grace to the lowly.
6 Humble yourselves, therefore, under the strong hand of God,
that he may exalt you in due season. 7 Cast all your cares on
him, for he cares for you.

8 Be sober, be watchful: for your adversary, the devil, like a
roaring lion, walks about, seeking whom he may devour. 9 Being
firm in the faith, resist him, knowing that the same afflictions
are accomplished in your brethren who are in the world.

10 But may the God of all grace, who has called us to his eternal
glory by Christ Jesus, after you have suffered a while, make you
perfect, establish, strengthen, confirm you. 11 To him be glory
and dominion from age to age. Amen.

12 By Sylvanus, a faithful brother to you, as I suppose, I have
written briefly, exhorting, and testifying that this is the true
grace of God in which you stand. 13 The church in Babylon,
elected together with you, salutes you, and so does Marcus my
son. 14 Salute one another with a kiss of love. Peace be with
you all that are in Christ Jesus.

SECOND LETTER OF PETER.

I. 1 SIMON PETER, a servant and apostle of Jesus Christ,
to those who have obtained faith, equally as precious
as our own, in the righteousness *revealed by* our God and Savior
Jesus Christ: 2 grace be to you, and peace be multiplied in the
acknowledgment of God, and Jesus our Lord.
3 As his divine power has given us all things that pertain to
life and godliness, through the acknowledgment of him who has
called us by his glorious power, 4 through which things very
great and precious favors that were promised have been given
us, that through these you may become partakers of the divine
nature, having escaped the corruption that is in the world
through desire: 5 so, even for this very purpose, uniting to these
things all diligence, add to your faith, virtue; and to virtue,
knowledge; 6 and to knowledge, temperance; and to temperance,
patience; and to patience, godliness; 7 and to godliness, brotherly kindness; and to brotherly kindness, love. 8 For if these
things be in you, and abound, they cause you to be neither idle,
nor unfruitful as it respects the acknowledgment of our Lord
Jesus Christ. 9 But he who is wanting in these things is blind,
and closes his eyes, and has forgotten that he was cleansed from
his old sins. 10 Wherefore, brethren, give the greater diligence
to make your calling and election sure: for if you do these
things, you will never fall. 11 For thus will an entrance be
given you abundantly into the eternal kingdom of our Lord and
Savior Jesus Christ.
12 Wherefore, I will not neglect to remind you always of these
things, though you know them, and are established in the present
truth. 13 Indeed, I think it right, as long as I am in this tabernacle, to arouse you by putting you in remembrance. 14 For I
know that the putting off of this my tabernacle is near at hand,
even as our Lord Jesus Christ showed me. 15 But I will earnestly
endeavor that you may be able, even after my decease, to have
these things always in remembrance.
16 For we did not follow cunningly devised fables, when we
made known to you the power and coming of our Lord Jesus
Christ; but we were eye-witnesses of his majesty. 17 For he received from God the Father honor and glory, when there came
to him from the magnificent glory a voice, such as this: This is
my beloved Son, in whom I delight. 18 And this voice, which

came from heaven, we heard when we were with him in the holy
mount; 19 and we have the prophetic word better established.
You do well to attend to this, as to a lamp that shines in a dark
place, till the day dawn, and the morning star arise in your
hearts; 20 knowing this first, that no prophecy of the Scripture
came from private interpretation: 21 for the prophecy came not
at any time by the will of man, but holy men of God spoke as
they were moved by the Holy Spirit.

II. 1 But there were false prophets among the people, as there
will be false teachers also among you; and these will stealthily
introduce ruinous sects, and deny the Lord that bought them,
bringing upon themselves swift destruction: 2 and many will
follow their dissolute ways, on account of whom the way of
truth will be reviled; 3 and, with delusive words, they will,
through covetousness, make gain of you: the condemnation,
long ago denounced against these, delays not, and their destruction does not slumber.
4 For if God spared not the angels that sinned, but cast them
down to Tartarus, and delivered them over to chains and darkness, to be kept for judgment; 5 and if he spared not the old
world, but brought a flood on the world of the ungodly, and
saved Noah, the eighth person, who was a preacher of righteousness; 6 and if, turning the cities of Sodom and Gomorrah into
ashes, he condemned them with an overthrow, making them an
example to those who should afterward live in an ungodly manner, 7 and delivered righteous Lot, wearied out with the licentious
conduct of the lawless,—8 for that righteous man dwelling among
them, in seeing and hearing, vexed his righteous soul from day
to day with their unlawful deeds: 9 *then*, the Lord knows how
to deliver the godly out of temptation, and to keep the ungodly
for the day of judgment, to be punished; 10 but especially those
who walk after the flesh in unclean lust, and who despise government. Presumptuous, willful men! they are not afraid to
speak evil of dignitaries: 11 whereas angels, who excel in might
and in power, bring no railing accusation against them in the
presence of the Lord. 12 But these men, like beasts without
reason, which follow the instinct of nature, and are made to be
taken and destroyed, speaking evil of things that they understand not, shall utterly perish in their own corruption, 13 and
receive the reward of unrighteousness. Counting it a pleasure
to riot in the day-time, they are spots and stains, rioting in

their delusions, while feasting with you; [14]having eyes that are
full of the adulteress, and that can not cease from sin, deceiving
unstable souls, having a heart exercised in covetousness, accursed children, [15]who have forsaken the right way and gone
astray, following the way of Balaam the son of Beor, who loved
the wages of unrighteousness; [16]but he was rebuked for his iniquity,—the dumb beast, speaking with man's voice, restrained
the madness of the prophet. [17]These men are fountains without
water, clouds driven by a tempest, for whom the gloom of darkness is reserved forever.

[18]For by speaking boastful words of folly, they allure through
the lusts of the flesh, and through lasciviousness, those who had
really escaped from those who live in error. [19]While they promise them freedom, they themselves are the servants of corruption: for by whatever any man is overcome, he is also enslaved.
[20]For if, after they have escaped the pollutions of the world,
through the knowledge of the Lord and Savior Jesus Christ,
they are again entangled in these, and overcome by them, the
last state of such is worse than the first. [21]For it would be
better for them not to have known the way of righteousness,
than, after having known it, to turn from the holy commandment delivered to them. [22]But it has happened to them according to the true proverb: The dog has turned again to his own
vomit; and, The sow that was washed, to her wallowing in the
mire.

III. [1]This second letter I now write to you, beloved; in both
of these I arouse your pure mind to remembrance, [2]that you
may be mindful of the words formerly spoken by the holy
prophets, and of the commandment of us the apostles of the
Lord and Savior: [3]knowing this first, that there will come in
the last days scoffers, walking after their own lusts, [4]and saying: Where is the promise of his coming? for since the fathers
fell asleep, all things continue as they were from the beginning
of the creation.

[5]For they are willingly ignorant of this, that by the word of
God, the heavens of old had their being, as also the earth con-
sisting of water and subsisting by water, [6]by which things the
world that then was, having been overflowed with water, perished. [7]But the heavens and the earth that now are, by the
same word are kept in store, reserved for fire against the day
of judgment, and perdition of ungodly men.

8 But, beloved, be not ignorant of this one thing, that one day
with the Lord is as a thousand years, and a thousand years as
one day. 9 The Lord does not delay concerning his promise, as
some men count delay, but he is long-suffering toward us, not
wishing that any should perish, but that all should come to repentance. 10 But the day of the Lord will come as a thief, in
which the heavens shall pass away with a great noise, and the
elements shall melt with fervent heat, and the earth, and the
works that are on it, shall be burned up.

11 Seeing, then, that all these things shall be dissolved, what
sort of persons ought you to be in all holy behavior, and godliness, 12 looking for and earnestly desiring the coming of the day
of God, because of which coming the heavens shall dissolve in
fire, and the elements shall melt with fervent heat. 13 But we,
according to his promise, look for new heavens and a new earth,
in which dwells righteousness.

14 Wherefore, beloved, seeing that you expect such things, earnestly strive, by being spotless and blameless, to be found by
him in peace: 15 and count the long-suffering of our Lord, salvation, even as our beloved brother Paul, according to the wisdom given him, has written to you; 16 as also in all his letters,
speaking in them of these things, in which are some things hard
to be understood, which the unlearned and unstable wrest, as
they do also the other Scriptures, to their own destruction.

17 Do you, therefore, beloved, since you know these things beforehand, beware, lest, being led away with the error of the
wicked, you fall from your own steadfastness. 18 But grow in
grace, and in the knowledge of our Lord and Savior Jesus
Christ. To him be glory both now and to the day of eternity.
Amen.

FIRST LETTER OF JOHN.

I. 1 THAT which was from the beginning, which we have
heard, which we have seen with our eyes, which we
have looked upon, and our hands have handled concerning the
Word of life; (2 the life also was manifested, and we have seen,
and do testify, and declare to you that eternal life, which was
with the Father, and was manifested to us;) 3 that which we
have seen and heard, we declare it to you, that you also may
have fellowship with us: and truly our fellowship is with the

Father, and with his Son Jesus Christ. 4 And these things we
write to you, that your joy may be full.
5 And this is the message that we heard from him, and do declare to you : that God is light, and in him is no darkness at all.
6 If we say that we have fellowship with him, and walk in darkness, we lie, and do not the truth. 7 But if we walk in the
light, as he is in the light, we have fellowship one with another, and the blood of Jesus Christ his Son cleanses us from
all sin.
8 If we say that we have no sin, we deceive ourselves, and the
truth is not in us. 9 If we confess our sins, he is faithful and
just, so that he will forgive us our sins, and cleanse us from all
unrighteousness. 10 If we say that we have not sinned, we make
him a liar, and his word is not in us.

II. 1 My little children, I write these things to you, that you
may not sin : and yet, if any one sin, we have an advocate with
the Father, Jesus Christ the righteous. 2 And he is the expiation for our sins : not for ours only, but for the sins of the whole
world.
3 And by this we know that we do know him, if we keep his
commandments. 4 He that says, I know him, and keeps not his
commandments, is a liar, and the truth is not in him. 5 But
whoever keeps his word, in him truly is the love of God perfected: by this we know that we are in him. 6 He that says,
he abides in him, ought himself also so to walk, even as he
walked.
7 Beloved, I write no new commandment to you, but an old
commandment, which you have had from the beginning: the
old commandment is the word, which you have heard from the
beginning. 8 Again, a new commandment I do write to you,
which is true as it respects him and you; because the darkness
is past, and the true light now shines.
9 He that says he is in the light, and hates his brother, is in
darkness till now. 10 He that loves his brother abides in the
light, and there is in him no cause for offense. 11 He that hates
his brother is in darkness, and walks in darkness; and he
knows not whither he goes, because darkness has blinded his
eyes.
12 I write to you, little children, because your sins are forgiven for his name's sake. 13 I write to you, fathers, because you
have known him that is from the beginning. I write to you,

young men, because you have overcome the wicked one. I write to you, my little children, because you have known the Father. 14 I have written to you, fathers, because you have known him that is from the beginning. I have written to you, young men, because you are strong, and the word of God abides in you, and you have overcome the wicked one. 15 Love not the world, nor the things that are in the world. If any man loves the world, the love of the Father is not in him. 16 For all that is in the world, the desire of the flesh, and the desire of the eyes, and the pride of life, is not of the Father, but is of the world. 17 And the world and its desire passes away: but he that does the will of God, abides forever.

18 Little children, it is the last time; and, as you have heard that the antichrist is coming, even now there are many antichrists; by which we know that it is the last time. 19 They went out from us, but they were not of us: for, if they had been of us, they would have remained with us; but they went out, that they might be made manifest that they were, all, not of us. 20 And you have an anointing from the Holy One, and know all things. 21 I have not written to you because you do not know the truth, but because you know it, and because no lie is of the truth. 22 Who is a liar, but he that denies that Jesus is the Christ? He is antichrist, who denies the Father and the Son. 23 Whoever denies the Son, has not the Father: he that confesses the Son, has the Father also.

24 Let that, therefore, abide in you which you have heard from the beginning. If that abide in you which you have heard from the beginning, you also shall abide in the Son and in the Father. 25 And this is the promise which he has promised us, even eternal life. 26 I have written these things to you concerning those who deceive you. 27 And the anointing which you have received from him abides in you; and you have no need that any one should teach you: but, as the same anointing teaches you concerning all things, and is true and is no lie, even as it has taught you, abide in it.

28 And now, little children, abide in him, that when he appears, we may have confidence, and may not be made ashamed by him at his coming. 29 If you know that he is righteous, you know that every one that works righteousness has been begotten by him.

III. 1 Behold, how great love the Father has bestowed on us, that we should be called the children of God! For this reason,

the world knows us not, because it knew him not. 2 Beloved,
now are we the children of God, and it does not yet appear
what we shall be: but we know that, when he shall appear, we
shall be like him; for we shall see him as he is. 3 And every
one that has this hope in him purifies himself, even as He is
pure. 4 Every one that works sin, works also transgression of
law: and sin is transgression of law. 5 And you know that he
was manifested, that he might take away our sins; and in him
there is no sin. 6 Whoever abides in him, sins not. Whoever
sins, has neither seen him nor known him.

7 Little children, let no one deceive you: he that works righteousness is righteous, even as he is righteous. 8 He that works
sin is of the devil, for the devil sins from the beginning: for
this purpose was the son of God manifested, that he might destroy the works of the devil. 9 Whoever has been begotten of
God does not work sin; because his seed remains in him: and
he can not sin, because he has been begotten of God. 10 By this
the children of God are manifest, and the children of the devil.
Whoever does not work righteousness is not of God; neither is
he that loves not his brother. 11 For this is the message that
you have heard from the beginning, that we should love one
another. 12 Not as Cain, who was of the wicked one, and slew
his brother: and for what reason did he slay him? because his
own works were evil, and his brother's, righteous. 13 Wonder
not, my brethren, if the world hates you. 14 We know that we
have passed from death to life, because we love the brethren:
he that loves not his brother, abides in death. 15 Whoever hates
his brother is a murderer: and you know that no murderer has
eternal life abiding in him.

16 By this we know the love of *Christ*, because he laid down his
life for us: and we ought to lay down our lives for the brethren.
17 Whoever has this world's goods, and sees his brother have
need, and shuts his heart against him, how dwells the love of
God in him? 18 My little children, let us not love in word, nor
in tongue, but in deed, and in truth. 19 And by this we know
that we are of the truth; and we shall have our hearts at rest
before him: 20 for if our heart condemn us, *we know* that God is
greater than our heart, and knows all things. 21 Beloved, if our
heart condemn us not, we have confidence toward God, 22 and
whatever we ask, we receive from him, because we keep his commandments, and do the things that are pleasing in his sight.
23 And this is his commandment: That we should believe on the

name of his Son Jesus Christ, and love one another, as he gave
us commandment. 24 And he that keeps his commandments
abides in him, and he in him. And by this we know that he
abides in us, by the Spirit which he has given us.

IV. 1 Beloved, believe not every spirit; but prove the spirits,
whether they are from God: for many false prophets have gone
out into the world. 2 By this you know the Spirit of God: every
spirit that confesses that Jesus Christ came in the flesh, is from
God: 3 and whatever spirit confesses not that Jesus Christ came
in the flesh, is not from God: and this is the spirit of antichrist,
of which you have heard that it comes, and is now already in
the world. 4 You are of God, little children, and have overcome
them; because he that is in you, is greater than he that is in
the world. 5 They are of the world: therefore, they speak of
the world, and the world hears them. 6 We are of God: he that
knows God, hears us: he that is not of God, does not hear us:
by this we know the spirit of truth, and the spirit of error.

7 Beloved, let us love one another; for love is of God: and
every one that loves, has been begotten of God, and knows God.
8 He that loves not, does not know God; for God is love. 9 In
this the love of God was manifested toward us, that God sent
his only-begotten Son into the world, that we might live through
him. 10 In this is love; not that we loved God, but that he loved
us, and sent his Son to be the expiation for our sins. 11 Beloved,
if God so loved us, we also ought to love one another. 12 No one
has seen God at any time. If we love one another, God dwells in
us, and his love is perfected in us. 13 By this we know that we
dwell in him, and he in us, because he has given us of his Spirit.

14 And we have seen, and we do testify, that the Father sent
the Son to be the Savior of the world. 15 Whoever confesses that
Jesus is the Son of God, God dwells in him, and he in God.
16 And we have known and believed the love which God has for
us. God is love; and he that dwells in love, dwells in God, and
God in him. 17 By this is our love made perfect, that we may
have boldness in the day of judgment; because, as he is, so are
we in this world. 18 There is no fear in love; but perfect love
casts out fear, because fear has torment: he that fears is not
made perfect in love. 19 We love him, because he first loved us.

20 If any man say, I love God, and yet hate his brother, he is a liar:
for he that loves not his brother, whom he has seen, how can he love
God, whom he has not seen? 21 And this commandment we have
from him: That he that loves God, must love his brother also.

V. 1 Whoever believes that Jesus is the Christ, has been begotten of God: and every one that loves him that begot, loves
him also that is begotten of him. 2 By this we know that we
love the children of God, when we love God, and keep his commandments. 3 For this is the love of God, that we keep his commandments; and his commandments are not burdensome. 4 For
whatever is begotten of God, overcomes the world; and this is
the victorious principle that overcomes the world, even our faith.
5 Who is he that overcomes the world, but he that believes that
Jesus is the Son of God?

6 This is he that came by water and by blood, Jesus the Christ;
not by water only, but by water and by blood: and it is the
Spirit that testifies, because the Spirit is truth. 7 For there are
three that testify, the Spirit, and the water, and the blood;
8 and the three agree in one. 9 If we receive the testimony of
men, the testimony of God is greater: for this is the testimony
of God, which he has borne concerning his Son. 10 He that believes on the Son of God has the testimony in himself: he that
believes not God, has made him a liar, because he has not believed
the testimony which God has borne concerning his Son. 11 And
this is the testimony, that God has given us eternal life: and
this life is in his Son. 12 He that has the Son, has life: he that
has not the Son of God, has not life.

13 I have written these things to you that believe on the name
of the Son of God, that you may know that you have eternal
life, and that you may believe on the name of the Son of God.
14 And this is the confidence that we have toward him, that if
we ask any thing according to his will, he hears us. 15 And if
we know that he hears us, whatever we ask, we know that we
have the petitions which we have asked of him. 16 If any one
see his brother sinning a sin not to death, he shall ask, and he
will give him life for those who sin not to death. There is a sin
to death: I do not say concerning this, that he should ask.
17 All unrighteousness is sin; and there is a sin not to death.
18 We know that whoever has been begotten of God, does not sin:
but he that is begotten of God, keeps himself, and the wicked
one touches him not. 19 We know that we are of God, and the
whole world lies under the wicked one. 20 And we know that
the Son of God has come, and has given us understanding, that
we may know him that is true: and we are in him that is true,
in his Son Jesus Christ. This is the true God, and life eternal.
Little children, keep yourselves from idols.

SECOND LETTER OF JOHN.

1 THE elder to the elect lady, and to her children, whom I love
in the truth: and not I only, but also all who know the
truth; 2 *we all love you*, on account of the truth that dwells in
us, and which will be with us forever: 3 grace be with you,
mercy and peace from God the Father, and from the Lord Jesus
Christ, the Son of the Father, in truth and love. 4 I rejoiced
greatly because I found some of your children walking in the
truth, as we received commandment from the Father. 5 And
now I beseech you, lady, not as though I wrote a new commandment
to you, but that which we had from the beginning,
that we love one another. 6 And this is love, that we walk according
to his commandments. This is the commandment, as
you have heard from the beginning, that you should walk in it.
7 For many deceivers have entered into the world, who confess
not that Jesus Christ came in the flesh: this is the deceiver
and the antichrist. 8 Look to yourselves, that we lose not the
things that we have gained, but that we receive a full reward.
9 Whoever transgresses, and abides not in the teaching of the
Christ, has not God: he that abides in the teaching of the Christ,
has both the Father and the Son. 10 If any one comes to you,
and brings not this teaching, receive him not into your house,
and do not wish him well: 11 for he that wishes him well, is partaker
of his evil deeds.
12 Though I have many things to write to you, I determined
not to communicate them by means of paper and ink: for I
hope to come to you, and to speak mouth to mouth, that our joy
may be full. 13 The children of your elect sister greet you.

THIRD LETTER OF JOHN.

1 THE elder to the beloved Gaius, whom I love in the truth.
2 Beloved, I pray above all things that you may prosper
and be in health, even as your soul prospers. 3 For I rejoiced
greatly when the brethren came and testified to the truth that
is in you, even as you walk in the truth. 4 I have no greater
joy than to hear that my children walk in the truth.
5 Beloved, you do faithfully whatever you do to the brethren, and
to strangers, 6 who have testified to your love before the church:

if you conduct these on their journey, in a manner worthy of
God, you will do well: [7] for, on account of his name, they went
out, taking nothing from the Gentiles. [8] We, therefore, ought
to receive such, that we may be fellow-helpers to the truth.

[9] I wrote to the church; but Diotrephes, who loves to have
the pre-eminence among them, receives us not. [10] Therefore, if
I come, I will remember his works which he does, prating
against us with malicious words: and not content with these
things, he does not himself receive the brethren, but both for-
bids those who are willing, and casts them out of the church.
[11] Beloved, do not imitate that which is evil, but that which is
good. He that does good is of God: he that does evil has not
seen God. [12] A good report is given of Demetrius by all, and
by the truth itself: and we also give our testimony, and you
know that our testimony is true.

[13] I had many things to write, but I will not communicate
them to you with ink and pen. [14] But I trust that I shall
shortly see you, and we will speak mouth to mouth. [15] Peace
be to you. Our friends *here* salute you. Salute our friends *with
you* by name.

LETTER OF JUDE.

[1] JUDE, a servant of Jesus Christ, and brother of James, to
those who are sanctified in God the Father, and preserved
in Jesus Christ, and called: [2] mercy be to you, and peace and
love be multiplied.

[3] Beloved, using all diligence to write to you of the common
salvation, I thought it necessary to write to you, and exhort
you to contend earnestly for the faith once delivered to the
saints. [4] For some men have stealthily entered in, who were
long ago appointed to this condemnation; ungodly men, who
pervert the grace of our God, and use it for lascivious purposes,
and deny our only Sovereign and Lord, Jesus Christ.

[5] But I wish to remind you, though you once knew this, that
the Lord, having saved the people from the land of Egypt, then
destroyed those who believed not. [6] The angels also that kept
not their own dominion, but left their proper habitation, he has
reserved, in eternal chains under darkness, to the judgment of
the great day. [7] So Sodom and Gomorrah, and the cities which
were about them, in like manner giving themselves over to lewd-

ness, and following after other flesh, are set forth as an example, suffering the punishment of eternal fire. 8 Yet, these dreamers also in like manner defile the flesh, despise government, and speak evil of dignitaries. 9 But Michael the archangel, when, contending with the devil, he disputed about the body of Moses, durst not bring a railing accusation, but said: The Lord rebuke you. 10 But these speak evil of the things which they know not: and those things which they know naturally, as animals without reason, in these they corrupt themselves. 11 Alas for them! for they have gone in the way of Cain: and, in the error of Balaam, they have rushed headlong after reward, and have perished in the rebellion of Korah.

12 These, while feasting with you, are spots in your love-feasts, feeding themselves without fear; they are clouds without water, driven along by winds; trees of autumn, without fruit, twice dead, torn up by the roots: 13 raging waves of the sea, foaming up their own shame: wandering stars, for whom the blackness of darkness is reserved forever. 14 And Enoch, the seventh from Adam, also prophesied with reference to these men, saying: Behold, the Lord comes with his holy myriads, 15 to execute judgment upon all, and to convict all the ungodly of all their ungodly works, which they have impiously committed, and of all the hard words which ungodly sinners have spoken against him. 16 These are murmurers, fault-finders, walking according to their own desires; and their mouth speaks boastful words, while they admire persons for the sake of gain.

17 But do you, beloved, remember the words that were formerly spoken by the apostles of our Lord Jesus Christ; 18 that they said to you, There should come, in the last days, scoffers walking according to their own ungodly desires. 19 These are they who separate themselves, animal, not having the Spirit.

20 But you, beloved, building yourselves up on your most holy faith, praying in the Holy Spirit, 21 keep yourselves in the love of God, looking for the mercy of our Lord Jesus Christ, in order to eternal life. 22 And on some, have compassion, making a distinction: 23 and others, save by fear, snatching them from the fire, hating even the garment spotted by the flesh.

24 Now to him that is able to keep you free from stumbling, and to present you blameless in the presence of his glory with exceeding joy, to the only God our Savior, be glory and majesty, strength and authority, both now and throughout all the ages. Amen.

THE REVELATION.

I. 1 THE Revelation of Jesus Christ, which God gave to him,
that he might show to his servants the things that
must shortly come to pass; and he sent it by his angel, and
made it known to his servant John, 2 who bore testimony to the
word of God, and recorded the testimony of Jesus Christ, whatever things he saw. 3 Blessed is he that reads, and those who
hear the words of this prophecy, and keep the things that are
written in it; for the time is at hand.

4 John to the seven churches that are in Asia, grace be to you
and peace from him who is, and who was, and who is to come;
and from the seven spirits which are before his throne; 5 and
from Jesus Christ, who is the faithful witness, the first born
from the dead, and the Prince of the kings of the earth. To
him that loves us, and that has washed us from our sins in his
own blood, 6 and has made us a kingdom, priests to his God and
Father; to him be glory and might from age to age. Amen.

7 Behold, he comes with clouds, and every eye shall see him,
and those also who pierced him: and all the tribes of the land
shall lament because of him. Even so. Amen. 8 I am the
Alpha and the Omega, says the Lord God, who is, and who was,
and who is to come, the Almighty.

9 I John, your brother and companion in the affliction, and
in the kingdom and patience of Jesus Christ, was in the island
called Patmos, on account of the word of God, and on account
of the testimony of Jesus Christ. 10 I was in spirit on the
Lord's day, and I heard behind me a great voice like that of a
trumpet, 11 saying: What you see, write in a book, and send to
the seven churches; to Ephesus, and to Smyrna, and to Pergamos, and to Thyatira, and to Sardis, and to Philadelphia, and to
Laodicea.

12 And I turned to see the voice that spoke with me: and having turned, I saw seven golden candlesticks, 13 and in the midst
of the seven candlesticks, one like the Son of man, clothed in a
robe reaching to his feet, and girded about the breast with a
golden girdle. 14 His head and his hair were white as white
wool, as white as snow; and his eyes were as a flame of fire;
15 and his feet were like fine brass, as if they burned in a furnace: and his voice was like the voice of many waters. 16 And
he had in his right hand seven stars; and out of his mouth went

a sharp, two-edged sword: and his face was as the sun when it
shines in its strength.

17 And when I saw him, I fell at his feet as dead; and he laid
his right hand upon me, saying: Fear not, I am the First and
the Last, 18 and I am he that lives; and I was dead, and behold,
I am alive from age to age: and I have the keys of hades and
of death. 19 Write, therefore, the things which you have seen,
and the things which are, and those which shall be hereafter;
20 the mystery of the seven stars which you saw in my right
hand, and the seven golden candlesticks. The seven stars are
the angels of the seven churches; and the seven candlesticks
are the seven churches.

II. 1 To the angel of the church in Ephesus, write: These
things says he that holds the seven stars in his right hand, that
walks in the midst of the seven golden candlesticks; 2 I know
your works, and your labor, and your patience; and that you
can not bear with those who are evil, and that you have tried
those who say they are apostles, and are not, and have found
them liars; 3 and that you have patience, and have endured for
my name's sake, and have not fainted. 4 But I have this against
you, that you have left your first love. 5 Remember, therefore,
whence you have fallen, and repent, and do your first works;
if not, I will come to you quickly, and I will remove your candlestick from its place, unless you repent. 6 But you have this,
that you hate the works of the Nicolaitanes, which I also
hate.

7 He that has an ear, let him hear what the Spirit says to the
churches: To him that overcomes, I will give to eat of the tree
of life, which is in the paradise of God.

8 And to the angel of the church in Smyrna, write: These
things says the First and the Last, who was dead, and is alive:
9 I know your works, and your affliction, and your poverty, (but
you are rich,) and the impious words of those who say they are
Jews, and are not, but are the synagogue of Satan. 10 Fear
none of the things which you are about to suffer; behold, the
devil will throw some of you into prison, that you may be tried:
and you shall have affliction ten days. Be faithful till death,
and I will give you the crown of life.

11 He that has an ear, let him hear what the Spirit says to the
churches. He that overcomes shall not be hurt by the second
death.

12 And to the angel of the church in Pergamos, write: These
things says he that has the sharp, two-edged sword: 13 I know
your works, and where you dwell, even where the throne of
Satan is: and yet you hold fast my name, and have not denied
my faith, even in those days in which Antipas was my faithful
witness, who was slain among you, where Satan dwells. 14 Yet
I have a few things against you, that you have there those who
hold the teaching of Balaam, who taught Balak to put a stumbling-block before the sons of Israel, to eat things sacrificed to
idols, and to practice lewdness. 15 So, also, you have those who
hold the teaching of the Nicolaitanes. 16 Repent, therefore; if
not, I will come to you quickly, and I will fight against them
with the sword of my mouth.

17 He that has an ear, let him hear what the Spirit says to
the churches. To him that overcomes, I will give of the hidden
manna; and I will give him a white stone, and on the stone a
new name written, which no one knows but he that receives it.

18 And to the angel of the church in Thyatira, write: These
things, says the Son of God, who has his eyes like a flame of fire,
and his feet like fine brass; 19 I know your works, and your love,
and your faith, and your service, and your patience, and your
works, the last greater than the first. 20 But I have against
you that you suffer that woman Jezebel, who calls herself a
prophetess, and teaches and deceives my servants to practice
lewdness, and to eat things sacrificed to idols. 21 And I have
given her time to repent; and she will not repent of her lewdness. 22 Behold, I will cast her into a bed, and those who commit
adultery with her into great affliction, unless they repent of
their deeds. 23 And I will kill her children with death; and all
the churches shall know that I am he that searches the reins
and the hearts: and I will give to every one of you according
to your works. 24 But I say to you, the rest who are in Thyatira, as many as have not this teaching, and who have not
known the depths of Satan, (as they call them,) I will lay on
you no other burden: 25 but what you have, hold fast till I
come.

26 And to him that overcomes, and keeps my works to the end,
will I give authority over the nations; 27 and he shall rule them
with a rod of iron; as the vessels of a potter shall they be broken
in pieces, as I have received from my Father: 28 and I will give
him the morning star. 29 He that has an ear, let him hear what
the Spirit says to the churches.

III. 1 And to the angel of the church in Sardis, write: These
things says he that has the seven spirits of God, and the seven
stars; I know your works, that you have a name, that you live,
and are dead. 2 Be watchful, and strengthen the things that
remain, which are about to die; for I have not found your works
perfect before God. 3 Remember, therefore, how you have received and heard, and be watchful and repent. If, therefore,
you do not watch, I will come upon you as a thief, and you
shall not know at what hour I will come upon you. 4 Yet you
have a few names in Sardis that have not defiled their garments;
and they shall walk with me in white, for they are worthy.

5 He that overcomes, shall be clothed in white raiment; and
I will not blot his name out of the book of life: and I will confess his name before my Father, and before his angels. 6 He
that has an ear, let him hear what the Spirit says to the
churches.

7 And to the angel of the church in Philadelphia, write: These
things says he that is holy, he that is true, he that has the key
of David, he that opens and no man shuts, and shuts and no
man opens; 8 I know your works: behold, I have set before you
an open door that no one is able to shut, because you have a
little strength, and have kept my word, and have not denied
my name. 9 Behold, I will make those who are of the synagogue of Satan, who say they are Jews, and are not, but do lie;
behold, I will make them come and worship before your feet,
and know that I have loved you. 10 Because you have kept the
word of my patience, I also will keep you from the hour of trial
that is about to come on the whole world, to try those who
dwell on the earth. 11 I come quickly: hold fast that which
you have, that no one take your crown.

12 Him that overcomes, I will make a pillar in the temple of
my God, and he shall go out no more; and I will write upon
him the name of my God, and the name of the city of my God,
the new Jerusalem, which comes down out of heaven from my
God, and I will write upon him my new name. 13 He that has
an ear, let him hear what the Spirit says to the churches.

14 And to the angel of the church in Laodicea, write: These
things says the Amen, the faithful and true witness, the beginning of the creation of God; 15 I know your works, that you
are neither cold, nor hot: I wish that you were cold, or hot.
16 So, then, because you are lukewarm, and neither cold nor hot,
I will vomit you out of my mouth. 17 Because you say I am

rich, and abound in wealth, and have need of nothing, and know
not that you are miserable and pitiable and poor and blind and
naked, 18 I counsel you to buy of me gold that has been tried in
the fire, that you may be rich; and white raiment, that you may
be clothed, and that the shame of your nakedness may not appear; and anoint your eyes with eye-salve, that you may see.
19 As many as I love, I rebuke and chasten; be zealous, therefore, and repent. 20 Behold, I stand at the door and knock; if
any one hear my voice, and open the door, I will come in to him,
and will sup with him, and he with me.

21 To him that overcomes, I will give to sit with me in my
throne, even as I also have overcome, and have taken my seat
with my Father in his throne. 22 He that has an ear, let him
hear what the Spirit says to the churches.

IV. 1 After these things I saw, and behold, a door was opened
in heaven; and the first voice which I heard, like the voice of a
trumpet speaking with me, said: Come up hither, and I will
show you things that must be hereafter.

2 And immediately I was in spirit; and behold, a throne was
set in heaven, and one sat on the throne; 3 and he that sat was,
in appearance, like a jasper and sardine-stone: and there was
round about the throne a rainbow, in appearance like an emerald. 4 And round about the throne were twenty-four thrones;
and on the thrones there sat twenty-four elders, clothed in white
raiment; and on their heads were crowns of gold. 5 And out
of the throne there went lightnings and thunderings and voices;
and seven lamps of fire were burning before the throne: these
are the seven spirits of God. 6 And before the throne there was
a sea of glass, like crystal. And in the midst of the throne, and
round about the throne, were four living creatures full of eyes
before and behind. 7 And the first living creature was like a
lion, and the second living creature was like a calf, and the
third living creature had the face of a man, and the fourth
living creature was like a flying eagle.

8 And the four living creatures had each of them six wings
about him; and they are full of eyes within; and they have no
rest day and night, saying, Holy, holy, holy is the Lord God, the
Almighty, who was, and is, and is to come. 9 And when the living creatures give glory and honor and thanks to him that sits
on the throne, who lives from age to age, 10 the twenty-four
elders fall down before him that sits on the throne, and worship

him that lives from age to age, and throw their crowns before
the throne, saying: Thou art worthy, O Lord, to receive glory
and honor and power: for thou hast created all things, and by
thy will they exist, and were created.

V. 1 And I saw in the right hand of him that sits on the
throne, a book written within and without, sealed with seven
seals. 2 And I saw a strong angel crying with a great voice:
Who is worthy to open the book, and to break its seals? 3 And
no one in heaven, or on earth, or under the earth, was able to
open the book, or to look upon it. 4 And I wept much, because
no one was found worthy to open the book, or to look upon it.
5 And one of the elders said to me: Weep not: behold, the Lion
of the tribe of Judah, the root of David, has the power to open
the book and its seven seals.

6 And I saw in the midst of the throne, and of the four living
creatures, and in the midst of the elders, a Lamb standing, like
one that had been slain, having seven horns and seven eyes,
which are the seven spirits of God that are sent into all the
earth. 7 And he came, and took the book out of the right hand
of him that sits on the throne. 8 And when he had taken the
book, the four living creatures, and the twenty-four elders fell
down before the Lamb, having, each of them, harps, and golden
cups full of incense, which is the prayers of the saints. 9 And
they sung a new song, saying:

Thou art worthy to take the book, and to open its seals: for
thou wast slain, and hast redeemed us to God by thy blood, out
of every tribe and tongue and people and nation: 10 and hast
made us to our God kings and priests, and we shall reign on the
earth.

11 And I saw, and I heard the voice of many angels round
about the throne and the living creatures and the elders; and
the number of them was myriads of myriads, and thousands of
thousands. 12 And they said, with a loud voice: Worthy is the
Lamb that was slain, to receive power and riches and wisdom
and strength and honor and glory and blessing. 13 And every
creature that is in heaven, and on the earth, and under the
earth, and such as are on the sea, even all that are in them, I
heard saying: To him that sits on the throne, and to the Lamb,
be blessing and honor and glory and strength from age to age.
14 And the four living creatures said, Amen; and the elders fell
down, and worshiped.

VI. 1 And I saw when the Lamb opened the first of the seven
seals, and I heard one of the four living creatures saying, with
a voice like thunder, Come and see. 2 And I saw, and behold,
a white horse, and he that sat on him had a bow; and a crown
was given to him; and he went forth conquering, and to conquer.
3 And when he had opened the second seal, I heard the second
living creature say, Come and see. 4 And there went forth another horse, which was red; and to him that sat on him was
given to take peace from the earth, and that they should kill
one another; and there was given to him a great sword.
5 And when he had opened the third seal, I heard the third
living creature say, Come and see. And I saw, and behold, a
black horse; and he that sat on him had a pair of scales in his
hand. 6 And I heard a voice in the midst of the four living
creatures, saying: A chœnix of wheat for a denarius, and three
chœnices of barley for a denarius; and as to the oil and the
wine, see that you do no injustice.
7 And when he had opened the fourth seal, I heard the voice
of the fourth living creature say, Come and see. 8 And I saw,
and behold, a pale horse; and the name of him that sat upon
him was Death: and Hades followed with him. And authority
was given to him over the fourth part of the earth, to kill with
the sword, and with famine, and with death, and with the
beasts of the earth.
9 And when he had opened the fifth seal, I saw under the altar
the souls of those who had been slain for the word of God, and
for the testimony which they had borne: 10 and they cried with
a loud voice, saying: How long, O Sovereign, holy and true,
dost thou not judge and avenge our blood on them that dwell on
the earth? 11 And a white robe was given to each of them: and
it was said to them, that they should yet rest for a time, till the
number of their fellow-servants, and of their brethren, who
should be killed as they had been, should be completed.
12 And I saw when he had opened the sixth seal; and there
was a great earthquake, and the sun became black as sackcloth
of hair, and the moon became like blood: 13 and the stars of
heaven fell to the earth, as a fig-tree casts its unripe figs when
shaken by a violent wind: 14 and the heaven departed as a volume when it is rolled up, and every mountain and island was
moved out of its place: 15 and the kings of the earth, and the
great men, and the officers, and the rich men, and the mighty
men, and every bondman, and every freeman, hid themselves in

the caves, and in the rocks of the mountains, 16 and said to the
mountains and to the rocks, Fall on us, and hide us from the
face of him that sits on the throne, and from the wrath of the
Lamb: 17 for the great day of his wrath has come, and who is
able to stand?

VII. 1 And after this I saw four angels standing on the four
corners of the earth, holding the four winds of the earth, that
the wind might not blow on the earth, nor on the sea, nor on
any tree. 2 And I saw another angel ascending from the east,
having the seal of the living God: and he cried with a loud
voice to the four angels, to whom it was given to hurt the earth
and the sea, 3 saying: Hurt not the earth, nor the sea, nor the
trees, till we have sealed the servants of our God on their foreheads.

4 And I heard the number of those who were sealed: a hundred and forty-four thousand were sealed out of all the tribes
of the sons of Israel. 5 Of the tribe of Judah, twelve thousand
were sealed: of the tribe of Reuben, twelve thousand were
sealed: of the tribe of Gad, twelve thousand were sealed: 6 of
the tribe of Asher, twelve thousand were sealed: of the tribe of
Naphtali, twelve thousand were sealed: of the tribe of Manasseh, twelve thousand were sealed: 7 of the tribe of Simeon,
twelve thousand were sealed: of the tribe of Levi, twelve thousand were sealed: of the tribe of Issachar, twelve thousand were
sealed: 8 of the tribe of Zabulon, twelve thousand were sealed:
of the tribe of Joseph, twelve thousand were sealed: of the tribe
of Benjamin, twelve thousand were sealed.

9 After this I saw, and behold, a great multitude, that no one
could number, out of all nations and tribes and peoples and
tongues, standing before the throne, and before the Lamb, clothed
with white robes, and there were palms in their hands; 10 and
they cried with a loud voice, saying: Salvation to our God, who
sits on the throne, and to the Lamb. 11 And all the angels
stood round about the throne and the elders and the four living
creatures; and they fell on their faces before the throne, and
worshiped God, 12 saying, Amen: blessing and glory and wisdom
and thanks and honor and power and strength be to our God
from age to age. Amen.

13 And one of the elders answered, and said to me: Who are
these that are clothed in white robes, and whence came they?
14 And I said to him: Sir, thou knowest. And he said to me:

These are they who have come out of great affliction, and have
washed their robes, and made them white in the blood of the
Lamb. 15 Therefore, they are before the throne of God, and
serve him day and night in his temple; and he that sits on the
throne shall dwell among them. 16 They shall hunger no more,
nor shall they thirst any more, nor shall the sun fall upon them,
nor any heat. 17 For the Lamb that is in the midst of the throne
will be their shepherd, and will lead them to living fountains
of water: and God will wipe away every tear from their eyes.

VIII. 1 And when he had opened the seventh seal, there was
silence in heaven for about half an hour.

2 And I saw the seven angels that stood before God, and seven
trumpets were given to them. 3 And another angel came, and
stood at the altar, having a golden censer; and much incense
was given to him, that he might offer it with the prayers of all
the saints upon the golden altar that is before the throne.
4 And the smoke of the incense, with the prayers of the saints,
ascended before God out of the hand of the angel. 5 And the
angel took the censer, and filled it with fire from the altar, and
threw it into the earth; and there were voices and thunderings
and lightnings and an earthquake. 6 And the seven angels that
had the seven trumpets prepared themselves to sound.

7 And the first angel sounded; and there were hail and fire
mingled with blood, and they were thrown into the earth: and
the third part of the earth was burned up, and the third
part of the trees was burned up, and all the green grass was
burned up.

8 And the second angel sounded; and, as it were, a great mountain, burning with fire, was thrown into the sea: and the third
part of the sea became blood. 9 And the third part of the creatures that were in the sea, that had life, died: and the third part
of the ships was destroyed.

10 And the third angel sounded; and there fell from heaven a
great star, that burned as a lamp; and it fell upon the third
part of the rivers, and upon the fountains of waters. 11 And the
name of the star is called Wormwood; and the third part of the
waters became wormwood: and many men died of the waters,
because they were made bitter.

12 And the fourth angel sounded; and the third part of the
sun, and the third part of the moon, and the third part of the
stars was smitten, that the third part might be darkened, and

that the day might not shine for the third part of it, and the
night in like manner.
13 And I saw, and heard an eagle, as he flew in mid-heaven,
saying, with a loud voice, Woe, woe, woe to the inhabitants of
the earth, because of the remaining voices of the trumpets of
the three angels which are yet to sound.

IX. 1 And the fifth angel sounded; and I saw a star fall from
heaven to the earth; and there was given to him the key of the
pit of the abyss; 2 and he opened the pit of the abyss; and there
arose a smoke out of the pit, like the smoke of a great furnace;
and the sun and the air were darkened by the smoke of the pit.
3 And out of the smoke there came locusts upon the earth; and
power was given to them, as the scorpions of the earth have
power. 4 And they were commanded not to hurt the grass of the
earth, nor any green thing, nor any tree, but the men who have
not the seal of God in their foreheads. 5 And they were permitted, not to kill them, but to torment them five months; and
the torment inflicted by them was like the torment inflicted by
a scorpion, when he stings a man. 6 And in those days men will
seek for death, and shall not find it; and they will desire to die,
and death shall flee from them.
7 And the shapes of the locusts were like horses prepared for
battle; and on their heads were, as it were, crowns of gold; and
their faces were like the faces of men. 8 And they had hair like
the hair of women; and their teeth were like the teeth of lions.
9 And they had breastplates like breastplates of iron; and the
sound of their wings was like the sound of chariots of many
horses running to battle. 10 And they had tails like scorpions,
and there were stings in their tails; and they had power to hurt
men five months. 11 And they had over them a king, the angel
of the abyss: his name, in Hebrew, is Abaddon, and, in Greek,
he has the name Apollyon.
12 The first woe is past: behold, there are coming, after this,
two woes more.
13 And the sixth angel sounded: and I heard a voice from the
four horns of the golden altar that is before God, 14 saying to
the sixth angel, who had the trumpet: Loose the four angels
that are bound at the great river Euphrates. 15 And the four
angels were loosed, who were prepared for an hour, and a day,
and a month, and a year, to slay the third part of men. 16 And
the number of the armies of horsemen was two myriads of

myriads: I heard the number of them. 17 And thus I saw the
horses in the vision, and those who sat on them; they had
breastplates, fiery, and hyacinthine, and sulphurous: and the
heads of the horses were like the heads of lions, and out of their
mouths issued fire and smoke and brimstone. 18 By these three
plagues was the third part of men killed, by the fire, and the
smoke, and the brimstone that issued out of their mouths.
19 For their power was in their mouth and in their tails; for
their tails were like serpents, and had heads, and with them
they do injury.

20 And the rest of men that were not killed by these plagues,
repented not of the works of their hands, that they might not
worship demons, and idols of gold, and of silver, and of brass,
and of stone, and of wood, which can neither see, nor hear, nor
walk; 21 and they repented not of their murders, nor of their
sorceries, nor of their lewdness, nor of their thefts.

X. 1 And I saw another mighty angel coming down from
heaven, clothed with a cloud; and the rainbow was upon his
head, and his face was like the sun, and his feet like pillars of
fire. 2 And he had in his hand a little book opened; and he
placed his right foot on the sea, and his left foot on the land;
3 and he cried with a loud voice, as when a lion roars: and when
he had cried, the seven thunders uttered their voices. 4 And
when the seven thunders had spoken, I was about to write; and
I heard a voice from heaven, saying: Seal up the things which
the seven thunders spoke, and write them not.

5 And the angel that I saw standing on the sea and on the
land, lifted up his right hand to heaven, 6 and swore by him
that lives from age to age, who created the heaven and the
things that are in it, and the earth and the things that are in
it, and the sea and the things that are in it, That time should
no longer intervene, 7 but in the days of the voice of the seventh angel, when he shall sound his trumpet, the mystery of
God should be finished, as he has declared to his servants the
prophets.

8 And the voice that I heard from heaven spoke to me again,
and said: Go and take the little book that is open in the hand
of the angel that stands on the sea and on the land. 9 And I
went to the angel, and said to him: Give me the little book.
And he said to me: Take it, and eat it up, and it will make
your stomach bitter, but it will be in your mouth as sweet as

honey. 10 And I took the little book out of the angel's hand,
and ate it up, and it was in my mouth as sweet as honey; and
when I had eaten it, my stomach was bitter. 11 And he said to
me: You must prophesy again before many peoples and nations
and tongues and kings.

XI. 1 And a reed like a rod was given to me; and it was said:
Rise and measure the temple of God, and the altar, and those
who worship in it. 2 But the court that is without the temple
leave out, and measure it not: for it is given to the Gentiles,
and the holy city they shall tread under foot forty-two months.
3 And I will give to my two witnesses, that they may prophesy
a thousand two hundred and sixty days, clothed in sackcloth.
4 These are the two olive-trees, and the two lamps that stand
before the Lord of the earth. 5 And if any man will injure them,
fire proceeds out of their mouth, and devours their enemies; and
if any one will injure them, he must be killed in this way.
6 These have authority to shut heaven, that it may not rain in
the days of their prophecy; and they have authority over the
waters, to turn them to blood, and to smite the earth with every
plague, as often as they wish.

7 And when they shall have finished their testimony, the beast
that ascends out of the abyss will make war with them, and
overcome them, and kill them. 8 And their dead bodies shall
lie in the street of the great city, which, spiritually, is called
Sodom and Egypt, where also our Lord was crucified. 9 And
some of the peoples and tribes and tongues and nations will see
their dead bodies three days and a half, and will not suffer their
dead bodies to be put into sepulchers. 10 And those who dwell
on the earth will rejoice over them, and make merry, and will
send gifts to one another, because these two prophets tormented
those who dwelt on the earth.

11 And after the three days and a half, the spirit of life from
God entered into them, and they stood upon their feet; and
great fear fell upon those who saw them. 12 And they heard a
great voice from heaven, saying to them: Come up hither. And
they went up into heaven in a cloud, and their enemies beheld
them. 13 And in that hour there was a great earthquake, and the
tenth part of the city fell; and in the earthquake there were
slain names of men, seven thousand: and the rest were frightened,
and gave glory to the God of heaven.

14 The second woe is past: behold, the third woe comes quickly.

15 And the seventh angel sounded; and there were great voices
in heaven, saying: The kingdom of the world has become our
Lord's and his Christ's, and he shall reign from age to age.

16 And the twenty-four elders that sat before God on their
thrones, fell upon their faces, and worshiped God, 17 saying: We
give thee thanks, O Lord God Almighty, who art, and who wast,
because thou hast taken thy great power, and hast reigned.
18 And the nations were angry, and thy wrath has come, and the
time of the dead, that they should be judged, and that thou
shouldst give reward to thy servants the prophets, and to the
saints, and to those who fear thy name, both small and great,
and that thou shouldst destroy those who corrupt the earth.

19 And the temple of God was opened in heaven, and there
was seen in his temple, the ark of the covenant of the Lord;
and there were lightnings and voices and thunderings, and an
earthquake, and great hail.

XII. 1 And a great sign appeared in heaven, a woman clothed
with the sun; and the moon was under her feet, and on her
head was a crown of twelve stars; 2 and, being with child, she
cried out in travail, and in the pains of delivery.

3 And there appeared another sign in heaven; and behold, a
great dragon, fiery-red, that had seven heads, and ten horns:
and on his heads seven diadems. 4 And his tail drew along the
third part of the stars of heaven, and did cast them to the earth.
And the dragon stood before the woman who was about to bring
forth, that, when she had brought forth, he might devour her
child. 5 And she brought forth a male child, that was to rule
all nations with a rod of iron; and her child was caught away
to God, even to his throne. 6 And the woman fled into the
wilderness, where she has a place prepared by God, that they
should feed her there for a thousand two hundred and sixty
days.

7 And there was war in heaven; Michael and his angels fought
with the dragon; and the dragon and his angels fought, 8 and
prevailed not: nor was their place found any more in heaven.
9 And the great dragon, that old serpent, called the Devil, and
Satan, who deceives the whole world, was cast into the earth,
and his angels were cast out with him. 10 And I heard a great
voice in heaven, saying: Now has come the salvation, and the
power, and the kingdom of our God, and the authority of his
Christ: for the accuser of our brethren, he that accused them

before our God day and night, is cast down. 11 And they over-
came him by the blood of the Lamb, and by the word of their
testimony; and they loved not their lives even to death. 12 Therefore, rejoice you heavens, and you that dwell in them. Alas
for the land and for the sea! for the devil has come down to you
with great anger, because he knows that he has but a short time.
13 And when the dragon saw that he was cast into the earth,
he persecuted the woman that brought forth the male child.
14 And two wings of a great eagle were given to the woman, that
she might fly into the wilderness into her place, where she is
nourished for a time, and times, and half a time, away from
the presence of the serpent. 15 And the serpent threw out of
his mouth water like a river, after the woman, that he might
cause her to be carried away by the river. 16 And the earth
helped the woman; and the earth opened her mouth, and swallowed up the river that the dragon threw out of his mouth.
17 And the dragon was angry with the woman, and went away
to make war with the rest of her children, that keep the commandments of God, and that hold the testimony of Jesus.

XIII. 1 And I stood on the sand of the sea, and saw a beast
coming up out of the sea, and he had seven heads and ten horns,
and on his horns ten diadems, and on his heads names impiously
irreverent. 2 And the beast that I saw was like a leopard, and
his feet were as those of a bear, and his mouth was as the mouth
of a lion. And the dragon gave him his power, and his throne,
and great authority. 3 And I saw one of his heads as if it had
been wounded even to death; and his deadly wound was healed;
and all the earth wondered after the beast. 4 And they worshiped
the dragon, because he gave authority to the beast: and they
worshiped the beast, saying, Who is like the beast? and, Who
is able to make war with him?
5 And there was given him a mouth that spoke great things
and impious words; and authority was given to him to continue
forty-two months. 6 And he opened his mouth in impious
speeches against God, to utter impious words against his name,
and his tabernacle, and against those who dwell in heaven.
7 And it was given him to make war with the saints, and to
overcome them: and authority was given him over every tribe
and people and tongue and nation. 8 And all that dwell upon
the earth will worship him, those whose names are not written
in the book of life of the Lamb that was slain from the founda-

tion of the world. [9] If any one has an ear, let him hear. [10] If
any one leads into captivity, he shall go into captivity. If any
kills with the sword, he must be killed with the sword. Here is
the patience and faithfulness of the saints.

[11] And I saw another beast coming up out of the earth; and
he had two horns like a lamb, and he spoke as a dragon. [12] And
he exercises all the authority of the first beast in his presence;
and he causes the earth and those who dwell in it to worship
the first beast, whose deadly wound was healed. [13] And he does
great signs, and even causes fire to descend from heaven upon
the earth in the sight of men. [14] And he deceives those who
dwell on the earth, by means of the signs which he is allowed
to do in the presence of the beast, saying to those who dwell on
the earth, that they should make an image for the beast which
had the wound by the sword, and did live. [15] And it was granted
him to give spirit to the image of the beast, that the image of
the beast should both speak, and cause as many as would not
worship the image of the beast, to be killed. [16] And he causes
all, small and great, rich and poor, free and bond, to receive a
mark on their right hand, or on their forehead, [17] and that no
one should be able to buy or sell, but he that had the mark, the
name of the beast, or the number of his name. [18] Here is wisdom.
Let him that has understanding, count the number of the beast:
for it is the number of a man, and his number is six hundred
and sixty-six.

XIV. [1] And I saw, and behold, the Lamb stood on the mount
Zion, and with him a hundred and forty-four thousand, that
had his name and his Father's name written in their foreheads.
[2] And I heard a voice from heaven like the voice of many waters,
and like the voice of loud thunder; and I heard the voice of
harpers harping with their harps. [3] And they sung a new song
before the throne, and before the four living creatures, and the
elders: and no one was able to learn the song, but the hundred
and forty-four thousand that had been redeemed from the earth.
[4] These are they that were not defiled with women; for they
are virgins; these are they that follow the Lamb wherever he
goes: these were redeemed from among men, the first-fruits to
God and to the Lamb. [5] And in their mouth was found no guile;
for they are blameless.

[6] And I saw another angel flying in mid-heaven, having the
eternal gospel to preach to those who dwell on the earth, even

to every nation and tribe and tongue and people; 7 and he said
with a loud voice: Fear God, and give glory to him, for the
hour of his judgment has come; and worship him that made
the heaven, and the earth, and the sea, and the fountains of
waters.

8 And another angel followed, saying: Babylon the great has
fallen, has fallen; because she has made all nations drink of the
maddening wine of her lewdness.

9 And the third angel followed them, saying, with a loud voice:
If any one worship the beast and his image, and receive his
mark in his forehead, or on his hand, even he shall drink of
the wine of the wrath of God, which is prepared without mixture in the cup of his indignation; 10 and he shall be tormented
with fire and brimstone in the presence of the holy angels, and
in the presence of the Lamb: 11 and the smoke of their torment
ascends from age to age: and they who worship the beast and
his image, and whoever receives the mark of his name, have no
rest day or night.

12 Here is the patience of the saints, who keep the commandments of God and the faith of Jesus. 13 And I heard a voice
from heaven, saying: Write, Blessed are the dead that die in
the Lord from this time. Yes, says the Spirit, that they may
rest from their labors, and their works do follow them.

14 And I saw, and behold, a white cloud, and on the cloud sat
one like the Son of man, who had on his head a crown of gold,
and in his hand a sharp sickle. 15 And another angel came out
of the temple, and cried with a loud voice to him that sat on
the cloud: Thrust in your sickle and reap, for the time has
come for you to reap, for the harvest of the earth is fully ripe.
16 And he that sat on the cloud thrust in his sickle on the earth,
and the earth was reaped.

17 And another angel came out of the temple that is in heaven,
and he also had a sharp sickle. 18 And another angel that had
power over fire, came out from the altar: and he cried with a
loud cry to him that had the sharp sickle, and said: Thrust in
your sharp sickle, and gather the clusters of the vine of the
earth, for its grapes are fully ripe. 19 And the angel thrust in
his sickle on the earth, and gathered the vine of the earth, and
threw it into the great wine-press of the wrath of God. 20 And
the wine press was trodden without the city; and blood came
out of the wine-press, even to the bridles of the horses, to the
distance of a thousand and six hundred furlongs.

XV. [1] And I saw another sign in heaven, great and wonderful: seven angels that had seven plagues which are the last; for
by them the wrath of God is brought to an end.
[2] And I saw, as it were, a sea of glass mingled with fire, and
those who had obtained the victory over the beast, and over his
image, and over the number of his name, standing on the sea
of glass, having the harps of God. [3] And they sung the song
of Moses the servant of God, and the song of the Lamb, saying:
Great and wonderful are thy works, Lord God Almighty; just
and true are thy ways, thou King of saints. [4] Who will not
fear thee, O Lord, and glorify thy name? For thou alone art
holy; for all nations shall come and worship before thee: because thy judgments are made manifest.
[5] And after this I saw, and the temple of the tabernacle of
the testimony in heaven was opened; and the seven angels that
had the seven plagues came out of the temple, clothed in pure
white linen, and girded about the breasts with golden girdles.
[7] And one of the four living creatures gave to the seven angels
seven golden cups full of the wrath of God, who lives from age
to age. [8] And the temple was filled with smoke from the glory
of God, and from his power; and no one was able to enter the
temple, till the seven plagues of the seven angels were completed.

XVI. [1] And I heard a great voice out of the temple, saying
to the seven angels: Go and pour out the seven cups of the
wrath of God upon the earth.
[2] And the first angel went, and poured out his cup on the
land; and there came a hurtful and afflictive sore upon the men
that had the mark of the beast, and that worshiped his image.
[3] And the second angel poured out his cup on the sea; and it
became blood, like that of a dead man: and every soul in the
sea died.
[4] And the third angel poured out his cup on the rivers and the
fountains of waters; and they became blood. [5] And I heard the
angel of the waters, saying: Just art thou, who art and who
wast, the Holy One, because thou hast thus judged. [6] For they
have shed the blood of saints and of prophets, and thou hast
given them blood to drink, and they are worthy. [7] And I heard
a voice from the altar saying: Even so, Lord God Almighty, true
and just are thy judgments.
[8] And the fourth angel poured out his cup on the sun; and

it was given to him to scorch men with fire. [9] And men were
scorched with great heat; and they uttered impious words
against the name of God who has power over these plagues; and
they repented not, that they might give him glory.

[10] And the fifth angel poured out his cup on the throne of the
beast; and his kingdom was filled with darkness; and they
gnawed their tongues because of pain; [11] and they spoke impiously against the God of heaven because of their pains, and
because of their sores; and they repented not of their works.

[12] And the sixth angel poured out his cup on the great river
Euphrates; and its water was dried up, that the way of the
kings of the east might be prepared. [13] And I saw three unclean spirits, like frogs, come out of the mouth of the dragon,
and out of the mouth of the beast, and out of the mouth of the
false prophet. [14] For they are the spirits of demons that do
signs, and they go forth to the kings of the whole world, to
bring them together to the battle of that great day of God Almighty. [15] Behold, I come as a thief: blessed is he that watches,
and keeps his garments, that he may not walk naked, and that
men may not see his nakedness. [16] And they brought them
together into a place that is called, in the Hebrew tongue,
Armageddon.

[17] And the seventh angel poured out his cup into the air; and
there came a great voice from the temple of heaven, from the
throne, saying: It is done. [18] And there were lightnings and
voices and thunders; and there was a great earthquake, such as
has not been since men were on the earth,—so great an earthquake, and so mighty. [19] And the great city was divided into
three parts, and the cities of the nations fell: and Babylon the
great was remembered before God, that he might give her the
cup of the wine of his fiercest wrath. [20] And every island fled,
and the mountains were not found. [21] And great hail, every
stone about the weight of a talent, fell from heaven upon men;
and men spoke impiously against God, because of the plague of
the hail: for the plague of it was very great.

XVII. [1] And there came one of the seven angels that had the
seven cups, and talked with me, saying: Come, I will show you
the judgment of the great harlot that sits on many waters, [2] with
whom the kings of the earth have practiced lewdness, and with
the wine of whose lewdness the inhabitants of the earth have
been made drunk. [3] And he carried me away in spirit into the

wilderness; and I saw a woman sitting on a scarlet beast, that
was full of impious names, and that had seven heads and ten
horns. 4 And the woman was clothed in purple and scarlet,
and adorned with gold, and precious stones, and pearls; and she
had in her hand a golden cup full of idolatrous pollutions, and
the impurities of her lewdness. 5 And on her forehead was a name
written: MYSTERY, BABYLON THE GREAT, THE MOTHER
OF HARLOTS, AND OF THE IDOLATROUS POLLUTIONS
OF THE EARTH. 6 And I saw the woman drunk with the blood
of the saints, and with the blood of the witnesses of Jesus; and
when I saw her, I wondered with great astonishment.

7 And the angel said to me: Why did you wonder? I will tell
you the mystery of the woman, and of the beast that carries
her, that has seven heads and ten horns.

8 The beast that you saw, was, and is not, and will come out
of the abyss, and go to perdition; and those who dwell on the
earth, whose names were not written in the book of life from the
foundation of the world, will wonder, when they see the beast
that was, and is not, though he is yet present.

9 Here is the mind that has wisdom: the seven heads are seven
mountains, on which the woman sits. 10 And there are seven
kings: five have fallen, one is, and the other has not yet come;
and when he comes, he must remain but a little while. 11 And
the beast that was, and is not, even he is the eighth, and is of the
seven, and goes to perdition.

12 And the ten horns which you saw are ten kings, who have
received no kingdom as yet, but receive authority as kings at
the same time with the beast.

13 These have one mind, and will give their power and authority to the beast. 14 These will make war with the Lamb,
and the Lamb will overcome them, for he is Lord of lords, and
King of kings: and those with him are called and chosen and
faithful.

15 And he said to me: The waters which you saw, where the
harlot sits, are peoples and multitudes and nations and tongues.
16 And the ten horns that you saw, and the beast, these will
hate the harlot, and will make her desolate and naked, and will
eat her flesh, and burn her up with fire. 17 For God has put into
their hearts to fulfill his will, and to agree, and to give their
kingdom to the beast, till the words of God be accomplished.

18 And the woman that you saw is that great city, which reigns
over the kings of the earth.

XVIII. 1 And after these things I saw another angel come
down from heaven, having great power; and the earth was
lighted with his glory. 2 And he cried with a strong voice, saying: Babylon the great has fallen, has fallen, and has become
the habitation of demons, and the haunt of every unclean spirit,
and the resort of every unclean and hateful bird. 3 For she has
made all nations drink of the maddening wine of her lewdness;
and the kings of the earth have practiced lewdness with her,
and the merchants of the earth have become rich by the power
of her voluptuousness.

4 And I heard another voice from heaven, saying: Come out
of her, my people, lest you become partakers of her sins, and
lest you receive of her plagues. 5 For her sins reach even to
heaven, and God has remembered her iniquities. 6 Reward her
as she has rewarded you, and render back to her double, according to her works: in the cup that she has mixed, mix for her
double. 7 As much glory and voluptuousness as she has given
to herself, so much torment and sorrow give her: for she says
in her heart, I sit a queen, and am no widow, and shall see no
sorrow. 8 Therefore, her plagues shall come in one day, death
and mourning and famine; and she shall be utterly burned with
fire: for strong is the Lord God who judges her.

9 And the kings of the earth, who have practiced lewdness
and lived voluptuously with her, shall weep and lament for
her, when they see the smoke of her burning, 10 standing far
off for fear of her torment, saying: Alas, alas, that great city
of Babylon, that mighty city! for in one hour has your judgment come.

11 And the merchants of the earth shall weep and lament over
her, because no one buys their merchandise any more; 12 the
merchandise of gold and silver and precious stones, and of
pearls, and of fine linen and purple, and of silk and scarlet;
and every kind of thyine wood, and every kind of vessel of
ivory, and every kind of vessel of most costly wood, and of
brass, and of iron, and of marble: 13 and cinnamon and amo-
mum and incense, and ointment, and frankincense, and wine
and oil, and fine flour and wheat, and beasts and sheep, and
horses and chariots, and bodies and souls of men. 14 And the
fruits that your soul desired have departed from you; and all
things that are dainty and sumptuous have perished from you,
and you shall find them no more at all.

15 Those who traded in these things, who were made rich by

her, shall stand far off for fear of her torment, weeping and
mourning and 16 saying: Alas, alas, that great city, that was
clothed in fine linen and purple and scarlet, and adorned with
gold and precious stones and pearls! for in one hour, so great
riches have been brought to ruin. 17 And every master of a
ship, and every one in ships, and sailors, and as many as trade
by sea, stood far off, 18 and cried, when they saw the smoke of
her burning, saying: What city is like the great city? 19 And
they threw dust on their heads, and cried, weeping and mourning and saying: Alas, alas, that great city, by which all that
had ships in the sea became rich by means of costly merchandise! for in one hour she is made desolate. 20 Rejoice over her,
O heaven, and you saints and apostles and prophets: for God
has avenged you on her.

21 And a mighty angel took up a stone like a great millstone,
and threw it into the sea, saying: Thus, with violence shall
Babylon, that great city, be thrown down, and shall be found
no more at all. 22 And the voice of harpers and musicians, and
of pipers and trumpeters, shall be heard no more at all in you:
and no artist of any art whatever, shall be found any more in
you: and the sound of the millstone shall be heard no more in
you: 23 and the light of a lamp shall shine no more in you: and
the voice of the bridegroom and of the bride shall be heard no
more in you: for your merchants were the great men of the
earth: for by your sorcery were all nations deceived. 24 And
in her was found the blood of prophets and of saints, and of
all that were slain upon the earth.

XIX. 1 After these things, I heard the great voice of a vast
multitude in heaven, saying: Alleluia; Salvation and glory and
honor and power to our God: 2 for true and righteous are his
judgments, for he has judged the great harlot that corrupted
the earth with her lewdness; and he has avenged the blood of
his servants at her hand. 3 And again they said: Alleluia;
and her smoke rises up from age to age. 4 And the twenty-four
elders, and the four living creatures, fell down, and worshiped
God that sits upon the throne, saying: Amen, Alleluia. 5 And
a voice came out of the throne, saying: Praise our God, all you
his servants, and you that fear him, both small and great.

6 And I heard as it were the voice of a great multitude, and
as the voice of many waters, and as the voice of mighty thunderings, saying: Alleluia; for the Lord God the Almighty

reigns. 7 Let us rejoice and be glad, and give glory to him:
for the marriage of the Lamb has come, and his wife has made
herself ready. 8 And to her was given that she should be clothed
in fine linen, clean and white; for the fine linen is the righteousness of the saints. 9 And he said to me: Write, Blessed are they
that are called to the marriage-supper of the Lamb. And he
said to me: These are the true words of God. 10 And I fell at
his feet to worship him; and he said to me: See that you do it
not; I am your fellow-servant, and of your brethren that have
the testimony of Jesus; worship God: for the testimony of
Jesus is the spirit of prophecy.

11 And I saw heaven opened, and behold, a white horse, and he
that sat on him was called faithful and true, and in righteousness does he judge, and make war. 12 His eyes were like a flame
of fire, and on his head were many diadems; and he had a name
written which no one knew, but he himself. 13 And he was
clothed with a garment dipped in blood; and his name is called
The Word of God. 14 And the armies that were in heaven followed him on white horses; and they were clothed in fine linen,
white and clean. 15 And out of his mouth goes a sharp, two-
edged sword, that with it he may smite the nations; and he
shall rule them with a rod of iron; and he treads the wine-press
of the fiercest wrath of God, the Almighty. 16 And he has, on
his raiment and on his thigh, a name written, King of kings,
and Lord of lords.

17 And I saw an angel standing in the sun; and he cried with
a loud voice, saying to all the birds that fly in mid-heaven:
Come, gather yourselves to the great supper of God, 18 that you
may eat the flesh of kings, and the flesh of officers, and the flesh
of mighty men, and the flesh of horses, and of those who sit on
them, and the flesh of all, both freemen and servants, both small
and great.

19 And I saw the beast, and the kings of the earth, and their
armies, assembled together to make war with him that sat on
the horse, and with his army. 20 And the beast was taken, and
the false prophet that was with him, who did signs in his presence, with which he deceived those who received the mark of
the beast, and those who worshiped his image. These two were
thrown alive into the lake of fire, which burns with brimstone.
21 And the rest were slain with the sword of him that sat on the
horse, which sword proceeded out of his mouth: and all the
birds were filled with their flesh.

XX. 1 And I saw an angel come down from heaven, having
the key of the abyss, and a great chain in his hand. 2 And he
laid hold of the dragon, that old serpent, which is the devil and
Satan, and bound him for a thousand years, 3 and threw him
into the abyss, and shut him up, and set a seal upon him,
that he should deceive the nations no more, till the thousand
years should be completed: and after this he must be loosed for
a little while.

4 And I saw thrones, and they sat upon them, and the power
of judging was given to them; and I saw the souls of those who
had been beheaded for the testimony of Jesus, and for the word
of God; and of those who had not worshiped the beast, nor his
image, and had not received his mark on their forehead, nor on
their hand: and they lived and reigned with Christ a thousand
years. 5 But the rest of the dead lived not till the thousand
years were completed. This is the first resurrection. 6 Blessed
and holy is he that has part in the first resurrection; over such
the second death has no power: but they shall be priests of God
and of the Christ, and shall reign with him a thousand years.

7 And when the thousand years shall have been completed,
Satan shall be loosed from his prison, 8 and shall go out to deceive the nations that are in the four corners of the earth, Gog
and Magog, to bring them together to battle: the number of
these is as the sand of the sea. 9 And they went up on the
breadth of the earth, and encompassed the camp of the saints,
and the beloved city: and fire came down out of heaven from
God, and devoured them. 10 And the devil who deceived them
was thrown into the lake of fire and brimstone, where the beast
and the false prophet are: and they shall be tormented day and
night from age to age.

11 And I saw a great white throne, and him that sat upon it,
from whose face the earth and the heaven fled away; and no
place was found for them. 12 And I saw the dead, small and
great, stand before the throne; and the books were opened; and
another book was opened, which is the book of life: and the
dead were judged out of the things that were written in the
books, according to their works. 13 And the sea gave up the
dead that were in it; and death and hades gave up the dead that
were in them; and they were judged, every one according to his
works. 14 And death and hades were cast into the lake of fire:
this is the second death. 15 And if any one was not found written in the book of life, he was thrown into the lake of fire.

XXI. 1 And I saw a new heaven and a new earth; for the
former heaven and the former earth had passed away: and the
sea was no more. 2 And I saw the holy city, New Jerusalem,
coming down out of heaven, from God, prepared as a bride
adorned for her husband. 3 And I heard a great voice out of
heaven, saying: Behold, the tabernacle of God is with men, and
he will dwell with them: and they shall be his people, and God
himself will be with them, their God. 4 And he will wipe every
tear from their eyes, and there shall be no more death; neither
shall there be any more sorrow, nor crying, nor pain; for the
former things have passed away.

5 And he that sat upon the throne said: Behold, I make all
things new. And he said to me: Write, for these words are
true and faithful. 6 And he said to me: It is done; I am the
Alpha and the Omega, the Beginning and the End. To him that
thirsts, I will give of the fountain of the water of life freely.
7 He that overcomes, shall inherit these things, and I will be his
God, and he shall be my son. 8 But the fearful, and the unbelieving, and the detestable, and murderers and lewd persons and sorcerers and idolaters and all liars, shall have their part in the lake
that burns with fire and brimstone, which is the second death.

9 And there came one of the seven angels that had the seven
cups full of the seven last plagues; and he talked with me,
saying: Come hither, and I will show you the bride, the Lamb's
wife. 10 And he carried me away in spirit to a mountain, great
and high, and showed me the holy city, Jerusalem, coming down
out of heaven from God, 11 having the glory of God: that which
gave it light was like a most costly stone, like jasper-stone,
brilliant as crystal. 12 It had a wall, great and high; and it had
twelve gates, and at the gates twelve angels, and names written
on them, which are the names of the twelve tribes of the sons
of Israel; 13 on the east, three gates; on the north, three gates;
on the south, three gates; and on the west, three gates. 14 And
the wall of the city had twelve foundations, and on them were
the names of the twelve apostles of the Lamb.

15 And he that talked with me had a measure, a golden reed,
that he might measure the city, and its gates, and its wall.
16 And the city lies square: and its length is as great as its
breadth. And he measured the city with the reed, twelve thousand furlongs: the length, and the breadth, and the hight of it
are equal. 17 And he measured the wall of it, a hundred and
forty-four cubits, the measure of a man, that is, of an angel.

18 And the wall of it was built of jasper; and the city was
pure gold, like clear glass. 19 And the foundations of the wall of
the city were adorned with every costly stone: the first foundation was jasper; the second, sapphire; the third, chalcedony;
the fourth, emerald; 20 the fifth, sardonyx; the sixth, sardius;
the seventh, crysolite; the eighth, beryl; the ninth, topaz; the
tenth, chrysoprase; the eleventh, hyacinth; the twelfth, ame-
thyst. 21 And the twelve gates were twelve pearls; every gate
was of one pearl: and the street of the city was pure gold, like
clear glass.

22 And I saw no temple in it; for the Lord God the Almighty,
and the Lamb, are its temple. 23 And the city had no need of
the sun, nor of the moon, to shine in it: for the glory of God
gave it light, and the lamp of it is the Lamb. 24 And the nations shall walk by the light of it; and the kings of the earth
bring their glory and their honor into it. 25 And its gates shall
not be shut at all by day: for there shall be no night there.
26 And they shall bring the glory and honor of the nations into
it. 27 And there shall not enter it any thing unclean, or that
does what is detestable, or that makes a lie: but those who are
written in the Lamb's book of life.

XXII. 1 And he showed me a river of water of life, clear as
crystal, coming out from the throne of God and of the Lamb.
2 In the midst of the street of the city, and on each side of the
river, was the tree of life, which bore twelve kinds of fruit, and
yielded its fruit every month; and the leaves of the tree were
for the healing of the nations. 3 And there shall be no more
curse; and the throne of God and of the Lamb shall be in it:
and his servants shall serve him. 4 And they shall see his face,
and his name shall be in their foreheads. 5 And there shall be
no more night; and they have no need of the lamp, nor of the
light of the sun: for the Lord God will give them light: and
they shall reign from age to age.

6 And he said to me: These words are faithful and true; and
the Lord God of the spirits of the prophets has sent his angel
to show his servants the things that must shortly take place.
7 And behold, I come quickly; blessed is he that keeps the words
of the prophecy of this book. 8 And I, John, am he that saw
and heard these things. And when I had heard and seen, I fell
down to worship before the feet of the angel that showed me
these things. 9 And he said to me: See that you do it not; I

am your fellow-servant, and of your brethren the prophets,
and of those who keep the words of this book: worship God.

10 And he said to me: Seal not the words of the prophecy of
this book: for the time is at hand. 11 He that is unjust, let him
be unjust still; he that is polluted, let him be polluted still; and
he that is righteous, let him be righteous still; and he that is
holy, let him be holy still. 12 Behold, I come quickly, and my
reward is with me, to give to every one as his work shall be.
13 I am the Alpha and the Omega, the First and the Last, the
Beginning and the End. 14 Blessed are those who do his commandments, that they may have right to the tree of life, and
that they may go through the gates into the city. 15 Without
are dogs and sorcerers and lewd persons and murderers and idolaters, and every one that loves and makes a lie.

16 I, Jesus, have sent my angel to testify these things to you
for the churches. I am the root and the offspring of David,
the bright, morning star. 17 And the Spirit and the bride say,
Come; and let him that hears, say, Come; and let him that is
thirsty, come; and let him that is willing, take the water of
life freely.

18 I testify to every one that hears the words of the prophecy
of this book: if any one add to these things, God will add to
him the plagues that are written in this book. 19 And if any
one take away from the words of the book of this prophecy,
God will take away his part from the tree of life, and from the
holy city; which things are written in this book.

20 He that testifies these things, says: Surely, I come quickly.
Amen: come, Lord Jesus.

21 The grace of the Lord Jesus Christ be with all the saints.

EXPLANATION OF CERTAIN TERMS.

DENARIUS—The earlier, equal to 8½*d.*, 17 cents; the later, 7½*d.*, 15 cents.

DRACHMA, equal to the denarius, or 15 cents.

DIDRACHMA, equal to 30 cents.

STATER, equal to 60 cents.

CHŒNIX, equal to about a quart.

YOD, is the name of the smallest letter of the Hebrew alphabet.

PEDAGOGUE, (Gal. iii, 24,) was a servant that led the children of his master to school. The literal meaning of the word is, "a leader of children." The pedagogue did not teach, but conducted his master's children to the schoolmaster.

CANAANITE, the same as *Zealot.*

The word *Canaanite* is of Hebrew or Aramaic origin; and the word *Zealot* is its meaning. The reader will observe that I have given the true spelling to a word misspelled in the Common Version—*Canaan.* It should be, and is so, spelled *Chanaan.*

In 1 Cor. xi, 29, I have given the reading as found in Codex Alexandrinus and Tischendorf's text.

In Rev. viii, 13, the word *eagle* is according to the reading of the best texts. The cherubim are described, chap. iv, 7: One of them was like a flying eagle.

In Matt. vi, 1, the reading of the best texts requires the term *righteous* instead of *charitable.* So, in chap. xxiii, 8, for *leader,* I now read *teacher.*

THE TRANSLATOR.

THE END.

www.ingramcontent.com/pod-product-compliance
Lightning Source LLC
LaVergne TN
LVHW020559110826
845149LV00002B/321

* 9 7 8 1 4 1 8 1 8 8 2 4 5 *